McGRAW-HILL

5 Steps to a 5

AP U.S. History

Other books in McGraw-Hill's *5 Steps to a 5* Series include:

AP Biology
AP Calculus AB
AP Chemistry
AP English Language
AP English Literature
AP Psychology
AP Spanish Language
AP Statistics
AP U.S. Government and Politics
Writing the AP English Essay

McGRAW-HILL

5 Steps to a 5

AP U.S. History

Stephen Armstrong
Diagnostic and Practice Exams by
Edward McBride

McGraw-Hill

New York   Chicago   San Francisco   Lisbon   London   Madrid   Mexico City
Milan   New Delhi   San Juan   Seoul   Singapore   Sydney   Toronto

Contents

Preface

So, you have decided to take AP U.S. History. Prepare to be continually challenged in this course; this is the only way you will attain the grade that you want on the AP exam in May. Prepare to read, to read a lot, and to read critically; almost all students successful in AP U.S. History say this is a necessity. Prepare to analyze countless primary source documents; being able to do this is critical for success on the exam as well. Most importantly, prepare to immerse yourself in the great story that is United States history. As your teacher will undoubtedly point out, it would be impossible to make up some of the people and events you will study in this class. What really happened is much more interesting!

This study guide will assist you along the journey of AP U.S. History. The chapter review guides give you a succinct overview of the major events of U.S. history. At the end of each chapter is a list of the major concepts, a time line, and sample multiple-choice questions for that chapter. In addition, a very extensive glossary is included in the back of this manual. All of the underlined words throughout the book can be found in the glossary (it would also be a good study technique to review the entire glossary before taking the actual AP exam).

The first two chapters of the manual describe the AP test itself and suggest some test-taking strategies. There are also two entire sample tests, with answers. These allow you to become totally familiar with the format and nature of the questions that will appear on the exam. On the actual testing day you want absolutely no surprises!

In the first chapter you will also find time lines for three approaches to preparing for the exam. It is obviously suggested that your preparation for the examination be a yearlong process; for those students unable to do that, two "alternative calendars" also appear. Many students also find that study groups are very beneficial in studying for the AP test. Students who have been successful on the AP test oftentimes form these groups very early in the school year.

Many students feel frustrated when their AP class doesn't make it all the way to the present day. Don't worry—The number of questions on the test that deal with events after the 1970s will be relatively small.

I hope this manual helps you in achieving the "perfect 5." That score is sitting out there, waiting for you to reach for it.

PART I

HOW TO USE THIS BOOK

Chapter 1

The Five-Step Program

BEFORE WE BEGIN

Reading This Guide

This guide provides you with the specific format of the AP U.S. History test, two sample AP U.S. History tests, and a comprehensive review of U.S. history. After each review chapter you will find a time line and several sample questions that might appear on the AP test.

Reading this guide is a great start to getting the grade you want on the AP U.S. History test, but it is important to read on your own as well. Several groups of students who have all gotten a 5 on the test maintain the key to success is to *read* as much as you can on U.S. history as you possibly can.

Reading this guide will not guarantee you a 5 when you take the U.S. history exam in May. However, by carefully reviewing the format of the exam and the test-taking strategies provided for each section, you will definitely be on your way! The review section that outlines the major developments of U.S. history should augment what you have learned from your regular U.S. history textbook. This book won't "give" you a 5, but it can certainly point you firmly in that direction.

Thinking Historically

Even if you have a photographic memory, there is more to do to get a 5 on the AP U.S. History exam. Unfortunately, knowing all of the dates, names, and important events of U.S. history is not enough. It is important that you develop the ability to analyze these events: to judge their importance, to analyze why they occurred, and to understand what the ramifications of these events were. Historical analysis is somewhat different than the analysis you do in an English or a physics class. There are plenty of examples in this book to help you to develop the skill of historical analysis, or to reinforce the skill if you already have it.

The Importance of Studying U.S. History

Please do not approach U.S. history as a study of old, irrelevant names, places, and dates. U.S. history is *not* an old, dead topic. The events you study in your U.S. history course all, either indirectly or directly, have an influence on the United States today. Also, at the risk of sounding incredibly corny, U.S. history is a *great* story! Allow yourself to become familiar with some of the bizarre and humorous events and people in U.S. history as well. Let the subject come alive! This will put you in the right frame of mind to seriously study the subject matter.

> *"I strongly encourage my students to keep up with current events. It helps to provide some context to the history they are studying."*
> —AP Teacher

Why This Particular Guide

The author of this book has taught U.S. history for over 20 years and is very familiar with the AP test and why students succeed (or don't succeed) when taking it. In a sense, my students have taught me a lot of what is in this book; I have seen over the years what works for them, and I have tried to include as much of this as possible in this book. I have also tried to keep this book user-friendly for you. I teach U.S. history to eleventh graders (which I suspect the vast majority of readers of this book are), and I have written the book in the language in which I converse with my students. I sat down and had lengthy conversations with seven groups of AP students (from seven different schools) before beginning this guide; many of their suggestions are included here.

Some of the other specific advantages of this guide are that it will

- Give you a very comprehensive review of the key events and trends of U.S. history
- Anticipate and answer many of the questions you have about the test
- Explain strategies for being successful in each part of the test to you
- Help you to "think historically" (as noted previously)
- Provide you with numerous opportunities to practice the types of questions that will be on the test
- Provide you with a comprehensive glossary of U.S. history terms
- Make you aware of the **Five-Step Program** for mastering the AP U.S. History exam

Organization of This Book

The introductory chapters of this book give you critical information on the AP U.S. History exam in general, and then specific detail on the multiple-choice and the essay sections of the exam. Specific strategies for success are given in each of these sections. Even though the major reason for getting this guide might have been to go through the section that reviews the details of U.S. history, it is strongly advised that you read these sections carefully. Taking the time to do the Diagnostic Exam will give you a good idea of where you stand before you start your preparations.

A 23-chapter review of the major events of U.S. history follows, with sample questions at the end of each chapter. A glossary of key terms used in these chapters is found at the very back of the book.

Two complete sample exams are also included, with all of the correct answers (and why they are correct) also noted.

INTRODUCTION TO THE FIVE-STEP PROGRAM

The **Five-Step Program** is a powerful tool designed to provide you with the best-possible skills, strategies, and practice to help lead you to the perfect 5 on the AP U.S. History examination. Each of these five steps provides you with the opportunity to get closer and closer to the 5, which every AP student strives to achieve.

STEP ONE leads you through a brief process to help determine which type of exam preparation is most comfortable for you:

1. Month-by-month: September through May
2. The calendar year: January through May
3. Basic training: the 4–6 weeks before the exam

STEP TWO helps develop the knowledge you need to do well on the exam:

1. A comprehensive review of the exam
2. A thorough review of the type of questions asked on the exam
3. Explanation of multiple-choice answers
4. A comprehensive review of the two types of essays asked for on the exam
5. A review of the major events and trends of U.S. history
6. A glossary of important terms in U.S. history

STEP THREE helps develop the skills necessary to take the exam and do well:

1. Practice activities in historical thinking
2. Practice activities in multiple choice questions
3. Practice document-based essay questions

STEP FOUR helps you develop strategies for taking the exam:

1. Learning about the test itself
2. Learning to read multiple-choice questions
3. Learning how to answer multiple-choice questions, and the value of guessing
4. Learning what to look for in the essay question
5. Learning how to plan the essay

 STEP FIVE helps you develop you confidence in using the skills demanded on the AP U.S. History exam:

1. The opportunity to evaluate yourself with many practice questions
2. Time management techniques and skills
3. Two practice exams that test how well-honed your skills are
4. The opportunity to show you that you know more than you think you do about U.S. history

GRAPHICS USED IN THIS BOOK

To emphasize particular skills, strategies, and practice, we use seven sets of icons throughout this book.

The first icon is an hourglass, which indicates the passage of time during the school year. This hourglass icon will appear in the margin next to an item that may be of interest to one of the three types of students who are using this book (mode A, B, or C students).

 For the student who plans to prepare for the AP U.S. History exam during the entire school year, beginning in September through May, I use an hourglass that is full on the top.

For the student who decides to begin preparing for the exam in January of the calendar year, I use an hourglass that is half full on the top and half full on the bottom.

 For the student who wishes to prepare during the final 6 weeks before the exam, I use an hourglass that is almost empty on the top and almost full on the bottom.

The second icon is a footprint, which indicates which step in the five-step program is being emphasized in a given analysis, technique, or practice activity.

Plan   Knowledge   Skills   Strategies   Confidence Building

The third icon is a clock, which indicates a timed practice activity or a time management strategy. It will indicate on the face of the dial how much time to allow for a given exercise. The full dial will remind you that this is a strategy which can help you learn to manage your time on the test.

The fourth icon is an exclamation point, which will point to a very important idea, concept, or strategy point that you should not pass over.

The fifth icon is a checkmark, which will alert you to pay close attention. This activity will be most helpful if you go back and check your own work, your calendar, or your progress.

The sixth icon is a lightbulb, which indicates strategies that you may want to try.

The seventh icon is the sun, which indicates a tip that you might find useful.

Boldfaced and <u>underlined</u> words indicate terms that are included in the glossary at the end of the book.

THREE APPROACHES TO PREPARING FOR THE AP U.S. HISTORY EXAM

> *"It really helps to develop a plan for studying for the test; once you have a plan, stick with it."* —AP Student

You are the only person who knows which schedule listed below is right for you. If you were to ask me, I would strong suggest using approach A, but I know that not everyone can or will. This manual is designed to help you, no matter which of the schedules you decide to adopt.

You're a full-year prep student (Approach A) if

1. You have a definite love of U.S. history.
2. You are certain that history will be your major in college.
3. You are not a procrastinator; you like to get things done.
4. You like detailed planning and everything in its place.
5. You feel you must be thoroughly prepared.
6. You have been successful with this approach in this past.

You are a one-semester prep student (Approach B) if

1. You are pretty interested in U.S. history.
2. You usually plan ahead but sometime skip some of the little details.
3. You feel more comfortable when you know what to expect, but a surprise or two does not floor you.
4. You are always on time for appointments.
5. You have been successful with this approach in the past.

You are a 4- to 6-week prep student (Approach C) if

1. United States history is somewhat interesting to you.
2. You work best under pressure and close deadlines.
3. You think the work you have done in your U.S. history class has prepared you fairly well for the AP test.
4. You decided late in the year to take the exam.
5. You like surprises.
6. You have been successful with this approach in the past.

"Do all the reading on U.S. history you possibly can. This WILL help you do better on the test." —*AP Student*

CALENDARS FOR PREPARING FOR THE AP U.S. HISTORY EXAM

Calendar for Approach A: Year-Long Preparation for AP U.S. History Exam

Although its primary purpose is to prepare you for the AP U.S. History exam you will take in May, this book can enrich your study of U.S. history.

SEPTEMBER–OCTOBER (Check off the activities as you complete them)

_____ Determine into which student mode you would place yourself.

_____ Carefully read the first three chapters of this manual.

_____ Get on the World Wide Web and see what is said on the College Board AP Web site.

_____ Skim the Comprehensive Review Questions (go to this section all year if you have specific questions).

_____ Buy a highlighter, and use it on this manual and, if possible, your regular textbook (in many schools AP students buy their textbooks ahead of time for this very purpose).

_____ Coordinate the materials in this manual with the curriculum of your AP History class.

_____ Begin to do outside reading on U.S. history topics.

_____ Begin to use this book as a resource.

NOVEMBER (The first 10 weeks have elapsed.)

_____ Do some of the sample questions found throughout the manual.

_____ Look at the one of the sample tests to get an idea of what the big picture is.

_____ Intensify your reading of outside sources.

_____ Remind yourself to do historical analysis when you read.

DECEMBER

_____ Review the section on document-based questions, or DBQs. (You will probably have one on your midterm exam in class.)

_____ Carefully review the historical survey sections found in this manual for the areas you have already studied in class. Do the interpretations of events generally match up? If they don't, why might this be so?

JANUARY

_____ Using the eras of U.S. history you have studied in class, create your own document-based question for two of the units, and try to answer it.

_____ Form a study group to prepare for the AP exams. Many successful students on the AP maintain that a good study group was critical to their success

FEBRUARY–MARCH

_____ Further intensify your outside readings.

_____ Take two U.S. history textbooks and compare and contrast their handling of three events in U.S. history. What do your results tell you?

_____ Carefully analyze the materials in the comprehensive review section of U.S. history for the units you are now studying in your U.S. history class. What events are you studying that directly impact the United States today?

APRIL

_____ Take Practice Exam 1 in the first week of April.

_____ Evaluate your strengths and weaknesses.

_____ Study appropriate chapters to correct weaknesses.

_____ Practice creating and answering multiple-choice questions in your study group.

_____ Develop and review worksheets for and with your study group.

MAY—First Two Weeks (It's Almost Showtime!)

_____ Highlight materials in your textbook (and in this manual) that you are unsure of, and ask your teacher about them.

_____ Write two or three historical essays under timed conditions.

_____ Take Practice Exam 2.

_____ Score and evaluate your performance.

_____ You are well prepared for the test. Go get it!

> "The more sample questions and essays you can go over before the test the better. Definitely take more than one practice exam from start to finish." —AP Student

Calendar for Approach B:
Semester-Long Preparation for the AP U.S. History Exam

Working under the assumption that you've completed one semester of U.S. History,
use this calendar and the skills you've learned to prepare for the May exam.

JANUARY–FEBRUARY

_____ Carefully read the introductory three chapters of the book.

_____ Write two or three document-based essay questions, sample multiple choice questions.

_____ "Think historically" about the material you are reading in class.

_____ Read at least on source outside of class on a topic you are studying.

MARCH

_____ Carefully analyze the historical review sections on the material you are now studying in class. Are the interpretations of historical events the same in your textbook and in this manual? If not, why might that be?

_____ Form a study group (these are pivotal to success).

_____ In your study group, practice creating and answering multiple-choice questions.

APRIL

_____ Take Practice Exam 1 in first week of April.

_____ Evaluate your strengths and weaknesses.

_____ Study appropriate chapters to correct weaknesses.

_____ Practice creating and answering historical essays with your study group.

_____ Develop and review worksheets for and with your study group.

MAY—First Two Weeks (It's Almost Showtime!)

_____ Ask your teacher to clarify things in your textbook or in this manual that you are unclear about.

_____ Carefully review the historical review section for as much of the year as you can.

_____ Take Practice Exam 2.

_____ Score yourself and analyze what you did wrong.

_____ Try to get answers to as many of the nagging details as you can before the test.

_____ Its almost time for the test: Let's do it!

Calendar for Approach C:
4- to 6-Week Preparation for the AP U.S. History Exam

You have been in an AP U.S. History class since September. Undoubtedly, you have read much and learned a lot. The purpose of this guide is not to start from the beginning, but to refine and to further develop all that you have been learning since September.

APRIL

_____ Carefully read the first three chapters about the format of the test.

_____ Read the comprehensive review sections on the events of U.S. history.

_____ Write one sample DBQ question, provided as a sample in this manual.

_____ Complete Practice Exam 1.

_____ Score yourself and analyze your errors.

_____ Go back to chapters on essays or multiple-choice question format if needed.

_____ Develop a weekly study group to prepare for the test (many students say this is crucial).

_____ Skim and highlight the glossary.

MAY

_____ Complete Practice Exam 2.

_____ Score yourself and analyze your errors.

_____ Review entire historical review section to refresh yourself on historical detail.

_____ Be sure to be familiar with the format of the test. Review chapters two and three if needed.

_____ **The test is almost here: Be ready for it!**

> _"Three of my friends and I worked together in a study group last year and it helped us a lot!"_ —AP Student

RAPID REVIEW

- Familiarize yourself with the Five-Step Program:
  - Know yourself.
  - Know the plan.
- Develop knowledge:
  - Know the test.
  - Carefully review the section on U.S. history and the glossary.
  - Check out AP Web sites.
- Develop skills:
  - Practice multiple-choice questions.
  - Practice historical essays
  - Practice thinking historically.
- Develop strategies:
  - Explore multiple-choice approaches.
  - Plan the DBQ.
  - Plan the historical essay.
- Develop confidence:
  - Practice time management skills.
  - Find your mode of preparation.
  - Familiarize yourself with the icons used in the text.
  - Choose your calendar.

PART II

WHAT YOU NEED TO KNOW ABOUT THE AP U.S. HISTORY EXAM

Chapter 2

Introduction to the AP U.S. History Exam

BACKGROUND INFORMATION

What Is the Advanced Placement Program?

The Advanced Placement program was begun by the College Board in 1955 to construct standard achievement exams that would allow highly motivated high school students the opportunity to be awarded advanced placement as freshmen in colleges and universities in the United States. Today, there are 35 courses and exams with well over a million students taking the annual exams in May

There are numerous AP courses in the social studies besides United States History, including Modern European History, World History, and Government. The majority of students who take AP tests are juniors and seniors; however, some schools do offer AP courses to freshmen and sophomores.

Who Writes the AP U.S. History Exam? Who Corrects Them?

Like all AP exams, the U.S. History exam is written by college and high school instructors of U.S. history. This group is called the AP United States History Development Committee. This group constantly evaluates the test, analyzing the test as a whole and on an item-by-item basis. All questions on the AP U.S. History exam are field-tested before they actually appear on an AP exam.

A much larger group of college and secondary school teachers meet at a central location in early June to correct the exams that were completed by students the previous month. The scoring procedure of each grader during this procedure is carefully analyzed to ensure that exams are being evaluated on a fair and consistent basis.

How Are AP Exams Graded?

Sometime in July the grade you receive on your AP exam is reported. You, your high school, and the colleges you listed on your initial application will receive scores.

There are five possible scores that you may receive on your exams:

- 5 indicates that you are extremely well qualified. This is the highest-possible grade.
- 4 indicates that you are well qualified.
- 3 indicates that you are qualified.
- 2 indicates that you are possibly qualified.
- 1 indicates that you are not qualified to receive college credit.

What Are the Benefits of Taking the AP U.S. History Exam?

There are several very practical reasons for enrolling in an AP U.S. History course and taking the AP U.S. History exam in May. In the first place, during the application process colleges look very favorably upon students who have challenged themselves by taking Advanced Placement courses. Although few would recommend this, it is possible to take any AP exam without taking a preparatory course for that exam.

Most importantly, most colleges will reward you for doing well on your AP exams. Although the goal of this manual is to help you achieve a 5, if you get a 3 or better in your AP U.S. History exam, most colleges will either (a) give you actual college credit for introductory U.S. History or (b) allow you to be exempt from introductory U.S. History courses. You should definitely check beforehand with the colleges you are applying to find out their policy on AP scores and credit. They will vary.

Taking a year of AP U.S. History (or any AP) course will be a very exacting and challenging experience. If you have the capabilities, allow yourself to be challenged! Many students feel a sense of great personal satisfaction after completing an AP course, regardless of the score they eventually receive on the actual AP exam.

THE AP U.S. HISTORY EXAMINATION

The AP U.S. History exam consists of both multiple-choice and essay questions. Each is worth 50 percent of the total exam grade.

Multiple-Choice Questions

!

This section consists of 80 questions. Each question had five possible answers. You will have 55 minutes to complete this section.

The College Board annually publishes material on the breakdown of questions on the multiple-choice test. According to their most recently published information, the multiple-choice is broken down as follows:

HISTORICAL ERAS:

- 1/6 of the questions deal with events from 1600 to 1789.
- 1/2 of the questions deal with events from 1790 to 1914.
- 1/3 of the questions deal with events from 1914 to the present.

TOPICS:

- 37 percent of the questions deal with political institutions and public policy.
- 36 percent of the questions deal with social change.
- 13 percent of the questions deal with diplomacy and international relations.
- 8 percent of the questions deal with economic changes and developments.
- 4 percent of the questions deal with cultural and intellectual developments.

The information provided above is extremely valuable as you prepare for the multiple-choice section of the test. As you study, you should obviously concentrate your efforts on the nineteenth and twentieth centuries. In addition, there are fewer questions on events of the twentieth century than on the nineteenth: The makers of the AP realize how difficult it is to "make it to the present" in the AP U.S. History course. Few questions will be asked on events that occurred after 1970.

It is obviously essential to spend most of your time preparing for questions on political and social changes that have taken place in the United States (again, mostly since 1789). Even though most instructors spend time on cultural and intellectual developments, there will be only a few questions on the AP test on those topics.

Question Format

As stated above, all multiple-choice questions will have five possible answers. In all probability, your teacher will give you plenty of practice on these as the year progresses. A question that might appear on the exam might be as follows:

America during the Great Depression experienced

A. severe drought across the vast majority of the country
B. a vast increase in the number of Americans opposed to the policies of Franklin Roosevelt
C. widespread unemployment in both urban and rural sectors
D. increased employment possibilities for women and blacks
E. an increased sense of militarism

You may also have questions on your exam asking you to interpret a political cartoon or a graph. To answer these, rely on the social studies skills you have developed from all of your social studies courses.

The hardest type of questions that many students encounter on their exam are the "which of the following is *not* correct" kind. Here is an example:

All of the following are true about America during the Great Depression except:

A. Americans were put to work by programs such as the W.P.A.
B. Americans saw an increase in the power of labor unions through acts such as the Wagner Act.
C. By the end of the decade many Americans favored the policies of Father Coughlin and Charles Townshend.
D. The majority of Americans rejected socialist solutions to the problems of the Great Depression.
E. The majority of Americans favored the programs of the New Deal.

Some Useful Hints on the Multiple-Choice Section

The most commonly asked question about this section is whether or not to guess if you are not completely sure of a question. If you can eliminate at least one of the answers as definitely wrong, the answer is this: Do it! As the College Board notes in its most recent publication on the AP U.S. History exam:

> *Many candidates wonder whether or not to guess the answers to questions about which they are not certain. In this section of the examination, as a correction for haphazard guessing, one-fourth of the number of questions you answer incorrectly will be subtracted from the number of questions you answer correctly. It is improbable, therefore, that mere guessing will improve your score significantly; it may even lower your score, and it does take time. If, however, you are not sure of the best answer but have some knowledge of the question and are able to eliminate one or more answer choices as wrong, your chance of getting the right answer is improved, and it may be to your advantage to answer such a question.*

> *"Go with your gut on multiple-choice questions: you don't have a real lot of time to do much thinking on individual questions."* —AP Student

Another suggestion is to make sure you read the question and all of the answers completely before you answer it. Sometimes the question asks you something other than what you think it will be asking. Always use the process of elimination when answering these questions. On the other hand, you have 80 questions to do in 55 minutes, giving you about 40 seconds per question. If you are sure you have the right answer, don't dwell on the question; you can certainly use the time for other questions that you are less certain on.

The Essay Questions

There are two types of essays you will be asked to write in your AP U.S. History exam: the document-based question (DBQ) and the "free-response" question. In the DBQ you will be asked to analyze 7 to 10 documents about a certain period in U.S. history to answer a question; the free-response questions are more traditional essay questions (you will be expected to write two of these on the exam). For the DBQ question you will have 15 minutes to read the documents and 45 minutes to construct your essay; for the free-response section you will have 70 minutes to write two essays. The essay section of the exam is also worth 50 percent of your final score.

DBQ Questions

In this section you are asked to analyze a number of documents and to utilize previously acquired knowledge on an era to answer a question. All of the information needed to earn a 5 is not included in the documents: You need to bring what you know to the table as well. In a typical question, you might be presented with a several political speeches, the results of public opinion polls, and several political cartoons from the 1960s and be asked to discuss the reasons for political unrest in the decade.

There has been a critical change in the DBQ format beginning with the May 2003 test. Unfortunately, this will not be to your advantage. In prior years, the 50-year period for the DBQ for that year was announced beforehand. This obviously assisted both teachers and students in preparing for the exam. However, the College Board has decided that beginning with the May 2003 exam, the DBQ period will not be released beforehand. It was felt that many historical trends have lasted longer than 50 years and that the 50-year limit was restricting the types of questions that could be asked.

> *"My students hated me during the year for giving them so many DBQs. After the test, they agreed it had been worth it."* —AP Teacher

Here are some hints for answering the DBQ questions. Use the standard essay format you have used for all historical essays. Of course, write out an outline before you actually start writing the essay. Students report that it is not always necessary to use every single document to construct your answer; use as many as possible, but make sure that their inclusion in your essay is relevant. In addition, students that have done well on this section note that the *order* of the documents presented to you is crucial. If the documents are presented in chronological order, your answer should also be chronological in nature.

It is not necessary to spend every second of the 45 minutes writing the essay. Answer the question, including what the documents say and what you can say about them, and be done with it. To repeat: *Some of what you already know has to be included in your answer.* As with all historical essays, there must be a logic to your answer. Organization as well as knowledge is important. Please remember that there is no "right answer" to the DBQ question.

Many students ask whether spelling counts. The answer is, generally, no. Scorers know that you are rushed on these essays; in all probability, if you think your writing is bad, they have probably seen worse. Nevertheless, do what you can to make your presentation as readable as possible. I know from personal experience as an instructor that it is hard to give a good grade to a student if you can hardly read what the student is saying.

Free-Response Questions

> *"Don't relax after the DBQ; you still have a big chunk of the test to go!"* —AP Student

Immediately after taking the DBQ, you will answer two free-response questions. You will receive two questions about the United States before the Civil War, and you will have to answer one of these. You will receive two questions about the United States after the Civil War, and you will have to answer one of these. Most free-response questions ask you to utilize higher-order thinking skills; you will be asked to analyze events and trends of the past. As stated above, you will have 70 minutes to answer these questions.

A typical question might be (again, picking one of the two) this:

I. What were the most important reasons for increased tensions between the American colonies and Great Britain between 1760 and 1776.
II. Analyze the major reasons for the defeat of the Confederacy in the Civil War.

Here are some hints for taking the free-response questions. You probably have had many of these questions in your AP class all year, so use the organizational approaches you have utilized during the year. Always make an outline before you begin to write. *Make sure to answer the question.* Don't just go around in circles with information you know about the topic in question.

Also, this may be obvious, but be sure to pick the questions that you know the most about to answer. I have had students say they chose a question because it "looked easier." Avoid that approach. In addition, *watch your time!* I have had students so intent on constructing the perfect essay for the first free-response question that they didn't realize until it was too late they only had 15 minutes to answer the second question.

One final note: Many teachers spend a great deal of time preparing their students for the DBQ question and stressing the importance of this part of the test to their students. Several students have reported to me that once the DBQ is over, they relaxed a bit. You should keep in mind that immediately after the DBQ is over, you will be beginning the free-response essays. Be ready for them.

TAKING THE EXAM

When you come to the exam, bring the following:

- Several pencils (for the multiple-choice)
- Several black pens (for the essays)
- A watch
- Something to drink—water is best
- A quiet snack, such as Lifesavers
- Tissues
- Your driver's license and some other ID, in case there is a problem with your registration

Other Recommendations

Here are some more tips:

- Don't work the night before. Allow yourself to come to the test refreshed.
- Wear comfortable clothing
- Eat a light breakfast before the test.
- You are well prepared! As you come to the test, remember that.

Final Preparations for the Exam

Some students have reported spending the entire day and night before the test studying, reviewing their notes, and so forth. If you have properly prepared yourself, don't bother; it's not going to improve your score. A quick review of your notes in the early evening of an hour or two might be in order, but by and large, relaxing yourself is the best way to prepare for the test.

> *"Last year a couple of kids in my class crammed for two straight days before the exam. Both ended up getting a "2" on the test."* —AP Student

GETTING STARTED:
THE DIAGNOSTIC/MASTER EXAM
AP U.S. HISTORY

Section I

Time—55 minutes

80 questions

Directions: Each of the questions or incomplete statements below is followed by five suggested answers or completions. Select the one that is best in each case, and write your answer neatly on the answer sheet.

1. The Compromise of 1820 averted sectional conflict by

   A. removing federal troops from the South
   B. preserving the balance of power between free and slave states
   C. implementing a more stringent Fugitive Slave Law
   D. lowering tariff rates
   E. eliminating the constitutional ban on the importation of the slaves

2. All of the following relate to the McCarthy Era *except*

   A. Alger Hiss trial
   B. McCarran Act
   C. Federal Loyalty Program
   D. "Palmer raids"
   E. "Hollywood Ten"

3. Samuel Gompers

   A. used the state militia to break up the Boston police strike
   B. led the American Federation of Labor
   C. directed President Franklin D. Roosevelt's War Labor Board
   D. was a Populist candidate for governor in Kansas
   E. advocated Socialism as head of the Industrial Workers of the World

4. During the Second New Deal, President Franklin D. Roosevelt

   A. sought passage of more long-lasting reform measures
   B. experienced less opposition from conservatives in Congress
   C. attempted to cooperate with business leaders to promote recovery
   D. averted a financial crisis with the Emergency Banking Act
   E. focused primarily on the creation of relief agencies such as the Civilian Conservation Corps

5. The trial of John Peter Zenger in 1735 contributed to the codification of which of the following principles in the Constitution?

   A. Freedom of religion
   B. Freedom of the press
   C. Separation of powers
   D. Checks and balances
   E. Taxation by elected representatives

6. "Vietnamization" of the Vietnam War took place under which of the following presidents?

   A. Harry S. Truman
   B. Dwight D. Eisenhower

C. John F. Kennedy
D. Lyndon B. Johnson
E. Richard M. Nixon

7. The Wilmot Proviso heightened sectional tensions by proposing

   A. to ban the importation of slaves in 1808
   B. to repeal the "three-fifths" compromise
   C. a constitutional amendment to free the slaves
   D. that all Western lands must be purchased with specie rather than paper money
   E. to ban the importation of slaves into land acquired from Mexico

8. Harvard College was founded primarily to

   A. promote the study of science and technology
   B. accommodate new movements in theology
   C. train Puritan ministers
   D. offer women a classical education
   E. give technical training to African-Americans in the South

9. Which of the following statements best summarizes the Rosenberg case?

   A. It represented the height of racial tensions in the 1890s.
   B. It was influenced by the nativism of the 1920s.
   C. It decentralized the power of the federal government in the 1930s.
   D. It exemplified the anticommunist hysteria of the 1950s.
   E. It ensured the rights of those accused of crimes in the 1960s.

10. In response to the disgusting conditions he or she witnessed in the meatpacking houses of Chicago,

which of the following individuals wrote *The Jungle*?

   A. Upton Sinclair
   B. Henry George
   C. John Spargo
   D. Jacob Riis
   E. Ida Tarbell

11. The Civil Rights Act of 1964

   A. completed the desegregation of the armed forces
   B. integrated all colleges and universities
   C. banned segregation in public places
   D. outlawed poll taxes and literacy tests
   E. proposed the Equal Rights Amendment

12. During his administration, President Theodore Roosevelt sought to limit the effects of industrial consolidation. He directed his attorney general to bring suit against specific monopolies under the Sherman Antitrust Act (1890). In *Northern Securities Company* v. *United States* (1904), the Supreme Court ordered the dissolution of a proposed monopoly in which of the following industries?

   A. Steel
   B. Railroad
   C. Oil
   D. Meatpacking
   E. Automotive

13. The following cartoon refers to a scandal that marred the administration of

   A. Ulysses S. Grant
   B. William J. Clinton
   C. Richard M. Nixon
   D. Grover Cleveland
   E. Warren G. Harding

JUGGERNAUT.

The political cartoon, "Juggernaut," April 1924; courtesy of the Library of Congress.

14. The Tea Act (1773) angered American colonists because it

   A. passed a revenue tax on a popular consumer item
   B. pitted eastern merchants against western farmers
   C. followed the closing of Boston Harbor
   D. granted the East India Company a virtual monopoly on the tea trade
   E. ruined colonial trade with the West Indies

15. Federalists opposed the purchase of the Louisiana territory primarily because

   A. it threatened the balance of power between the political parties
   B. they feared a war with Spain
   C. they rejected the idea of the federal government accumulating debt
   D. it would not improve Western commerce
   E. it might jeopardize their goal of purchasing Canada

16. Which of the following Civil War battles resulted in Union control of the Mississippi River?

   A. Vicksburg
   B. Gettysburg
   C. Shiloh
   D. Chancellorsville
   E. New Orleans

17. All of the following were part of President Woodrow Wilson's "New Freedom" legislation *except* the

   A. Federal Trade Commission Act
   B. Pure Food and Drug Act
   C. Underwood Tariff

D. Clayton Antitrust Act
E. Federal Reserve Act

18. In his message to Congress, President Grover Cleveland resisted the annexation of Hawaii mainly because he

   A. feared the influx of cheap labor to the West Coast
   B. did not want to extend citizenship rights to nonwhites
   C. believed that the provisional government had unjustly undermined the existing government
   D. had little support for annexation from Republicans in Congress
   E. was more concerned with mounting tensions with Spain

19. Cesar Chavez is significant because he

   A. led the AIM occupation of Alcatraz Island
   B. wrote the *Pentagon Papers*
   C. integrated the University of Mississippi in 1962
   D. was the first Hispanic mayor of a major U.S. city
   E. organized farm workers into a powerful union

20. A "flapper" was

   A. a mass-produced automobile
   B. a young woman who challenged traditional gender roles in the 1920s
   C. a steel ship introduced at the turn of the century
   D. an electric record player of the 1930s
   E. a jazz instrument

21. The Marshall Plan was

   A. an international agreement that outlawed war
   B. the blueprint for the Allied invasion at Normandy on June 6, 1944
   C. an effort to root out communists from the State Department during the Truman administration
   D. an effort to provide economic aid to countries devastated by World War II
   E. designed to send military aid to Middle Eastern nations battling communism

22. The "Great Migration," which involved the movement of African-Americans from the South to the industrial cities of the North and West, occurred primarily

   A. during the Civil War
   B. in the 1880s
   C. during and after World War I
   D. after World War II
   E. during and after the Vietnam War

23. Which of the following statements best expresses the pro-business stance of the Republican administrations of the late nineteenth century?

   A. They maintained very high tariff rates to protect American industry.
   B. They lowered corporate and income taxes for the wealthy industrialists.
   C. They bargained with labor leaders to forestall crippling strikes.
   D. They passed legislation limiting investments abroad.
   E. They expanded the federal government's role in regulating economic growth.

24. Throughout the 1920s, American farmers suffered from depressed agricultural prices. As a result, President Franklin D. Roosevelt hoped to stabilize the farm economy by attempting to control production and fixing the price of farm goods. The agency in charge of monitoring the agricultural sector of the economy was the

   A. Farmer's Holiday Association
   B. NRA
   C. RFC
   D. AAA
   E. Farm Board

25. The "supremacy clause" of the Constitution

   A. distributed power among the executive, legislative, and judicial branches of the government
   B. made presidential authority superior to Congress through the chief executive's veto powers
   C. empowered the Chief Justice of the Supreme Court to supervise impeachment proceedings
   D. ensured that all states would be equally represented in the Senate
   E. forced the state legislatures to conform to federal laws

26. During the Spanish-American War, the Teller Amendment stated that

   A. the residents of the Philippines automatically became American citizens with annexation
   B. the United States did not intend to annex Cuba
   C. all of the property of Spanish landholders would be returned after the war
   D. the United States reserved the right to intervene in Cuban affairs after the war
   E. France must abandon its claims to build a canal in Central America

27. "Education, beyond all other devices, is a great equalizer of the conditions of men, the balance wheel of the social machinery. . . . The spread of education, by enlarging the cultivated class or caste, will open a wider area over which the social feelings will expand; and if this education should be universal and complete, it would do more than all things else to obliterate factitious distinctions in society."

   The antebellum reformer who asserted these beliefs was

   A. John Dewey
   B. Lucretia Mott
   C. Horace Mann
   D. Theodore Dwight Weld
   E. Mary Montessori

28. Herbert Hoover oversaw the most successful of President Woodrow Wilson's war boards during World War I. That agency was the

   A. Food Administration
   B. Red Cross
   C. War Industries Board
   D. Committee on Public Information
   E. UNIA

29. In an effort to stabilize the economy, President Kennedy attempted to implement voluntary "wage-price" guidelines for American businesses. Although several industries adopted these standards, one in particular tried to resist the president's initiatives. In response Kennedy threatened to terminate federal contracts and bring suit unless this industry complied. Which industry lowered its prices because of Kennedy's reaction?

   A. Automobile
   B. Oil
   C. Steel
   D. Textiles
   E. Railroad

30. Which of the following contributed to the growth of suburbs before 1900?

   A. Generous federal land grants
   B. Mass production of the automobile
   C. Implementation of the Newlands Act
   D. Developments in mass transit
   E. Corruption of municipal governments

31. All of the following statements about the election of 1860 are true except

   A. Abraham Lincoln won the election with a minority of the popular vote

B. the Democratic party was split between two candidates

C. more votes were cast in 1860 than any previous antebellum election

D. Abraham Lincoln's name did not appear on many Southern ballots

E. Southern Unionists did not vote, as no party represented their interests

32. Which of the following represents an attempt to curb the arms race during the Nixon administration?

A. Test Ban Treaty
B. SALT I
C. War Powers Act
D. Strategic Defense Initiative
E. INF Treaty

33. In 1943, Allied leaders met at the Teheran Conference and decided to

A. launch a cross-Channel invasion of France
B. invade Sicily and eliminate Hitler's primary ally
C. outlaw war
D. limit fleet construction as a means to naval disarmament
E. divide German possessions in Africa

34. In the decade preceding the War of 1812, which of the following Indian chiefs attempted to organize a confederation of tribes to halt white expansion?

A. Metacomet (King Philip)
B. Tecumseh
C. Osceola
D. Geronimo
E. Pontiac

35. The Fourteenth Amendment, which ensured the citizenship rights of African-Americans, was ratified

A. when the Southern states seceded from the Union
B. after the Union victory at Antietam

C. as a requirement of "Radical" Reconstruction
D. as part of President Theodore Roosevelt's "Square Deal"
E. as part of the Compromise of 1877

36. Which of the following presidential candidates pursued a "give 'em hell," whistle-stop campaign in which he blasted the "do-nothing" 80th Congress?

A. Thomas Dewey
B. Franklin D. Roosevelt
C. Dwight D. Eisenhower
D. Adlai Stevenson
E. Harry S. Truman

37. The Ballinger-Pinchot Controversy (1909) was

A. a dispute between the Secretary of the Interior and the Chief Forester over the sale of public lands
B. a conflict between a reform governor and a corrupt urban boss
C. an investigation of communist infiltration of the State Department
D. the result of the sinking of an American merchant ship in French waters
E. a reaction to the passage of antitrust legislation

38. "The United States is now involved in a sizeable and 'open-ended' war against communism in the only country in the world which won freedom from colonial rule under communist leadership. . . . My own view is that there is a kind of madness in the facile assumption that we can raise the many billions of dollars necessary to rebuild our schools and cities and public transport and eliminate the pollution of air and water while also spending tens of billions to finance an 'open-ended' war in Asia."

A notable "dove" on the Vietnam War, he wrote an incisive critique of American foreign policy in Southeast Asia (excerpted above) entitled *The Arrogance of Power*. This man was

A. Robert McNamara.
B. Dean Acheson.
C. Dean Rusk.
D. J. William Fulbright.
E. Robert F. Kennedy.

39. The Treaty of Guadalupe Hidalgo

A. formalized the annexation of Texas in 1845
B. ended the Mexican War in 1848
C. ended the war between Mexico and the Texans in 1836
D. applied the Monroe Doctrine to Venezuela in 1824
E. gave Stephen F. Austin the right to sell land titles in Mexico in 1821

40. In 1965, a riot occurred that served as a symbol of African-American frustration to some and rampant lawlessness to others. That riot took place in

A. Oxford, Mississippi
B. Birmingham, Alabama
C. Kent State, Ohio
D. Little Rock, Arkansas
E. Watts, Los Angeles, California

41. The American victory at Yorktown

A. forced the British evacuation of Boston
B. induced Great Britain to negotiate an end to the Revolutionary War
C. ended Pontiac's Rebellion
D. caused French troops to withdraw from British North America
E. led to the removal of General William Howe

42. The United States matched the Soviet Union when the first American (Alan Shepard) was put into space during the administration of

A. Dwight D. Eisenhower
B. John F. Kennedy
C. Lyndon B. Johnson
D. Richard Nixon
E. Jimmy Carter

43. Which of the following statements about immigration to the United States during the period 1890 to 1910 is true?

A. Most immigrants settled in the South to take advantage of agricultural opportunities.
B. Most immigrants tended to be Protestant, skilled workers.
C. Most new immigrants came from Southern and Eastern Europe.
D. All immigrants were accepted into established urban communities.
E. No immigrants went to California or the West Coast during this period.

44. The WCTU promoted

A. prohibition of alcohol in the 1880s
B. isolationism in the 1930s
C. abolitionism in the 1840s
D. suffrage for African-Americans in the 1950s
E. religious fundamentalism in the 1860s

45. In 1830, President Andrew Jackson vetoed the Maysville Road Bill. The bill provided for federal financing, in the amount of $150,000, for construction of a 60-mile road near Maysville, Kentucky. Which of the following statements best summarizes Jackson's reason for vetoing the bill?

A. Westerners opposed the bill because they would have to bear the greatest burden of the taxes demanded by Congress.
B. As a strict constructionist, he never signed internal improvements bills.

C. He wanted to assist his long-time ally, Henry Clay, who opposed the bill.

D. Since the road would run within the borders of one state, he believed that Congress did not have the constitutional authority to finance the road.

E. As a resident of Tennessee, Jackson bore much ill will against Kentuckians.

46. Which of the following individuals presented a direct challenge to President Franklin D. Roosevelt's New Deal with the introduction of his "Share the Wealth" program?

A. Al Smith
B. Alf Landon
C. Thomas E. Dewey
D. Huey Long
E. Francis Townsend

47. Which of the following statements best expresses a tenet of the Puritan faith?

A. The church and state must remain separate entities.
B. Worldly events could be explained through science and reason.
C. Individuals could attain salvation through emotional appeals to God.
D. After creating the universe, God allowed worldly events to operate according to natural law.
E. An omnipotent God predestined some individuals for salvation.

48. During the 1950s, the United States experienced a "baby boom." Doctors and child development specialists spurred the national focus upon the family. The polio vaccine, which prevented the spread of a crippling childhood disease, was developed by

A. Jonas Salk
B. Allen Ginsburg
C. Benjamin Spock

D. John Foster Dulles
E. Albert Einstein

49. Which of the following contributed to the onset of the Great Depression?

A. Overspeculation in Western lands
B. Overproduction of consumer goods
C. Collapse of the Bank of the United States
D. Elimination of the gold standard
E. Significant cuts in federal spending on public works projects

50. In 1896, the *Plessy* v. *Ferguson* decision

A. outlawed monopolies
B. reversed child labor legislation
C. legalized racial segregation
D. empowered the federal government to place Plains Indians on reservations
E. limited free speech through the "clear and present danger" clause

51. In the early nineteenth century, mounting hostilities between France and Great Britain caused a war that threatened American interests abroad. When both nations violated American neutrality, the United States attempted to use economic coercion to force both nations to respect shippers' rights. The Embargo Act, which banned American international commerce, was passed under

A. George Washington
B. John Adams
C. Thomas Jefferson
D. James Madison
E. James Monroe

52. Which of the following best explains the witchcraft phenomenon that swept New England in the late seventeenth century?

A. Conflicts with the Creeks and Seminoles caused widespread panic among Puritan settlers.

B. The Second Great Awakening had undermined many elements of the Puritan faith.
C. New England colonies were more superstitious than other colonies.
D. Polluted water caused physiological disturbances among young women in Massachusetts.
E. Social strains were not being contained within Puritan communities.

53. The immediate cause of the Korean War was

A. an attack upon the USS *Maddux* in the Gulf of Tonkin
B. the assassination of Ngo Dinh Diem
C. U-2 incident
D. North Korean invasion of South Korea
E. creation of the National Security Council

54. Nat Turner's Rebellion (1831) had which of the following results?

A. It shattered the perceptions of those who believed that a bond of mutual affection existed between slaves and their masters.
B. It led to the repeal of the "gag rule" in Congress.
C. It induced Congress to ban the future importation of slaves into the United States.
D. It cemented the bond between North and South on the issue of fugitive slaves.
E. It led to the rapid emancipation of slaves in the Upper South.

55. During World War II, the OPA

A. promoted the purchase of Victory Bonds
B. fixed prices and promoted the rationing of consumer goods

C. led a propaganda campaign that contributed to the persecution of German-Americans
D. attempted to limit the Asian immigration into the United States
E. regulated the purchase of industrial resources and halted nonessential production

56. The Albany Congress (1754) was significant because it

A. was the first effort by American women to win equal rights
B. ended the French and Indian War
C. passed a series of resolutions opposing the passage of the Quebec Act
D. formulated the first bill of rights in the colonies
E. proposed a colonial union for defense against the Indians

57. By 1830, which of the following opened the Great Lakes to Eastern commerce?

A. The National Road
B. The Oregon Trail
C. The Erie Canal
D. The Baltimore and Ohio Railroad
E. The Natchez Trace

58. During Reconstruction, the Freedmen's Bureau achieved a significant measure of success in

A. redistributing the land of former slave masters
B. promoting educational opportunities for African-Americans
C. stripping power from former Confederate leaders

D. eliminating the influence of the Ku Klux Klan

E. revitalizing the devastated Southern economy

59. All of the following attempted to promoted collective security during the Cold War *except*

A. NATO
B. SEATO
C. CENTO
D. Kellogg-Briand Pact
E. the United Nations

60. Which of the following statements is true about Shays's Rebellion, 1787?

A. It was suppressed when President George Washington implemented the powers granted to him under the Constitution.
B. It hurt the Federalist party in the next election.
C. It ended when Daniel Shays was killed by federal troops in a barn in Virginia.

D. It demonstrated the power of the federal government over the states.
E. It alarmed conservatives and landowners in several states.

61. The Lend-Lease Act was designed to

A. help Great Britain in the war against Germany
B. get the nation out of the depths of the Great Depression
C. strengthen Japan against the Soviet Union
D. expand consumer credit
E. improve relations with Middle Eastern nations

62. The following newspaper headline was intended to stir up American hostility toward

A. Germany
B. Spain
C. Great Britain
D. Mexico
E. the USSR

The newspaper article, "Destruction of the Warship Maine," *New York Journal*, February 17, 1898; courtesy of PBS.

63. The concept of "republican mother-hood" emerged after which of the following?

   A. The establishment of the Massachusetts Bay colony, 1620
   B. The First Great Awakening, 1734 to 1746
   C. The American Revolution, 1775 to 1783
   D. The end of the Jackson administration, 1837
   E. The election of the first Republican president, 1860

64. Which of the following best represents the results of the election of 1976?

   A. The Republican party regained control of the executive office after 20 years of Democratic administrations.
   B. The Democratic candidate lost support in many Southern states.
   C. The Republicans capitalized upon popular unrest over the Vietnam War.
   D. The Democratic party portrayed his Republican candidate as a war monger.
   E. The Watergate scandal undermined the position of the Republican party.

65. The CIO was founded in order to

   A. organize industrial unions
   B. "pump prime" the economy during the Kennedy administration
   C. achieve diplomatic goals through sabotage and covert operations
   D. monitor the economy during World War I
   E. support passage of the Equal Rights Amendment

66. The phrase "54°40' or fight" was a rallying cry that referred to

   A. the boundary line Confederate soldiers vowed to protect at all costs
   B. a dispute between American and Canadian loggers on the Maine border
   C. a means of tax relief demanded after the Panic of 1819
   D. a border dispute between the United States and Great Britain
   E. the conflict between American farmers and the Mexican government in Texas

67. All of the following were powers that the Articles of Confederation granted to Congress *except* the power to

   A. make treaties
   B. declare war
   C. borrow money
   D. organize a post office
   E. tax

68. In *McCulloch* v. *Maryland,* the Supreme Court

   A. reaffirmed the ability of Congress to regulate interstate commerce
   B. endorsed the constitutionality of the Bank of the United States
   C. attempted to halt the state's efforts to remove Indians from their tribal lands
   D. upheld President Lincoln's suspension of habeas corpus
   E. freed Clement Vallandigham, who had criticized Lincoln's war measures

69. The most significant expansion of American highways began during the administration of

   A. Richard M. Nixon
   B. Franklin D. Roosevelt
   C. Harry S. Truman
   D. Dwight D. Eisenhower
   E. Herbert Hoover

70. In the antebellum period, which of the following contributed to the growth of nativism?

    A. Conflicts with Indian tribes along the frontier
    B. The political beliefs of the Democratic party
    C. The rapid influx of Irish and German immigrants
    D. New congressional restrictions on naturalization
    E. The feeling that Southerners were trying to spread slavery into the territories

71. In response to mounting Anglo-French tensions and French claims that the United States was bound by the Treaty of Alliance of 1778, which of the following presidents issued a proclamation of neutrality that became the cornerstone of American foreign policy?

    A. George Washington
    B. John Adams
    C. Thomas Jefferson
    D. James Madison
    E. James Monroe

72. President Lyndon Johnson was able to enact his "Great Society" programs primarily because the

    A. nation's economy had improved dramatically
    B. Republican party favored reform
    C. Democrats controlled Congress
    D. business community supported the program
    E. Supreme Court favored Republican policies

73. All of the following statements about the election of 1928 are true *except* that

    A. voters endorsed the pro-business policies of the Republican party
    B. the Democratic candidate received support from urban centers
    C. the Republican candidate won some support in southern states
    D. the Republican candidate supported the repeal of Prohibition
    E. it was the first election to feature a Catholic presidential candidate

74. Which of the following statements about life in the colonial South is *not* true?

    A. Life expectancy was lower than in the New England colonies.
    B. Gender ratios were relatively equal in the South.
    C. Disease took more lives than in the New England colonies.
    D. Patriarchal authority exerted far less control than in New England.
    E. The rivers were critically important to the regional economy.

75. Which of the following statements is true about the Battle of the Bulge, 1944?

    A. It was the first battle American soldiers fought upon French soil.
    B. It prevented Japan from invading Australia.
    C. It swept all Nazi forces from Italy.
    D. It enabled American naval vessels to protect Allied merchants ships as they crossed the Atlantic Ocean.
    E. It so weakened the Nazi army that it could no longer stop the Allied advance toward Berlin.

76. Which of the following men was beaten on the floor of the Senate in 1856 because of his "Crime against Kansas" speech in which he scathingly attacked the institution of slavery and insulted fellow senator Andrew Butler?

    A. Charles Sumner
    B. Thaddeus Stevens
    C. Stephen Douglas
    D. John Bell
    E. William Seward

77. During the late nineteenth century, bimetallism received the support of those who wanted to

    A. retire federal bank notes
    B. weaken the Populist party
    C. promote copper mining in the West
    D. inflate the currency and alleviate debts
    E. allow state banks to produce their own currency

78. Although Andrew Jackson is credited for the increasing democratization of the United States in the early ante-bellum period, state governments also expanded democracy by

    A. changing the process for the election of senators
    B. overturning the restrictive Supreme Court decisions of John Marshall
    C. extending manhood suffrage by removing property requirements
    D. granting women the right to vote
    E. passing "slave codes" that gave slaves certain rights in white society

79. All of the following represented social unrest in the 1960s *except*

    A. the SDS
    B. the Black Panthers
    C. the Yippies
    D. Mario Savio and FSM
    E. VISTA

80. "I challenge the warmest advocate of separation to show a single advantage that this continent can reap by being connected with Great Britain. . . . But the injuries and disadvantages we sustain by that connection are without number; and our duty to mankind at large, as well as to ourselves, instruct us to renounce that alliance. . . . Everything that is right or natural pleads for separation. The blood of the slain, the weeping voice of nature cries, 'TIS TIME TO PART.' "

    In an effort to rally popular support for war with Great Britain, which of the following penned these words from *Common Sense*?

    A. Patrick Henry
    B. Thomas Paine
    C. John Adams
    D. Samuel Adams
    E. George Washington

END OF SECTION I

Section II

Part A

(Suggested writing time—45 minutes)

Directions: The following question requires you to construct a coherent essay that integrates your interpretation of Documents A to H *and* your knowledge of the period referred to in the question. High scores will be earned only by essays that both cite key pieces of evidence from the documents and draw on outside knowledge of the period.

1. To what extent did the Federalist administrations of the George Washington and John Adams promote national unity and advance the authority of the federal government?

Document A
Source: George Washington's First Inaugural Address, April 30, 1789

> *I behold the surest pledges that as on one side no local prejudices or attachments, no separate views or party animosities, will misdirect the comprehensive and equal eye which ought to watch over [Congress] so . . . that the foundation of our national policy will be laid in the pure and immutable principles of private morality, and the preeminence of free government be exemplified by all the attributes which can win the affections of its citizens and command the respect of the world.*

Document B
Source: Virginia Resolutions on the Assumption of State Debts, December 16, 1790

> *The General Assembly of the Commonwealth of Virginia . . . represent [that] . . . in an agricultural country like this . . . to perpetuate a large monied interest, is a measure which . . . must in the course of human events produce . . . the prostration of agriculture at the feet of commerce, or a change in the present form of federal government, fatal to the existence of American liberty.*

Document C
Source: Thomas Jefferson's Opinion on the Constitutionality of the Bank, February 15, 1791

> *I consider the foundation of the Constitution as laid on this ground—that all powers not delegated to the United States, by the Constitution, nor prohibited by it to the states, are reserved to the states, or to the people. To take a single step beyond the boundaries thus specially drawn around the powers of Congress, is to take possession of a boundless field of power.*

Document D
Source: Alexander Hamilton's Opinion on the Constitutionality of the Bank, February 23, 1791

> *This restrictive interpretation of the word necessary is also contrary to this sound maxim of construction; namely, that the powers contained in a constitution of government, especially those which concern the general administration of the affairs of a country, its finances, trade, defense, etc., ought to be construed liberally in advancement of the public good.*

Document E
Source: George Washington's Proclamation on the Whiskey Rebellion, August 7, 1794

> *Whereas combinations to defeat the execution of the laws laying duties upon spirits distilled within the United States . . . have . . . existed in some of the western parts of Pennsylvania; and whereas the said combinations, proceeding in a manner subversive equally of the just authority of government and the rights of individuals; . . . it is in my judgement necessary under the circumstances to take measures for calling forth the militia in order to suppress the combinations of the combinations aforesaid, and to cause the laws to be duly executed.*

Document F

Source: Jay's Treaty, November 19, 1794

> *His Majesty will withdraw all of his troops and garrisons from all posts and places within the boundary lines assigned by the treaty of peace to the United States. . . . His Majesty consents that the vessels belonging to the United States of America, shall be admitted and hospitably received, in all the seaports of the British territories in the East-Indies.*

Document G

Source: The Sedition Act, July 14, 1798

> *That if any person shall write, print, utter, or publish, any false, scandalous, and malicious writing or writings against the government of the United States . . . with the intent to defame said government, . . . then such person, being convicted before any court of the United States having jurisdiction thereof, shall be punished by a fine not exceeding two thousand dollars, and by imprisonment not exceeding two years.*

Document H

Source: Kentucky Resolutions, November 16, 1798

> *Resolved, that the several States composing the United States of America, are not united on the principle of unlimited submission to their general government; . . . that [the States] retain to themselves the right of judging how far the licentiousness of speech and press may be abridged without lessening their useful freedom . . . therefore [the Sedition Act], which does abridge the freedom of the press, is not law but is altogether void.*

Section II

Part B and Part C

(Suggested total planning and writing time: 70 minutes)

Part B

Directions: Choose *one* question from this part. You are advised to spend 5 minutes planning and 30 minutes writing your answer. Cite relevant historical evidence in support of your generalizations and present your arguments clearly and logically.

2. Explain the reaction of the American colonists to *two* of the following acts of Parliament:

   Proclamation of 1763

   Stamp Act, 1765

   Coercive Acts, 1774

3. To what degree were the reform movements of the 1840s liberal or conservative?

Part C

Directions: Choose *one* question from this part. You are advised to spend 5 minutes planning and 30 minutes writing your answer. Cite relevant historical evidence in support of your generalizations and present your arguments clearly and logically.

4. Discuss the impact of third-party candidates in *two* of the following elections:

1912, 1948, 1968

5. In what ways did World War II unleash the movements for racial and gender equality?

END OF SECTION II

ANSWERS TO DIAGNOSTIC/MASTER EXAM

Section I

1. B	21. D	41. B	61. A
2. D	22. C	42. B	62. B
3. C	23. A	43. C	63. C
4. A	24. D	44. A	64. E
5. B	25. E	45. D	65. A
6. E	26. B	46. D	66. D
7. E	27. C	47. E	67. E
8. C	28. A	48. A	68. B
9. D	29. C	49. B	69. D
10. A	30. D	50. C	70. C
11. C	31. E	51. C	71. A
12. B	32. B	52. E	72. C
13. E	33. A	53. D	73. D
14. D	34. B	54. A	74. B
15. A	35. C	55. B	75. E
16. A	36. E	56. E	76. A
17. B	37. A	57. C	77. D
18. C	38. D	58. B	78. C
19. E	39. B	59. D	79. E
20. B	40. E	60. E	80. B

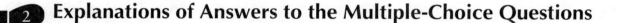

Explanations of Answers to the Multiple-Choice Questions

1. **B.** The Compromise of 1820, also known as the Missouri Compromise, admitted Maine as a free state and Missouri as a slave state, and established the 36°30′ line as a demarcation between free and slave territories in the Louisiana Purchase. The Compromise of 1877 removed federal troops from the Southern states. The Compromise of 1850 included the Fugitive Slave Act. The Compromise of 1833 reduced tariff rates to end the Nullification Crisis.

2. **D.** The Palmer Raids attempted to root out subversives in the years following World War I. All other responses pertain to McCarthyism. The House Un-American Activities Committee (HUAC), founded in 1938, raised public concern about subversive activities in the early 1940s. In 1947, the Truman administration warned against the dangers of international communism and began to investigate federal employees. Chaired by J. Parnell Thomas, HUAC began its investigations of the motion picture industry that same year. Alger Hiss, a former member of Franklin D. Roosevelt's State Department, faced perjury charges for denying that he had given top secret government information to the Soviets. In 1950 President Truman signed the

McCarran Internal Security Act requiring all communist organizations to register with the federal government.

3. **C.** Active in unionism through out his career, Gompers served as president of the American Federation of Labor (A.F.L.) from 1886 until his death in 1924. Although some industrial workers were attracted to Populism, Gompers never joined the party. He criticized Socialists and their goals. Gompers opposed Governor Calvin Coolidge's use of the militia to break up the Boston Police Strike. President Roosevelt established the National War Labor Board after Gompers's death.

4. **A.** Roosevelt passed most of his reform legislation (i.e., Social Security Act, Fair Labor Standards Act) during the Second New Deal (1935 to 1939). The First New Deal focused primarily on recovery and relief. He passed the Emergency Banking Act as one of his first measures as president. He also created the Civilian Conservation Corps during his first "hundred days." When business leaders failed to cooperate with his National Recovery Administration, he adopted a more regulatory policy toward industry. Opposition from conservatives in Congress increased throughout the New Deal, as many believed that New Deal measures exceeded constitutional limits on power and approached socialism.

5. **B.** Zenger published articles criticizing New York's unpopular royal governor William Crosby. The governor issued a proclamation condemning the actions of the newspaper. Zenger was arrested for seditious libel in 1734. Noted Philadelphia lawyer Andrew Hamilton defended Zenger. Chief Justice of the New York Supreme Court James Delany, an ally of Crosby, sat on the bench. Hamilton argued the editor's case directly to the jury. The jury acquitted Zenger on the grounds that public statements could not be considered libelous if they could be proven to be true. The Bill of Rights later ensured this freedom of the press.

6. **E.** Vietnamese forces defeated French troops at Dienbienphu in 1954. When France withdraws from North Vietnam, Eisenhower pledges American aid to the noncommunist government of Ngo Dinh Diem in Saigon. Kennedy began sending American military advisors in 1961. By the time of Kennedy's assassination in 1963, the number of advisors in Vietnam rose to 15,000. Congress issued the Tonkin Gulf Resolution in 1964, granting Johnson broad powers to wage war against communism in Southeast Asia. By the time of Nixon's victory in 1968, the number of American ground troops in Vietnam rose to over 500,000. Nixon began withdrawing American troops from Vietnam in 1969, thereby initiating the policy of "Vietnamization".

7. **E.** Congressman David Wilmot (R-PA) feared that the addition of new territory would increase the number of potential slave states. He introduced an amendment to an appropriations bill that would impede the creation of new slave states in any land acquired from the

Mexican War. The Constitution banned the importation of slaves into the United States after 1808. No constitutional amendment abolishing slavery would be introduced until the Civil War. Students should not focus upon the reference to the specie circular, which also pertained to expansion and western lands.

8. **C.** Puritans believed that only trained ministers could propagate the faith. Puritans eschewed the Enlightenment philosophy that science and reason could explain worldly events. They resisted any challenge or alternative teaching of the Puritan orthodoxy. However, seventeenth century women were not admitted. E refers to the Tuskegee Institute, founded in the nineteenth century.

9. **D.** Ethel and Julius Rosenberg were convicted of espionage in 1951 for allegedly organizing a conspiracy to provide the Soviet Union with atomic secrets. They were executed in 1953. Students should avoid the references to *Plessy* v. *Ferguson* (1896), Leopold-Loeb case (1924), and Sacco-Vanzetti case (1920 to 27).

10. **A.** Upton Sinclair wrote *The Jungle* (1906). Henry George identified the great disparity of wealth between the rich and poor in *Progress and Poverty* (1879). The other four authors were "muckrakers." Jacob Riis wrote *How the Other Half Lives,* based on his photographs of urban poverty, in 1890. Ida Tarbell published an exposé of the monopoly practices of Standard Oil Trust in 1904. John Spargo examined the problems of child labor in *The Bitter Cry of Children* (1906).

11. **C.** The Civil Rights Act ordered the desegregation of public accommodations. President Eisenhower completed the integration of the military in 1954. The *Brown* v. *Board of Education* decision required the integration of schools. President Kennedy used military force to integrate public universities before 1964. In the wake of the Selma march, Johnson signed the Voting Rights (Civil Rights) Act of 1965.

12. **B.** Financier J. P. Morgan attempted to orchestrate the merger of the Union Pacific, Burlington, and Northern Pacific railroad lines. This monopoly would virtually eliminate competition among the largest commercial carriers from the Pacific coast to the Midwest. The Supreme Court ordered the dissolution of the Northern Securities Company for "combining to restrain free trade," a violation of the Sherman Antitrust Act. Suits against Swift and Company (1905), and Standard Oil (1911) followed.

13. **E.** Scandal touched the administrations of all five presidents. The "whiskey ring" and Credit Mobilier scandals occurred under Grant. President Clinton faced impeachment charges for lying about his involvement with intern Monica Lewinsky. Nixon resigned after the Watergate scandal surfaced. Cleveland acknowledged that he had an illegitimate child. At the request of his Secretary of the Interior Albert Fall, President Warren G. Harding transferred control of naval oil reserves at Elk Hills, California, and Teapot Dome, Wyoming. Fall

accepted bribes from Harry F. Sinclair and Edward L. Doheny, two wealthy oilmen. He was sentenced to one year in prison.

14. **D.** Parliament passed a revenue tax on tea as part of the Townshend Acts (1767). After colonial boycotts, Lord North repealed most of the duties in 1770, except the tax on tea. The Tea Act enabled the British East India Company to sell its tea directly to its agents in the colonies, thus bypassing the tax on tea. The act bankrupted many colonial merchants who continued to pay the duty. Popular unrest over the Tea Act led to the Boston Tea Party. Parliament closed the port of Boston in the Coercive (Intolerable) Acts (1774) in response to the destruction of the property of the British East India Company.

15. **A.** The election of 1800 marked a transition of power from the Federalists to the Jeffersonian Republicans. Jefferson seemed to favor a limited government and agrarian interests. Many Federalists saw that the acquisition of the vast Louisiana territory portended the creation of several new Republican states, thus further eroding their political power and influence in the federal government.

16. **A.** Vicksburg remained in Confederate hands after New Orleans fell to Admiral David Farragut in 1862. General Grant's victory at Shiloh gave the Union control of much of western Tennessee. His siege at Vicksburg finally gave the Union forces control of the Mississippi River in 1863. Both Gettysburg and Chancellorsville occurred in the eastern theater of war.

17. **B.** During his first administration, Woodrow Wilson intended to address what he called the "triple wall of privilege." To achieve his goals, he lowered tariff rates with the Underwood Tariff. He addressed the problem of trusts by signing the Clayton Act and creating the Federal Trade Commission. He reformed the banking system by passing the Federal Reserve Act, which created the Federal Reserve Board. Theodore Roosevelt previously signed the Pure Food and Drug Act.

18. **C.** In spite of strong Republican support in Congress, President Cleveland opposed the treaty for annexation. He stated before Congress in 1893 that the Americans who had deposed Queen Lilioukalani had committed "an act of war . . . without the authority of Congress" and committed a "substantial wrong [to] our national character as well as the rights of the [Hawaiians]."

19. **E.** Chavez formed the United Farm Workers Union in 1966. He led a boycott that forced grape growers to sign contracts with the UFW. James Meredith integrated the University of Mississippi in 1962. Members of the American Indian Movement occupied Alcatraz Island in 1969. Daniel Ellsberg published the *Pentagon Papers* in 1971. The CIA funded a military junta that overthrew Chilean president Salvador Allende in 1973. The city of San Antonio, Texas elected Henry Cisneros mayor in 1981.

20. **B.** Changing views of women during the 1920s eroded traditional Victorian mores. Some women, especially among the lower-middle and working class, began to smoke, drink, dance, and wear makeup. The "flapper" image emerged during the "Jazz Age" but was not a musical instrument. Mass-produced automobiles of the era were sometimes called "flivvers."

21. **D.** In June 1947, Secretary of State George C. Marshall announced plans to give economic aid to all European nations willing to participate in recovery efforts. The Soviet Union and Eastern bloc nations rejected the plan as "Yankee imperialism." Nevertheless, the United States contributed over $12 billion dollars by 1950 to revive struggling European economies. The Kellogg-Briand Pact (1928) futilely attempted to outlaw war by international agreement. "Operation Overlord" was the code name for the Normandy invasion. The Federal Loyalty Program investigated the loyalty of federal employees. The Eisenhower Doctrine sent military aid to the Middle East.

22. **C.** Although Union forces occupied most of the Confederate states by 1865, former slaves did not leave the South in large numbers. The end of Reconstruction in 1877 did not spark massive migration in the following decade. World War I expanded employment opportunities in the industrial North. Massive migration began in 1915 as thousands of African-Americans sought to escape the poverty, racism, and violence.

23. **A.** During post-Civil War industrial expansion, most Republicans advocated high tariffs to protect American products from foreign competition. Both the McKinley Tariff (1890) and Dingley Tariff (1897) kept rates above 45 percent. Protectionists also succeeded in undermining efforts to lower rates in the Wilson-Gorman Tariff by adding high-tariff revisions to the bill. Republican policy of the era typically avoided significant regulation of the economy and often sided with management during strikes. Republican Secretary of the Treasury Andrew Mellon revised corporate and income taxes during the 1920s.

24. **D.** Headed by Milo Reno, the Farmers' Holiday Association attempted to raise agricultural prices by withholding commodities from the market. Their efforts failed to increase prices. President Hoover's Federal Farm Board failed to control the farm surplus. His Reconstruction Finance Corporation (RFC) also failed to revitalize the industrial economy. President Franklin D. Roosevelt created the National Recovery Administration (NRA) to address industrial recovery and the Agricultural Adjustment Administration (AAA) to regulate the farm economy. Both met with limited success.

25. **E.** Article VI states that the Constitution and federal legislation "shall be the supreme law of the land." All senators, representatives, judges, and members of state legislatures must swear to uphold the Constitution.

26. **B.** Although nationalists readily supported war with Spain, Congress denied any intention of annexing Cuba. American policy seemed to shift after hostilities ceased. In 1901, Congress passed the Platt Amendment and induced Cuba to accept its terms. The Platt Amendment limited Cuba's ability to make treaties, enabled the United States to establish a naval base on the island, and granted the United States the right to intervene in Cuban affairs.

27. **C.** Both John Dewey and Mary Montessori pushed for education reform during the Progressive era. The other three individuals participated in antebellum reform movements. Initially an abolitionist, Lucretia Mott helped organize the Seneca Falls Convention. Weld published abolitionist tracts. Horace Mann served on the Massachusetts Board of Education and revitalized the Massachusetts school system. Other states followed his model.

28. **A.** Herbert Hoover headed the Food Administration, which supervised a highly successful food rationing campaign. The War Industries Board, led by Bernard Baruch, failed to mobilize the American economy fully by the end of the war. George Creel supervised the Committee on Public Information, which produced propaganda.

29. **C.** Kennedy battled a slight recession and above-normal unemployment figures with legislation designed to foster economic expansion. He convinced steelworkers to abandon demands for higher wages temporarily. When U.S. Steel and other companies announced a price increase, Kennedy denounced the industry's actions in a news conference in April 1962. U.S. Steel lowered its prices three days later.

30. **D.** Federal land grants contributed to the construction of railroads in the West. Mass production of automobiles did not occur until the 1920s. Streetcars allowed people to move outside the city limits.

31. **E.** Lincoln won approximately 40 percent of the popular vote. Democrats split their votes between Stephen Douglas and John C. Breckinridge. Some Southern states refused to recognize Lincoln's candidacy. However, many Unionists in the South cast their vote for John C. Bell, the Constitutional Union candidate.

32. **B.** The United States and the Soviet Union signed the Strategic Arms Limitation Talks (SALT I) at the end of Nixon's first term. The War Powers Act set limits on the president's ability to commit troops abroad. The INF Treaty and Strategic Defense Initiative are connected to the Reagan administration. Kennedy negotiated the Test Ban Treaty in 1963.

33. **A.** Roosevelt and Churchill assured Stalin of an impending invasion of France. At Casablanca earlier in 1943, Roosevelt and Churchill had agreed to invade Italy. The Washington Conference (1921 to 1922) attempted naval disarmament; the Kellogg-Briand Pact (1928) sought to eliminate war.

34. **B.** Metacomet fought British colonists in the seventeenth century. Pontiac led his tribe in an uprising in colonial Virginia in the 1760s. Tecumseh forged a loose alliance of tribes in the Northwest that broke down after the defeat at Tippecanoe in 1811 and ended with his death in 1813. Osceola led the Seminoles in war against Americans in the 1830s. Geronimo raided settlements in the Southwest until the mid-1880s.

35. **C.** Congress sent the Fourteenth Amendment to the states in 1866. Tennessee was the only Southern state to ratify it. The next congressional elections increased the power of the "Radical" Republicans. They passed the Reconstruction Act of 1867, which dismantled the existing state governments in the South in favor of military districts. Republicans made ratification of the amendment a requirement for states seeking readmission to the Union.

36. **E.** Many pollsters picked Thomas E. Dewey to win the election of 1948. Truman, who ascended to the presidency upon Roosevelt's death, faced challenges from both the left and right of the Democratic party. He adopted an aggressive campaign style and traveled across the country by train. He delivered over 350 speeches, attacking Republican policy toward organized labor and the agricultural economy. He garnered nearly 50 percent of the popular vote to win an unexpected victory.

37. **A.** President Theodore Roosevelt set aside thousands of acres of public lands for parks. Richard Ballinger, Taft's Secretary of the Interior, attempted to open forests and mineral reserves to private corporations. Chief Forester Gifford Pinchot criticized Ballinger's actions and was eventually dismissed by Taft. Conservationists and progressives generally sided with Pinchot.

38. **D.** McNamara and Rusk favored American involvement in Vietnam. Both Fulbright and Kennedy opposed sending more troops to Vietnam, but Fulbright wrote the book.

39. **B.** Texans defeated General Santa Anna's forces in 1836. Nevertheless, the Mexican government did not recognize Texan independence. President Jackson resisted annexation in spite of the support of Texans for joining the Union. A joint resolution of Congress annexing Texas heightened simmering tensions that subsequently led to war. The Treaty of Guadalupe Hidalgo followed the war, granting the United States the territory from Texas to California.

40. **E.** In 1957 white mobs attempted to prevent black students from entering Little Rock Central High School. Whites rioted over the admission of James Meredith to the University of Mississippi in 1962. Police used fire hoses and police dogs to disrupt nonviolent demonstrations in Birmingham. A week of violence and destruction of property followed an incident of police brutality in Watts in 1965.

Four students died when National Guardsmen fired into a crowd of antiwar protestors on the campus of Kent State University in 1970.

41. **B.** British troops evacuated Boston early in the Revolutionary War, only to return later with reinforcements. William Howe had been removed from his command in 1778. The American victory on the Virginia coast indicated that Britain's former colonies would continue to sustain the war effort. As a result, the possibility of continuing a costly conflict heightened public opposition to the war in Great Britain.

42. **B.** The Soviet Union launched *Sputnik,* an unmanned satellite, into space in 1957. Cosmonaut Yuri Gagarin became the first man in space in April 1961. Alan Shepard followed in May. Neil Armstrong walked on the moon after the inauguration of Richard Nixon.

43. **C.** The agricultural economy had not improved dramatically in the South since the end of the Civil War. Most Southern farmers faced an unending cycle of poverty and debt. Immigrants at the turn of the century differed significantly from their antebellum predecessors. A large percentage of these new Americans were Catholic or Jewish and came from Italy or Russia.

44. **A.** The Women's Christian Temperance Union sprang from the Progressive era. Formed in 1873, this organization led a publicity campaign against the negative effects of alcohol. It reached the pinnacle of its membership before World War I.

45. **D.** Residents of the Western states would benefit from the expansion of the National Road. The proposed route could improve the movement of crops and expand regional commerce. Although Jackson had previously signed some internal improvements bills, he vetoed the Maysville bill. Jackson believed that the federal government had no authority to finance the project, since it did not run between several states and promote interstate commerce.

46. **D.** Landon and Dewey ran against Roosevelt in the presidential elections of 1940 and 1944, respectively. Neither Republican candidate promoted higher taxes as part of their platform. Francis Townsend proposed the creation of a pension program to alleviate the suffering of elderly Americans hit hard by the Depression. Louisiana senator Huey P. Long proposed confiscatory taxes on the wealthy to be redistributed among average Americans.

47. **E.** In Puritan communities, church leaders directed town affairs. Puritans believed in predestination. The Enlightenment, deism, and the First Great Awakening challenged the traditional Puritan view of worldly events and salvation.

48. **A.** Jonas Salk developed the polio vaccine, which the federal government began to distribute in the mid-1950s. Dr. Benjamin Spock promoted a child-centered approach to raising young people in his book *Baby and Child Care.*

49. **B.** Overspeculation in Western land sales and the demise of the Bank of the United States contributed to the Panic of 1837. The United States remained on the gold standard until Franklin Roosevelt took office. The federal government did not begin to spend significant amounts of money on works projects until the New Deal. Over-production of consumer goods during the 1920s depressed prices by the end of the decade.

50. **C.** During Reconstruction, Congress passed a Civil Rights Act, which outlawed discrimination in public places. Many state legislatures complied until the Supreme Court narrowed the interpretation of the law in the *Civil Rights Cases* (1883). When Homer Plessy challenged segregation laws in New Orleans, the Court ruled in favor of "separate but equal" facilities for blacks and whites. As a result, states applied the principle of segregation to all public accommodations, including restaurants, hotels, and drinking fountains. *Hammer* v. *Dagenhart* (1918) overturned the Keating-Owen Act, which regulated child labor. The Court's decision in *Schenck* v. *U.S.* (1919) limited the interpretation of "free speech."

51. **C.** Washington annunciated the cornerstone of early American foreign policy in his Neutrality Act and Farewell Address. When France and Great Britain began to seize American ships, Jefferson replied with the Embargo Act. He hoped that being cut off from American trade would force the belligerent nations to respect American neutrality. Instead, the act exacerbated economic problems in the United States and revitalized Federalist opposition to Jefferson.

52. **E.** Economic and social tensions increased as Puritan communities grew. Class distinctions emerged and friction followed. Historians differ on explanations of events in Massachusetts. Some point to the economic rivalry between Salem Village and Salem town; others note that the accused transgressed the traditional roles of colonial women. The Second Great Awakening did not occur until the eighteenth century. The Creeks and Seminoles lived primarily in the Southern colonies.

53. **D.** Both the United States and Soviet Union sent troops into Korea during World War II, and agreed to a temporary partition at the 38th parallel. Soviet and American forces withdrew in 1949. The Soviets supported a pro-communist government in the North, while the United States endorsed the pro-Western government of Syngman Rhee in the South. North Korea invaded South Korea in June 1950. Truman mobilized American forces and sought the support of the United Nations. The alleged attack on the *Maddux* led to the Tonkin Gulf Resolution and American involvement in Vietnam.

54. **A.** Antebellum defenders of slavery frequently used paternalistic terminology to describe a purportedly affectionate relationship between masters and slaves. Nat Turner and his followers collected weapons

and attacked families in Southhampton County, Virginia. Nearly 60 whites died; federal and state troops killed over 100 blacks when suppressing the insurrection. Widespread fear of similar slave revolts led to the passage of stricter "slave codes." This fear persisted throughout the antebellum period. Some Southerners believed that Northern abolitionists had inspired the rebellion, which exacerbated sectional tensions. This belief later led to the passage of a "gag rule" in Congress that prevented discussion of abolitionist petitions on the floor of the House.

55. **B.** Franklin Roosevelt created the Office of Price Administration (OPA) in 1942 to combat inflation. As more Americans found employment in the booming war industries, prices increased. The OPA capped prices and wages and promote rationing with coupon books. Roosevelt's War Production Board (WPB) struggled to convert the economy to wartime production and control military purchases. The Committee on Public Information (CPI) directed the propaganda campaign during World War I.

56. **E.** Tensions with Indians along the frontier brought representatives from several colonies together at Albany. Benjamin Franklin's "Plan of Union" proposed a form of government to administer to colonial affairs. Most colonial assemblies rejected the Albany Plan by the onset of the French and Indian War. The war ended in 1763 with the Treaty of Paris. Parliament did not pass the Quebec Act until 1774. The women's rights convention at Seneca Falls occurred in 1848.

57. **C.** Construction of the Erie Canal began in 1817. Upon its completion in 1825, it linked Lake Erie to the commerce of New York City. The National Road did not extend to Illinois until 1837. Few railroad routes extended as far as the Erie Canal in this period.

58. **B.** Although many former slaves hoped to become landowners, no concerted effort was made to redistribute the property of former slaveholders. The Confiscation Act of 1862 yielded few free homesteads. Some redistribution occurred in the Sea Islands (South Carolina), but the model was not followed throughout the South. The Freedmen's Bureau established schools in several Southern states. Staffed by white and black teachers, these schools enrolled thousands of black students. Military Reconstruction and the election of Republican governments limited the influence of former Confederate leaders to some degree. However, the Ku Klux Klan and similar organizations terrorized white and black Republicans, leading to the reestablishment of Democratic (Conservative) governments.

59. **D.** In the Kellogg-Briand Pact (1928), signatory nations pledged to outlaw war "as an instrument of national policy." Although signed by over 60 nations, the treaty provided no enforcement mechanism. At the end of World War II, delegates from several nations created the United Nations. The Security Council retained the power to

investigate international issues, recommend actions, and use military force when necessary to maintain international peace. The North Atlantic Treaty Organization (NATO) created a defensive alliance among the United States and several European nations in 1949. Similar alliances followed for Southeast Asia (SEATO) and the Middle East (CENTO).

60. **E.** Daniel Shays and followers used armed resistance to prevent collection of taxes and confiscation of property among hard-pressed farmers in western Massachusetts. The Confederation government and state legislature had little money or power to suppress domestic unrest. Perceiving a threat to property, wealthy merchants financed the state militia to end the rebellion. President George Washington used powers granted under the Constitution to call up state militias and suppress the Whiskey Rebellion in 1794.

61. **A.** By 1941, Great Britain faced an uncertain future in their fight against Nazi aggression. Bombing raids and submarine attacks disrupted the British economy. President Franklin Roosevelt favored the lend-lease policy over "cash-and-carry" because it enabled the United States to provide greater assistance to the beleaguered nation. Roosevelt extended lend-lease to the Soviets after Hitler's forces invaded the USSR.

62. **B.** At the end of the nineteenth century, a combination of events drew the United States into war with Spain. In 1898, an explosion on the USS *Maine* killed over 260 sailors in Havana harbor. The "yellow journalism" of newspapers such as William Randolph Hearst's *New York Journal* intensified the war fever in the United States. "Remember the *Maine*" became a popular rallying cry for advocates of war.

63. **C.** One result of the American Revolution was the widespread belief that an effective republic rested upon the active participation of its citizens. Although the Revolution did not significantly alter the social and legal position of women, it placed great emphasis on their influence upon children. Women were expected to instill their children with the virtues of liberty, thus creating the next generation of loyal citizens.

64. **E.** Watergate and his pardon of Richard Nixon cost Gerald Ford a number of votes in 1976. Dwight D. Eisenhower was elected in 1952 after 20 years of Democratic administrations. Dissent over Johnson's Vietnam policy helped the Republican party in 1968. In 1964, Republican candidate Barry Goldwater was cast as imprudent in foreign affairs.

65. **A.** Workers in mass-production industries remained outside the scope of the American Federation of Labor, which organized craft unions. Supporters of industrial unions strove to organize all workers in a particular industry without concern for their particular skill

or function. John L. Lewis, head of the United Mine Workers, attempted to unionize mass-production workers from within the A.F.L. A.F.L. leaders dismissed Lewis and his committee after a series of bitter conflicts. Lewis reestablished the committee as the Congress on Industrial Organization in 1936.

66. **D.** The United States and Great Britain both claimed territory in the Pacific Northwest. President Polk proposed a division of the Oregon Territory at the 49th parallel. When a British ambassador rebuffed Polk's offer, advocates of manifest destiny clamored for action. In spite of nationalistic rhetoric, Polk wanted a peaceful resolution to the issue. The United States and Great Britain avoided armed conflict by settling on the original proposal.

67. **E.** The American states ratified the Articles of Confederation in order to create a loose alliance to fight the Revolutionary War. Individual state legislatures retained a great deal of authority. The states granted the Continental Congress limited powers to wage the war. Each state jealously guarded its authority to tax its citizens.

68. **B.** The state of Maryland attempted to tax the operations of a local branch of the Bank of the United States (B.U.S.). Maryland indicted James McCulloch, cashier for the B.U.S., for refusing to pay the state tax. Chief Justice Marshall ruled that the state tax law violated the supremacy clause of the Constitution and was thus void. Marshall affirmed the "necessary and proper" clause that afforded the creation of the Bank. In *Gibbons* v. *Ogden* (1824), Marshall confirmed congressional authority to regulate interstate commerce in a dispute between steamboat companies. Marshall attempted to counter the Indian removal of the 1830s but was opposed by Andrew Jackson.

69. **D.** Eisenhower signed the Federal Highway Act of 1956, which initiated the construction of tens of thousands of miles of interstates. New Deal public works projects did not complete as many miles of interstate.

70. **C.** Severe economic distress in both Ireland and Germany impelled millions of immigrants to American shores in the antebellum period. The emergence of the American or "Know-Nothing" party reflected the widespread nativism of the era. The Democratic party tended to welcome these new Americans into their ranks. Legislation to restrict naturalization and immigration was not passed until later in the century and in the early twentieth century.

71. **A.** Smoldering friction between Great Britain and France erupted in war in 1793. Washington stated that the United States would "pursue a conduct friendly and impartial towards the belligerent powers." He repeated his position in the Neutrality Act of 1794 and his Farewell Address.

72. **C.** Johnson enjoyed sizable Democratic majorities in the House and Senate during his first years as president. He promoted a "War on Poverty" with job training programs, aid to education, and urban renewal.

73. **D.** The election of 1928 pitted Republican Herbert Hoover against Democrat Al Smith. Hoover seemed to represent a continuation of Republican prosperity. He enjoyed the support of rural America and made inroads into the South. As such, he opposed the repeal of Prohibition. Al Smith, the first Catholic presidential candidate, favored the repeal of Prohibition, a policy popular in the Northern cities.

74. **B.** Many single males moved to the Southern colonies in search of economic opportunities. More family units migrated to the New England colonies. Climate and the prevalence of unfamiliar diseases contributed a lower life expectancy in the colonial South. As a result, frequent deaths undermined patriarchal authority. The river system provided valuable transportation routes for the regional economy.

75. **E.** After the Normandy invasion in June 1944, Allied forces gained ground in France. The Allies marched into Paris in August. The Nazi army mounted its last major offensive in December 1944 along the Belgian-German border. Allied forces retreated to Bastogne and suffered heavy casualties. However, the Allied line did not break and a successful counteroffensive opened Germany to an invasion from the west.

76. **A.** Douglas maintained that the residents of a territory should be able to decide the question of slavery. Seward, Stevens, and Sumner opposed the institution of slavery. On May 20, 1856, Sumner launched into a diatribe against the Kansas-Nebraska Act and the expansion of slavery into Kansas. He focused his invective on Senator A. P. Butler of South Carolina. Butler's nephew, Representative Preston Brooks, sought to avenge this insult to his family. Brooks accosted Sumner on the floor of the Senate and beat him with a cane. Brooks and Sumner came to represent opposite sides of the sectional debate brewing in the 1850s.

77. **D.** Facing rising debts in the late nineteenth century, farmers advocated the free coinage of silver. Adherence to a gold standard contracted the federal money supply; an inflated currency would raise the price of farm goods, providing farmers the income to repay their debts. The Populists endorsed bimetallism in the elections of 1892 and 1896.

78. **C.** A number of states lifted property or tax-paying qualifications for voting during the first three decades of the nineteenth century. However, the states did not extend voting privileges to women. The states also passed legislation to restrict the freedoms of African slaves. In 1913 the Seventeenth Amendment gave citizens the right to elect senators directly.

79. **E.** Volunteers in the Service of America (VISTA) enlisted idealistic young people to address poverty in urban and rural communities. The Free Speech Movement, led by Mario Savio, and Students for a Democratic Society exemplified the student protest groups of the decade. Both addressed a wide range of issues, from the Vietnam War to university policies. The outlandish Yippies, members of the Youth International Party, clashed with police outside of the 1968 Democratic Convention in Chicago. The militant Black Panther party rejected the nonviolent protests of moderates within the civil rights movement.

80. **B.** A recent immigrant from Great Britain, Paine was an effective propagandist of the rebel cause. Unlike some other colonial writers, Paine focused American hostility on King George III rather than Parliament. To Paine, "common sense" dictated that Americans should declare their independence. Americans bought over 100,000 copies of *Common Sense* within its first few months of publication.

Section II

Part A

Summary Response to Document-Based Question

1. Although the Federalists intended to unify the nation and strengthen the federal government, their political and economic policies split the nation into rival partisan factions. Students might note that debates over ratification of the Constitution set the stage for the emergence of political parties by the end of the 1790s. They could briefly discuss the supporters and opponents of ratification, the Antifederalists, and *The Federalist Papers,* particularly *The Federalist,* no. 10. Students should examine the ideological conflict between loose and strict interpretations of the Constitution, as well as federal versus state authority. They should identify the leading Federalists (Washington, Adams, Hamilton) and Republicans (Jefferson, Madison, Randolph). Document A indicates Washington's desire that Congress may set policy without party division. Students may note, however, that friction stemmed from Hamilton's financial program. They should examine his intention to establish a sound financial foundation for the new nation by creating a national bank, addressing the public debt (Assumption Act, Funding Bill), and raising revenue (excise taxes, tariffs). While Hamilton's program strengthened the federal government, it fostered dissent among the Republicans. Document B reflects Virginia's opposition to the assumption of state debts. Students will note that the conflict over the Bank of the United States in Document C, and D reflects Jefferson's and Hamilton's interpretation of the "necessary and proper clause" of the Constitution. Students may also contrast the Republican view of an agricultural economy in Document B. with Federalist support for the Tariff of 1789 and Hamilton's Report on Manufactures. They may note that opposition to the excise tax led to the Whiskey Rebellion. In Document E, Washington states his intention to enforce federal law and implement powers granted under the Constitution. Washington demonstrated federal authority by calling forth the militias from three states to suppress the rebellion. Some students may refer to Shay's Rebellion. Students may begin a discussion of diplomatic policy with Washington's Neutrality Proclamation (1793) and Neutrality Act (1794). They may explain how the neutrality policy survived the challenge of "Citizen Genet." However, Great Britain challenged the policy by seizing American ships. Students should discuss partisan perceptions of Jay's Treaty (Document F). They may note that it achieved some of its nationalistic goals regarding the Northwest territory and promoting commerce with Great Britain. However, they should also address Republican views of its shortcomings. Some students may address Pinckney's Treaty. Students should discuss Washington's views on parties in his Farewell Address.

They will note how the election of 1796 yielded a Federalist president (Adams) and a Republican vice president (Jefferson). Students will note how the strife in the executive office reflected party differences in the United States. A discussion of the undeclared naval war with France will reveal the pro-British views of Federalists and pro-French sympathies of the Republicans. Students will discuss how opposing perceptions of the war and the XYZ Affair led to the Alien and Sedition Acts of 1798 (Document G). Students will observe how Madison and Jefferson penned the Virginia and Kentucky Resolutions (Document H), which asserted the theory of nullification. They might conclude how the problems of the Adams administration led to the election of Jefferson in 1800.

Part B and Part C

Summary Responses to Standard Free-Response Questions

2. Students may assert that the colonists increasingly believed that Parliament overstepped its legitimate authority. Students should briefly discuss the results of the French and Indian War. They should examine the development of the colonial assemblies and address the differences between virtual and actual representation throughout the essay. Parliament prohibited colonial expansion in the Proclamation of 1763. The policy intended to reduce the costs of governing the empire, prevent war with Indians along the frontier, and advance the British economy over the colonial economy. The colonists ignored the proclamation and expanded west. They grew restive under parliamentary restrictions on land speculation and the fur trade. Students may explain how Parliament passed the Stamp Act to cover the costs of administering an empire. They should note that the tax fell on all paper products, from legal documents to newspapers. Colonists angrily reacted to the imposition of a revenue tax not passed by their assemblies. Students might discuss Patrick Henry, James Otis, the Stamp Act Congress, Thomas Hutchinson, the Sons of Liberty, and/or colonial boycotts. Parliament passed the Coercive (Intolerable) Acts in response to the Boston Tea Party. Some students may address the Tea Act of 1773. Parliament intended to punish Massachusetts, long considered a source of rebellion. Students should address the Boston Port Act, Massachusetts Government Act, new Quartering Act, and/or a provision allowing officials accused of crimes in the colonies to be tried in England. Students will note how the other colonies rallied in support of Massachusetts with legislative resolutions and a new round of boycotts. Some might refer to the formation of the First Continental Congress.

3. A response to this question might begin by examining the results of industrialization, immigration, and the question of slavery. Students will measure the extent to which the reform movements promoted change or

attempted to arrest new developments. They should touch upon the Second Great Awakening. Students may address the education and temperance movements as reactions to the rapid influx of Irish and German immigrants. Discussions of education should refer to Horace Mann and the goals of public schools. However, students might also address the more liberal emphasis on republicanism or the development of female education. In an examination of temperance movement, students might address the various temperance organizations, Lyman Beecher, Neil Dow, and/or state temperance laws. Students might discuss the emergence of utopian communities such as New Harmony, Oneida, and Brook Farm as reactions to industrialization and/or as representations of new social views. They might discuss Dorothea Dix and the movement to improve asylums and hospitals. An examination of efforts to improve women's rights might include the "cult of domesticity," Quakers, Emma Willard, Catherine Beecher, Lucretia Mott, Elizabeth Cady Stanton, and/or the Seneca Falls Convention. A discussion of the antislavery movement could include the American Colonization Society, major abolitionists (including William Lloyd Garrison, Frederick Douglass, Theodore Dwight Weld, Elijah Lovejoy and/or the Grimkes). Students might address the division within the movement over the inclusion of women and/or immediate versus gradual abolitionism.

4. Students might argue that third-party candidates address the interests of groups feeling isolated from the two major parties. These individuals may attract support away from mainstream candidates. In 1912, the Democratic party nominated Woodrow Wilson; incumbent William Howard Taft headed the Republican ticket. However, Taft's candidacy did not satisfy the liberal Republicans. Reformers within the G.O.P. bristled over Taft's apparent support for the policies of the Old Guard Republicans. Students might discuss the passage of the Payne-Aldrich Tariff, the Ballinger-Pinchot Controversy, and the conflict between Speaker of the House Joseph Cannon (R-IL) and progressive Republicans such as George Norris. Students might address Theodore Roosevelt's Osawatomie speech and progressive proposals known as "New Nationalism" (i.e., increased federal regulation of corporations, tariff revision, income tax, etc.). Students might note the final split between Roosevelt and Taft over the U.S. Steel suit in 1911. They would examine how Taft's renomination at the Republican convention in Chicago led to Roosevelt's candidacy for the Progressive ("Bull Moose") party. Roosevelt attracted may progressive Republicans and other liberals to the Progressive banner. Students may note the differences between Roosevelt's New Nationalism and Wilson's New Freedom proposals (regulation versus eradication of monopolies).

Students will observe that the rift in the Republican party ushered in Wilson as the next president. Some students might indicate that Debs' candidacy for the Socialist party, by comparison, did little to take votes away from Wilson. Harry Truman faced third-party candidacies from both the left and right in 1948. Students might review some elements of the Truman administration before the election, including but not limited to the Truman Doctrine, labor issues, postwar inflation, President's Committee on Civil Rights/*To Secure These Rights*, congressional elections of 1946, and/or rejection of "Fair Deal" policies. Students may note that Truman's eroding position spawned the candidacies of Henry Wallace and Strom Thurmond. Students might argue Wallace's candidacy for the Progressive party represented liberals and Democrats alienated by Truman's containment policy, reaction to the UMW strike, and failure to implement effective social reform. Thurmond's States' Rights party opposed Truman primarily because of his stance on civil rights. The "Dixiecrats" advocated the maintenance of segregation. Students should address the candidacy of Republican Thomas E. Dewey and his favorable position before the election. Students may note that some conservatives may have supported Thurmond over Dewey. Others may argue that Truman's aggressive "whistle-stop" campaign enabled him to defeat the third parties as well as his Republican challenger. In 1968 students may begin with Johnson's withdrawal from the race and touch upon the escalation of Vietnam, popular protest, the mixed results of his "Great Society" programs, and/or challenges led by Eugene McCarthy and Robert F. Kennedy. Students may again note the division within the Democratic party and the emergence of Hubert Humphrey. Wallace's American Independent party fed upon the social dislocations of the decade. He won votes from conservatives who opposed Johnson's civil rights legislation and who rejected the disorder fomented Vietnam protestors. Wallace advocated states rights over "big government." Students will want to address Nixon's bid for the votes "Middle America," aspects of his platform (law-and-order, deregulation, Vietnam) and his "Southern strategy." Students may note that Wallace may have attracted votes away from both Humphrey and Nixon, contributing to the slim margin of victory in the popular vote.

5. Student might first examine how the war affected American women. They could discuss employment in war industries ("Rosie the Riveter" versus discrimination in the workplace), increased participation service-sector jobs (clerical, etc.), and enlistment in the military (WAACs, WAVEs). They could explain the impact of this work upon women themselves. Students might discuss the evaporation of wartime advances with the "baby boom" and return of men to the workplace. Students should address the participation of African-Americans in war industries (opportunity versus discrimination) and the armed forces (segregated units). They should examine the effects of increased opportunities or treatment abroad upon African-Americans. They may include a discussion of the second "Great Migration," FEPC (effects/limitations), CORE, and individuals such as A. Philip Randolph, James Farmer, and Bayard Rustin. Some students may also include a discussion of Japanese-Americans (internment, 442nd Combat Team), Native Americans ("code talkers," departure from reservations), and Mexican-Americans (*braceros,* urban migration, "zoot suit riot").

PART III

A COMPREHENSIVE REVIEW OF UNITED STATES HISTORY

Chapter 3

The Settling of the Western Hemisphere and Colonial America (1450–1650)

NATIVE AMERICANS AND EUROPEAN EXPLORATION

Initial Settlement of the Americas

The first settlers in the Western Hemisphere came from Asia beginning about 25,000 B.C. There is some evidence that some of these early Americans arrived by boat, but the vast majority arrived across the Bering Strait and through Alaska when the last Ice Age create a land-bridge across the strait. It is possible that these settlers were not consciously migrating but were simply following animals that they hunted.

By the time that the Spanish arrived in the Americas in the late fifteenth century, there were approximately 4 million Native Americans living in Canada and the United States and over 20 million living in Mexico. Most groups of Native Americans in the Americas were **hunter-gatherers**, although some were farmers.

European Exploration of the Americas

There are several important reasons why Europeans were interested in the Americas in the period 1450 to 1500. Some historians emphasize that only limited economic growth appeared possible in Europe itself. European monarchs and entrepreneurs therefore had to look abroad for future profits. Europeans could now travel faster and further, because of better ship-building techniques and the perfection of the **astrolabe** and the compass. The **Crusades** had whetted the appetites of Europeans for the luxury goods provided by Asia, thus further encouraging exploration abroad. In addition, the growth of nation-states (governed by kings) during this period increased the competition between European powers for both wealth and territory.

A BRINGING TOGETHER OF THREE PEOPLES BY THE SPANISH

It is important to understand that early European exploration and settlement actually brought together people from three societies: European, Native American, and African. It is crucial to understand the complex and sophisticated nature of Native American and African civilization before each came into contact with the Europeans.

The explorations and conquests of Hernando Cortes and Francisco Pizarro should be carefully studied. Both stated a desire to convert as many natives as possible to Catholicism, and economic factors were also careful considerations in their exploits. In 1519 Cortes invaded Mexico and encountered the rich and powerful **Aztecs**, centered at Tenochtitlán (now Mexico City). The Aztecs were defeated two years later by the Spanish, largely because of Spanish technological advantages (they had guns, while the Aztecs did not) and because of the diseases, such as smallpox, that the Europeans gave to the Native Americans. Ten years later Pizarro defeated the **Inca Empire**, located in the Andes Mountains. The effects of these conquests were that shipload after shipload of gold were shipped from the Americans back to Spain; in addition, a large Spanish empire was created in the Americas. In North America both missionaries and economic opportunists from Spain eventually settled in what is now the southwestern United States and in Florida.

The effects of the Spanish conquests were numerous. The number of Native Americans living in the Americas decreased, with disease brought by the Spanish also devastating the Pueblo tribes of the Southwest and other groups in Florida and the Southeast. Territories ruled by the Spanish were harshly maintained; Native Americans were forced to work as near-slaves on Spanish plantations. In addition, horses introduced by the Spanish did much to alter Native American life in both North and South America. Plants, animals, and diseases from the Americas were also introduced for the first time to Europeans.

THE FRENCH IN CANADA

The French didn't have any permanent settlements in Canada until 1608, when Samuel de Champlain founded Quebec. Few colonists ever came to the French territory in Canada: The climate was considered undesirable, and the French government provided few incentives for them to leave France. In addition, the dissident **Huguenots** were legally forbidden from emigrating. It should be noted that over 65 percent of all those who did come to Quebec ended up returning to France.

The French also desired to convert Native Americans to Catholicism but used much less coercive tactics than the Spanish. Samuel de Champlain actually entered into alliances with the Huron and other Native American tribes, largely for protection for his somewhat unstable settlement. The French actually joined with the Huron and the Algonquians in a battle against the Iroquois tribe in 1608.

Those settlers who did stay in Quebec turned from farming to trapping and fur trading. French explorers ventured into the interior of North America to develop the fur-trading industry. **Jesuit** Jacques Marquette and fur trader Louis Joliet reached the Mississippi River, Wisconsin, and Arkansas; Robert La Salle continued to explore along the Mississippi River and named the territory Louisiana (after Louis XIV).

The impact of the French on Native Americans they came into contact with was profound. The diseases they brought wiped out an estimated 30 percent of all tribes they came into contact with. Many Native American tribes desired to dominate the fur trade desired by the French; this created a serious of very bloody wars between these tribes. Jesuit priests were effective in converting thousands of Native Americans to Christianity. Jesuits were more successful than the Spanish **Franciscans** were in converting natives, largely because natives were also asked to become forced laborers in Spanish territories. When the French fought the British and British colonists in the French and Indian wars in the late seventeenth and early eighteenth centuries, most Native American tribes sided with the French.

In short, the French territories were successful as a fur-trading enterprise and a place where natives were converted to Christianity; the territories were a failure in the sense that a large number of settlers never took root there.

It should also be noted that during this period the Dutch made their initial entry into the Americas. The Dutch were largely interested in the commercial possibilities that the Americas offered them. In 1609 Henry Hudson discovered and named the Hudson River, and proceeded to establish trading settlements on the island of Manhattan, at Fort Nassau (soon renamed Albany), and in present-day Connecticut, New Jersey, and Pennsylvania. Like the French, the Dutch were unable to attract large numbers of settlers to the Dutch territories. Like the French, the Dutch were successful in fur trading. However, the aggression of the Dutch in expanding their territory brought them into bloody conflict with several Native American tribes, thus limiting the success of Dutch economic endeavors.

THE ENGLISH IN THE AMERICAS

Several factors encouraged English entrepreneurs and settlers to come to America. After 1550 there was huge population growth in England, with high inflation and a decline in wages for many workers. The number of landless laborers increased dramatically; thousands entered London and other English cities. Many observers noted that England appeared to be dangerously overcrowded, and leaders became increasingly convinced that settlement in America could help relieve the population problem.

Many English people became increasingly attracted to the possibility of resettlement in the Americas.

In addition, many English **Puritans** were increasingly disenchanted with the **Church of England**, feeling that the church was too close to Catholicism. Puritans, who followed the Protestant teaching of **John Calvin**, had some measure of religious freedom under Elizabeth I. After her death in 1603, the position of Puritans in England became more difficult, with some Puritan clergymen removed from their pulpits. Thus, by the 1630s many Puritans felt that by moving to the Americas they would be able to practice their religion without interference from either English civil or religious authorities. Another religious group opposed to the Church of England was the **Separatists**. After several of its leading spokespersons were arrested, this group fled to Holland; from here a percentage of Separatists decided to go to the Americas.

Settlement in Jamestown

The first permanent English settlement in America was the Jamestown colony, founded in 1607 by Captain John Smith. King James I had granted the **London Company** a charter permitting them to establish this colony. The swampy site of the Jamestown colony encouraged disease; in addition, several years of poor harvests created severe food shortages. In addition, early conflict with the **Powhattan Confederacy** of Native Americans placed additional strains on the colony.

Because of a severe shortage of food, John Smith created a trade alliance with the Powhattans; the corn received from the Native Americans kept the colony alive. Pocahontas, the daughter of the Powhattan chief married one of the more influential men in the Jamestown colony, John Rolfe. This marriage helped to temporarily prevent further conflict with Native Americans. Rolfe's main contribution, however, was to begin the cultivation of tobacco in Jamestown. Rolfe's system of cultivation ensured that tobacco would become the main cash crop of Virginia; the demand for tobacco in England helped to ensure the economic success of the colony.

Large numbers of workers were needed in Virginia to harvest the tobacco crop. To meet this demand, **indentured servants** began to arrive in Virginia; many of these men were unemployed, ex-criminals, or both. As an additional measure to meet the demand for labor the first African slaves arrived in Virginia in 1619, the same year that the first white women arrived there. It should be noted that the Virginia colony created the House of Burgesses in 1619; this was the first representative government in any British colony.

Settlement in Massachusetts

Colonization in New England was different. Where economic gain was the major motivation for settlement in Virginia, many religious dissenters settled in New England, thus making religious zeal a primary factor in the colonization of that region.

A group of Separatists received a charter to settle southeast of the Hudson River. The purpose of this journey was to spread the "gospell"; these men saw their journey as a "pilgrimage," and thus became known as Pilgrims. This group, led by William Bradford, encountered a storm as they neared America and landed on Plymouth Rock in Massachusetts. Before landing they produced the Mayflower Compact (1620), a document that promised that their settlement would have a government answerable to the will of the governed. As in the case of Plymouth, the first year of settlement proved to be very difficult, and the settlers were forced to rely on help from the Native Americans. However, after the first year the Pilgrims had some amount of economic success; many of the diseases that ravaged the Virginia colony were absent in colder New England. By 1691 this group joined with the other major settlement in the region, the Massachusetts Bay colony.

The Massachusetts Bay colony was established in 1629 by the Puritans. This colony was established as a location of earth where the will of God could be truly manifested; the colony was established as a commonwealth and was based on the Calvinist view of man's relation to God. By 1640 nearly 25,000 English people had migrated to Massachusetts Bay. Nearly half of these were fleeing bad economic times in England; the remainder were Puritans, who used the Bible as their religious and their legal guide.

In 1629 John Winthrop was elected governor of the Massachusetts Bay colony, a position he held for 20 years. Winthrop envisioned the colony as a "city upon a hill," away from the corrupting influences of England. Here, he felt, residents could freely live according to the precepts of God. Church, community, and political participation were all emphasized.

Massachusetts Bay did not have the devastating first several years experienced by other colonies. The colony came to be governed by a "General Court," which was an assembly elected by Puritan males in good standing. Thus, in both Virginia and in Massachusetts representative government (albeit in a limited form) were established. Additional towns were chartered in the years following the initial arrival of the Puritans near Boston.

It should be noted that there were profound differences between the Virginia and Massachusetts Bay colonies. The slave labor of Virginia never existed in Massachusetts; while many families settled in Massachusetts, Virginia was mostly settled by single men. In Massachusetts religion and political participation went hand in hand, while in Virginia land ownership was a necessity for political participation.

Effects of Religious Dissent: Development in Massachusetts Bay was steady, but leaders continued to emphasize that the main purpose of the colony was to be a place where God would be served. Religious dissent was simply not tolerated, obviously alienating some within the colony. As a result, four new colonies were created. Roger Williams believed that the Puritans in Massachusetts were still too close to the ways of the Church of England, and he preached on the necessity of the total separation of church and state (this was obviously not practiced in Massachusetts Bay).

Williams was finally asked to leave Massachusetts, and he settled in Providence, Rhode Island. Thomas Hooker was another dissenter who was hounded out of the colony; he ended up settling near Hartford, Connecticut. Anne Hutchinson claimed to have received special revelations from God; as a result, she was invited to leave and founded Portsmouth near Narragansett Bay. Finally, John Davenport and other Puritans founded a colony in New Haven. In 1662 Hooker's colony combined with Davenport's to create the colony of Connecticut.

Maryland and the Carolinas

By 1640 the English kings began to create proprietary colonies, which were given to a single individual or groups of individuals and not to a stock company. Maryland was settled in 1632 by George Calvert and was designed as a refuge for English Catholics. North Carolina was very similar to Virginia, while planters in South Carolina used slaves from almost the very beginning. Plantation owners found both Native Americans and indentured servants to be good workers; their search for large numbers of workers inevitably made them turn to slavery as a possible solution.

The importation of slaves will become crucial to the economies of several southern colonies in the seventeenth and eighteenth centuries. It is estimated that over 20 million Africans were brought to the Americas before slavery was outlawed. By the late 1600s laws had been made in several southern colonies regulating the institution of slavery.

EFFECTS OF ENGLISH, FRENCH, AND BRITISH SETTLEMENT

Many effects, intended and otherwise, were created by European settlement in the Americas. Diseases and agricultural products introduced by Europeans dramatically changed the ecosystem of the Americas. Settlement fundamentally altered population patterns in Africa (with the loss of slaves) and in the Americas (with the loss of Native American populations). Settlements in America gradually introduced representative government and freedom of religion when these concepts were not popular in much of Europe.

CHAPTER REVIEW

Rapid Review Guide

To achieve the perfect 5, you should be able to explain that

- Economic difficulties in Europe, the desire to acquire raw materials, and religious tensions all caused Europeans to become interested in the Americas.

- Cortes, Pizarro, and other Spanish conquistadors entered much of Central America, South America, the southeastern section of North America, and the area now known as Florida, conquering the Aztecs, the Incas, and other Native American tribes. Guns, horses, and diseases brought from Europe all aided the Spanish in their efforts to defeat the native tribes.

- French settlers in Canada were less oppressive than the Spanish. Jesuit priests converted thousands of Native American to Christianity. French settlers became increasingly interested in fur trading.

- Puritans and other religious dissidents came to the Americas because they felt the Church of England was too close to Catholicism.

- The first English settlement in America was the Jamestown colony, founded in 1607. Tobacco became the main crop in Jamestown, and the first slaves arrived in 1619.

- A group of religious Separatists arrived in Plymouth, Massachusetts, in 1620. The first year of settlement was difficult for these Pilgrims, who had to rely on help from the Native Americans to survive.

- The Massachusetts Bay colony was established in 1629 by the Puritans. This colony was established as a "city upon a hill," where the will of God could be manifested. A limited representative government was established. Religious dissent was not tolerated in this colony: Dissenters were thrown out and founded new colonies in Rhode Island, Connecticut, and Portsmouth.

- The ecosystem of the Americas was tremendously altered by European settlement.

Time Line

10,000 B.C.E.: Migration of Asians to the Americas across the Bering Straight begins

1492: Voyage of Columbus to the Americas

1520–1530: Smallpox epidemic helps wipe out Native American tribes of South and Central America

1519: Cortes enters Mexico

1534–1535: French adventurers explore the St. Lawrence River

1541–1542: Spanish explorers travel through southwestern United States

1607: English settle in Jamestown

1619: Virginia establishes House of Burgesses (first colonial legislature)

1620: Plymouth colony founded

1629: Massachusetts Bay colony founded

1634: Maryland colony founded

1636: Roger Williams expelled from Massachusetts Bay colony and settles in Providence, Rhode Island; Connecticut founded by John Hooker

1642: City of Montreal founded by the French

✓ Review Questions

1. By the seventeenth century, Spain had

   A. monopolized New World trade
   B. reached the height of its power and began to decline
   C. failed in its effort to build a New World empire
   D. swept across northern Africa and seized control of the slave trade
   E. pioneered new routes to the East Indies

(Correct Answer: **B.** By this point England was catching up to the Spanish in terms of naval power, and Spanish power in the Americas had reached its highest point.)

2. Which of the following was *not* a religious dissenter in Massachusetts Bay?

   A. William Bradford
   B. Roger Williams
   C. John Davenport
   D. Anne Hutchinson
   E. Thomas Hooker

(Correct Answer: **A.** Bradford was a governor of Massachusetts Bay for twenty years; all of the others left for religious reasons and founded colonies elsewhere.)

3. A colony designated as a refuge for English Catholics was:

   A. North Carolina
   B. Pennsylvania
   C. South Carolina
   D. Maryland
   E. Virginia

(Correct Answer: **D.** George Calvert settled this colony in 1632 for exactly that purpose.)

4. English people came to the New World because of

   A. their dislike for the Church of England
   B. overcrowding in English cities
   C. economic opportunity
   D. A and C
   E. All of the above

(Correct Answer: **E.** The overcrowding of cities was an additional factor in convincing some English people to "try their lot" in the New World)

5. The very first Americans

   A. lived in South America
   B. were nomadic wanderers
   C. lived in permanent sites
   D. were subsistence farmers
   E. predated Spain's arrival in the New World by only two centuries

(Correct Answer: **B.** Almost all early Native American tribes were nomadic in nature.)

Chapter 4

The British Empire in America: Growth and Conflict (1650–1750)

THE IMPACT OF MERCANTILISM

The dominant economic philosophy of the period in Europe was **mercantilism**. This theory proclaimed that it was the duty of the government to strictly regulate a state's economy. Mercantilists believed that it was crucial for a state to import more than it exported, since the world's wealth was limited. The possession of colonies (so a nation wouldn't have to rely on other nations for raw materials), tariffs, and monopolies were other mercantilist tactics of the era. The American colonies were more than adequate from a mercantilist point of view, as they could provide crops such as tobacco and rice from the southern colonies and raw materials such as lumber from the colonies of the north.

Charles II came to the throne in England in 1660 and desired to increase British trade at the expense of its main trading rival, the Dutch. Charles influenced the British Parliament to pass the **Navigation Acts** of 1660 and 1663. These bills had great influence on colonial trade. These stated that certain products from the colonies, such as sugar, tobacco, and indigo, could only be shipped to England; in an effort to help British merchants, the acts required that all goods going from anywhere in Europe to the American colonies must pass through England first.

Resistance to the Navigation Acts came from both the Dutch and the American colonies. Three commercial wars between the Dutch and the British took place in the late 1600s (with one result being the ending of the Dutch monopoly over the West African slave trade). In New England, many wanted to be able to continue to trade with the Dutch, who offered them better prices for their goods. Edmund Randolph, the chief British customs official in Massachusetts Bay, noted that colonial officials welcomed non-British traders, and he called upon the British government to "reduce Massachusetts to obedience." In 1684 a British court ruled that

Massachusetts Bay colony had intentionally violated the Navigation Acts (as well as restricting the Church of England). The charter of the colony was thus declared invalid, and the colony was placed under direct British control. The **Dominion of New England** was created, which revoked the charters of all the colonies from New Jersey to Maine and placed immense powers in the hands of Sir Edmund Andros, the governor.

Similar feelings of resentment against the Navigation Acts developed in Virginia. The price of tobacco dropped sharply after 1663, with many landowners blaming Royal Governor Sir William Berkeley, who was thought to be profiting greatly from his position in Virginia. Some landowners joined in opposition to Berkeley under **Nathaniel Bacon.** In a dispute over policy toward Native Americans (specifically, how the government could protect farmers against Native American attacks) and how the colony would be governed, Bacon and his followers took control of the colony and burned the city of Jamestown. Some historians view this revolt as a rebellion of poor western farmers against the "eastern elite." The rebellion ended in October 1676 when Bacon and several of his followers died from dysentery. The results of Bacon's Rebellion were a limitation of the power of the royal governor by the Virginia gentry and an increase in the slave trade (some of Bacon's supporters were former indentured servants; the leaders of Virginia believed that African slaves would be much more docile.)

AFRICAN SLAVERY IN THE AMERICAS

For both political and economic reasons, African slavery became widely introduced in the Chesapeake colonies in the 1670s and 1680s. Cultivation of goods such as tobacco required a large number of workers, and by this point fewer and fewer English people were willing to come to Virginia as indentured servants (with increased prosperity, more workers were remaining in England, while others viewed the economic possibilities of the Middle Colonies as more appealing.) The Portuguese and other European powers had engaged in slave trading as early as the 1440s, and African slaves had been imported to the Spanish possessions in the Americas. The first Africans entered Virginia as workers in 1619; few legal differences existed between white and black workers at that time. By 1662 servitude for blacks in Virginia was a legal fact when it was stated that a child born to a mother who was a slave was also a slave.

The trading of slaves was a pivotal part of the **triangular trade system** that tied together the economies of North America, South America, the Caribbean, Africa, and Europe in the late seventeenth century. Under this system, finished products from Europe went to Africa and the Americas, while raw materials from various colonies went to Europe. The shipping of slaves from Africa to America became known as the **middle passage**, as it served as the foundation of the entire trading system.

Until the 1670s the financial risk of owning African slaves was too much for most Virginia plantation owners, who still could be guaranteed a supply of British indentured labor. Yet as that labor force eroded, the desire to own African slaves increased. This desire only expanded when the Dutch monopoly on the slave trade ended in 1682, drastically reducing the prices of slaves in British colonies. Many landowners in the region that could not afford slaves ended up moving westward.

The **middle passage** or journey of African slaves on European slave ships to the Americas is well documented. Disease and death were common on these ships for both the Africans kept chained under the decks and the European crews of the ships. It is estimated that almost 20 percent of all Africans who began the journey on one of these ships perished before reaching the Americas.

Until the 1730s most slaves in the region worked on small farms with two or three other slaves and the plantation owner. Under these conditions it was difficult to create a unique slave culture. However, slaves cultures did slowly develop, combining elements of African, European, and local traditions. African religious traditions were sometimes combined with Christianity to create a unique religious culture. Slaves used various methods to demonstrate their hatred of the slave system that had been thrust on them. Many owners reported examples of broken tools, stolen supplies, and imagined illnesses.

Slaves were used in other colonies as well. The most oppressive conditions for slaves existed in South Carolina, where they were used to harvest rice. Overwork and mosquito-borne epidemics caused thousands of slaves to die an early death there.

Slave owners lived in fear of slave revolts, which occasionally did occur. The most famous slave uprising occurred near Charleston, South Carolina, in 1739 and was called the **Stono Rebellion**. Nearly 100 slaves took up arms and killed several plantation owners before they were killed or captured and executed. The effect of the rebellion was that slaves were treated more harshly than they had been before.

CONTINUED UNREST IN NEW ENGLAND

The New England colonies chafed under the harsh and arbitrary rule of Sir John Andros as governor. In 1688 they saw an opportunity to remove him. The **Glorious Revolution** in England removed James II from the throne and replaced him with William of Orange and Mary, who pledged their support to a parliamentary system. Andros was jailed in Massachusetts; colonists there wrote to the new monarchs pledging their loyalty to them and asking what form of government they should adopt. A Protestant revolt also took place in Catholic Maryland, while in New York a revolt put Jacob Leisler, a military officer, in charge.

The colonists soon discovered that William and Mary, like the Stuart monarchs that proceeded them, believed in firm control by Britain over colonial affairs. They sanctioned the rebellion in Maryland because of its religious overtones but ordered Jacob Leisler hung and again established Massachusetts as a royal colony with a governor appointed by the crown.

However, the authoritarian nature of the Dominion of New England ended, as representative political institutions at the local level were restored.

THE SALEM WITCH TRIALS

The Massachusetts colony underwent great economic and social change in the last half of the seventeenth century. Tensions developed between the Puritan ideal of small, tightly knit farming communities and the developing ideal of a colony based on trade and commerce, with less emphasis on strict Puritan beliefs. These tensions were largely responsible for the **Salem Witch Trials** of 1692.

Several women had been killed earlier in the century in Massachusetts for suspicion of witchcraft, but in 1692 a larger group of women were reported to display strange behavior. Observers testified many had strange fits and experienced "great distress." By the end of August over 100 people were jailed for suspicion of witchcraft; 19 people (18 of them women) had already been executed. The new royal governor to Massachusetts arrived and ended the trials, freeing those in prison. As stated previously, the trials demonstrated the social clashes existing in the colony; almost all of the accusers were members of the older farm communities, while the accused all were part of the newer "secular" class.

WARS IN EUROPE AND THEIR IMPACT ON THE COLONIES

Beginning in 1689 and continuing through much of the eighteenth century, England and France fought a series of wars to see which of them would be the dominant power of Western Europe. Various other countries also became involved in these wars in Europe; predictably, English and French colonists would also become involved. Both England and France also used Native American tribes as allies during various campaigns in the American continent.

The War of the League of Augsburg (known in American textbooks as **King William's War**) lasted from 1689 to 1697. During this war, troops from New England fought with allies from the Iroquois tribe against French soldiers, who were allied with the Algonquians. The French destroyed the British settlement in Schenectady, New York, while troops made up largely of residents of Massachusetts captured Port Royal (in present-day Nova Scotia). The Treaty of Ryswick ended this war, reaffirming prewar colonial boundaries and allowing the French to maintain control over half of Santo Domingo (now Haiti).

The War of the Spanish Succession (in American books called **Queen Anne's War**) took place between 1702 and 1713; in this war Spain was also allied with France.

Anticipating an attack by the Spanish from Florida, the British attacked first from South Carolina, burning the settlement at St. Augustine and then arming many Native Americans who had fled the near-slavelike working conditions in the Spanish missions. These Indians attacked the missions, as well as the Spanish settlement at Pensacola. Native Americans allied with the French attacked English settlements in Maine. In 1704 the Iroquois, also allied with the French, attacked Deerfield, Massachusetts, killing 48 settlers there and taking 112 into captivity.

Neither side could conclusively claim victory in several other battles that were to follow, but victories in Europe allowed the British to make sizable gains in the Treaty of Utrecht. In this treaty, France had to give the British Newfoundland, Acadia (Nova Scotia), territory along the Hudson Bay, as well as more access to the Great Lakes region.

THE GROWTH OF THE COLONIAL ASSEMBLIES

After these wars the British attempted to reform their control of the colonies in general but were unable to do that. American colonies existed in a variety of forms. Many were royal colonies, with governors appointed by the Crown; other colonies, such as Connecticut and Rhode Island, elected their own governors and other local officials. Colonies such as the Carolinas, Maryland, and Pennsylvania were **proprietorships**, with residents who owned property-electing assemblies and governors appointed by the proprietors themselves.

One disturbing development during this period for the British was the rise in the independence of **colonial assemblies**. In the 1720s the Massachusetts assembly resisted on three occasions instructions from the Crown to pay the royal governor a permanent salary; similar acts of resistance took place in other assemblies. These developments should not be seen as a move toward democracy in any way; assemblies were made up of members of the landowning elite in every colony. Nevertheless, popular opinion did begin to be expressed during New England town meetings and in political discussions throughout the colonies. Some colonial legislators perceived that the "power of the purse" could be a powerful tool against the British in the future.

THE ERA OF "SALUTARY NEGLECT"

British politics during the reigns of George I (1714–1727) and George II (1727–1760) helped to foster a desire for more self-government in the American colonies. During this period of "**salutary neglect**" British policies were most concerned with defending British territory at home and abroad and strengthening the British economy and trade. Strict control of political affairs in the colonies was not a priority in this era. Many officials appointed to positions in the Americas during this era were appointed because of political connections and not because of political skill. British politics during this era weakened the British political hold in the Americas.

The British did impose policies in this era that increased their economic control over the American colonies. Under the terms of the Navigation

Acts, all "finished products" owned by colonists had to be made in Great Britain. English officials passed additional regulations prohibiting the colonists from producing their own textiles (1699), hats (1732), and iron products (1750). However, the Navigation Acts allowed the colonies to own ships and to transport goods made in the colonies. Colonial ships carried on a lively trade with the French West Indies, importing sugar from there instead of from British colonies producing sugar in the Caribbean. In 1733 Parliament enacted the **Molasses Act**, which tightened British control over colonial trade. By 1750 Charles Townshend and others on the British Board of Trade were convinced that the colonies had far too much economic freedom, and they were determined to bring the era of salutary neglect to an end.

THE GREAT AWAKENING

A great religious revival, the **Great Awakening**, swept through the American colonies from the 1720s through the 1740s. Ministers of the movement claimed that local ministers were not devoted enough to God and practiced "cold" preaching. Preachers such as Jonathan Edwards preached of the pitiful condition of man and the terrors of hell that most will confront when they die. Entire congregations were stirred to greater religious devotion; thousands turned up to hear Anglican George Whitefield as he toured the colonies in 1740. Some congregations also split over the message and the tactics of the "Awakeners."

The Great Awakening had several major effects on the colonies. Yale, Harvard, Brown, Dartmouth, Princeton, and Rutgers were all founded to train ministers during this period, yet preachers without college degrees preaching during the Great Awakening claimed to "know God" as well; several historians claim that the movement introduced a sense of social equality to the colonies. By challenging the existing the religious establishment, the Great Awakening introduced a sense of social rebellion to colonial thought that became amplified in the ensuing years. In addition, some historians maintain that the debate and the questioning of religious authority that took place in the Great Awakening reinforced the idea that the questioning of political authority was also acceptable.

CHAPTER REVIEW

Rapid Review Guide

To achieve the perfect 5, you should be able to explain the following:

- The dominant economic theory of the era was mercantilism; British mercantilist measures such as the Navigation Acts created resentment in the American colonies.

- The importation of African slaves became increasingly important for the continued economic growth of several southern colonies.

- The Salem Witch Trials demonstrated the social conflict present in the American colonies.

- Eighteenth-century European wars between the British and the French spilled over to the Americas, with British and French colonists becoming involved.

- In the early eighteenth century, colonial assemblies became increasingly powerful and independent in several colonies, including Massachusetts.

- Even during the era of "salutary neglect," the British attempted to increase their economic control over the colonies.

- The religious revival called the Great Awakening caused some in the colonies to question many of the religious, social, and political foundations on which colonial life was based.

Time Line

1651: First of several Navigation Acts approved by British parliament
1676: Bacon's Rebellion takes place in Virginia
1682: Dutch monopoly on slave trade ends, greatly reducing the price of slaves coming to the Americas
1686: Creation of Dominion of New England
1688: Glorious Revolution in England; James II removed from the throne
1689: Beginning of the War of the League of Augsburg
1692: Witchcraft trials take place in Salem, Massachusetts
1702: Beginning of the War of the Spanish Succession
1733: Enactment of the Molasses Act
1739: Stono slave rebellion in South Carolina
1740: George Whitefield tours the American colonies—the high point of the Great Awakening

✓ Review Questions

1. The creation of the Dominion of New England

    A. increased democracy in the colonies
    B. increased the power of the governor of the area
    C. allowed New England colonies to discuss common grievances
    D. guaranteed direct control of the King over affairs in the New England colonies
    E. was largely a symbolic gesture

    (Correct Answer: **B.** This occurred after resistance in Massachusetts to the Navigation Acts, and it gave increased power to Sir Edmund Andros.)

2. A major effect of the Stono Rebellion was

   A. an increase in the number of slaves brought into the southern colonies
   B. increased fortifications around several southern cities
   C. an attempt by slave owners to lessen the horrors of the "middle passage"
   D. the passage of legislation in southern assemblies calling for mandatory capital punishment for escaped slaves
   E. harsher treatment of slaves in many parts of the south.

(Correct Answer: **E.** Many plantation owners were fearful of additional rebellions and felt that harsh treatment of slaves would prevent rebellious behavior.)

3. The growth of colonial assemblies alarmed the British for all of the following reasons *except:*

   A. At meetings of these assemblies anti-British feelings were expressed.
   B. Assemblies holding the "power of the purse" could ultimately undermine British control.
   C. The assemblies increased democratic tendencies in the colonies.
   D. The assemblies occasionally ignored or resisted instructions from Great Britain.
   E. Governors appointed in Britain had little control over these assemblies in most colonies.

(Correct Answer: **C.** These assemblies were in no way democratic, as in every colony they were dominated by the landowning elite.)

4. For the British, the major economic role of the American colonies was

   A. to produce manufactured goods the English did not want to produce
   B. to produce crops such as tobacco
   C. to provide food and materials for the other British colonies
   D. to produce raw materials such as lumber
   E. B and D above

(Correct Answer: **E.** The role of the colonies under mercantilism was to provide England with crops and raw materials.)

5. What changes in the slave system of the southern colonies began in the 1730s?

   A. The Dutch lost the monopoly on slave trading, thus increasing the number of slaves being brought into the Americas.
   B. Conditions during the "middle passage" began to slightly improve.
   C. Under pressure from religious leaders, slave conditions in South Carolina became less oppressive.
   D. More slaves began to live and work on larger plantations.
   E. A series of slave rebellions created much harsher treatment for slaves.

(Correct Answer: **D.** Before the 1730s, most slaves worked on small farms. The Dutch lost their monopoly on slave trading back in 1682. The Stono Rebellion was the first major slave rebellion and occurred in 1739.)

Chapter 5

Resistance, Rebellion, and Revolution (1750–1775)

PROBLEMS ON THE FRONTIER

An energetic traveler going west of the Appalachian Mountains in 1750 would discover a land inhabited by Native American tribes who had no desire to release their territory to colonial or European settlers. The Iroquois and other tribes of the region had traded and allied with both the English and the French, depending on who offered the best "deal" at the time.

Beginning in the 1740s, English and French interests in this region began to come into conflict. Land speculators from Virginia and other colonies began to acquire land in the Ohio Valley, and they tried to broker further treaties with Native Americans who resided there. French colonial officials viewed this with alarm, as their ultimate aim was to connect Canada and Louisiana with a series of forts and settlements through much of the same region.

In 1754 delegates from seven northern and middle colonies met at the **Albany Congress**, at which the colonies attempted to coordinate their policies concerning further westward settlement and concerning Native Americans. While the representatives couldn't agree on several main points, Governor Robert Dinwiddie of Virginia sent a young militia officer to attempt to stop the French construction of a fort at what is now the city of Pittsburgh. The young officer, George Washington, was defeated in battle there. Several Native American tribes, noting the incompetence of Washington and the colonial army, decided to cast their lot with the French. After hearing of this defeat in early 1756, the British sent a seasoned general, Edward Braddock, to stop French construction of Fort Duquesne. Braddock's army was routed by the French, and he was killed in the battle. When London heard of this, war was officially declared against the French. This was the beginning of the Seven Years War (in American textbooks called the **French and Indian War**).

79

ADDITIONAL CONFLICTS BETWEEN THE BRITISH AND THEIR COLONIAL "ALLIES"

The war went very badly for the British and the colonial Americans in 1756 and 1757. Much of New York was captured by the French, and even the western New England territories appeared to be in jeopardy. Other than the Iroquois, most Native American tribes sided with the French. The British finally put the war in the hands of William Pitt, who sent nearly 25,000 to the Americas to fight against the French. The British had had little luck in convincing the colonies to supply many men or much material to the war effort. To get the support of the colonies, Pitt agreed to reimburse them for expenses during the war and put the recruiting of troops totally in local hands (Pitt's willingness to incur large debts for Great Britain to finance the war effort should be noted). As a result, a colonial army of nearly 24,000 joined with the British army to battle the French. The French stronghold at Quebec was defeated in 1759, and Montreal was taken one year later.

The **Treaty of Paris** ending the French and Indian War effectively in 1763 ended French influence in the Americas. Most French territory in the New World was given to the British, who now controlled over half of the continent of North America. France also gave Spain (its ally in the war) the Louisiana territory west of the Mississippi River.

The American colonists and the British both shared a sense of victory in 1763, yet resentments between the two festered. The colonist resented the patronizing attitude that the British had toward them; in addition, many British soldiers had been quartered in the homes of colonists without compensation. Many colonial soldiers viewed with horror the harsh punishments given to British soldiers for trivial infractions. The British felt that the colonists never did their fair share in the war; they also noted that some colonists continued to trade with the French during the first two years of the war.

THE POLICIES OF GEORGE GRENVILLE

George II died in 1660 and was succeeded by his grandson, George III. George III never exhibited even average political skills and was more than willing to give his ministers (who he rapidly replaced) a large amount of political power. In 1763 he selected George Grenville as prime minister.

Grenville faced a difficult financial task. Great Britain had great debt, largely because of the lengthy wars that had taken place both on the continent and in the colonies. British citizens were already very heavily taxed. Grenville felt that one way to relieve the financial burden facing the Crown would be for the American colonists to pay a greater share for colonial administration. Grenville was convinced that Britain should be making more money than it was in the Americas; he was personally disturbed by the illegal trading carried out by colonists during the Seven Years War.

Grenville took measures to "reform" the trading relationship between Britain and the Americas. The <u>Currency Act</u> of 1764 made it illegal to print paper money in the colonies. Because of the lack of hard currency in the colonies, the impact of this bill was significant. The <u>Sugar Act</u> of the same year conceded that the colonies were importing large amounts of French molasses, but it increased the penalties for colonial smuggling and ensured that colonists would pay the British a duty for all molasses brought into the colonies. In the years after the French and Indian War, colonial economies were already suffering from depression; the Grenville Acts only served to make that depression worse.

Debate over the reforms of Grenville appeared in many colonial newspapers, with many editorials pondering the proper relationship between decisions made in Great Britain and the American colonies.

A SENSE OF CRISIS: THE STAMP ACT

The act proposed by Grenville that created the greatest furor in the colonies was the <u>Stamp Act</u>. This act would require a purchased stamp on virtually all printed material purchased in the colonies: Newspapers, wills, dice, official documents, and countless other written documents would require this stamp. This was controversial in the colonies because this was the first time the Parliament would directly tax the colonies; before, this all taxation was self-imposed. Grenville's purpose was two-fold: The Stamp Act would raise needed revenue and would uphold "the Right of Parliament to lay an internal Tax upon the Colonies."

For many colonists the final straw was the <u>Quartering Act</u>, which insisted that colonial governments provide food and accommodations for British troops stationed in the colonies.

In several colonies, such as Massachusetts, reaction against the Stamp Act was swift. During July of 1765 the <u>Sons of Liberty</u> was created in Boston, led by Samuel Adams. Demonstrations by this group forced the stamp agent in Massachusetts, Andrew Oliver, to resign. Similar outbursts in other colonies forced stamp agents to resign. Some politicians also began to speak in state assemblies against the act. Patrick Henry proclaimed in the Virginia Houses of Burgesses that the act demonstrated the tyranny of George III; several members of the assembly demanded that he be arrested for treason. James Otis from Massachusetts and Benjamin Franklin from Philadelphia both proposed that the colonists be directly represented in the British Parliament. In October of 1765, nine colonies met together at the <u>Stamp Act Congress</u>, where representatives reaffirmed the principal that taxation of the colonies be imposed only from within the colonies.

The Repeal of the Stamp Act

The uproar from the colonies may have helped the British Parliament to repeal the Stamp Act. However, the real pressure for repeal came from

British merchants, who feared the act would destroy the profits they made by trading with the colonies. Economic boycotts were threatened in numerous colonies. Lord Rockingham, the new prime minister, urged repeal of the bill not for philosophical but for economic and political reasons. Celebration occurred in many colonies when news of the repeal came from Britain. These celebrations became muted when word arrived that the Parliament had also passed a **Declaratory Act**, which stated that Parliament had the right to tax and pass legislation regarding the colonies "in all cases whatsoever."

MORE PROTEST: THE TOWNSHEND ACTS

In 1766 George III appointed the aging and infirm William Pitt as prime minister. Ill health made him unable to concentrate on his duties concerning the colonies. As a result, Charles Townshend, the **Chancellor of the Exchequer**, had a large hand in creating policy concerning the American colonies. Townshend decided to follow the policies of Grenville and try to extract more income for the government from colonial trade. In 1767 he proposed new duties on glass, paper, and tea. These **Townshend Acts** were different than previous duties on colonial trade; these were for goods produced in Britain. In addition, income from these acts would be used to pay the salaries of certain ranks of British officials in the colonies; colonial assemblies had always authorized these salaries. Townshend also created new courts in the colonies, the Admiralty courts, to try smuggling cases and ordered British soldiers to be stationed in major port cities (to hopefully prevent the protests that had followed the Stamp Act).

The opposition to the Townshend Acts in the colonies was immediate and sustained. Newspaper editorials and pamphlets renounced the acts with vehemence. John Dickinson from Pennsylvania best expressed the colonial position in his **Letters from a Farmer in Pennsylvania** (1767). Dickinson said that Parliament had the right to regulate colonial trade, but not to use that power to raise revenue. By this argument, only duties used to control trade or regulate the affairs of the empire were legal. Benjamin Franklin expressed a different view of the situation. Franklin stated that "Either Parliament has the power to make all laws for us, or Parliament has the power to make no laws for us; and I think the arguments for the latter more numerous and weighty than those of the former."

In early 1768 Samuel Adams in Massachusetts composed a document opposing the Townshend Acts, proclaiming that "taxation without representation is tyranny." The Massachusetts Assembly voted to approve this document and send it along to other colonial assemblies for approval. The royal governor stated that this **Circular Letter** was a form of sedition, and Parliament suggested that and state assembly passing such a resolution be dissolved. Yet similar resolutions were passed in five other colonies. Boycotts of British goods again took place to protest the Townshend Acts. In 1770 a new prime minister came into power in Britain, Lord North. North repealed all of the Townshend Acts except the tax on tea; the tea tax remained to remind the colonists that the British had the right to collect such taxes if they desired to.

CONTINUED TENSIONS IN MASSACHUSETTS

British customs officials and merchants in Massachusetts continued to clash over the smuggling of goods into Boston harbor. In 1768 officials seized a vessel belonging to a well-known smuggler, John Hancock; in the next several days several customs officials were roughed up. As a result, two regiments of regular British soldiers were assigned to the city. Tensions increased notably in the city; many local workers became incensed when, in their off-hours, British soldiers took jobs that had previously been held by Bostonians. Soldiers were taunted on a regular basis. On March 5, 1770, the event that became known as the **Boston Massacre** took place. A confrontation occurred, with laborers throwing snowballs filled with rocks at the soldiers. The soldiers, acting against orders, finally shot into the crowd, killing five men and wounding eight. Sam Adams and others made much of the "massacre," yet members of the **Sons of Liberty** opposed uncontrolled violence. Seven soldiers were later put on trial for the "massacre"; five were acquitted and two were branded on the thumb and then freed.

THE CALM BEFORE THE STORM: 1770–1773

There was an apparent calm in relations between the British and the colonies between 1770 and 1773. Import duties were collected on a regular basis. The tea tax was still in effect; some colonists boycotted British tea, but some drank it openly. Resistance again occurred first in Massachusetts. Samuel Adams established a **Committee of Correspondence** in Boston. Similar groups were created throughout Massachusetts, Virginia, and other colonies as well. These groups were designed to share information on British activities in the Americas, as well as to share details of demonstrations, protests, and so on. Some historians argue that these Committees of Correspondence were the first permanent machinery of protest in the colonies.

THE BOSTON TEA PARTY

The Boston Tea Party occurred because of an effort by the British government to save the near-bankrupt East India Tea Company. American boycotts and smuggled Dutch tea had hurt this company; they asked the government for permission to sell their tea directly to the American colonies without going through English merchants as middlemen. The old tax on tea would remain, but tea would now be cheaper to purchase for the colonists. Lord North and Parliament approved the passage of the **Tea Act** that would legalize these changes.

Colonial leaders were furious. Some pointed out that this measure reaffirmed that Parliament could tax the colonies; others feared a monopoly of the East India Company on all colonial trade. In the fall of 1773, crowds prevented tea from being unloaded in several port cities. Predictably, Boston was the city where resistance was the strongest. On December 16, 1773, in an event called the **Boston Tea Party**, 65 men dressed as Mohawk Indians boarded the tea ships and dumped nearly 350 chests of tea in the harbor.

THE INTOLERABLE ACTS

The British were extremely quick to act in punishing the colonists. The **Intolerable Acts** all took effect by May of 1774. The port of Boston was closed except for military ships and ships specifically permitted by British custom officials. The upper house of the Massachusetts Assembly would now be appointed by the king instead of being elected by the lower house. Town meetings could not be held without the governor's consent, and the Quartering Act was again put into effect. Many concerned citizens in other colonies feared that similar actions could easily occur elsewhere. As a result, several colonial legislatures suggested a meeting of representatives from all the colonies to discuss the situation in Massachusetts. The passage of the Quebec Act by the British further alarmed many colonial leaders. Among other things, this act increased the religious freedom of French Catholics. To many Protestants in the colonies, Catholicism was easily equated with the absolutist French monarchy of the eighteenth century.

THE FIRST CONTINENTAL CONGRESS

Fifty-six delegates from every colony except Georgia attended the Continental Congress in Philadelphia on September 5, 1774. Some of those present, such as Sam Adams, pushed for a total boycott of British goods; others proposed further negotiations with Parliament. John Adams worked out a compromise entitled the **Declaration of Rights and Grievances**, which stated that the colonists would not object to measures designed to regulate their external commerce. The colonies would, however, resist any measures that taxed them without their consent. The mood of the meeting was even clearer when the **Suffolk Resolves** were adopted. This act stated that colonies would continue to boycott English imports and approve the efforts of Massachusetts to operate a colonial government free from British control until the Intolerable Acts were rescinded. Colonies were also urged to raise and train militias of their own.

Before they adjourned, the Continental Congress sent a petition to George III requesting the repeal of all regulatory acts since 1763 and informing him of the continued boycott of British goods. Colonial leaders returned home, wondering what the response of George III to their petition would be.

CHAPTER REVIEW

Rapid Review Guide

To achieve the perfect 5, you should be able to explain the following:

- Tensions between the British and the French intensified in the 1740s when land speculators from the English colonies began to acquire land in the Ohio Valley.
- The Seven Years War (the French and Indian War in American textbooks) was between the English and colonial militias and the French; Native Americans fought on both sides.
- The defeat of the French in this war largely ended their influenced in the Americas; after the war, the British attempted to make the colonies pay their fair share for the war effort.
- Parliamentary efforts during this era to produce money for Great Britain by imposing various taxes and duties on the colonies resulted in great unrest in the colonies.
- The impact of the Stamp Act on the colonies was great; as a result, nine colonies met at the 1765 Stamp Act Congress and the Sons of Liberty formed in Boston.
- Boston remained a center of opposition to British policy; the Boston Massacre in 1770 and the Boston Tea Party in 1773 helped to create resistance to the Crown in other colonies as well.
- The 1774 Intolerable Acts, which closed the port of Boston and curtailed freedom of speech in Massachusetts, outraged many in the colonies.
- The 1774 First Continental Congress passed a resolution that firmly stated the colonies would firmly resist measures that taxed them without their consent. At this meeting it was also decided that individual colonies should start to raise and train state militias.

Time Line

1754: Representatives of colonies meet at Albany Congress to coordinate further western settlement
1756: Beginning of Seven Years War
1763: Signing of Treaty of Paris ending Seven Years War
1764: Parliament approves Sugar Act, Currency Act
1765: Stamp Act approved by Parliament; Stamp Act Congress occurs and Sons of Liberty are formed, both in opposition to the Stamp Act
1766: Stamp Act repealed, but in Declaratory Act, Parliament affirms its right to tax the colonies
1767: Passage of the Townshend Acts

> 1770: Boston Massacre occurs
> 1773: Boston Tea Party takes place in December in opposition to the Tea Act
> 1774: Intolerable Acts adopted by Parliament
> First Continental Congress held in Philadelphia

✓ Review Questions

1. William Pitt was able to convince the colonies to fight in the Seven Years War by

   A. convincing Native American tribes to attack colonial settlements in the Ohio valley
   B. threatening military reprisals by the British army
   C. threatening to make the colonists fight the French by themselves
   D. putting the recruiting of troops in the colonies totally in the hands of the colonies themselves
   E. paying colonial soldiers generous bonuses to fight against the French

(Correct Answer: **D.** Pitt put the recruiting of colonial troops totally in local hands and agreed to reimburse the colonies for all their expenses during the war.)

2. The Stamp Act created great fury in the colonies because

   A. it imposed massive duties on the colonies
   B. colonial legislatures had expressed opposition to it beforehand
   C. it was the first time Parliament had imposed a duty on the colonies
   D. it took badly needed revenue away from colonial legislatures
   E. this was the first time that Parliament imposed a direct tax on the colonies

(Correct Answer: **E.** All previous taxation of the colonies had been self-imposed.)

3. The statement "taxation without representation is tyranny" was first proclaimed by

   A. Benjamin Franklin
   B. John Hancock
   C. Samuel Adams
   D. John Dickinson
   E. Patrick Henry

(Correct Answer: **C.** This statement was first made by Adams in 1768 in an article he wrote opposing the Townshend Acts.)

4. After the Seven Years War, resentment between the British and the colonists existed for all of the following reasons *except*

   A. the British resented the fact that few colonists had actually helped them in the war against the French
   B. British soldiers had been quartered in colonial homes
   C. the British resented the fact that some colonists continued to trade with the French at the beginning of the war
   D. colonial militiamen felt the British exhibited a patronizing attitude toward them
   E. many colonial militiamen were appalled at the incredibly harsh discipline that British officers imposed on their soldiers

(Correct Answer: **A.** The colonies contributed nearly 24,000 men to the war effort—while the British contributed 25,000.)

5. Most delegates at the First Continental Congress of 1774

   A. felt that there should be a total boycott of British goods by the colonies
   B. felt that the colonies should firmly resist measures to tax them without their consent
   C. felt that it was time to seriously consider military measures against the British
   D. wanted the British to totally refrain from regulating trade to the colonies
   E. proposed sending Benjamin Franklin and John Dickinson as representatives to the British parliament

(Correct Answer: **B.** Although some, including Sam Adams, wanted a boycott of all British goods, John Adams crafted a compromise that called for the colonies to oppose "taxation without representation.")

Chapter 6

The American Revolution and the New Nation (1775–1787)

THE AMERICAN REVOLUTION

Prelude to Revolution: Lexington and Concord: April, 1775

Events in the colonies had little effect on attitudes in Britain. George III and Lord North both still insisted that the colonies comply with edicts from England. What they failed to realize was that royal authority in the colonies was routinely being ignored. General Thomas Gage was the acting governor of Massachusetts, and in early 1775 he ordered the Massachusetts Assembly not to meet. They met anyway.

Gage also wanted to stop the growth of local militias. On April 19 he sent a group of regular British troops to Concord to seize colonial arms stored there and to arrest any "rebel" leaders that could be found. As you learned in second grade, Paul Revere and other messengers rode out from Boston to warn the countryside of the advance of the British soldiers. At dawn on April 19 several hundred British soldiers ran into 75 colonial militiamen on the town green in <u>Lexington</u>. The British ordered the colonists to disperse; in the confusion, shots rang out, with 8 colonists killed and 10 wounded.

The British marched on to <u>Concord</u>, where a larger contingent of militiamen awaited them. The British destroyed military stores and food supplies and were ready to return to Boston when the colonists opened fire, with three British soldiers killed and nine wounded. The British were attacked at they retreated to Lexington; they lost 275 men, compared to 93 colonial militiamen killed. At Lexington the British were saved by the arrival of reinforcements.

Several weeks later Ethan Allen and his Green Mountain Boys captured Fort Ticonderoga from the British. Cannons from the fort were dragged to

Boston, where they would be a decisive factor in forcing the British to leave Boston harbor in March 1776.

THE SECOND CONTINENTAL CONGRESS

The purpose of the <u>Second Continental Congress</u>, which met in Philadelphia in May of 1775, was clear: to get the American colonies ready for war. It authorized the printing of paper money to buy supplies for the war, established a committee to supervise foreign relations with other countries, and created a Continental Army. George Washington was appointed commander in chief of this new army. Washington was chosen because of his temperament, because of his experiences in the French and Indian Wars, and because he was *not* from Massachusetts, considered by George III the place where the "rabble" were.

The Congress made one final gesture for peace when moderates drafted, and the Congress approved, the sending of the "Olive Branch Petition" to George III. This document, approved on July 5, 1775, asked the king to formulate a "happy and permanent reconciliation." The fact that the king refused to even receive the document strengthened the hand of political radicals throughout the colonies.

The Impact of *Common Sense*

The impact of Thomas Paine's <u>*Common Sense*</u> on colonial thought was immense. Paine was a printer and had only been in the colonies for two years when his pamphlet was published in January of 1776. Virtually every educated person in the colonies read this document (within three months 120,000 copies were sold). Paine proclaimed that "monarchy and hereditary succession have laid the world in blood and ashes" and called George III a "royal brute." Paine attacked the entire system of monarchy and empire, expressing confidence that the colonies would flourish once they were removed from British control. Many saw in Paine's document very sensible reasons why the Americas should break from Britain. When discussing the document, one New York <u>loyalist</u> bitterly complained that "the unthinking multitude are mad for it . . . ."

THE DECLARATION OF INDEPENDENCE

On June 7, 1776, Henry Lee of Virginia made a motion at the meeting of the Second Continental Congress in Philadelphia. His motion proposed that American colonies should be considered independent states, that foreign relations should begin with other countries, and that a confederate form of government be prepared for future discussion by the colonies. It was decided that the motion would be voted on July 1 (giving delegates time to win the resistant middle colonies over). In the meantime, one committee worked on a potential constitution, while another was appointed to write a declaration of independence. This committee gave the job of writing the first draft to Thomas Jefferson. Jefferson was a perfect choice: He was a student of the thinkers of the **Enlightenment** and other thinkers of the era.

Jefferson's argument maintained that men had certainly "unalienable rights," which included "Life, Liberty, and the pursuit of Happiness." Jefferson stated that when a government "becomes destructive of these ends" those who live under it can revolt against it and create a government that gets its "just powers from the consent of the governed." Jefferson also listed many things the British had done that were oppressive to the colonies. Unlike others who had criticized certain ministers or Parliament, Jefferson personally blamed George III for many of these misdeeds. This document was formally approved on July 2, 1776; this approval was formally announced on July 4.

THE OUTBREAK OF THE REVOLUTION: DIVISIONS IN THE COLONIES

The celebrations surrounding the announcement of the Declaration of Independence took place in every colony, but not every citizen living in the Americas took part. Many loyalists were members of the colonial economic elite and feared the repercussions on their pocketbooks of a break with Great Britain. Other loyalists saw the legitimacy of Britain's control over the colonies; some loyalists were also very practical men, who predicted the easy defeat of the colonies by the seemingly immense British army.

Blacks in America greeted the Declaration of Independence with enthusiasm. Many free blacks saw the a possible revolution as a chance to improve their position; slaves saw the possibilities of freedom from slavery (during the war some slaves managed to escape their masters, and a few even fought on the side of the British). During the fighting, British troops freed slaves in Georgia and South Carolina. In the North, some slaves fought in colonial militias, winning their freedom through military service. The British courted Native American tribes, but their determination to definitively help the British in battle was never strong.

STRATEGIES OF THE AMERICAN REVOLUTION

It is easy to see how the British thought that they would be able to defeat the colonists quickly and decisively. Britain had a strong navy, one of the finest armies of Europe, and considerable support from approximately 150,000 loyalists in the colonies. In addition, in the first years of the war, the Continental Army suffered from poor discipline, frequent desertions, a lack of supplies and money, and a virtually nonexistent navy. However, an obviously long supply line (four to six weeks by ship), divided British policies in London, and a army used to fighting the more "formal" European type of war would end up hindering British efforts. The leadership of George Washington, the willingness to use defensive tactics and only attack when needed, and the fact that they were fighting on home territory all helped aid the colonial military efforts. Washington felt that a lengthy war would assist the colonists, since they were fighting on home ground.

In May of 1775 a bloody battle had taken place at **Bunker Hill** in Boston. The colonists were defeated, but at the expense of nearly 1,000 British dead or wounded.

WASHINGTON AS COMMANDER

The British approach under General William Howe was to slowly move his army through the colonies, using the superior numbers of the British army to wear the colonists down. However, from the beginning things did not go as planned for the British. In March 1776, the British were forced to evacuate Boston. The British then went to New York, which they wanted to turn into one of their major military headquarters (a large number of loyalists lived there). Washington and his troops attempted to dislodge the British from New York in late August of 1776; Washington's army was routed and chased back into Pennsylvania.

During November and December of 1776, Washington's army faced daily desertions and poor morale. On Christmas night Washington boldly led the **Battle of Trenton** against the **Hessian** allies of the British, defeating them. On January 3 Washington defeated a small British regiment at Princeton. These victories bolstered the morale of the colonial army greatly.

Another tremendous advantage for the colonists were the arms shipments from the French that they began receiving in late 1776. French aid for the colonies did not come from any great trust that developed between the two sides; for over a century, France and Britain had been bitter rivals, and the French saw the American Revolution as another situation that they could exploit for their gain against the British. Massive British naval superiority in the Americans was at least partially counterbalanced by the entry of the French navy into the war.

The "British Blunder" of 1777

The British decided on a strategy to strike a decisive blow against the colonists in 1777. Three separate British armies were to converge on Albany, New York, and cut off New England from the rest of the colonies. The British effort is called a blunder because of the poor execution of military plans that might have been effective. An army led by General Howe headed toward Philadelphia for obvious strategic reasons it should have been heading toward Albany. Howe was intent on taking on Washington's army in Philadelphia and decisively defeating it. An army under "Gentleman Johnny" Burgoyne carried much heavy equipment that could be carried in preparation for European battles but not through the forests of North America. On October 17, 1777, Burgoyne was forced to surrender at Saratoga. Some military historians claim this defeat was the beginning of the end for the British. The colonial victory convinced the French to send troops to aid the war effort.

Women became increasingly important to the war effort of the colonies. Women were prominent in the boycott of British goods, provided support services for the Continental Army, spied on British troops, and ran numerous households when the "man of the house" was off fighting the British. In a March 1776 letter to her husband John, Abigail Adams reminded him to "Remember the Ladies . . . Do not put such unlimited power in the hands of the Husbands."

THE WAR MOVES TO THE SOUTH

After their defeat at Saratoga, the British abandoned their strategy of fighting in New York and New England and decided to concentrate their efforts in the Southern colonies, where they imagined more loyalists to live. Despite their victory at Saratoga, the winter of 1777–1778 was the low point for the Continental Army. The British camped for the winter in Philadelphia, while Washington's army stayed at **Valley Forge**. Cold weather, malnutrition, and desertion horribly hurt the army. Morale improved when daily drilling began under the leadership of Baron von Steuben, a Prussian who had volunteered to help the colonists. As a result, the Continental Army that emerged in the spring was a much tougher and more disciplined unit.

Nevertheless, at first the British southern strategy was successful. By the summer of 1780, the British captured Georgia and South Carolina. Desertions continued, and General Benedict Arnold went over to the British side.

Things soon turned against the British. A Virginia army under George Rogers Clark defeated a British force and their Native American allies at Vincennes, Indiana, securing the Ohio River region for the colonies. By the summer of 1781, French army forces joined the Continental Army as two regiments marched from New York to Virginia. The British southern campaign, now headed by General Cornwallis, was constantly hampered by attacks by colonial guerrilla bands, led by Francis Marion and other rebel leaders.

Cornwallis decided to abandon the southern strategy and went into Virginia, where he was ordered to take up a defensive position at **Yorktown**. Once the British troops began to dig in, they were cut off by a combination of French and continental forces. Cornwallis hoped to escape by sea, but ships of the French navy occupied Chesapeake Bay. For three weeks Cornwallis tried to break the siege; on October 17, 1781, he finally surrendered. Fighting continued in some areas, but on March 4, 1782, Parliament voted to end the British military efforts in the former colonies.

THE TREATY OF PARIS

British, French, Spanish (also allies with the colonists in the war), and American diplomats gathered in Paris in 1783 to make the treaty ending the war. The British and French diplomats were initially not impressed with the diplomatic efforts of the Americans, but soon the American team of John Jay, Benjamin Franklin, and John Adams demonstrated shrewd diplomatic skills. The Americans negotiated separately with the British, and on September 3, 1783, the <u>Treaty of Paris</u> was signed. (Please note that this is a different Treaty of Paris from the one ending the French and Indian War.) By this treaty Great Britain formally recognized American independence. Britain held on to Canada, but all of the territory they had received from France after the French and Indian War (territory between the Appalachian Mountains and the Mississippi River) was given over to the Americans. The American diplomats also negotiated for fishing rights off the coasts of Newfoundland and Nova Scotia. The British insisted on, and received, promises that British merchants would be free to recover prewar debts and that loyalists would be treated as equal citizens and would be able to recover property seized from them during the war. (As might be expected, many loyalists were leaving the Americas during this period.)

THE ESTABLISHMENT OF GOVERNMENTAL STRUCTURES IN THE NEW NATION

The Drafting of State Constitutions

By the end of 1777, 10 new state constitutions had been written. Written into these constitutions were safeguards to prevent the evils that Americans had seen in the colonial governments established by the British. The governor was the most oppressive figure in many colonies; as a result, many new constitutions gave limited power to the governor, who was usually elected by the state assembly. All states except Pennsylvania and Vermont adopted a **bicameral legislature**, with much power usually given to the upper house. Most states also lowered the property qualifications for voting, thus allowing people to vote who had not voted before the Revolutionary War. Many historians comment that writers of these constitutions were making a conscious attempt to broaden the base of American government. Most state constitutions also included some form of a bill of rights.

THE ARTICLES OF CONFEDERATION

In the fall of 1777, the Continental Congress send a proposed constitution out to the individual states for ratification. This document, called the

<u>Articles of Confederation</u>, intentionally created a very weak national government.

The main organ of government was a <u>unicameral legislature</u>, in which each state would have one vote. Executive authority was given to a <u>Committee of Thirteen</u>, with one representative from each state. For both amendment and ratification, the unanimous consent of all 13 state legislatures was required.

The national government was given the power to conduct foreign relations, mediate disputes between states, and borrow money. The weakness of the national government was shown by the fact that it could not levy taxes, regulate commerce, or raise an army. Because of disputes over land claims in the West, all 13 states didn't ratify the Articles of Confederation until 1781.

Economic Distress

Financial problems plagued the new nation in the years immediately after the war. Many merchants had overextended themselves by importing foreign goods after the war. Large numbers of Revolutionary War veterans had never been paid for their service. The national government had large war debts. By the terms of the Articles of Confederation, the national government could not tax, so the national government began to print a large amount of paper money. These bills, called "<u>Continentals</u>," were soon made worthless by inflation. Proposals for the national government to impose import tariffs came three times, and all three times they were defeated. Loans from foreign countries, especially France, propped up the national government during this period.

THE NORTHWEST ORDINANCES

The sale of lands in the West was one way that the national government *could* make money, and westward settlement was encouraged. By 1790 nearly 110,000 settlers were living in Kentucky and Tennessee, despite the threat of Native American attack. The <u>Northwest Ordinances</u> of 1784, 1785, and 1787 regulated the sale of lands in the Northwest Territory and established a plan to give these settled territories statehood. The 1784 Ordinance provided governmental structures for the territories and a system by which a territory could become a state. The Ordinance of 1785 spelled out the terms for the orderly sale of land in the Northwest Territory. The Ordinance of 1787 stated that any territory with 60,000 white males could apply for statehood, provided a bill of rights for settlers, and prohibited slavery north of the Ohio River. Controversy over whether slavery should be allowed in these territories was a foreshadowing of the bitter conflicts that would follow on the issue of slavery in newly acquired American territories.

SHAY'S REBELLION

Like farmers in other parts of colonies, farmers in western Massachusetts were in desperate shape in the years after the Revolution. Many owed large amounts to creditors, inflation further weakened their economic position, and in 1786 the Massachusetts Assembly raised taxes. Farmers took up arms, closing government buildings and freeing farmers from debtor's prisons. This rebellion was called Shay's Rebellion, after one of its leaders, war veteran Daniel Shays. The rebellion spread throughout Massachusetts and began to gain supporters in other New England states. The rebellion was put down by an army paid for by citizens of Boston and by a lowering of taxes. To many, Shay's Rebellion demonstrated that stronger state and national governments were needed to maintain order.

CHAPTER REVIEW

Rapid Review Guide

To achieve the perfect 5, you should be able to explain the following:

- The first armed resistance to the British army occurred at Lexington and Concord.
- The Second Continental Congress began to prepare the American colonies for war against the British, but by passing the Olive Branch Petition, they tried to accommodate colonial interests with those of the Crown.
- The impact of the message presented in *Common Sense* by Thomas Paine was widespread throughout the colonies.
- Many loyalists lived in the colonies at the outbreak of the Revolutionary War; many were members of the economic elite.
- Blacks and women played a large role in the war effort of the colonies.
- The defensive tactics of George Washington as leader of the continental forces proved decisive, since a longer war was disadvantageous to the British army.
- French assistance to the continental war effort proved invaluable; the French navy proved to be especially critical as the war progressed.
- The Treaty of Paris ended the Revolutionary War. In this treaty, American independence was recognized by the British and large amounts of territory west of the Appalachian became American territory.
- The Articles of Confederation created a weak national government, partially to avoid replicating the "tyranny" of the Crown in England.
- To many colonial observers, Shay's Rebellion demonstrated that a stronger national government was needed.

Time Line

1775: Battles of Lexington and Concord Meeting of Second
Continental Congress
1776: *Common Sense* published by Thomas Paine
Declaration of Independence approved
Surrender of British forces of General Burgoyne at Saratoga
1777: State constitutions written in 10 former colonies
1777–1778: Continental Army encamped for the winter at
Valley Forge
1778: French begin to assist American war efforts
1781: Cornwallis surrenders at Yorktown Articles of Confederation
ratified
1783: Signing of the Treaty of Paris
1786–1787: Shay's Rebellion in Massachusetts
1787: Northwest Ordinance establishes regulations for settlement of
territories west of the Appalachian Mountains

✓ Review Questions

1. The purpose of the Olive Branch petition was to

   A. rally colonial support for war against Great Britain
   B. petition the king for redress of economic grievances suffered by the colonies
   C. ask the king to craft a solution to end the tensions between Great Britain and the colonies
   D. request formal support of each colony for the formulation of the Second Continental Congress
   E. ask the king to grant independence to the colonies

(Correct Answer: **C.** Although the Second Continental Congress began to prepare for colonies for war against Great Britain, the delegates also voted to send this petition to George III, asking him to create harmony between Great Britain and the colonies.)

2. At the beginning of the Revolutionary War, the British were extremely confident of victory because all of the following reasons *except*

   A. they had outstanding generals that would be commanding British forces in the Americas
   B. there were many loyalists throughout the American colonies
   C. the Continental Army suffered from poor discipline
   D. the British had an outstanding navy
   E. the Continental Army was continually lacking in supplies

(Correct Answer: **A.** Several of the main generals commanding British troops in the Revolutionary War proved early on to be quite ordinary in tactical and leadership skills.)

3. All of the following were contained in the Treaty of Paris of 1783 *except*

   A. Americans got fishing rights off the coast of Newfoundland
   B. territory west of the Appalachian Mountains was ceded to the Americans

C. American independence was recognized by Great Britain
D. Quebec and the area immediately surrounding it was ceded to the Americans
E. former loyalists in the colonies could retrieve property seized from them during the Revolutionary War

(Correct Answer: **D.** None of the British territory in Canada was taken from them as a result of the treaty.)

4. Women were important in the war effort because they

A. provided much of the financial backing for the colonial cause
B. provided several delegates to the Second Continental Congress
C. wrote influential articles in colonial newspapers urging the colonies to resist the British
D. provided clothing and blankets for the frozen troops at Valley Forge
E. maintained economic stability in the colonies by managing households across the colonies while men were off fighting the British

(Correct Answer: **E.** Although women assisted the war effort in many ways, they made an important contribution by in managing estates and farms while their husbands were serving in the colonial militias or in the Continental Army.)

5. The weakness of the national government created by the Articles of Confederation was demonstrated by the fact that it was *not* given the power to

A. mediate disputes between states
B. raise an army
C. conduct foreign relations
D. borrow money
E. print money

(Correct Answer: **B.** The national government was not given the power to issue taxes, regulate commerce, or raise an army.)

Chapter 7

The Establishment of New Political Systems (1787–1800)

DESIRES FOR A STRONGER CENTRAL GOVERNMENT

Many Americans viewed the flaws of the national government established by the Articles of Confederation with dismay. As Alexander Hamilton stated, the American Revolution had taught those living in the former colonies to think "<u>continentally</u>"; yet the government in existence did not foster continental thought or action. To many, a stronger national government was a necessity.

In 1787 delegates from the 13 states went to Philadelphia to amend the Articles of Confederation. Many of the great men of the age were present at this meeting, including Alexander Hamilton, George Washington, James Madison, and Benjamin Franklin (John Adams and Thomas Jefferson were both in Europe during this convention). Debates quickly turned away from reforming the Articles of Confederation to creating a new national government. Most delegated believed that the central government had to be much stronger, with the ability to raise an army, collect taxes, and regulate commerce.

However, some delegates at the convention had doubts about how strong a new central government should actually be. They feared that too much power might fall into the hands of a small group, who would use it to their own advantage. In addition, small states and large states had very different ideas about how representation in a new national legislature should be determined. Smaller states favored the model provided by the Articles of Confederation with one vote per state; larger states proposed that population should determine representation. In addition, Southern and Northern states began to view each other suspiciously. Debates also took place over the future relationship of the national government to the various state governments.

GOVERNMENT UNDER THE NEW CONSTITUTION

Virginia plantation owner Edmund Randolph presented the **Virginia Plan**, which proposed a bicameral legislature with the number of representatives in each house determined by **proportional representation**. The guiding force behind this plan was really James Madison, a 36-year-old scholar and member of the Virginia legislature. Madison also proposed a structure of three branches of government: judicial, legislative, and executive. The importance of the contributions of James Madison in the creation of the Constitution cannot be overemphasized; by proposing branches of government, Madison dispelled the fears held by many critics that in the new government too much power would be placed in the hands of a small number of leaders.

Smaller states, while favoring a strong central government, were opposed to Madison's concept of a national legislature, fearing it would be dominated by the larger states. Smaller states supported the **New Jersey Plan**, which proposed a unicameral legislature where every state would receive one vote. This plan was equally unpopular with the larger states. Delegates from Connecticut finally proposed the plan that was ultimately adopted, the **Great Compromise**. This plan included an upper house, called the Senate, which would have two representatives per state, and a lower house, the House of Representatives, whose members would be elected by proportional representation.

Many representatives remained skeptical of a national government with massive powers. To diminish these fears, it was voted that the chief executive of the national government would be elected by an **Electoral College**, membership to which would be chosen by individual states. In addition, senators would be elected by state legislatures and not by the voters.

THE ISSUE OF SLAVERY

The issue of slavery was discussed several times during the deliberations of the Convention. It was decided that the new national government could not regulate slavery for 20 years. Much debate took place over how slaves should be counted when determining representation for states in the House of Representatives; slave states wanted to count the slaves in their total populations. This issue was resolved by the **Three-Fifths Compromise**, which stated that three-fifths of a state's slave population would be counted when determining representation in the House of Representatives. Southern states applauded the section of the Constitution promising national aid to any state threatened with "domestic violence"; Southern politicians assumed that this meant that federal troops would be utilized to help dispel any future slave revolts.

RATIFICATION OF THE CONSTITUTION

The writers of the new document wanted it to be approved by <u>ratifying</u> <u>conventions</u> that would be held in each state. Supporters of the new Constitution began to call themselves <u>Federalists</u>, a term used at the time for a supporter of strong *national* government. Federalists had faith that the elites that would come to dominate both federal and state governments would act in the interest of the entire nation. Those opposed to the new, stronger national government were soon called <u>Antifederalists</u>. Antifederalists sometimes equated the potential tyranny they saw in the new government with the tyranny that had been practiced by British monarchs. Antifederalists felt that the best protection against the tyranny of a strong central government would be the power of the individual states. In the end, they said that the major problem was that the new government was not based on republican principles and, without a Bill of Rights, was not interested in individual rights. After especially tough fights in New York, Virginia, and Massachusetts, the new Constitution was finally passed by all states (with New York being last) on July 26, 1788.

THE PRESIDENCY OF GEORGE WASHINGTON

Although he did not seek the presidency, the national reputation of George Washington made him the most logical choice to be the first chief executive of the United States of America. For at least the first term of Washington's administration, the future of the United States remained uncertain. Washington felt that it was crucial to establish respect for the office of President of the United States. Washington believed it was his job to administer the laws and not to make them; he almost never made legislative proposals to the Congress.

THE BILL OF RIGHTS

When the Constitution was being written, James Madison opposed including a bill of rights, fearing that such a document might actually limit the rights of citizens. By 1791, he saw the wisdom of such a document, and proposed 12 amendments to the Constitution. Antifederalists unanimously supported the addition of a bill of rights; they felt these would be added protections against the tyranny of the federal government. By the end of year 10, amendments had been ratified by the individual states. The **<u>Bill</u>** **<u>of Rights</u>** contains the basic protections that Americans hold dear today; politically it quieted the Antifederalists and their fears of authoritarian government. The Bill of Rights guaranteed the right of free speech, ensured freedom of worship, gave citizens the right to bear arms, forbid the quartering of troops in private homes, and said that warrants were needed before searches took place. In addition, persons could not be forced to testify against themselves, citizens were guaranteed a trial by jury, "due process of law" was guaranteed, and "cruel and unusual punishments" were outlawed. The Ninth Amendment stated that these were not the only rights that Americans had, while the Tenth stated that any powers not specifically given to the federal government belonged to the states. Some historians point out that the basis of the entire American political system can be found in these 10 amendments.

COMPETING VISIONS: ALEXANDER HAMILTON AND THOMAS JEFFERSON

Two of the most brilliant men in the Washington administration were Secretary of State Thomas Jefferson and Secretary of the Treasury Alexander Hamilton. Hamilton was a huge admirer of the British economic system and wanted to turn America, which was still largely agrarian, into a manufacturing society like Britain. Hamilton wanted to institute strong **mercantilist** policies and proposed economic union with Great Britain. Hamilton believed that a strong national government was necessary for economic growth and believed in a broad interpretation of the Constitution. By this interpretation, the federal government had many powers not specifically mentioned in the Constitution and was only denied those powers specifically given to the states.

Jefferson (supported by James Madison) proposed a radically different view of America. He proposed an America that would remain largely agricultural, with industry serving only as "a handmaiden to agriculture." While Hamilton supported the mercantilist policy of high tariffs on foreign goods, Jefferson proposed a system of **free trade** (which would keep prices low). Jefferson came to be influenced by the events of the French Revolution and was fearful of the power of the federal government (emphasizing the importance of state power instead). Jefferson also favored a strict interpretation of the Constitution; by this interpretation the federal government only had the powers it was specifically given in the Constitution.

From these differences emerged the two-party system in the United States. Hamilton and his supporters called themselves **Federalists**; mercantilism would impel them to propose a strong government hand in economic affairs. Jefferson and his followers were called **Republicans**; as stated previously, they favored **laissez-faire economic principles** and the continued vision of America as a largely agricultural nation. The plans of Hamilton were most popular in the commercial cities of the Northeast and the port cities of the South, while the Republican plan was most popular in the Western and Southern sections of the country.

The Plan of Alexander Hamilton

Determined to turn the United States into a manufacturing power, Hamilton began a gigantic economic reform of America. In his "**Report on the Public Credit**" Hamilton proposed that the United States had the obligation to redeem in full all notes that had been issued by the government established by the Articles of Confederation. In addition, he proposed that the federal government take over all of the debts of the individual states. Hamilton also proposed the chartering of a **national bank,** which could provide loans to developing industries. Hamilton proposed that the federal government use subsidies and tax incentives to spur industrial growth. Hamilton proposed that these measures could be paid for largely by high tariffs on foreign imports.

Jefferson and Madison opposed these plans on both practical and philosophical grounds. They maintained that the commercial elite would be the ones to benefit from these programs, largely at the expense of the farmer. Most of Hamilton's programs were adopted, although the plan to increase industrial growth was not. Hamilton's economic vision provided a system of public credit and a steady stream of government revenue through tariffs.

THE FRENCH REVOLUTION

The French Revolution broke out as George Washington was taking over as president in 1789. By 1793 a continent-wide war pitted revolutionary France against most of Europe. Within months Washington issued a **Declaration of Neutrality,** which allowed American merchants to prosper by trading with both sides. Many Americans sided with the democratic principles that the Revolution appeared to be based on; **Democratic-Republican clubs** in many cities carefully followed events in France. Many of the people supporting the Revolution also supported Jefferson and his republican ideals in America. The entire Revolution and especially the Terror appalled other Americans; many of these men supported federalism in the United States.

Pennsylvania farmers who supported the **Whiskey Rebellion** of 1796 were inspired by the French Revolution (they actually carried signs proclaiming "Liberty, Equality, and Fraternity"). They opposed a tax Alexander Hamilton had placed on distilled alcohol, which reduced the profits on the whiskey that they produced and sold. The tax was necessary because the federal government needed more money; Hamilton's plan of having the federal government assume certain debts of state governments had recently been instituted. Hamilton demonstrated his political skill by taxing whiskey; the grain from which it was made came from Western farmers, most of whom supported Jefferson. Washington raised an army and put the whiskey revolt down; by the time the army was ready to fight, the rebellion had largely ended.

FOREIGN POLICY AND JAY'S TREATY

The war between France and the rest of Europe continued. By 1794 British officials became concerned that the Americans were trading mostly with the French West Indies during their period of "neutrality." The British began to search, and then to seize, American merchants ships, many times imploring that the crews of these ships join the British navy. Washington sent Chief Justice John Jay to negotiate with the British, and the results were mixed at best. Jay was unable to get the British to promise not to undermine American freedom of the seas, and he was forced to comply with the British demand that they had the right to remove French products and materials from American ships. The British did agree to leave some of the forts they still occupied in the Northwest Territory.

Bitter political battles took place in America over **Jay's Treaty**. On the other hand, the treaty negotiated by Thomas Pinckney with Spain was extremely popular; by this treaty the United States gained navigating rights along the Mississippi River. The transport of farm produce from the South and the West got to markets much quicker as a result of this treaty.

WASHINGTON'S FAREWELL ADDRESS

Increased political battles between Federalists and Republicans convinced George Washington not to stand for a third term as president. In his Farewell Address, Washington spoke against party politics, asking political leaders to work together and not against each other. He also warned America not to "interweave our destiny with any part of Europe" and stated that America should not enter into alliances that would cause them to get involved in foreign wars. Political leaders for the next 200 years would invoke the words of Washington when opposing American plans to ally with foreign nations.

THE PRESIDENCY OF JOHN ADAMS

John Adams had been Washington's vice president, was also a Federalist, and served one term as president (1796 to 1800). Adams was opposed in the 1796 election by Thomas Jefferson, running as a Republican. Adams won, but Jefferson came in second in the Electoral College, thus putting candidates of two different parties in as president and vice president.

Despite recent biographies that suggest otherwise, Adams had four largely unsuccessful years in office. Adams spent a great deal of time back home in Quincy, Massachusetts, thus allowing his Cabinet members to make major decisions with little input from the president.

Problems with France

The French were unhappy with a series of American laws and policies that economically favored the British at their expense. For many in France, Jay's Treaty was the last straw. The French impounded several American ships going to England and announced that American sailors doing duty on British ships would be treated as "pirates." A three-member diplomatic delegation went to Paris in 1798 to negotiate with the French. French Minister Talleyrand, through third and fourth parties, informed the Americans that a bribe would have to be paid before negotiations could begin. The American diplomats refused to pay, and word of this caused outrage at home. This affair came to be know as the "<u>XYZ Affair</u>," named for the unnamed "assistants" of Talleyrand who made the bribe offer.

Adams announced the buildup of the American navy in preparation for a potential war against France. Trading with France was temporarily suspended, and American ships were authorized to attack French ships at sea. In 1800 the French and the Americans met again (Napoleon was now in power in France) and tensions decreased. The Convention of 1800 gave the United States compensation for ships that had been seized by the French. In addition, the United States was freed from its diplomatic entanglements with the French.

THE ALIEN AND SEDITION ACTS

During the undeclared war against France, the policies of Adams were attacked by some in the press; several pamphlets written by French emigrants were especially vindictive. As a result, Adams and his administration supported several measures that would threaten the rights of Americans. The <u>Alien Act</u> gave the president the right to deport any immigrant who was felt to be "dangerous to the peace and safety of the United States." The <u>Sedition Act</u> stated that the administration could prohibit any attacks on the president or Congress that were deemed to be "malicious." Twenty Republican journalists and politicians were arrested under the Sedition Act, with some going to jail. State legislatures in Virginia and Kentucky passed the <u>Kentucky and Virginia Resolves</u>, stating that states have the right to not enforce laws that were unconstitutional, such as the Sedition Act. This would later be the philosophy of some Southern states in the years leading up to the Civil War and again in the civil rights struggles of the 1950s and 1960s.

The negative publicity generated by the Sedition Act certainly did not help John Adams as he ran for president against Thomas Jefferson in 1800.

CHAPTER REVIEW

Rapid Review Guide

To achieve the perfect 5, you should be able to explain the following:

- The 1787 meeting on amending the Articles of Confederation turned into a historical session where the Constitution of the United States was drafted.

- The importance of James Madison in the formulation of the Constitution cannot be overemphasized.
- The format of the bicameral legislature, the branches of power established at the federal level, and the division of powers between federal and state governments made the U.S. Constitution a unique document for its time.
- The division between Federalists and Antifederalists demonstrated that very different visions of America and the scope of the federal government existed in the United States at this time.
- The Bill of Rights established the basic freedoms that Americans cherish today.
- During the Washington administration, very different visions of America were expressed by Alexander Hamilton and Thomas Jefferson; the ideas of Hamilton helped spur American economic growth during the Washington administration.
- The United States had a great deal of trouble convincing the British and the French that the United States was a major power during this era.
- Many critics viewed the Alien and Sedition Acts of John Adams as gross overextensions of the power given to the federal government by the Constitution.

Time Line

1787: Constitutional Convention ratifies U.S. Constitution
1788: U.S. Constitution ratified by states
1789: Washington sworn in as first president
1790: Hamilton issues plans proposing to protect infant U.S. industries
1791: Establishment of First National Bank
      Ratification of the Bill of Rights
1793: Democratic-Republican clubs begin to meet
1794: Whiskey Rebellion begins
1795: Jay's Treaty with England/Pinckney's Treaty with Spain
1796: John Adams elected president, Thomas Jefferson vice president (each from a different political party)
1798: XYZ affair
      Sedition Act of John Adams issued
      Kentucky and Virginia Resolves
1800: Convention of 1800
      Thomas Jefferson elected president

✓ Review Questions

1. The Connecticut Plan presented to the Constitutional Convention of 1787

   A. proposed a one-house legislature based on population

   B. proposed a two-house legislature based on proportional representation

   C. proposed a one-house legislature based on proportional representation

D. proposed a two-house legislature, with one house based on proportional representation

E. proposed a balance of power between executive, legislative, and judicial branches

(Correct Answer: **D.** The Connecticut plan, also called the Great Compromise, was ratified by the delegates. Under this plan representation in the House of Representatives would be by population, while in the Senate all states would have equal representation.)

2. The Kentucky and Virginia Resolves

A. expressed support for the new U.S. Constitution

B. expressed opposition to the government actions in putting down the Whiskey Rebellion

C. stated that individual states do not have to enforce laws the states consider unconstitutional

D. were written to support John Adams' support of the Sedition Act

E. were written in opposition to the economic policies of Alexander Hamilton

(Correct Answer: **C.** After the passage of the Sedition Act, legislatures in Kentucky and Virginia passed resolutions stating that states do not have to enforce laws they consider to be unconstitutional.)

3. Many in America felt that the English and the French failed to treat the United States as a major power in this era; all of the following are evidence of that *except*

A. the Convention of 1800

B. the treatment of American ships by the French during the 1890s

C. Jay's Treaty

D. the treatment of American ships by the British during the 1890s

E. the XYZ Affair

(Correct Answer: **A.** As a result of the Convention of 1800, the French agreed to compensate the United States for ships seized during the previous decade. Events mentioned in all of the other choices demonstrate that the French and English had little respect for American rights in diplomatic matters and on the high seas during this era.)

4. Thomas Jefferson and Alexander Hamilton had different views on all of the following *except*

A. whether America should be a commercial or agrarian society

B. the amount of power the federal government should have

C. the tariff policy of the United States

D. the importance of a National Bank

E. their belief in the power of the U.S. Constitution

(Correct Answer: **E.** Both believed in the power of the Constitution, although their interpretation of the Constitution was different. Jefferson believed in a strict interpretation of the Constitution, while Hamilton believed in a broad interpretation.)

5. Under the Electoral College system

A. voters directly elect the president of the United States

B. state legislatures elect the president of the United States

C. voters approve electors, who elect the president of the United States

D. it is possible to win the popular vote and lose the election in the Electoral College

E. C and D above

(Correct Answer: **E.** As demonstrated in the presidential election of 2000, it is possible to get the most number of votes nationwide but to lose the presidential election in the Electoral College. This also occurred in the presidential election of 1876.)

Chapter 8

The Jeffersonian Revolution (1800–1820)

THE ELECTION OF 1800

John Adams, despite much criticism over the **Sedition Act**, stood for reelection in 1800. The vice presidential candidate of the Federalists was Charles Pinckney. The candidate for the Republicans was Thomas Jefferson, with Aaron Burr running for vice president. At this point all candidates were eligible for votes in the Electoral College; Jefferson and Burr each received 73 votes (the **Twelfth Amendment** of 1804 would change this, stating that the Electoral College would vote for president and vice president separately). The Constitution in 1800 threw the election to the House of Representatives, where each state received one vote. Federalists supported Burr, and it was only on the thirty-sixth ballot that Jefferson was elected president. Jefferson's victory was only assured when Alexander Hamilton convinced some Federalists to switch their votes to Jefferson, telling them that Burr was "the most unfit man in the United States for the office of president." Some historians term this election the "Revolution of 1800"; as previously stated, Jefferson's vision of America had almost no similarity with the views of the Federalists who had been in power since the beginning of the republic, yet they peacefully gave up power when the balloting was completed in the House of Representatives.

Some historians maintain that Thomas Jefferson was one of the most brilliant men ever to be elected president. Recent movies and exposés on the life of Jefferson have largely ignored his immense political skills and intellect. Jefferson had been a diplomat, was familiar with European affairs, was a skillful politician, and was a distinguished political philosopher. He implemented Republican policies almost as soon as he took office, with the goal of cutting back on the growth of the federal government that had taken place under Adams. The Alien and Sedition Acts of Adams were not renewed, taxes such as the whiskey tax were eliminated, and Jefferson opposed further expansion of the national debt. On the other hand, Jefferson remained a pragmatist. As a member of Washington's Cabinet, he had vigorously opposed the creation of a National Bank, yet as president he supported it (he reasoned that American economic growth was dependent on the existence of the Bank.)

REFORM OF THE COURTS

When Jefferson was inaugurated in 1801, virtually every justice in the court system was a Federalist, since they had all been appointed by either Washington or Adams. Several weeks before Jefferson took office, Congress passed the **Judiciary Act**, creating a large number of new federal courts. In a series of "**midnight appointments**" made just hours before he left office, Adams appointed Federalists to all of these positions.

Jefferson's Republican allies in the Congress repealed the Judiciary Act almost immediately and also impeached two Federalists judges. John Marshall was a Federalist who had been appointed Chief Justice of the Supreme Court by Adams and continued in office during Jefferson's presidency and beyond. Marshall served as Chief Justice from 1801 to 1835 and served to dramatically improve the prestige and the functioning of the federal court system.

Marshall also dramatically increased the power of the Supreme Court itself in the 1803 ***Marbury v. Madison*** decision. John Adams had appointed John Marbury to be justice of the peace for the District of Columbia in one of his final appointments before leaving office. James Madison, secretary of state under Jefferson, refused to issue the appointment letter signed by Adams. Marbury sued, demanding that the Supreme Court force Madison to release the appointment letter.

Marshall ruled that the Supreme Court did not have the power to force Madison to act. However, the ruling also stated that the Supreme Court did have the right to judge the constitutionality of federal laws and decisions. This began the principal of **judicial review**, making the judiciary an equal branch in every way with the executive and legislative branches.

WESTWARD EXPANSION

As previously mentioned, Thomas Jefferson had a very different view of America than had been held by Alexander Hamilton and many other Federalists. While Hamilton had envisioned America as evolving into a mighty industrial power, Jefferson's view of an ideal America was one made up largely of yeoman farmers, who would possess a spirit of fierce independence and pride. To accomplish this end, Jefferson encouraged further expansion westward (into the area between the Appalachian Mountains and the Mississippi River). Over 1 million settlers lived there in 1800; in 1804 it became even easier to purchase land in this territory, when it became possible to buy 160 acres of land for an initial down payment of $80. New settlers streamed into the area, sometimes settling on land legally owned by Native American tribes.

Jefferson publicly stated that the best approach to Native Americans would be to show them the benefits of farming. He felt that if Native Americans could be turned into farmers that they would not need all of their forest land and they might incorporate themselves as citizens of the U.S. However, Jefferson's desire for western settlement far outweighed his desire for fair treatment for Native Americans. The pattern that began under Jefferson and continued for decades was one where Native Americans were forced to sign treaties in which they gave up more and more of their lands with virtually nothing given in return.

The Louisiana Purchase

In secret treaties between France and Spain signed in 1800 and 1801 France regained the Louisiana territory. Americans did not hear of this until 1802 and were worried that Napoleon's France might attempt to reassert their power in the Americas. Napoleon also expressed his desire to place Haiti back under French control. Concerns increased when in the last two months of their control there the Spanish refused to allow American ships to store products in New Orleans (which had been common practice).

Jefferson feared war with France and sent Virginia governor James Monroe to France to see if France would sell part of the territory to the United States. Napoleon had been unable to recapture Haiti and needed money to finance his army for his European conquests, so he offered to sell the Louisiana Territory to the United States for $15 million. The **Louisiana Purchase** doubled the size of the United States; for Jefferson this was the perfect opportunity to expand the "empire of liberty." Many Northeastern Federalists were opposed to the Louisiana Purchase, fearing it would decrease their economic and political power. Nevertheless, the purchase was overwhelmingly ratified by Congress in late 1803. Jefferson's pragmatism was also displayed when he approved the Louisiana Purchase. The Constitution did not mention that the federal government had the right to acquire new territory; Jefferson had always interpreted the Constitution strictly, and normally stated that the federal government has no powers that were not specifically mentioned in the Constitution. However, in Jefferson's eyes the acquisition of the Louisiana territory was absolutely essential for the continued growth of the United States.

Jefferson and many others in America wanted more accurate information about the geography, the peoples, and the economic possibilities of the rest of continent. In 1804 the **Lewis and Clark Expedition** began. This expedition of nearly 50 men took two years to complete; despite hardships they crossed the Rockies and eventually made it to the Pacific Ocean. The information they brought back about the possibilities of further expansion in the West intrigued many.

POLITICAL TENSIONS AND THE STRANGE CASE OF AARON BURR

Federalists feared that the country was being debased by virtually every move that Jefferson made. A group of Federalists called the **Essex Junto** existed in Boston and loudly campaigned against the "decline in public virtue" they saw personified in Jefferson. Thomas Pickering, senator from Massachusetts, saw Jefferson as a "Parisian revolutionary monster." A younger group of Federalists tried to improve the image of the party, although the Federalist candidate, Charles C. Pinckney, received only 14 electoral votes in the 1804 election.

Aaron Burr was vice president, but after the fiasco of the 1800 election, he had no meaningful role during Jefferson's first term. Some New England Federalists had spoke of leaving the Union after the Louisiana Purchase and forming a **Northern Confederacy**. The group tried to get Alexander Hamilton to join them. After he refused, they tried to recruit Aaron Burr, who, seeing no future role in a Washington run by Thomas Jefferson, was trying to become governor of New York. Hamilton accused Burr of attempting to ruin the United States. At this point, Burr challenged Hamilton to a duel (a practice that had been outlawed in the United States). Hamilton died in the duel, and Burr was indicted for murder.

After ending his term as vice president, Burr moved to the West (probably to avoid jail). While in Louisiana, he met up with General James Wilkinson, the military governor there. The two plotted to turn Louisiana into an independent nation, with Burr as its leader. Burr was betrayed by Wilkinson and arrested. Burr was acquitted, but his actions and the actions of other Federalists demonstrate the deep divisions that were developing in the United States. Federalists had plotted secession, President Jefferson wanted a conviction of Burr at all costs, and Federalist John Marshall, who presided over the trial, made several rulings that helped Burr (possibly to discredit the efforts of Jefferson).

EUROPEAN WARS SPILL OVER TO AMERICA (AGAIN)

The Napoleonic Wars of Europe that lasted from 1802 till 1815 had a large impact on the United States. America viewed its role in this war as a neutral, yet came into conflict with both France and Great Britain. By terms of the **Continental System**, American ships that traded in Britain were sometimes stopped and seized. British ships also seized ships trading with the French West Indies, made merchants pay heavily to get special licenses to send their ships through the British naval blockade of the continent, and practiced **impressment** (forcing deserted British sailors but also American citizens into the British navy). Jefferson banned British warships from American ports, yet impressment and the stopping and seizing of American ships continued.

Many in America wanted war, but Jefferson thought that economic pressure would cause the British and the French to respect the rights of

America as a neutral. He declared the **Embargo of 1807**, by which American ships could not enter the seas until England and France stopped their harassment of American shipping. Predictably, the effect on the American economy was disastrous. Exports dropped dramatically, with Northeastern merchants, Southern plantation owners, and even farmers dramatically affected.

The Embargo of 1807 was by far the most unpopular act championed by Jefferson. In the 1808 presidential election, Congressman James Madison was elected president, even though he was one of the architects of the embargo bill.

Seeing that America had actually fallen into economic depression, Madison in 1808 introduced the **Non-Intercourse Act**, which opened trade with all countries except England and France. An 1810 act again threatened to cut trade with any nation that interfered with Americans ships, which England and France continued to do.

THE WAR OF 1812

Reasons for War

Frustrated by the continued British policies of impressment and the seizure of ships, Madison formally asked Congress for a Declaration of War against Britain in June of 1812. Many Federalists opposed the war. They regarded Great Britain as a potential trading partner and viewed British citizens as people "like themselves." To many Americans, Madison's argument that the country's political and economic rights as a neutral power had been violated was convincing. A younger group of Republicans, personified by Henry Clay of Kentucky, were especially supportive of war. This group, called the "War Hawks," felt that war would enable the United States to acquire more territory in the West, leading to greater economic growth.

Another stated cause for war revolved around connections between the British and Native Americans. In 1812 two members of the Shawnee Tribe, Tecumseh and his brother Tenskwatawa, decided the time was right to take a stand against further settlement by whites in the region between the Appalachians and the Mississippi River. Tecumseh joined many tribes together, terrifying settlers in the region. James Madison was convinced by Western political leaders that the Native Americans were being encouraged (and being armed) by the British in Canada. The attack on Tecumseh's village by General William Henry Harrison in late 1811 intensified the conflict that would take place with Native Americans in the region.

The Outbreak of War

The United States was totally unprepared for war against Britain when war was first declared. In 1812 the army consisted of 6000 men, and the entire navy was made up of 17 ships. The first military effort was a three-pronged attack against Canada, with the intent of destroying Indian villages, defeating British troops, and taking Montreal. Military efforts were largely unsuccessful, and American troops soon retreated.

The American navy had some initial successes, but American ships were soon driven back and blockaded in their own ports. The naval victories of 1812 at least boosted the morale of the American nation. Native Americans, including Tecumseh and the Shawnee, were fighting on the side of the British. The first big victory for the Americans came in the summer of 1813 when William Henry Harrison and his forced defeated the British and the Native Americans at the Thames River (east of present-day Detroit), killing Tecumseh. In Tennessee a militiaman, Andrew Jackson, lead many victories over Indian forces.

The Attack on Washington

Napoleon was finally defeated in 1814. Many Americans rejoiced at the defeat of the French, but also realized that the United States was now Britain's only enemy. The British began an offensive in New York, but in August 1814, a second British army advanced on Washington. Most Washingtonians (including President Madison) left the city before the British arrived, but the British proceeded to sack the city, including the White House and the Capitol.

Ironically, as the British were burning the capitol, peace negotiations for ending the war were already in progress in Ghent, Belgium. With the European war over, many of the issues that had driven Britain and America apart, such as blockading and impressment, now appeared to be less important. After sustained battles against Napoleon, public opinion in England did not favor continued military action in the Americas. The strange **Treaty of Ghent**, which ended the war, actually said nothing about impressment or neutral trading rights, but simply restored diplomatic relations between Britain and the United States. Two weeks after peace was declared, Andrew Jackson defeated a large British force at the Battle of New Orleans.

Political Effects of the War

Nine days before the Treaty of Ghent was signed, a group of Federalists met at the **Hartford Convention**. They continued to see the war as disastrous to their interests and viewed with extreme suspicion the growing influence of politicians and military leaders from the West. Proposals regarding **nullification**, and even one concerning **secession**, were debated. When the ending of the war and the victory at New Orleans were announced, the actions of the Federalists appeared foolish. Their influence on political life in America was drawing to an end. With the decline of the Federalists, the United States was united more after the War of 1812 than it had been for years. As a result, the years 1816 to 1823 are called in textbooks the <u>Era of Good Feelings</u>, with James Monroe taking over the presidency in 1817.

THE AMERICAN SYSTEM

Henry Clay and other nationalists in Congress proposed the <u>American System</u> in the aftermath of the War of 1812. This plan was supported by James Madison and most fully implemented by James Monroe. The purpose of this plan was to make America less economically dependent on Europe by encouraging the production of goods in the United States that had previously been purchased abroad. Important to this economic growth would also be a second national bank, so that credit would be readily available, and a rather large protective tariff, which would encourage production and interstate commerce.

The <u>Tariff of 1816</u> raised tariff rates to nearly 22 percent, providing more than adequate protection for American business interests and revenues for improvements in the internal transportation system of the United States. A <u>Second National Bank</u> was also chartered in 1816. There was rapid economic growth in the postwar years, as Europeans and others traded for American tobacco, cotton, and grain. Economic growth could not last forever, and a depression gripped America in 1819.

THE MISSOURI COMPROMISE

The issue of slavery was one that increased as more settlers moved westward: Would the territories they were moving into be slave or free? In 1808 the further exporting of slaves was eliminated. Additional states had joined the Union, some slave and some free. By 1819 there were 11 slave states and 11 free states. The issue came to a head that year when Missouri petitioned to join the Union as a slave state. Debate in the Congress and in newspapers around the country was heated; to many Northerners, to have more slave states than free states was unthinkable. Speaker of the House Henry Clay engineered the Missouri Compromise, by which Maine entered the Union as a free state, Missouri entered as a slave state, and in the Louisiana Territory any states north of 36 degrees, 30 minutes had to come in as free states. Many at the time realized that this solution would only be a temporary one.

CHAPTER REVIEW

Rapid Review Guide

To achieve the perfect 5, you should be able to explain the following:

- The election of Thomas Jefferson in 1800 is called the "Revolution of 1800," as the new president had a completely different vision of America than the Federalists whom he replaced.

- Thomas Jefferson was one of the most brilliant men ever to serve as president, and he instituted many "Republican" policies during his eight years in office.
- The role of the federal courts was greatly strengthened during the tenure of John Marshall as Chief Justice of the Supreme Court.
- The Louisiana Purchase more than doubled the size of the United States and allowed the "empire of liberty" to continue to expand.
- The case of Aaron Burr showed the deep political divisions that existed in the United States during this period.
- The Napoleonic wars greatly impacted the relationship between the United States, England, and France.
- American entered the War of 1812 because President Madison convinced the nation that America's rights as a neutral power had been violated and because many in Congress felt that the British were encouraging resistance by Native American tribes.
- The American System of Henry Clay and others was proposed after the War of 1812 and outlined a plan for broad economic growth for the United States.
- The Missouri Compromise temporarily solved the issue of the number of slave versus the number of free states.

Time Line

1800: Thomas Jefferson elected president in "Revolution of 1800"
1801: John Marshall named as Chief Justice of Supreme Court
      Alien and Sedition Acts not renewed
1803: Louisiana Purchase
      Marbury v. *Madison* case established federal judicial review
1804: Alexander Hamilton killed in duel with Aaron Burr
      Thomas Jefferson reelected
      Twelfth Amendment ratified (separate voting for president, vice president)
      Beginning of Lewis and Clark expedition
1807: Embargo Act greatly harms foreign trade
1808: James Madison elected president
      Further importation of slaves into United States made illegal
1812: Beginning of War of 1812
1814: British army sacks Washington
      Treaty of Ghent formally ends War of 1812
      Indian removal from Southern territories begins in earnest
1814–1815: Hartford Convention (meeting of Federalists)
1815: Victory of Andrew Jackson at Battle of New Orleans (after War of 1812 was officially over)
      Henry Clay proposes the "American System"
1816: James Monroe elected president
1816–1823: Era of Good Feelings
1820: Missouri Compromise

✓ Review Questions

1. The *Marbury v. Madison* decision

   A. gave powers to the president that the Republicans of Thomas Jefferson claimed he didn't have
   B. gave broad judicial power to the state courts
   C. declared that the Alien and Sedition Acts were constitutional
   D. established the principle of judicial review
   E. legalized the removal of Native Americans from western lands

(Correct Answer: **D.** The decision stated that the Supreme Court had the right to decide on the constitutionality of federal rulings and laws.)

2. As a result of the election of Thomas Jefferson in 1800,

   A. more assistance was given to the commercial sector
   B. politicians in New York, Boston, and Philadelphia gained power
   C. American foreign policy became more pro-British
   D. the federal debt rose dramatically
   E. federal excise taxes were eliminated

(Correct Answer: **E.** All of the remaining answers would have been true if a Federalist had been elected president. Jefferson favored lessening the power of the federal government, and eliminating federal excise taxes was one way in which he did so.)

3. All of the following are reasons why America entered the War of 1812 *except*

   A. the impressment of American naval crews
   B. the existence of a strong American navy ready to demonstrate its capabilities
   C. the relationship between the British and Native American tribes in the western territories of North America
   D. the violation of America's rights as a neutral power
   E. the desire by American leaders to acquire additional western territories

(Correct Answer: **B.** The United States had an army of 6000 men and 17 ships when war began. All of the other choices are reasons that Americans supported the War of 1812.)

4. The Hartford Convention demonstrated that

   A. the Federalist party had remained a dominant party in American political life
   B. the War of 1812 brought political union to the United States
   C. the concept of nullification was not exclusively a Southern one
   D. the legacy of John Adams was large
   E. the Treaty of Ghent was a controversial treaty

(Correct Answer: **C.** Kentucky and Virginia spoke of nullification after the Sedition Act; New England Federalists saw the War of 1812 as a disaster and at the Hartford Convention also spoke of nullification.)

5. The American System of Henry Clay

   A. favored strong economic growth and a Second National Bank
   B. wanted to make the United States the military equivalent of Great Britain or France
   C. wanted to place a ceiling on the national debt
   D. favored lowering tariffs, so that more goods could be purchased from abroad
   E. advocated the elimination of slavery

(Correct Answer: **A.** The American System favored American economic growth, a national bank, and increased tariffs to protect American businesses and finance new transportation systems within the United States.)

Chapter 9

The Rise of Manufacturing and the Age of Jackson (1820–1845)

THE GROWTH OF THE FACTORY

 Economic growth was a key component of Henry Clay's American System, and in the aftermath of the War of 1812, measures were taken to expand American industry. American industries were protected by the Tariff of 1816, which raised import tariffs by 25 percent. At the same time state governments began improving road, river, and canal transportation systems.

Before 1820 almost all products made in America were completed using a system borrowed from Europe called the **putting-out system**. Under this system merchants would buy the raw materials, recruit dozens, or in some case hundreds, of farm families to do the work, and then sell the finished product. Many shoes in New England were made in this manner; women and children would make part of the shoe, which would be finished by experienced shoemakers.

Beginning in the late 1780s the textile industry started to use power-driven machines and interchangeable parts. All power in these early factories came from water, so the early factories all were located along rivers. Most were located in New England or the Middle states. In the 1790s factories like those in Lowell, Massachusetts, began to weave cotton imported from the south. With the introduction of the cotton gin in the same decade, more cotton became available, and production boomed. By 1840 the textile industry employed nearly 75,000 workers, with almost half of them women.

The workforce of many of the early factories was hired using the "**Lowell System**." Young women from surrounding areas were brought in to work. They worked for a pittance, worked in horrible conditions, and slept in dormitories provided by the factory. The young women saw this as temporary work, as many went home after several years after making some money (and in some cases spending it as well). This constant turnover of workers kept worker demands low, which pleased the factory owners. An economic middle class of manufacturers, bankers, and their families began to grow during this period. Factory towns such as Lowell, Massachusetts, began to grow rapidly in size.

An economic panic hit the United States in 1819, caused by the recovery of European economies after the Napoleonic wars, by money policies of the National Bank, and by the efforts of officials at several branch banks of the National Bank to enrich themselves through speculation. It was not until the 1830s that worker strikes began, along with drives to influence state legislatures to shorten the workday. A real **labor movement** did not develop in the textile industry until the 1840s.

THE MONROE DOCTRINE

The fact that America now was beginning to consider itself a major world power was demonstrated by the **Monroe Doctrine**, announced by President Monroe in 1823. Many Latin American nations had announced their independence in the Napoleonic era, and many in Latin America and in the United States felt that the Spanish and the French might send armies to reassert their control of the region. The Monroe Doctrine stated that countries in the Western Hemisphere were now off-limits to European control (these states "henceforth are not to be considered as subjects for future colonization by any European powers").

POLICY TOWARD NATIVE AMERICANS

In 1824 President James Monroe proposed that all Native Americans be moved west of the Mississippi River. Conflict had continued east of the Mississippi between settlers and various Native American tribes. Even though tribes had signed legal treaties for land, settlement constantly encroached on Native American territories. Monroe claimed that his proposal would benefit the Native Americans, stating that settlers would never bother them as long as they settled west of the Mississippi River Some tribes, such as the Cherokee, adopted systems of government similar to those used in many states, but even that did not stave off the pressure for removal.

The state of Georgia pressured the Cherokee to sell the land they held in that state. The Cherokee felt they held a valid treaty for the land that they lived on and decided to take their case to the federal court system. In a 1831 decision, ***Cherokee Nation v. Georgia***, Chief Justice Marshall stated that Native Americans had no real standing in court, since they were not a state or a foreign country. Nevertheless, Marshall affirmed that the Cherokee had a right to the lands that they possessed.

The Constitution states that it is the job of the executive branch to enforce the laws or decisions of the other two branches. Andrew Jackson was now president, and a large part of his reputation was as a successful Indian fighter. Jackson declined to take action to enforce this decision, stating "John Marshall has made his decision: let him enforce it." In his inaugural speech Jackson affirmed his support for Native American removal. During the War of 1812 Jackson led troops against the Creek tribe. As a result, the Creeks lost over 60 percent of their tribal lands. Congress had already passed and Jackson signed the **Removal Act of 1830**, which authorized the removal of all tribes east of the Mississippi.

Tribes were forced to move beginning in 1831; the horrors of these journeys, sometimes undertaken during winter months, are very well documented. In 1838 the Cherokees were finally marched west at gunpoint in what is now called the **Trail of Tears**; nearly one-third died of disease or exhaustion along the way. Many Native Americans were never able to adjust to the alien environment found west of the Mississippi. Indian resistance continued in Florida until 1841.

THE SECOND GREAT AWAKENING

The rise of industry, the growing commercialization of cities, and westernization all fundamentally altered America in the years 1800 to 1830. Transportation was rapidly changing; a National Road linked the Potomac and the Ohio rivers, and the Erie Canal was completed in 1825. The lives of vast numbers of ordinary people were being altered as a result of these economic and social changes.

In the midst of these transformations, the **Second Great Awakening** reaffirmed the role of religion in the lives of believers. The movement began in the late 1790s and reached its zenith in the 1830s. Where earlier Calvinist preachers had spoke of predestination, preachers of this era such as Timothy Dwight and Charles Finney proclaimed that one's actions on Earth played at least some role in an individual's fate after death. During this period **revival meetings**, some lasting as long as a week, would cause followers to faint, speak in tongues, or writhe uncontrollably. The Second Great Awakening began as a rural phenomenon, but by the 1820s, it spread to the cities as well. Evangelical sects such as the Methodists and the Baptists also grew in popularity.

Women played a significant role in the revivalism of the era. Many women became dedicated Christians and worked as volunteers for Protestant churches. In addition, many of these churches set up "academies" to educate women.

Other Reform Movements

Many individuals involved in the religious fervor of the era wanted to use that enthusiasm to reform society. Many wanted to act to improve the lives of those living in the cities and others with disadvantages. Dorothea Dix campaigned for better treatment of the mentally ill in the 1830s and

1840s. A prison reform movement also developed. In addition, a large **temperance movement** developed in this period, urging the working class to not drink to excess. Individuals such as Horace Mann spoke out for formal education for all children, the expansion of the school year, and the need for rigorous standards of teacher training.

Many Christians, especially in the North, began to speak out forcefully about the treatment of American slaves. In the 1820s and 1830s the **abolitionist movement** gained a large number of supporters. Abolitionists considered slavery to be a sin. The most prominent abolitionist was William Lloyd Garrison, who founded ***The Liberator***, his antislavery newspaper, in 1831. Some were against slavery for other reasons. The **American Colonization Society**, founded in the South in 1817, opposed slavery on the grounds that it encouraged contact between blacks and whites; members of this organization urged slave owners to free their slaves and return them to Africa.

Frederick Douglass, an ex-slave, was another leader of the abolitionist movement, who in 1845 would write the *Narrative of the Life of Frederick Douglass,* a key text for those who opposed slavery. In 1831 Nat Turner, a slave in Virginia, organized a bloody slave revolt that killed 60 whites. As was the case in the Stono Rebellion, the revolt was brutally repressed, and Black Codes and other restrictions on slaves in Southern states became more harsh.

POLITICAL REFORM: THE JACKSONIAN ERA (1829–1841)

Alexis de Tocqueville and other visitors from Europe noticed a different spirit in America than existed in European countries. de Tocqueville viewed with wonder the egalitarian system that he observed in virtually all aspects of American life. Many political changes both before and during the presidency of Andrew Jackson accentuated the sense that the "common man" reigned in this era.

Changes were already taking place in how presidential candidates were chosen. In 1800 only five states chose electors to the Electoral College by popular vote. By 1824, 18 out of 24 states chose electors in this manner. By the 1824 campaign, banners, posters, buttons, and hats were commonplace (the 1828 campaign was the first time when these were mass-produced).

In addition, more and more people could vote. By 1824 the property qualification, long a method to keep the "rabble" away from the political process, had been eliminated in most states. Blacks (even free blacks in the North) and women were still excluded from the political process.

THE ELECTION OF 1824

In this election Secretary of the Treasury William Crawford, Speaker of the House Henry Clay, Secretary of State John Quincy Adams, and

Tennessee's Andrew Jackson all ran for president. All of them considered themselves Republicans (the party was now referred to in many newspapers as **Democratic-Republican**). Jackson won the most popular votes, but only 38 percent of the electoral votes, so the election was turned over to the House of Representatives. Speaker of the House Clay threw his support to Adams, who won in the House and then appointed Clay to the position of Secretary of State.

For the next four years supporters of Jackson did everything they could to sabotage the presidency of John Quincy Adams, constantly reminding themselves of the "**corrupt bargain**" between Adams and Clay that had decided the 1824 election.

THE 1828 PRESIDENTIAL ELECTION

The 1828 presidential campaign was the model for many political campaigns of the future. Campaign rallies were held by supporters of both Quincy Adams and Jackson. Mudslinging was a daily occurrence during the campaign. Jackson's supporters claimed that Adams stole the 1824 election and gave too many fancy dinners; they also claimed that when he had been envoy to Russia, Adams had helped procure American prostitutes for the Russia tsar. Supporters of Adams said that Jackson was a murderer and an adulterer (the charge was made that his wife was an adulterer as well). Jackson won the election handily; under him the **Democratic party** became the first real political party of the United States.

JACKSON AS PRESIDENT

Andrew Jackson had been born in a log cabin, but when he was elected president in 1828, he was a planter and slaveholder. He was the first president from the West and had first achieved fame by fighting Native Americans. Jackson, however, was not naïve in terms of politics; he had been a congressman and a senator from Tennessee, as well as serving as territorial governor of Florida. Jackson was personally popular, especially with the common people.

Jackson also expressed loyalty to those who supported him politically. He infrequently consulted with his appointed Cabinet, relying instead on his "**Kitchen Cabinet**," the inner circle of his political supporters. Jackson also utilized the **spoils system** to give other political supporters jobs in the government.

Jackson also wanted to return to the Jeffersonian ideal of America as a nation of independent yeoman farmers. He opposed excessive government involvement in economic affairs, fearing that in most cases only wealthy interests benefited from that involvement. In modern terms, Jackson favored "smaller government" and was not afraid to use the power of the presidential veto to stop government programs he thought were excessive. At the end of his presidency Jackson appointed Roger B.

Taney as Chief Justice of the Supreme Court; the Taney court would validate almost all of Jackson's decisions favoring states rights.

To many of his opponents Jackson was a paradox. While he spoke of the need to limit the influence of government in society, he increased the power of the presidency. Opponents often referred to him as "King Andrew I." On the issue of slavery Jackson was no friend of abolitionists; he was a slave owner and was opposed to reform of the slave system.

THE NULLIFICATION CONTROVERSY

Jackson was forced early in his presidency to face the issue of the power of the states in relation to the power of the federal government. In 1828 Congress passed a bill authorizing new tariffs on imported manufacturing cloth and iron. The cost of these goods rose dramatically, and legislators in South Carolina began to revisit the doctrine of **nullification**, whereby individual states could rule on the constitutionality of federal laws. Jackson's own vice president, John C. Calhoun of South Carolina, stated that the practice of nullification was a necessity to protect states from the potential tyranny of the federal government.

In 1830 a debate in the U.S. Senate over western land sales between Robert Hayne of South Carolina and Daniel Webster of Massachusetts evolved into a debate on nullification. In the **Webster-Hayne Debate**, Daniel Webster argued that if nullification were to proceed, the results would be "states dissevered, discordant, belligerent; on a land rent with civil feuds, or drenched . . . in fraternal blood!" President Jackson was a believer in states' rights but firmly opposed the concept of nullification.

New tariffs were imposed on imported goods, and in November of 1832 a specially called convention in South Carolina voted to nullify the law imposing these tariffs. Jackson moved troops and federal marshals to South Carolina to collect the tariff payments there; Congress authorized these decisions when it passed the **Force Act**. John Calhoun resigned as vice president (Jackson suggested privately that he should be hung). A crisis was avoided when the Congress passed a bill, acceptable to South Carolina, that lowered the amount of the tariffs to be collected.

THE BANK CRISIS

The Second Bank of the United States was chartered in 1816 (it was a crucial part of Henry Clay's "American System"). The bank issued national currency, regulated loan rates, and controlled state banks. The bank had been run since 1823 by Nicholas Biddle. As stated previously, Jackson was suspicious of government involvement in the economy. These suspicions extended to the National Bank.

Henry Clay was going to run for president in the 1832 election and wanted to use the bank as a campaign issue. Clay began pushing to have the bank rechartered, even though its original charter did not expire until

1836. Clay was convinced that national support of the bank would swing supporters his way. Jackson vetoed the rechartering proposal, claiming it served special interests and few others. This increased his popularity with the public and helped to ensure his reelection in 1832.

Jackson wanted to destroy the National Bank, and in 1833, he ordered that money be removed from it and placed in state or local banks (Jackson's political enemies called these his "pet banks"). To keep the National Bank going, Biddle increased interest rates and called in loans that had been made to state banks. The results of this **Bank War** would eventually be the **Panic of 1837** and a depression that would last into the 1840s.

THE WHIG PARTY: A CHALLENGE TO THE DEMOCRATIC-REPUBLICANS

In the 1830s the **Whig party** emerged as the major opposition party to the party of Jackson. The Whigs and the Democratic-Republicans battled for elections throughout the 1830s and 1840s. Taking their lead from the legacy of Andrew Jackson, the Democrats generally favored a limited government. They saw urbanization and industrialization as necessary evils; the America they favored was still essentially a Jeffersonian one.

The Whigs favored more governmental involvement in commercial activities and favored the National Bank and industrial growth. They were opposed to rapid and uncontrolled settlement of the West. Consistent with their view of a more activist government, the Whigs also were more likely to sponsor reformist legislation. Predictably, businessmen from the North and Northeast supported the Whigs, as did Southern planters. The Democrats were generally supported by the "common man," which included small farmers, factory workers, and smaller merchants. A Democrat, Martin Van Buren, won the 1836 election, but Whig William Henry Harrison was elected in 1840. Harrison died after one month in office and was seceded by John Tyler. Developments in Texas and American expansionism would become important issues during his presidency.

CHAPTER REVIEW

Rapid Review Guide

To achieve the perfect 5, you should be able to explain the following:

- A new production system developed in textile mills, such as those that existed in Lowell, Massachusetts, in the early nineteenth century.
- The Monroe Doctrine boldly proclaimed that the Western Hemisphere was off-limits to European intrusion.
- Beginning in 1824, it was official American policy to move Native American tribes east of the Mississippi; the horrors of many of these relocations are well documented.

- The Second Great Awakening influenced many to become involved in reform movements, including the abolitionist movement.
- The presidency of Andrew Jackson is celebrated as an era where the "common man" reigned supreme, although Jackson greatly expanded the powers of the presidency.
- The Democratic party of Andrew Jackson was the first real political party in American history.
- Jackson's tariff policy caused a renewal of interest in the policy of nullification in several Southern state legislatures.
- In the 1830s the Whig party emerged as the major party opposing the Democratic party of Jackson.

Time Line

1790s: Beginning of Second Great Awakening
1816: Second Bank of United States chartered
        Tariff of 1816 imposes substantial import tariffs
        Election of James Monroe
1819: Panic of 1819 (unemployment lasts until 1823)
1820: Missouri Compromise
        Reelection of James Monroe
1820s: Growth of New England textile mills
1823: Monroe Doctrine
1824: Proposal by President Monroe to move Native Americans east of the Mississippi River
1825: John Quincy Adams elected president by House of Representatives (no candidate had won a majority in Electoral College)
1828: Andrew Jackson elected president
1830: Passage of Indian Removal Act in Congress
        Webster-Hayne debate
1830s: Growth of the Whig Party
1831: Cherokee nation goes to court to defend tribal rights in *Cherokee Nation* v. *Georgia*
        First issue of William Lloyd Garrison's *The Liberator* published
1832: Andrew Jackson reelected
        Nullification crisis after nullification of tariffs by South Carolina
1834: First strike of women textile workers in Lowell, Massachusetts
1836: Democrat Martin Van Buren elected president
1840: Whig William Henry Harrison elected president

✓ Review Questions

1. President Monroe claimed that westward relocation of Native Americans would be to the advantage of the Native Americans because

A. they would not be bothered west of the Mississippi

B. the American military would protect them during the journey

C. they would be well compensated for the tribal lands that they were leaving

D. they would not have to pay for the lands they were moving to

E. settlers west of the Mississippi were receptive to Native American settlement there

(Correct Answer: **A.** Monroe stated that Native Americans could not avoid being continually harassed if they lived east of the Mississippi, but that this would not happen after they moved.)

2. The concept of nullification became an issue during this period when

A. Georgia opposed congressional legislation concerning slavery

B. South Carolina nullified congressional legislation concerning the removal of Native Americans

C. South Carolina nullified congressional tariff bills

D. Southern representatives to the Electoral College switched their votes in the 1824 election

E. Virginia nullified congressional legislation concerning slavery

(Correct Answer: **C.** Because the tariff bills increased the prices of cloth and iron, the South Carolina legislature first nullified the Tariff of 1828.)

3. Critics of Andrew Jackson would make all of the following claims *except*

A. he was a very common man and not fit to be president

B. he gave too much power to the presidency

C. he gave political offices to his friends

D. his lack of experience in governmental affairs

E. he relied too much on his "Kitchen Cabinet"

(Correct Answer: **D.** All of the other criticisms were often made against Jackson. However, he did have an impressive background: Before becoming president, he had served as a congressman and a senator from Tennessee and as the territorial governor of Florida.)

4. The following are true about the textile mills of New England in the early nineteenth century *except*

A. a large percentage of their workforce was made up of women

B. they depended on water for power

C. they used a system called the putting-out system

D. Almost none still exist today.

E. there was little labor unrest in the mills until the 1830s and 1840s

(Correct Answer: **C.** It was the putting-out system that these mills replaced.)

5. Horace Mann is associated with

A. abolitionism

B. the temperance movement

C. prison reform

D. educational reform

E. reform for conditions of the mentally ill

(Correct Answer: **D.** Horace Mann wrote and spoke about the need to improve schools and to improve teacher training methods.)

Chapter 10

The Union Expanded and Challenged (1835–1860)

THE IDEOLOGY OF MANIFEST DESTINY

The idea of **manifest destiny** fueled the continued American expansion westward. Americans from the time of the Puritans spoke of America as a community with a divine mission. Beginning in the 1830s, some began to express the view that it was "God's plan" that America expand beyond the Mississippi River. Both political leaders and Protestant missionary organizations fervently supported western expansion. In 1845 Democratic newspaperman John O'Sullivan wrote that the most critical need for America was "the fulfillment of our manifest destiny to overspread the continent allotted by Providence for the free development of our yearly multiplying millions."

Americans had begin to settle in Oregon in the 1830s. The six-month, 2000-mile journey along the **Oregon Trail** brought settlers to the Oregon territory; many of them settled in the Willamette Valley. Many settlers in the Ohio Valley began to catch "Oregon Fever" by 1842; stories of a mild climate and the possibility of fur trading fueled the imaginations of many. Missionaries came to "tame" the Native Americans that lived in the region. By 1845 over 5000 had streamed into the Oregon territory. A section of Oregon was controlled by the British and a section by America. "Fifty-four Forty or Fight" became the rallying cry for expansionists who wanted all of Oregon to be under American control. The **Oregon Treaty** of 1846 gave most of Oregon to the Americans. The California territory, controlled by Spain, also attracted the interest of American settlers; American settlers first arrived there in the 1830s. The future of expansion in Oregon and California were key issues in the 1844 presidential campaign.

"REMEMBER THE ALAMO!"

The drive for expansion, which fueled the dreams of many Americans in the first half of the nineteenth century, made eventual conflict with Mexico inevitable. Mexico gained its independence from Spain in 1821 and encouraged the economic development of its northern province of Texas (which consisted of what we now know of as the state of Texas and parts of Kansas, Oklahoma, New Mexico, Wyoming, and Colorado). American economic investment was encouraged in the region: American settlers who would agree to become Mexican citizens, become Catholics, and encourage others Americans to come to Mexico were given large tracts of land for next to nothing. These settlers numbered nearly 30,000 by 1836.

Predictably, many Americans who settled in Texas were not diligent in fulfilling their obligations to the Mexican government, causing the Mexican government to act to reassert control over Texas. In 1836 the American settlers and some Mexicans living in Texas revolted against Mexican control of Texas. On March 2 they declared that Texas was an independent state and established a constitution (in which slavery was legal). Led by Davey Crockett and Jim Bowie, 165 Texans were defeated at the Alamo on March 6 by over 3000 Mexican soldiers, but their cry of "Remember the Alamo!" became the rallying cry for those fighting for the independence of Texas. A declaration of independence was issued in early March of 1836 by a convention of Texans opposed to continued Mexican rule.

Many American adventurers eager for land now poured into Texas and helped the Texans defeat the Mexican army on April 21, 1836. An independent Republic of Texas was proclaimed. General Sam Houston, who had led the army that defeated the Mexicans, became president of the Lone Star Republic. Most people living there (the vast majority being Americans) desired to become part of the United States. Andrew Jackson gave stirring speeches favoring the annexation of Texas and offered diplomatic recognition to the Lone Star Republic just before he left office. However, most Whigs were against annexation, fearing it would cause war with Mexico and domestic dissension. Abolitionists in the North were opposed to it, since they feared the entry of another slave state (which Texas would undoubtedly be) into the Union. Jackson feared that the annexation of Texas would hurt the chances of his chosen successor, Martin Van Buren, in the 1836 presidential election. He never acted on the annexation issue, causing the Republic of Texas to turn to Europe for potential allies.

Martin Van Buren also refused to support legislation that would make Texas part of the United States. William Henry Harrison, a Whig, defeated Van Buren in the 1840 presidential election but died after one month in office. Harrison's vice president was John Tyler, a Democrat who had been placed on the ticket to appeal to Southerners. Tyler favored the annexation of Texas and by mid-1844 had completed negotiations with the Texans on a treaty that would bring Texas into the United States. John C. Calhoun, the secretary of state, wrote a note to the British government concerning the situation in Texas; in the note he stated that the continuation of slavery would be good for Texas. This was enough to doom the treaty when it went to the Senate for approval.

THE PIVOTAL ELECTION OF 1844

Democrat James K. Polk was elected president in 1844. Polk was the first American **dark-horse candidate** for president, as he was not one of the announced candidates before the Democratic convention of that year. The campaign of that year showed several trends that would be pivotal to American political life in the 1840s and 1850s. The South and Southern interests increasingly influenced and were reflected in Democratic policies, and the Walker Tariff of 1846 established a very low tariff on imported goods, delighting many in the South and disgusting many Northern industrialists.

Abolitionism officially entered presidential politics in 1844. The Liberty party, with James Birney as its presidential candidate, was an abolitionist party. Although Birney attracted only 62,000 votes, abolitionism, and the sectional divisions it would help to foster, became a permanent part of the political landscape until the Civil War.

The 1844 election also demonstrated that desire for manifest destiny was the most important issue facing America at the time; most historians credit Polk's support of American expansionism as the major reason for his election. Polk was inaugurated in March of 1845. By December Texas had entered the Union. Expansionism and slavery also became increasingly intertwined as a single issue. The status of slavery in each newly acquired territory would have enormous political consequences, as forces in the North and the South were determined that the number of slave and free states remain equal.

WAR WITH MEXICO

The reasons for the Mexican-American War are numerous. Patriots in Mexico were outraged when Texas joined the United States, as they considered Texas still to be part of Mexico. The war served the economic interests of groups both in Mexico and the United States. However, the main reason for war was the determination of President Polk to fulfill what he perceived to be America's mission to occupy the lands all the way to the Pacific Ocean and his willingness to use force to accomplish this aim.

Polk did much to provoke war with the Mexicans. He encouraged settlers in Mexico to occupy territory all the way to the Rio Grande River, which the Mexicans considered to be outside of the territory of Texas (Mexico considered the Nueces River, north of the Rio Grande, as the border between Texas and the rest of Mexico). Polk also wanted to buy territory from Mexico that would allow the United States to expand all the way to California. In October 1845, he offered the Mexican government $5 million for the territory between the Nueces and the Rio Grande rivers, $25 million for California, and $5 million for other Mexican territory in the West. John Slidell, the diplomat sent to Mexico City with Polk's offer, was never even received by the Mexican government. Early in 1846 Polk sent an American force commanded by General Zachary Taylor to defend the territory between the Nueces and the Rio Grande rivers. In early April part of this force was ambushed by the Mexican army. Polk had to do little to convince the American Congress to issue a declaration of war against Mexico on May 13, 1846.

Many Whigs had hoped the conflict with Mexico could be peacefully negotiated; abolitionists feared the conflict with Mexico was little more than a Southern ruse to expand slavery in the American territories. Texas had never achieved real prosperity since its independence from Mexico, and the Mexican government was riddled with corruption. President Polk had predicted that the Mexicans would refuse American efforts to purchase western territories, and he proceeded through officials stationed there to let Americans and Mexicans living in California know that if they rose in opposition to Mexican control of the area, the American army would protect them. Not coincidentally, American naval and infantry forces arrived in California in late 1845 as a show of American force. Shortly after the American declaration of war against Mexico, settlers rose up in revolt, supported by American infantry forces commanded by John C. Fremont. On July 4, 1846, the **Bear Flag Republic** was officially proclaimed in the California territory.

American troops also entered into Mexico itself, easily defeating the Mexican army. Forces under Zachary Taylor were especially successful in winning battles over the Mexicans in late 1846 and early 1847. The Mexican government refused to surrender or negotiate with the Americans. President Polk then sent an American force under General Winfield Scott to Mexico to occupy Mexico City, the capital. Scott landed on Mexican territory at Veracruz on March 8, 1847, and was victorious in several battles against the Mexicans. Mexico still refused to settle for peace, and on September 13, 1847, Scott's army entered Mexico City. Mexican partisans continued guerrilla warfare well into 1848.

Effects of the Mexican War

The **Treaty of Guadalupe Hidalgo** was signed on February 2, 1848, and officially ended the Mexican-American War. Many who had favored war considered the treaty too generous to the defeated Mexicans. For $15 million the United States acquired the Texas territory north of the Rio Grande, New Mexico, and California (the exact territory they had previously offered to buy). The American government also assumed all claims of Americans against the Mexican government.

The territory of the United States increased by one-third as a result of this treaty, yet the controversy over slavery in the new territories was immense. In 1846 David Wilmont, a Democratic Representative from Pennsylvania, introduced an amendment to a bill authorizing funding for the Mexican-American War that stated slavery could not exist in any territory acquired from Mexico. The **Wilmont Proviso** was passed by the House of Representatives four times and rejected by the Senate each time. Nevertheless, each debate concerning the bill stirred up intense sectional differences concerning slavery in the territories. Southerners such as John C. Calhoun strenuously argued that the federal government had no right to outlaw something in an American territory that was legal in a number of American states. President Polk's compromise decision was to continue the line drawn by the **Missouri Compromise** out to the Pacific Ocean, with slavery allowed in territories south of the line and not allowed in territories north of the line.

To avoid being hurt by the controversies surrounding slavery, both the Democrats and the Whigs said little about it in the 1848 presidential election. Zachary Taylor ran as a Whig and was victorious, largely because of his war record in Mexico and because he made no comments whatsoever about the future of slavery in the territories. Some members of the Liberty party and defectors from the Whig and Democratic parties formed the **Free-Soil party**, whose main purpose was to oppose slavery in the newly acquired western territories. The Free-Soilers nominated former president Van Buren, who won 10 percent of the popular vote.

POLITICAL CHALLENGES OF THE 1850s

The controversies of the 1850s largely centered around slavery and its status in the newly acquired American territories. Americans had been able to compromise on such issues in the first half of the nineteenth century. By the 1850s the volatile nature of debate on the issue of slavery made compromise much harder to come by.

The discovery of gold in California in January of 1848 caused a flood of "diggers" to enter the territory. Within a year over 80,000 "forty-niners" entered the state. By the end of 1849 the territory's population swelled to over 100,000. Law enforcement and governmental controls were severely lacking in much of the territory. Zachary Taylor encouraged settlers in California and New Mexico to draft constitutions and to apply for statehood. By the end of 1849 California had adopted a constitution prohibiting slavery; New Mexico did the same six months later.

Taylor's proposal to allow California to enter the Union as a non-slave state infuriated many Southerners. Southern senators railed that much of the California territory was south of the **Missouri Compromise** line: Shouldn't slavery be allowed in that part of California? A convention was called for representatives of Southern states to come together and discuss leaving the Union. John C. Calhoun captured the feeling of many Southerners when he said, "I trust we shall persist in our resistance until restoration or all our rights, or disunion, one or the other, is the consequence."

Henry Clay, the author of the **Missouri Compromise**, spoke forcefully against many of Calhoun's arguments and wrote the parts of the legislation that together would be called the **Compromise of 1850**. Both the North and the South got some of what they wanted in this compromise. Northerners were happy that the legislation allowed California to enter the Union as a free state, that the residents of the New Mexico and Utah territories would decide if these areas would be slave territories, and that slave trading was eliminated in Washington, DC. Southerners were satisfied over several provisions found in the legislation: provisions of the **Fugitive Slave Law** were toughened, Congress stated that it didn't have jurisdiction over interstate slave trade, and slavery was allowed to continue in Washington. Eight months of debate were needed to pass all provisions of the compromise. Senator Stephen A. Douglas of Illinois was the most effective spokesperson for the cause of the compromise. California entering the Union as a free state gave the free states a majority; in the future, that majority would grow, helping to explain the increased tensions between the North and the South between 1850 and 1860.

The presidential election of 1852 was another campaign devoid of much discussion of the slave issue. The Free-Soilers got half the votes they had received in the 1848 election. General Winfield Scott was the candidate of the Whigs. Like Zachary Taylor in 1848, he made few public statements on political issues. Franklin Pierce was another **dark-horse candidate** who won the Democratic nomination and then the presidency.

EFFECTS OF THE COMPROMISE OF 1850

The part of the **Compromise of 1850** that most bothered abolitionists in the North was the strengthening of the **Fugitive Slave Act**. Under the new provisions of the bill, judges in the North determined the fate of blacks accused of being escaped slaves. Accused runaways were denied jury proceedings and often were denied the right to testify in their own trials. Heavy financial penalties were imposed on Northerners who helped slaves escape or who hid slaves. Harriet Beecher Stowe's *Uncle Tom's Cabin* was written as a response to the **Fugitive Slave Act**. Stowe demonstrated the immorality of slavery in her novel, which sold nearly 275,000 copies in its first year of publication.

THE PRESIDENCY OF FRANKLIN PIERCE

Pierce's foreign policy was pro-expansionist. In 1853 he sent a naval force under Commodore Matthew Perry to Japan to open Japan to American trade and diplomatic contact. American diplomats negotiated the **Gadsden Purchase** with Mexico, which gave America an additional southern route for trade (and territory for a proposed transcontinental railroad). Pierce also initiated efforts to purchase Cuba from the Spanish. When this effort proved unsuccessful, many in the Pierce administration favored the seizing of Cuba by force, which infuriated many in the North. Pierce's policies seemed to benefit Southern interests and were viewed with suspicion by many in the North.

The Whig party also died during this period. Many former Whigs became members of the American or **Know-Nothing party** that developed in response to rising immigration from Ireland and Germany, which had begun in the late 1840s. The Know-Nothing party was **nativist** and especially anti-Catholic. The Know-Nothings favored restrictions on further immigration and various schemes that would keep recent immigrants from voting. The fact that it was second most powerful party in America during the first years of the Pierce administration demonstrates the weakness of the two-party system in this period.

THE RETURN OF SECTIONAL CONFLICT

The desire to organize settlement in Kansas and Nebraska brought tensions between the North and the South back to the forefront. According to the provisions of the Missouri Compromise, slavery would be banned in both of these territories. Stephen A. Douglas, sponsor of the bill that proposed the creation of the Kansas and Nebraska territories, wanted to create a large region free of native Americans so that a transcontinental railroad could be built between Chicago and the West Coast. Douglas was pressured by Southern senators and included a provision in the bill that the existence of slavery in these territories would be decided by a vote of those that lived there. This **Kansas-Nebraska Act** infuriated many in the North. The bill was passed with the support of President Pierce.

The fury over the passage of the Kansas-Nebraska Act caused the creation of the **Republican party**. The party was an exclusively Northern one and was dedicated to the principle that slavery should be prohibited in all territories. Some former Democrats, Whigs, and Free-Soilers made up the base of the Republican party, which would quickly replace the Know-Nothings as the second most important political party in the United States.

"BLEEDING KANSAS": SLAVE OR FREE?

In preparations for elections that would be held in 1855, states and interests supporting and opposing slavery all were active in sending settlers into Kansas that would support their cause. Abolitionists financed the journey to Kansas of many settlers opposed to slavery; at the same time, many Southern states "encouraged" settlers to travel there. Conflicts, often involving bloodshed, erupted between the two sides. Many pro-slavery settlers flooded into Kansas from Missouri, thus ensuring the election of a pro-slavery legislature in 1855 by casting illegal ballots. The legislature enacted measures designed to protect slavery in the territory (the "Lecompton Constitution" made slavery legal in a constitutional sense). Free-Soilers proceeded to elect their own legislature and adopted equally harsh antislavery legislation. Violence continued in **"Bleeding Kansas"** in 1856: The free-soil settlement at Lawrence was attacked, and in response, abolitionist John Brown and his followers killed five pro-slavery settlers. Fighting between supporters and opponents of slavery continued throughout the year.

Democrat James Buchanan won the presidential election of 1856. The opposition to him was split, with John C. Fremont running as a Republican and ex-president Millard Fillmore running as the Know-Nothing candidate. It should be noted that Fremont and Fillmore together gained nearly 55 percent of the popular vote.

THE DRED SCOTT DECISION

The **Dred Scott case** finally made it to the Supreme Court docket in 1856. Many hoped it would decisively end the controversy over slavery in the territories. Dred Scott was a former slave who was suing for his freedom on the basis that his owner had taken him to stay first in a free state, Illinois, and then into a free territory, Wisconsin.

The final decision of the Supreme Court, in essence, supported the Southern position concerning slavery in the territories. The court ruled that Scott as a slave had no legal right to sue in federal court, that his time in a free state and a free territory did not make him a free man, and that Congress had no right to prohibit slavery in the territories, since the Constitution protected property rights and slaves were still considered property.

Instead of easing tensions between the North and South, the Dred Scott decision only made tensions between the sections worse. Southerners felt their position had been justified and felt little need to compromise with the North; Northerners were more convinced than ever that "slave interests" controlled all the branches of government.

President Buchanan further antagonized Northerners by recommending that Kansas be admitted to the Union as a slave state, even though the legislature in Kansas had been elected by largely illegal means (Kansas was finally admitted to the Union as a free state in 1861).

THE LINCOLN–DOUGLAS DEBATES

Stephen Douglas was opposed by Abraham Lincoln in the 1858 election for senator from Illinois. Lincoln had been a Whig but was now a Republican, having broken from the Whig party over slavery. Lincoln was a practicing attorney, had been in the U.S. Congress during the Mexican War, and narrowly lost an earlier bid for the Senate in 1852. Douglas and Lincoln debated at seven locations throughout Illinois in the months leading up to the election. The issues of slavery and the territories dominated all of these debates. At a debate in Freeport, Lincoln asked Douglas how the residents of a territory could exclude slavery in light of the Dred Scott decision. Douglas responded with the **Freeport Doctrine**, which maintained that a territory could exclude slavery if the laws and regulations written made slavery impossible to enforce. Douglas won the Senate seat, but Lincoln was recognized by many as an up-and-coming force in the Republican party.

JOHN BROWN'S RAID

Radical abolitionist John Brown and 18 followers seized the federal arsenal at Harper's Ferry, Virginia, on the evening of October 16, 1859. Brown hoped to incite a slave uprising by his actions. It would later become known that Brown's actions had been financed by several wealthy Northern abolitionists. Brown was captured, tried for treason, and hung. The response to Brown's death further intensified the tensions between the North and the South. Henry David Thoreau was one of many Northerners to consider Brown as "the bravest and humanest man in all the country," while Southerners were outraged by Northern support of Brown's actions.

THE PRESIDENTIAL ELECTION OF 1860

The election of Abraham Lincoln as president in 1860 virtually ensured that some Southern states would leave the Union. Lincoln campaigned on the need to contain slavery in the territories. The Democratic party split at their nominating convention, with Stephen Douglas receiving the support of Northern Democrats and John Breckinridge getting the backing of Southern Democrats. Douglas stated that the slave issue in the territories should be decided by a vote of those residing in each territory; Breckinridge proposed that slavery should be legally protected in the territories. John Bell also received some ex-Whig support as he ran as a candidate of the Constitutional Union party. Lincoln received nearly 40 percent of the popular vote and easily won the Electoral College vote.

To many Southerners, the election was an insult. A man had been elected president who virtually no one in the South had voted for. Since free states outnumbered slaves states, it was only natural that their representatives would dominate Congress and the Electoral College. Lincoln had repeatedly stated that Republicans had no interest in disturbing slavery in the South, but many Southerners did not believe him.

South Carolina was the first state to leave the Union on December 20, 1860. In the next six weeks, legislatures in Mississippi, Georgia, Florida, Alabama, Texas, and Louisiana all voted to do the same. Representatives of these seven states met in February of 1861 to create the **Confederate States of America**, with former moderate Jefferson Davis elected as president. The only question remaining was when the first shots between the North and the South would actually be fired.

CHAPTER REVIEW

Rapid Review Guide

To achieve the perfect 5, you should be able to explain the following:

- The concept of manifest destiny spurred American expansion into Texas and the far West.

- American settlers much more loyal to the United States than to Mexico entered Texas in large numbers and encouraged Texas to break away from Mexico and eventually become an American state.

- The issue of slavery and slavery in the territories came to dominate American political debate more and more in the 1840s and 1850s.

- California entered the Union as a free state under the Missouri Compromise, upsetting the balance between free and slave states and intensifying the conflict between them.

- The Kansas-Nebraska Act created violence in these territories as they "decided" on whether they would be slave or free; both abolitionists and pro-slavery forces shipped in supporters to help sway the elections in these territories.

- The Dred Scott decision only intensified tensions between the North and the South.

- The election of 1860 was seen as an insult to many in the South, and after its results were announced, the secession of Southern states from the Union was inevitable.

Time Line

1836: Texas territory repels against Mexico; independent republic of Texas created
1841: Beginning of expansion into Oregon territory
1844: James K. Polk elected president
1845: Texas becomes a state of the United States
1846: Oregon Treaty with Britain gives most of Oregon to United States
War with Mexico begins
Wilmont Proviso passed
1848: Gold discovered in California; beginning of California gold rush
Treaty of Guadalupe Hidalgo
Formation of Free-Soil party
Zachary Taylor elected president

1850: Passage of Compromise of 1850
1852: Franklin Pierce elected president
Uncle Tom's Cabin by Harriet Beecher Stowe published
1854: Kansas-Nebraska Act passed
Formation of the Republican party
1856: Democrat James Buchanan elected president
"Bleeding Kansas"
1857: Dred Scott decision announced
1858: Lincoln-Douglas debates
Freeport Doctrine issued by Stephen Douglas
1859: Harper's Ferry rail of John Brown
1860: Abraham Lincoln elected president
South Carolina secedes from the Union (December)

✓ Review Questions

1. Northerners approved all of the provisions of the Compromise of 1850 *except*

   A. the section of the document concerning slavery in California
   B. the section of the document concerning the Fugitive Slave Law
   C. the section of the treaty on slave trading in Washington, DC
   D. the section of the document concerning slavery in New Mexico
   E. the section of the document concerning slavery in Utah

(Correct Answer: **B.** In the Compromise of 1850, provisions of the Fugitive Slave Law were made tougher. California was to enter the Union as a free state, the residents of New Mexico and Utah could decided if they wanted to be slave or free, and slaving trading was outlawed in Washington, DC.)

2. During the presidential election of 1860

   A. the Democratic party had split and ran two candidates
   B. the new president was someone that almost no one in the South had voted for
   C. support for the Constitutional Union party demonstrated that ex-Whigs were not satisfied with either the Democratic or the Republican party
   D. the issue of the future of slavery in the territories was a major issue
   E. All of the above

(Correct Answer: **E.** All of the factors mentioned concerning the 1860 election are true.)

3. According to the concept of manifest destiny

   A. it was primarily economic factors that caused Americans to expand westward
   B. it was primarily political factors that caused Americans to expand westward
   C. the desires of the American military did much to force westward expansion
   D. westward expansion was the fulfillment of America's destiny
   E. overpopulation on the eastern seaboard forced westward expansion

(Correct Answer: **D.** The concept of manifest destiny stated that social, political, and social factors all came together to encourage western expansion, and that western expansion was actually "God's plan" for America.)

4. American settlers first came to Mexico in the early 1830s

    A. to avenge the attack on the Alamo
    B. for religious reasons; most that came were devout Catholics
    C. for political reasons; most that came were disenchanted with American policy toward Native Americans
    D. out of personal loyalty to Davey Crockett or Jim Bowie
    E. because they could receive a large plot of land for next to nothing

(Correct Answer: **E.** Settlers who came and became Mexican citizens and Catholics could receive very large plots of land for almost nothing. The incident at the Alamo did not occur until 1836.)

5. The political party of the era that supported nativist policies was the

    A. Liberty party
    B. Free-Soil party
    C. Democratic party
    D. Know-Nothing party
    E. Whig party

(Correct Answer: **D.** The Know-Nothing party, a popular party in the early 1850s, supported a number of anti-immigrant and anti-Catholic policies.)

Chapter 11

The Union Divided: The Civil War (1861–1865)

The Civil War was the culmination of nearly 40 years of tensions between the North and the South. Northern abolitionists looked forward to the war with great anticipation: Victory over the South would finally allow the dreaded institution of slavery to be eliminated. Northern industrialists saw the war as an opportunity, at long last, to expand their control of American industry. The majority of Southerners rejoiced at the onset of war; they perceived that victory would allow the "Southern way of life" to continue without constant criticism from the North. As in many wars, politicians and generals on both sides predicted a quick victory. Newspapers in both the North and the South declared that the war would be over by Christmas of 1861.

To state that the Civil War was just about slavery is an oversimplification. Certainly, criticism by Northern abolitionists of the "peculiar institution" of slavery, and Southern responses to that criticism, were important factors. However, other tensions between the North and the South also existed. The future of the American economy as seen by Northern industrialists differed drastically from the desires and needs of the leaders of Southern plantation society. Most importantly, the Southern view of "state's rights" differed most dramatically from the view of the Union held in the North. By 1861, many political leaders in the South fervently espoused the views that John C. Calhoun had formulated decades earlier: It was up to the individual state to decided on the validity of any federal law or federal action for that state. This position was intolerable to President Lincoln and most political leaders in the North. If anything, it was debate over the state's rights issue that made the Civil War inevitable.

Other factors increased the animosity between the North and the South. By this point slavery was synonymous with Southern identity; in Southern eyes any attack on slavery was an attack on the South as a whole. The fact that this struggle between the North and the South had gone on for 40 years served to harden positions on both sides. In addition, by this point the population of the North was greater than the population of the South, and the number of free states was greater than the number of slaves states. As a result, Southerners knew that Northern antislave interests would control the Congress (and the ability to influence Supreme Court appointments) and the Electoral College for the foreseeable future.

ADVANTAGES OF THE NORTH AND SOUTH IN WAR

Many Southerners were very excited when the Civil War finally began, yet there were some harsh realities facing them as war commenced. Most of the nation's wealth was situated in the North; the industrialization of the North would give Northerners an advantage in producing guns, bullets, and other materials needed for warfare. The Northern railway system was far superior to the existing railways in the South. Most influential banks and financial markets were located in the North. More people (by a nearly 3-to-1 margin) lived in the North. The South could at least say that they were larger than the North; conquering the South would be a formidable task. At the outset of the war, Southerners might also claim that their officer corps, led by men such as Robert E. Lee, was superior to the officer corps of the Union, led by Winfield Scott.

The Aftermath of Secession

As mentioned in the previous chapter, South Carolina, Mississippi, Florida, Louisiana, Texas, Georgia, and Alabama all voted to secede from the Union in late 1860 or early 1861. In February 1861, the **Confederate States of America** was officially created. States in the Upper South (such as Virginia and Kentucky) were not eager to join the secessionist movement (there were fewer slaves in these states). Leaders of Kentucky and Maryland proposed that Congress in Washington enact legislation that would protect slavery in any territory or state where it already existed; the desire of these leaders was the preservation of the Union. President James Buchanan did little to aid the situation. Buchanan stated in December of 1860 that secession from the Union was illegal, but that nowhere in the Constitution was it stated that any state could be forced to remain in the Union.

Politicians in South Carolina and elsewhere in the South interpreted Buchanan's statement as, in essence, stating that he would do nothing to bring back the seceded states and that they were now independent. Leaders in South Carolina demanded the surrender of **Fort Sumter**, a federal fort located in Charleston harbor. To test the will of the leaders of South Carolina, Buchanan sent an unarmed merchant ship to bring supplies to the fort. When the ship was fired on, Buchanan did not send the navy in (which many in South Carolina was sure he would do); "patri-ots" in South Carolina and elsewhere in the South now felt certain that independence was theirs.

As the crisis continued at Fort Sumter, Senator John Crittenden of Kentucky emerged with a compromise plan. The **Crittenden Plan** proposed that the federal government guarantee the existence of slavery in any state where it existed, and that the line of the Missouri Compromise be extended all the way to the Pacific, with territories to the north of the line being free from slavery and those south of the line having slavery. Republicans in Congress rejected this plan, since it went away from the concept of "free soil" that president-elect Lincoln had just been elected on.

THE ATTACK ON FORT SUMTER AND THE BEGINNING OF WAR

Abraham Lincoln had to walk a political tightrope upon his inauguration in March of 1861. It was necessary to maintain the authority of the fed-eral government, but at the same time to do nothing that would provoke war with the South. Many of Lincoln's advisors thought that negotia-tions could bring at least some of the states that had seceded back into the Union. In his inauguration speech, however, Lincoln stated that force would be used if necessary to preserve the Union.

The skill of Lincoln as president was immediately called upon. In April of 1861, Lincoln sent another ship to supply **Fort Sumter**. The gov-ernment of South Carolina was informed that the ship would be arriving and that no troops would land unless the delivery of these supplies was interfered with. Jefferson Davis and the Confederate government saw this as an opportunity to strike against the Union. Confederate guns bombed Fort Sumter for two days, and on April 14 the fort surrendered. Davis was hopeful that early victory would force states in the Upper South to turn to the Confederate cause; Confederates also hoped to obtain British and French assistance. Any thought of compromise between North and South ended with the attack on Fort Sumter.

Three days after the surrender of the fort, Virginia passed a resolu-tion favoring secession. On the same day, Robert E. Lee rejected an offer to command the Union army, resigned from the Union army, and took control of the Confederate army. In the end, Lincoln was able to keep four of the states of the Upper South in the Union (Kentucky, Missouri, Maryland, and Delaware).

WAR AIMS AND STRATEGIES

From the beginning of the war, the Southern defense of the slave system was unrelenting. This position greatly undermined the possibility of the Confederacy receiving aid from the French and the English. Economically, European support of the Confederacy would have made sense; Europeans nations were dependent on cotton cultivated in the American South. However, both France and England firmly opposed slavery and had outlawed it in their countries decades earlier. The South also overestimated the British need for Southern cotton; Britain soon proved that it could get cotton elsewhere.

Both sides began recruiting armies in the spring and early summer of 1861. Lincoln was able to summon support in the Northern states not from speeches on slavery but from the simple claim that the actions of the South was an attack on the very principles of the republican form of government. Both sides predicted early victory. The capital of the Confederacy was moved to Richmond, Virginia, after Virginia joined the Confederacy; cries of "On to Richmond!" filled the Northern newspapers. For political reasons, Lincoln pushed for an early attack against the South (Winfield Scott presented an alternative proposal, stating that the best policy for the North would be to blockade all Southern ports and starve the South into submission). A Union army advanced on Richmond. On July 21, 1861, at the **First Battle of Bull Run,** Union forces retreated in chaos back toward Washington. After this battle Northern political leaders and generals conceded that victory in this war would not be as easy as they initially thought it might be.

The Effects of Bull Run

The Battle of Bull Run showed both sides that new tactics would be necessary for victory. The plan proposed by Winfield Scott, now referred to as the **Anaconda Plan,** was reviewed more carefully by Abraham Lincoln. Lincoln had the United States Navy blockade Southern ports; as the war wore on, this became increasingly important. Industrial goods that the South had imported from the industrial North in earlier years now could not be gotten from Europe either. Also, later in the war Confederate states could not export cotton to Europe for very badly needed currency. Another part of the Anaconda Plan called for Northern naval forces to control the Mississippi River. The Union made major headway with this part of the plan in April of 1862 when a Union naval force captured New Orleans.

The Confederacy also made a major foreign trading mistake in early 1862. Cotton-producing states were convinced not to export cotton to England and France. Confederate leaders thought that textile factory owners in those countries would be so affected by this that they would pressure their governments to help the Confederacy and get their cotton back. Instead, Europeans turned elsewhere for cotton (especially India). As stated previously, when the South wanted to export cotton later in the war, they couldn't because of the naval blockade. It also became obvious that the organization of the South into a confederacy during a period of wartime was a disadvantage; individual state governments had the constitutional right to block critical tax programs and requisitions. The decision of the Confederacy to print paper money with no secure backing also would prove to be detrimental.

The Union Triumphant in the West

The Confederacy won several more battles in 1862, including the <u>Second Battle of Bull Run</u>. General George McClellan was named commander of the Union army and began formulating a plan to attack the Confederacy from the west. In February 1862, forces commanded by General Ulysses S. Grant captured Fort Henry and Fort Donelson, in Tennessee. Forces on both sides realized the importance of these victories. Grant continued to conquer Southern territory from this position. On April 6, 1862, the incredibly bloody but inconclusive <u>Battle of Shiloh</u> was fought. Up until this point it was the bloodiest battle ever fought in America. McClellan began to develop the reputation as a commander who was afraid to enter his troops into battle, even though the situation warranted it.

The Confederacy attempted to use technology to defeat the Northern naval blockade. In March of 1862 they presented their very first <u>ironclad</u> ship, the <u>Merrimack</u>. Shortly after the Union displayed the first Union ironclad, the <u>Monitor</u>. The two ironclads met once in battle, with neither ship able to do much to damage to the other.

DEVELOPMENTS IN THE SOUTH AND IN THE NORTH

Being a nation founded on the principle of <u>state's rights</u> was oftentimes a disadvantage for the Confederacy. Many Confederate soldiers who enlisted for one year in 1861 appeared ready to return home in 1862. General Robert E. Lee insisted that a system of <u>conscription</u> had to be introduced to ensure a steady supply of soldiers. In April 1862, the Confederate legislature passed laws requiring three years in the army for all white men from 18 to 35 (after the horrible losses of Antietam, this was extended to 45). Many advocates of state's rights violently objected to these regulations. Three Southern governors tried to block the conscription law in their states, saying that only the individual states had the right to make such laws. In some sections of the South nearly 60 percent of available manpower never served in the army. The Confederacy also adopted a plan to pay plantation owners who released their slaves to serve in the army; this was largely resisted because it was economically harmful to slave owners.

By late 1862 severe shortages of food and other materials began to spread throughout the South. Prices skyrocketed. Many soldiers deserted the army to return home to help their families through these difficult times. Large numbers of deserters and those who had resisted the draft became a problem in some sections of the South. The Confederacy instituted an income tax in order to get needed income for the government. Under existing circumstances, the actual collection of this money was sometimes difficult.

Many similar tensions existed in the North. In 1863 a system of conscription was introduced, requiring service of all men from ages 20 through 45. As in the South, draft dodgers could be found in the North. A provision of the Northern draft law that was very unpopular to many allowed a drafted person to avoid service by hiring a substitute or by paying the government $300; many of the "replacement" soldiers were Irish immigrants. Draft riots took place in New York City in July 1863, with nearly 200 people dying in these protests. Many taking part in the riots were Irish-Americans, and many of those killed were black. Draft offices and other buildings were destroyed; Irish-Americans did not want to take part in a war that would free the slaves, whom they perceived would be their competitors for jobs.

The North also had trouble financing the war. In 1861 a federal income tax was instituted. Still short of money, the government began issuing "greenbacks" in 1862; this money, not backed by gold, was considered official legal tender until the end of the war.

In every wartime setting in American history, the power of the executive has expanded. This was certainly true in the Civil War. President Lincoln assumed powers that no previous president had even considered. By executive order parts of Kentucky were placed under martial law for much of the war. Some Democrats in the North, nicknamed Copperheads, vigorously opposed the war, stating that it would lead to masses of freed slaves coming north and taking jobs. Copperheads were sometimes arrested, and three of them were actually deported from the North. Over 14,000 who opposed the war were imprisoned without trial. In several cases Lincoln ordered the writ of habeas corpus suspended.

THE EMANCIPATION PROCLAMATION

When he was elected president, Abraham Lincoln had no thought whatsoever of freeing the slaves; he repeatedly stated that he had no constitutional right to do that. However, on a practical level Lincoln realized that the continued existence of slavery in the South would make Northern victory harder; the existence of slavery allowed Southern landowners to leave their fields and fight in the Confederate army.

The Emancipation Proclamation was issued on January 1, 1863. The timing of this was a brilliant political move. Support for the war in the North had been waning; the Emancipation Proclamation gave Northerners a moral justification to continue fighting. This measure was received by different groups in predictable ways. Northern blacks were heartened by it, Southerners condemned it, and in Southern territories controlled by the Union army, slaves were actually freed. Many in England agreed with the proclamation; any last hopes that England might enter the war to aid the Confederacy were dashed at this point. Some whites in the North feared that ex-slaves would end up taking their jobs, and as a result, in the 1862 congressional elections Democrats picked up seats.

Blacks were not accepted into the Union army at the beginning of the war. After the Emancipation Proclamation many ex-slaves from Southern territories and free blacks from the North joined the Union army. By

1865, blacks made up almost 10 percent of the entire Union army. Black soldiers traditionally served in all-black units with white officers (the heroism of the 54th Massachusetts Infantry can be seen in the movie *Glory*).

1863: THE WAR TIPS TO THE NORTH

The darkest days of the war for the Union occurred in late 1862 and early 1863. The Union army suffered major defeats at the **Battle of Fredericksburg** (December 13, 1862) and at the **Battle of Chancellorsville** (May 1 to 3, 1863). Competent leadership of the Union army remained a major problem.

Yet time was an enemy of the Confederate army. As commander, General Robert E. Lee found it increasingly difficult to get men and resources (the Northern naval blockade definitely was affecting Southern military efforts by this point). In June of 1863, Lee decided to move the Confederate army out of Virginia into Pennsylvania. At the **Battle of Gettysburg** (July 1 to 3, 1863). Lee was defeated by the Union army, commanded by General George Meade. This was the bloodiest overall battle of the war, with 24,000 casualties suffered by the North and 28,000 by the South. Lee's army was forced to retreat to Virginia and would never again be able to mount an attack into Northern territory. Some military historians claim that the fate of the Confederate army was sealed by their defeat at Gettysburg.

The tide of the war continued to swing to the North as a result of several victories by armies commanded by Ulysses S. Grant. On July 4, 1863, Grant completed his victory at **Vicksburg**, ending a siege of the city that lasted six weeks. Victory at Vicksburg gave the Union virtual control of the Mississippi River. In November Grant was victorious at the Battle of Chattanooga (November 23 to 25, 1863). Abraham Lincoln's **Gettysburg Address** had been given four days earlier. In January of 1864 Grant was made commander of the Union army. At the same time, some in the Confederate government began speaking of the need for peace negotiations with the North.

Grant and the Army of the Potomac began to advance toward Richmond in the spring of 1864, while an army commanded by William T. Sherman began to advance toward Atlanta.

WAR WEARINESS IN THE NORTH AND SOUTH

In both the North and the South the pressures of a long war were obvious by 1864. To many in the South, it was clear that the Confederacy would be defeated. Severe food and material shortages continued. In the North, the presidential campaign of 1864 produced little excitement. Lincoln's Democratic opponent was General George McClellan. In early September of 1864 Lincoln confided to friends that he thought he would lose the presidency. However, word arrived that General Sherman had taken the key Confederate city of Atlanta. That, along with any real enthusiasm for (and by) McClellan, allowed Lincoln to easily win reelection.

THE END OF THE CONFEDERACY

Sherman employed a scorched earth policy as he marched from Atlanta to Savannah, Georgia, in November and December of 1864. In early April of 1865 General Lee took the Confederate army from Richmond and tried to escape to the south. The Union army caught up to him, and he finally surrendered on April 9, 1865, at the courthouse in **Appomattox**, Virginia. By the first week of June all other Confederate forces also surrendered and began to return home to oftentimes devastated homelands.

Lincoln only had time to begin to plan for what a post-Civil War America would look like. On April 14, 1865, he was assassinated by John Wilkes Booth at Ford's Theater. Booth was a pro-Southerner. He and a group of coconspirators also planned to kill Vice President Andrew Johnson and other members of the Lincoln cabinet. Booth was hunted down several days later and was killed by gunfire; several others conspiring with him were found and, after trials by military tribunals, hung. The incredibly difficult task of reconstruction would have to be handled by the new president, Andrew Johnson, a Tennessee Democrat who Lincoln had chosen to be his vice president.

CHAPTER REVIEW

Rapid Review Guide

To achieve the perfect 5, you should be able to explain the following:

- By 1861 various social, political, economic, and cultural factors made conflict between the North and the South inevitable.

- The North had numerous industrial, transportation, and financial advantages that they utilized throughout the Civil War.

- The Confederate States of America was created in February 1861; the fact that these states were organized as a confederacy had several disadvantages that would become obvious as the war progressed.

- Success for the Confederacy depended on European aid; Southerners overestimated the dependence of Europe on Southern crops.

- Confederate generals proved much more competent than their Union counterparts in several key battles in the first years of the war.

- By late 1862 the war had produced severe effects on the home fronts; food shortages were occurring in the South, and President Lincoln imposed martial law in several locations and suspended the writ of habeas corpus in the cases of some of his political opponents.

- The Emancipation Proclamation provided a moral justification for Northerners to continue the war.

- The war shifted decisively in favor of the North in 1863, with the battles of Gettysburg and Vicksburg proving to be critical victories for the North.

- The surrender of the Confederacy in April 1865 was caused by a severe lack of morale, manpower, and economic stability in the South.

Time Line

1860: Abraham Lincoln elected president
South Carolina secedes from Union
1861: Confederate States of America created
Attack on Fort Sumter
First Battle of Bull Run
Union begins blockade of Southern ports
1862: New Orleans captured by Union navy
Battle of Shiloh
Conscription begins in Confederate states
Emancipation of slaves in Southern states begins
Battle of Antietam
British announce they will not aid the Confederacy in any substantial way
1863: Emancipation Proclamation
Conscription begins in the North; draftees may hire "replacements"
First black soldiers enlist in Union army
Crucial Union victory at Gettysburg
Crucial Union victory at Vicksburg
Draft riots in New York City
1864: Abraham Lincoln reelected
General Sherman carries out his "march to the sea"
Desertion becomes a major problem in the Confederate army
1865: General Lee surrenders at Appomattox
Abraham Lincoln assassinated

✓ Review Questions

1. The North held many advantages at the beginning of the Civil War *except*

   A. most major financial institutions were in the North
   B. the North occupied more territory than the South
   C. the North had more railroad lines
   D. the North had more factories
   E. the North had a larger population

   (Correct Answer: **B.** All of the others were major advantages for the Union war effort.)

2. European states did not aid the Confederacy in the Civil War because

A. Union diplomats made many efforts to convince them not to
B. there were alternative sources of cotton and other crops that they could turn to
C. the Confederacy's position on slavery
D. they did not believe that the Confederacy could win
E. All of the above

(Correct Answer: **E.** All of the reasons given helped convince the Europeans not to assist the Confederacy. The Confederacy's position on slavery proved to be especially troublesome, since slavery had long been outlawed in Europe.)

3. The military draft was unpopular to many in the North because

A. the North already was lacking in men during this period
B. the draft allowed blacks to enter the armed forces
C. the draft allowed Irish-American immigrants to enter the army
D. the draft allowed those drafted to hire "replacements"
E. martial law was needed in many locations to enforce the draft provisions

(Correct Answer: **D.** The fact that replacement soldiers, oftentimes immigrants, could be hired or that a payment of $300 to the government could get a man out of the draft made the system very unpopular to many.)

4. The Battle of Vicksburg was an important victory for the Union because

A. it reversed several Union defeats in the same year
B. it came quickly, with a minimal loss of Union life
C. it gave the Union a pathway to Atlanta
D. it gave the Union virtual control of the Mississippi River
E. it demonstrated that General Lee could, in fact, be beaten

(Correct Answer: **D.** The six-week Battle of Vicksburg occurred in 1863 and helped turn the war in the Union's favor. As a result of Vicksburg, the Mississippi was virtually in the hands of the Union. Lee did not command the Confederate forces at Vicksburg.)

5. Copperheads were

A. Democrats in the North who opposed the war
B. Republicans in the North who suggested that Lincoln be replaced
C. Democrats in the North who switched over to Lincoln
D. Southern Democrats who wanted negotiations with the North as early at 1863
E. Northern Democrats who moved to the South during the war

(Correct Answer: **A.** Copperheads were Democrats in the North who claimed that the war would bring economic ruin to the North, with freed slaves taking jobs that whites now had. Some were arrested and deported.)

Chapter 12

The Era of Reconstruction (1865–1877)

"Some men are born great, some achieve greatness and others lived during the Reconstruction period"

Paul Laurence Dunbar, 1903

LINCOLN'S PLANS FOR RECONSTRUCTION

The preceding quote perfectly expresses the frustrations felt by many Americans during the <u>Reconstruction Era</u>. During this period, political leaders in the North had to decide how the former states of the Confederacy would be assimilated back into the Union. What should be done with former Confederate leaders? What should be done with former slaves? How much punishment (if any) should the former states of the Confederacy be made to endure? There were obviously incredibly complicated questions, and the results *had* to be imperfect in some manner.

Other factors increased the difficulty of the Southern assimilation after the Civil War. It was only when defeated Confederate soldiers returned to their homes that the extent of the devastation of the South during the war became widely known. Virtually the entire Southern railway system and many farms and cities were destroyed by the war. In addition, nearly one-third of all adult males residing in Confederate states died or were wounded during the war. For those plantation owners whose plantations were not destroyed, laborers now had to be hired; many of these owners were now strapped for cash. Many freed blacks wandered the countryside looking for work, while many poorer white men with jobs lived in fear of being replaced by freed black men.

The problems of Reconstruction were compounded by the assassination of Abraham Lincoln at the very end of the Civil War. Lincoln had begun constructing a Reconstruction plan as early as mid-1863. Lincoln devised a plan for former Confederate to rejoin the Union that was entitled the **Ten Percent Plan**. By the provisions of this plan, citizens of former Confederate states would be given the opportunity to swear allegiance to the government in Washington (high-ranking Confederate military and civilian authorities would not be offered this opportunity). When 10 percent of the registered voters in the state signed this pledge, the state was afforded the chance to form its own state government, which obviously had to be loyal to Washington.

Tennessee, Louisiana, and Arkansas all went through the appropriate procedures to form loyal state governments, yet their applications for renewed participation in the Union were not approved by the **Radical Republicans** who dominated the Congress. These men were determined to punish the Southern states in any way possible for their "betrayal" of the Union. This group, led by Thaddeus Stevens, included several who had been ardent abolitionists in the years before the Civil War. They believed that power in the Southern states had to be totally reorganized in order for blacks to achieve equality. The Radical Republicans also saw the creation of Reconstruction policy as a constitutional issue, stating that it was the job of the Congress and not the president to create this policy.

Radical Republicans felt that action was needed to counter the **Black Codes**, which had been passed by all Southern state legislatures in 1866. These sets of regulations limited movement by blacks, prohibited interracial marriage, and insisted that blacks obtain special certificates to hold certain jobs.

The Radical Republicans were insistent on immediate voting rights for blacks in the South; this desire was behind the **Wade-Davis Act**, which was passed by Congress in the summer of 1864. This bill stated that Congress would only authorize a state government in former Confederate states when the majority of voters took an "ironclad" oath, stating that they were not now disloyal to the Union nor had they ever been disloyal. Under these provisions, it would be impossible for any state to reenter the Union without a large number of black voters. President Lincoln killed this bill by a pocket veto.

ANDREW JOHNSON'S PLAN FOR RECONSTRUCTION

Much to the disappointment of the Radical Republicans, the Reconstruction plan announced by Andrew Johnson was also a relatively lenient one. Johnson stated that the United States should offer "amnesty and pardon" to any Southerner who would swear allegiance to the Union and the Constitution. Like Lincoln, Johnson felt that ex-Confederate leaders should not be eligible for amnesty; he also opposed amnesty for individuals (almost always plantation owners) whose property was worth over $20,000. Johnson had been a small farmer from Tennessee before he entered politics, and he possessed the typical hatred that small farmers had for plantation owners. Johnson also created a fairly simple plan for Confederate states to reenter the Union.

All of the former Confederate states followed the proscribed procedures and elected members to the Congress of the United States that met in December 1865. However, the "loyalty" of the former Confederate states was still questioned by some in the North. Many former Confederate officials and military officers were elected in local and even congressional elections. In no Southern state legislature were the issues of blacks getting the vote or education for former slaves even considered in the months following the Civil War. The **Radical Republicans** of the North found this totally unacceptable.

THE RECONSTRUCTION OF THE RADICAL REPUBLICANS

The Radical Republicans soon began to implement their own program for Reconstruction in the South. Although they differed on tactics, all agreed that their main goal in the South should be to advance the political, economic, and social position of the **freedmen**, or former slaves. In early 1865 Congress passed legislation creating the Freeman's Bureau, which was designed to help ex-slaves get employment, education, and general assistance as they adjusted to their new lives. By 1866 large numbers of freedmen were back on their original plantations (often against the advice of the Freeman's Bureau), working as **tenant farmers**. Under programs established by the Freeman's Bureau, ex-slaves could receive "40 acres and a mule."

Some Radical Republicans, such as Charles Sumner of Massachusetts, stated that the ex-slave's position would improve the quickest in the South if they were given the vote. Thaddeus Stevens felt that black voters would be strongly influenced by wealthy landowners who oftentimes employed them, and stated that the first goal of the federal government should be to take land from former Confederate leaders and give it to the freedmen. A Joint Committee on Reconstruction first met in January 1866.

The Joint Committee proposed, and the Congress passed, a bill authorizing the continuation of the Freeman's Bureau and a Civil Rights bill early in 1866. Johnson immediately vetoed both, stating they were unconstitutional and emphasizing the need to allow former Confederates to have more of a say in affairs in the South. It is at this point that tensions between the Congress and the president began to increase severely. Johnson gave a Washington's Birthday speech where he claimed the Radical Republicans were traitors and actually wanted to kill him.

Congress eventually overrode the presidential veto of both of these bills. Johnson's actions and demeanor were causing many moderate Republicans to join forces with the radical branch of the party. The **Civil Rights Act of 1866** granted freedmen all the benefits of federal citizenship and promised that federal courts would uphold these rights. In cases where these rights were violated, federal troops would be used for enforcement. The Civil Rights Act also helped to enforce the **Thirteenth Amendment** to the Constitution, which had been ratified in December 1865 and outlawed slavery and other forms of involuntary servitude.

The **Fourteenth Amendment** was passed by the Congress and sent to the states for ratification. The amendment declared that citizenship would be the same in all states, that states that did not give freedmen the vote would have reduced representation in the Congress, and that former Confederate officials could not hold public office. Anti-black riots in New Orleans and Memphis in early 1866 caused the Radical Republicans to push for the passage of the Fourteenth Amendment even more forcefully. President Johnson publicly opposed the ratification of the Fourteenth Amendment. However, Radical Republicans won by large margins in the 1866 congressional elections. After these elections, the Radical Republicans began to dictate the course of Reconstruction in the South.

A PERIOD OF RADICAL RECONSTRUCTION

With many Democrats and even moderate Republicans swept out of office in the 1866 congressional elections, Radical Republicans immediately put their plans for Reconstruction into action. The 1867 **Reconstruction Act** actually placed the Southern states under military rule, with the South being divided into five regions and a military general in control of each region. Former Confederate states were ordered to hold new constitutional conventions to form state constitutions that allowed qualified blacks to vote and provided them equal rights. The legislation barred former supporters of the Confederacy from voting and required that the Fourteenth Amendment be passed in all former Confederate states. To guarantee the assistance of the United States Army in these efforts, Congress also passed the **Army Act**, which reduced the control of the president over the army. To ensure that Secretary of War Edwin Stanton (an ally of the Radical Republicans) would not be dismissed, Congress passed the **Tenure of Office Act**, which stated that the president could not dismiss any Cabinet member without the approval of the Senate.

THE IMPEACHMENT OF ANDREW JOHNSON

In the fall of 1867 President Johnson tried to remove Edwin Stanton as Secretary of War. Radical Republicans loudly proclaimed that Johnson had flouted the United States Constitution by directly violating the Tenure of Office Act, and began **impeachment** proceedings against him. The House of Representatives voted to impeach Johnson on February 24, 1868, making him the first president of the United States to be impeached (Bill Clinton was the second). The trial of Johnson in the Senate began in May. By the Constitution, two-thirds of the Senate have to vote to convict the president for him to be removed; Andrew Johnson escaped conviction by one vote (the deciding vote was a Republican from Kansas by the name of Edmund Ross, who was opposed to Johnson but felt there was insufficient evidence to actually remove him from office).

Johnson served the remainder of his term without incident. In the 1868 presidential election, Ulysses S. Grant, a hero of the Civil War with little political knowledge and few stated political opinions, led the Republican party to victory.

RADICAL RECONSTRUCTION REINFORCED

With the election of Grant, Radical Republicans finally had an ally in the White House. In March of 1870 the final Reconstruction amendment was ratified. The **Fifteenth Amendment** stated that no American could be denied the right to vote "on account of race, color, or previous condition of servitude." Elections in the South in 1870 were regulated by federal troops stationed there. In these elections thousands of Southern blacks voted for the first time; predictably, many Southern whites did not vote in these elections and viewed the entire process with disgust.

In the 1870 elections nearly 630 blacks were elected as representatives in Southern state legislatures. Sixteen blacks were elected to Congress, one to the United States Senate, and a black, P.B.S. Pinchback, was elected governor of Louisiana.

It would be impossible to overstate the resentment with which many Southern whites viewed the entire Reconstruction process. Reconstruction was oftentimes blamed on **carpetbaggers**, who were Northerners who moved to the South during the Reconstruction period, or on **scalawags**, a Southern term for white Southern Republicans.

Groups such as the **Ku Klux Klan** (founded in Tennessee in 1866) fueled white resentment into violence against blacks and their "outside" supporters in the South. The Klan's activities ranged from trying to intimidate blacks at polling places to the burning of crosses to torture and murder. Various federal laws were passed to limit the activities of the Klan, with thousands of members being arrested. The group and its activities persisted, however.

THE END OF RECONSTRUCTION

Grant won reelection in 1872, yet during his second term, federal and Northern interest in the affairs of the South began to wane. The reasons for this were numerous. By this time in history many of the original Radical Republicans had died or no longer were active in government. There were numerous corruption scandals in the second Grant administration (some historians state that this was the most corrupt administration in American history). A recession in 1873 turned the interests of many Northerners to economic and not political and social issues. As a result, Northern troops were gradually removed from the South, allowing whites in Southern states to regain control of Southern governments.

Many Reconstruction-style reforms made by earlier state legislatures were overturned.

The political event that "officially" ended Reconstruction was the **Compromise of 1877**. In the presidential election of 1876, Samuel Tilden, governor of New York, was the Democratic party candidate, running against Republican Rutherford B. Hayes. Tilden won the popular vote and was leading in the electoral vote, but he needed the electoral votes of Florida, Louisiana, and South Carolina, all still occupied by federal troops and under Republican control. Both sides claimed victory in these three states. A special congressional commission was created to resolve this situation. The commission had more Republicans than Democrats on it and was ready to hand the election to Hayes, even though evidence indicated that Tilden had won enough electoral votes to win. When Democrats in Congress stated that they would loudly and publicly protest the Commission's findings, the **Compromise of 1877** was worked out. Hayes was named president; in return, the new president promised to remove all federal troops from the South and to stop the enforcement of much Reconstruction-era legislation concerning the South. As a result, blacks in the South were again reduced to the status of second-class citizens. In addition, Southern hatred of Reconstruction-era Republican policies would make the South solidly Democratic; white Southern support of the Democratic policy would last for nearly 100 years. It should be noted that whites who returned to power in state legislatures in the South in 1878 were called "the redeemers."

CHAPTER REVIEW

Rapid Review Guide

To achieve the perfect 5, you should be able to explain the following:

- Any plan to assimilate the Southern states back into the Union after the Civil War would have major difficulties; a problem was determining the appropriate post-war status of former supporters of the Confederacy.

- The plans for Reconstruction proposed by Abraham Lincoln, the Radical Republicans, and Andrew Jackson all varied dramatically.

- Radical Republicans instituted policies to improve the political and economic status of former slaves; this created great resentment in other segments of Southern society.

- The impeachment of Andrew Johnson went forward because of major disagreements over policy between Johnson and the Radical Republicans in Congress.

- The Thirteenth, Fourteenth, and Fifteenth Amendments outlawed slavery, established the rights of blacks, and established the framework by which Southern states could rejoin the union.

- Profits made by carpetbaggers and scalawags further angered the traditional elements of Southern society; many in the South, including members of the Ku Klux Klan, felt great resentment towards the carpetbaggers and scalawags and towards the political and economic power now held by some Southern blacks.

- The Compromise of 1877 ended Reconstruction in the South; as Union troops left, blacks were again reduced to the status of second-class citizens.

Time Line

1865: Andrew Johnson institutes liberal Reconstruction plan
Whites in Southern legislatures pass Black Codes
Thirteenth Amendment ratified

1866: Civil Rights Act, Freedman's Bureau Act approved by Congress (vetoed by Johnson)
Fourteenth Amendment passes Congress (fails to be ratified in Southern states)
Anti-black riots in New Orleans, Memphis
Republicans who favor Radical Reconstruction win congressional elections, in essence ending Johnson's Reconstruction plan
Ku Klux Klan founded

1867: Tenure of Office Act approved by Congress (Congress had to approve presidential appointments, dismissals)
Reconstruction Act approved by Congress (Southern states placed under military rule)
Constitutional conventions called by former Confederate states
Johnson tries to remove Edwin Stanton as Secretary of War, leading to cries for his impeachment

1868: Impeachment of Andrew Johnson: Johnson impeached in the House of Representatives, not convicted in the Senate
Southern states return to Union under policies established by Radical Republicans
Final ratification of Fourteenth Amendment
Former Civil War general U.S. Grant elected president

1870: Fifteenth Amendment ratified
Many blacks elected in Southern state legislatures

1872: Former Confederates allowed to hold office
U.S. Grant reelected

1876: Disputed presidential election between Tilden, Hayes

1877: Compromise of 1877 awards election to Hayes, ends Reconstruction in the South

✓ Review Questions

1. Radical Republicans favored all of the following *except*

   A. he continuation of the Freedman's Bureau
   B. the governing of the South by military generals
   C. the impeachment of Andrew Johnson
   D. the return of former Confederate leaders to positions of power in the South
   E. the election of newly enfranchised blacks to positions in Southern state legislatures

(Correct Answer: **D.** All of the other choices were favored by Radical Republicans; the Reconstruction Act of 1867 placed the former Confederate states under military rule.)

2. The official reason for impeachment proceedings against Andrew Johnson was

   A. he had violated the Tenure of Office Act
   B. he had violated the Reconstruction Act
   C. his Reconstruction policies were much too lenient to the South
   D. he had failed to enforce the Army Act
   E. he had failed to enforce the Civil Rights Act of 1866

(Correct Answer: **A.** By attempting to remove Edwin Stanton as Secretary of War, many in Congress stated that Johnson had knowingly violated the Tenure of Office Act, thus violating provisions of the United States Constitution.)

3. Black Codes were instituted to

   A. increase black participation in Southern politics during Reconstruction
   B. increase the effectiveness of the Freedman's Bureau
   C. prevent blacks from having certain jobs
   D. maintain slavery in some sections of the Deep South
   E. allow blacks to move more freely in the South

(Correct Answer: **C.** Black Codes were adopted by Southern legislatures in 1866 and limited movement by blacks, prevented them from having certain jobs, and prohibited interracial marriage.)

4. Reconstruction ended as a result of the Compromise of 1877 because

   A. a presidential mandate ordered that Reconstruction end
   B. by the provisions of the compromise, the U.S. Army was removed from Southern states
   C. the new president, Rutherford B. Hayes, was strongly against existing Reconstruction policy
   D. many blacks were now in positions of power in the South, and Reconstruction policies were no longer needed
   E. public opinion in the North no longer favored existing Reconstruction policies

(Correct Answer: **B.** After Hayes was given the presidency by the Compromise of 1877, the U.S. Army left control of the South to the South. Without the army present to enforce Reconstruction policies, these policies ended. Blacks were soon second-class citizens again.)

5. The Fifteenth Amendment

A. allowed Southern states to reenter the Union
B. outlawed slavery
C. stated that a person could not be denied the vote because of his color
D. said that former Confederate officials could not hold public office
E. stated that citizenship would be the same in all states

(Correct Answer: **C.** The Fifteenth Amendment stated that no American could be denied the right to vote "on account of race, color, or previous condition of servitude.")

Chapter 13

Western Expansion and Its Impact on the American Character (1860–1895)

FEDERAL LEGISLATION ENCOURAGES WESTERN SETTLEMENT

Adventurous Americans had settled west of the Mississippi and out to the Pacific in the decades prior to the Civil War. However, several acts passed by the federal government in 1862 set the stage for the massive movement westward that would take place after the Civil War.

The one act that gave land directly to settlers was the **Homestead Act**. This legislation allocated 160 acres to any settler who (1) was an American citizen, or who, in the case of immigrants, had at least filed for American citizenship; (2) was 21 years old and the head of a family; (3) was committed to building a house on the property and living there at least six months of the year; and (4) could pay a $10 registration fee for the land. After actively farming the land for five years, the farmer was given actual ownership of his 160-acre plot. By 1900 nearly 610,000 parcels of land had been given out under the provisions of the Homestead Act, allowing nearly 85 million acres of land to go over to private ownership.

A bill that indirectly gave land to settlers was the 1862 **Morrill Land-Grant Act**. To encourage the building of "land-grant" colleges in Western territories that had already been granted statehood, hundreds of thousands of acres of land were given to state governments. This land could be sold by the states to pay for these colleges. At 50 cents an acre (and sometimes less), settlers and **land speculators** received land from individual states.

The expansion of the railroad was closely tied to western expansion. In acts enacted in 1862 and 1864, the Union Pacific and Central Pacific Railroads received grants of land to extend their rail lines westward. Part of the legislation also gave the railroads 10 square miles on both sides of the track for every mile of track constructed. This land was sometimes sold to settlers as well, sometimes at exorbitant prices.

FARMING ON THE GREAT PLAINS

In the ideology of Thomas Jefferson, the yeoman farmer was the central figure in the development of the American character. The abilities, fortitude, and luck of the yeomen were severely tested as they moved to the Great Plains. Many settlers who went west were immigrants with families (unlike the single male immigrants who lived in New York, Boston, and other Eastern cities).

The harshness of life on the plains was simply too much to bear for many settlers and their families. Temperatures ranged from over 100 degrees in the summer to bitter cold in the winter, and many of the sod houses built by settlers did little to keep out the heat or the cold. Having enough water was a constant problem, with some of the water collected in barrels or buckets carrying "prairie fever" (typhoid fever). In a single year a settler and his land might be attacked by fierce blizzards, howling dust storms, and locusts or grasshoppers. The rosy picture of life on the Great Plains presented in recruitment brochures found in New York or in Currier & Ives prints popular in the East were a harsh contrast with reality. By 1900 two-thirds of the homestead farms failed, causing many ex-farmers to return to the East.

How did the settlers who survived on the Great Plains manage to do so? Survival on the plains largely depended on cooperation with other settlers that lived near you. Groups of men would put up new barns and construct fences; women on the plains would get support from wives of other settlers. In short, successful farmers on the plains were no longer the individual yeomen envisioned by Jefferson.

THE TRANSFORMATION OF AGRICULTURE ON THE PLAINS

More importantly, success on the plains became increasingly dependent on the use of technology and the introduction of business approaches to agriculture. The United States Department of Agriculture was established in 1862 and by late 1863 was distributing information to plains farmers on new farm techniques and developments. New plows and threshers (included some powered by steam) were introduced in the late 1860s and early 1870s.

Slowly, control of agricultural production on the plains was taken from individual farmers as large **bonanza farms** developed. While individual settlers were interested in producing enough for their families to survive, bonanza farms usually produced only one or two crops on them. Produce from these farms was sold to the Eastern United States or abroad. While individual settlers were being driven off of the land because of the hardships of farming on the plains, bonanza farms were run as large businesses and had the technology and professional backing to be successful.

Bonanza farms were plentiful by the late 1870s and demonstrated the transformation that had taken place in agriculture. These farms were truly capitalistic; their success was dependent on the machinery that existed on the farms and on the railroad that would take their crops away for export. Farm production increased dramatically with the advent of bonanza farms. At the same time, the numbers of Americans involved in agriculture decreased (from nearly 60 percent in 1860 to 37 percent in 1900).

The new business techniques practiced by bonanza farms were successful in the short run but created problems for both bonanza farms and individual farmers in the future. Several times in the 1880s and early 1890s there was simply too much grain being produced on these farms, dropping the prices drastically. To remain economically successful, farmers proceeded to do the only logical thing: produce even more, which drove prices down even more. Many plains farmers in this period were unable to pay their mortgages, and farms were foreclosed. Bonanza farms usually had the technology for the production of only one or two crops and could not diversify; they too faced financial distress. Many farmers felt that federal policies had to do more to protect them, and thus started to organize to protect themselves.

WOMEN AND MINORITIES ON THE PLAINS

As stated previously, most settlers came to the plains as families (there were a tiny number of women who filed for land claims on their own). Diaries of many women who lived on the plains spoke of the loneliness of their existence, especially in the non-harvest periods when many men left for other work and women were left on the farms. Perhaps the greatest novel describing prairie life is _O Pioneers!_ (1913) by Willa Cather. This book describes both the tremendous challenges and the incredible rewards found in life on the prairie. An equally compelling vision of prairie life is _Giants of the Earth_ (1927) by O. E. Rolvaag. In this novel the harshness of prairie life drives the wife of an immigrant settler to madness and to eventual death.

It was in the Western states where the first American women received the vote. In 1887 two towns in Kansas gave women the vote (with one of them electing a woman mayor to a single term in office). The state constitution of Wyoming was the first to give women the vote on a state-wide basis.

Thousands of blacks moved west after the Civil War to escape the uncertainty of life in the Reconstruction South. Many who ended in the plains and elsewhere lacked the finances and farming abilities to be successful, and faced many of the same racial difficulties they had faced in the American South. However, some black farmers did emerge successfully as plains farmers. The most prominent group of Southern blacks who went west was a 1879 group who called themselves the **Exodusters** (modeling their journey after the journey of the Israelites fleeing Egypt to the Promised Land). Less than 20 percent of this group became successful farmers in the plains region.

MINING AND LUMBERING IN THE WEST

The rumors of gold at Pike's Peak, Nevada, silver at Comstock, Nevada, and other minerals at countless other locations drew settlers westward in the quest for instant riches (it should be noted that a large number of Californians traveled eastward for exactly the same reason). Persons of all backgrounds, including women and some Chinese who had left their jobs in railroad construction, all took part in the search for riches. Stories of the wild nature of many early mining towns are generally accurate; stories of the failure of most speculators to find anything to mine are almost always true. Most prospectors who did find something in the ground found it much too difficult to dig for and then to transport; oftentimes they sold their claims to Eastern mining companies, such as the **Anaconda Copper Company**, who did the work for them. For many of these companies, minerals such as tin and copper became just as profitable as gold and silver to mine.

Lumber companies also began moving into the Northwest in the 1870s to start to cut down timber. The lumber industry benefited greatly from the federal **Timber and Stone Act**, passed in 1878. This bill offered land in the Northwest that was unsuitable for farming to "settlers" at very cheap prices. Lumber companies hired seamen from port cities and others who had no interest in "settling" to buy the forest land cheaply and then to transfer the ownership of the land to the companies.

RANCHING IN THE WEST

In Texas the ranching industry was profitable long before either farming or mining was fully developed. Settlers there had learned cattle ranching from the Mexicans. Much of the romantic view many still have of the West comes from of our vision of cowboys driving cattle on the "long drive" from Texas to either Kansas or Missouri (nearly one-third of the cowboys involved were either Mexicans or blacks).

The long drive was economically inefficient, and with the removal of Native Americans and buffalo from the Great Plains in the 1860s and 1870s (to be discussed in the next section), many cattle ranchers moved their herds northward, allowing them to be closer to the cattle markets of Chicago, Kansas City, and St. Louis.

However, conflicts between farmers and ranchers soon developed. Farmers often accused ranchers of allowing herds to trample their farmland. The invention of barbed wire by Joseph Glidden in 1873 was the beginning of the end for the cattle industry; as farmers began to contain their farmlands, the open range began to disappear.

A critical blow to the cattle industry occurred during two very harsh winters of 1885 to 1886 and 1886 to 1887. Many cattle froze to death or starved during these years, with some ranchers losing up to 85 percent of their cattle. Those ranchers that survived turned to the same business techniques that had saved many plains farms; scientific methods of breeding, feeding, and fencing were now utilized by those ranchers that survived. In reality, the independent cowboy present in our myths of the West also died during this transformation.

THE PLIGHT OF NATIVE AMERICANS

The westward stream of settlers in the mid-1800s severely disrupted the lives of Native Americans. The migration patterns of buffalo, which the Native Americans depended on, were disrupted; settlers thought nothing of seizing lands that previous treaties had given to Native Americans. Some tribes tried to cooperate with the onrush of settlers, while others violently resisted. It is unlikely that any Native American approach would have saved Native American territories from the rush of American expansionism. The completion of the transcontinental railroad required that rail lines run through territories previously ceded to Native American tribes. A congressional commission meeting in 1867 stated the official policy of the American government on "Indian affairs": Native Americans would all be removed to Oklahoma and South Dakota, and every effort would be made to transform them from "savages" into "civilized" beings.

The tribe that resisted the onrush of settlement most fiercely were the **Sioux**. In 1865 the government announced their desire to build a road through Sioux territory; the following year tribesmen attacked and killed 88 American soldiers. After negotiations in 1868 the Sioux agreed to move to a reservation in the Black Hills of South Dakota. Yet in late 1874 miners searching for gold began to arrive in the Black Hills. The chief of the tribe, Sitting Bull, and others of the tribe left the Dakota reservation at this point. General George Custer was sent to round up Sitting Bull and the Sioux. He and his force of over 200 men were all killed at the **Battle of the Little Bighorn** in June of 1876. This was the last major Native American victory against the American army. Large numbers of federal troops were brought into the region, returning the Sioux to their reservations.

Conflict with the federal army occurred again in 1890 after the death of Sitting Bull. Some Sioux again attempted to leave their reservation; these tribesmen were quickly apprehended by the federal army. As the male Sioux were handing in their weapons, a shot was fired by someone. The soldiers opened fire on the Native Americans, killing over 200 men, women, and children in the **Massacre at Wounded Knee**.

Other tribes such as the **Nez Perce** also initially resisted, only to be eventually driven to reservations. Nez Perce warriors ending up taking part in elaborate **Ghost Dances**, which were supposed to remove the whites from Native American territories, return the buffalo, and bring ancestors killed by the whites back to life. The Ghost Dances terrified white settlers who viewed them and served to bring more federal forces into territories nominally controlled by Native Americans.

The killing off of tribes of buffalo by white settlers for food, hides, and even for pure sport did much to destroy Native American life, since Native Americans depended upon the buffalo for their very existence. A fatal blow to remaining land owned by Native American tribes was the 1887 **Dawes Act**. This act was passed in the spirit of "civilizing" the Native Americans and was designed to give them their own plots of land to farm on. The real intent of the legislation was to attempt to destroy the tribal identities of Native Americans. Many Native Americans had little skill or interest in farming; many eventually sold "their" land to land speculators.

In 1889 there were still 2 million acres of unclaimed land in "Indian territory" in Oklahoma. On April 22 a mad rush took place by white settlers staking out claims on this territory (those who staked claims that day were called "boomers"; settlers who had entered Indian territory a day or more early to stake their claims were called "sooners").

By the end of the century virtually all Native Americans had been placed in reservations. Many young Indians attempted to dress, talk, and act like white men in schools established by white reformers, but their attempts to think like and become whites were much, much more difficult.

THE ORGANIZATION OF THE AMERICAN FARMER AND POPULISM

As stated previously, American farmers from the West were in economic trouble by the mid-1880s. Many farmers from the South shared their plight. Several policies were originating in Washington that farmers felt greatly hurt them economically. Congresses of this era favored high tariffs, which helped Eastern businessmen. Farmers felt they were hurt by the high tariff policy, as it kept foreigners from buying their produce. The issue that farmers were most upset about, however, concerned currency.

The Issue of the Gold Standard

After the Civil War, federal budget officials enacted a **"tight money"** policy and took the paper money used during the Civil War out of circulation. In addition, the dollar during this period was for the first time put on the **gold standard**, meaning that every dollar in circulation had to be backed by a similar amount of gold held by the federal government. This action also served to limit the amount of money in circulation. These financial measures ensured that inflation would not occur, but Western farmers were convinced that depressed farm prices were largely a result of these policies. Several congressional acts to increase the coining and mining of gold and silver met with limited success and were opposed by the presidents of the era.

The Beginning of Organization: The Grange and the Farmer's Alliances

In 1867 the <u>Grange</u> organization was founded by Western farmers. By 1875 it boasted of over 800,000 members. Through the Grange, farmer cooperatives were formed, allowing farmers to buy in large quantities (and at lower prices). Farmers were also convinced that railroad rates were disadvantageous to them, and legislators in farm states began to receive communications from farmers urging regulation of railroad rates and policies. Some farmers supported the <u>Greenback party</u>, which supported getting more paper money into circulation, in the 1878 election. The Greenbacks managed to elect several congressmen from farm states but got little support elsewhere.

While the Grange organization largely operated on the local level, development of the <u>Farmer's Alliances</u> joined farmers at the statewide and even regional level. By 1889 the Southern Alliance claimed 1 million members, while a separate Colored Farmers' National Alliance also had 1 million members on the books. Membership in the Farmer's Alliances on the Great Plains was nearly 2 million members. The policies endorsed by the Farmer's Alliances included federal regulation of the railroad, putting more money in circulation, the establishment of a state department of agriculture in every state, and readily available farm credits; it was proposed that the federal government have large warehouses where farmers could store their grain and get credit for it if prices were low during harvest season. These measures were spelled out in detail at a national Alliance convention held in 1890 in Ocala, Florida. The <u>Ocala Platform</u> stated the principles that motivated most political activity by farmers for the remainder of the century. Some federal policies did at least partially meet the demands of agricultural interests; the <u>Interstate Commerce Act</u> of 1887 stated that the federal government could regulate interstate railway rates, and the <u>Sherman Antitrust Act</u> of 1890 aimed to control the power of trusts and monopolies.

By 1890 some leaders of the Farmer's Alliances began to plan for political action on the national level. Alliance strength was particularly strong in the South, where four governors owed their election to Alliance support. Forty-seven congressmen in the South were also strongly supported by the Alliance. In the plains states Alliance candidates were successful on the local level. Alliance support extended to women as well; several women held important leadership positions at the top levels of the Farmer's Alliances.

The Populist Campaign of 1892

On July 4, 1892, in a convention held in Omaha, Nebraska, a national convention of Farmer's Alliances created the People's party, whose followers soon became known as Populists. The <u>Populist party</u> was intended to appeal to workers of all parts of the country. Populists desired a much greater role of government in American society. The party platform expressed support for increasing the circulation of money, a progressive income tax (by which wealthy Eastern industrialists would pay the most and farmers would pay the least), government ownership of communication and transportation systems, and more direct methods of democracy (greater use of direct primaries, recall, referendum, etc.). To appeal to urban workers, the platform also supported an eight-hour workday. The Populists nominated James B. Weaver, a Union general from the Civil War, as their candidate.

Despite a spirited campaign by Populist supporters, the party only received 1 million popular votes and 22 electoral votes in the 1892 election. Few voters in the Northeast supported the Populists, and Democratic control of the electoral process in the South remained strong. Only in the western United States did Populism do well.

Populism in the 1890s

The reelection of Grover Cleveland angered the agricultural interests greatly, as he announced his continued support of the gold standard during his inauguration speech. A great depression hit America in 1893, with workers from all parts of the country being laid off (in some cities up to 25 percent of laborers were unemployed). Populist marchers joined with marchers from many groups protesting government financial policy in Washington in 1894.

In the 1896 presidential election, the Republican candidate was William McKinley, who followed Cleveland in his support of the gold standard. The Democratic candidate, endorsed by the Populists, was William Jennings Bryan, campaigned on a policy of free silver and an expanded availability of currency, stating, "You shall not crucify mankind upon a cross of gold!" Many Populist leaders hit the campaign trail for Bryan, yet with little success. Bryan carried the South and the West, but was unable to garner support in the Midwestern or Northeastern states.

As the depression ended at the end of the decade, Populists and others in the agricultural sector began to recognize the massive changes that had taken place in the American economy since the end of the Civil War. The American economy was now a national economy and not a sectional one; the railroad had been largely responsible for this change. In addition, slowly but surely the United States was becoming an industrial nation and not an agricultural one.

THE IMPACT OF THE WEST ON AMERICAN SOCIETY

The myths we now associate with the frontier began to be created as early as the 1870s in dime-store novels by Edward L. Wheeler and others. Wheeler's story of _Deadwood Dick: The Prince of the Road_ portrayed a

Western America filled with gamblers, hard drinkers, and stagecoach robberies. The Wild West shows that began in 1883 and were promoted by Buffalo Bill Cody contributed to the myths begun by Wheeler: Spectators were shown log cabins, spectator rodeos, and mock battles between cavalrymen and seemingly deadly Indians.

A different view of the West was presented by Frederick Jackson Turner, an academic who in 1893 published his "frontier thesis." The **Turner Thesis** states that as Americans moved westward they were forced to adapt and to innovate, and how western expansion had helped to ingrain these characteristics into the fabric of American society. Turner stated that their frontier had created a society of men and women who were committed to self-improvement, who supported democracy, and who were socially mobile. In short, the Turner Thesis maintains that much of the nature of America comes from our experiences in the West.

Each of these views is partially correct. The view of western expansion espoused (and later partially rejected) by Turner ignores the fact that not everyone who settled the West were white Easterners. In addition, the massacre of large numbers of Native Americans violates the basic principles of democracy. There is also some truth to Buffalo Bill's view of western settlement, yet his view ignores the cultural and material progress that did take place in the West as a result of western expansion. In 1893 the Turner Thesis and Buffalo Bill's shows both drew incredible interest. During that year it was clear that the Western frontier was for all practical purpose closed, and Americans were attempting to make sense of what that actually meant for the country. Historians today still revisit this question on a regular basis.

CHAPTER REVIEW

Rapid Review Guide

To achieve the perfect 5, you should be able to explain the following:

- The Homestead Act and the Morrill Land-Grant Act encouraged thousands to go westward to acquire land for farming.

- Farming on the Great Plains proved to be very difficult and was oftentimes accomplished by help from one's neighbor; many farmers were not successful on the Great Plains.

- Bonanza farms were part of a transformation of agriculture that began in the late 1860s.

- Western states were the first states where women received the vote.

- Mining and lumbering also attracted many settlers to the West.

- Native American tribes were gradually forced off of their lands because of American expansion to the west; some resistance to this by

Native Americans did take place, such as at the Battle of the Little Bighorn and through the Ghost Dances.

- The 1887 Dawes Act did much to break up the remaining Native American tribal lands.

- American farmers organized beginning in the late 1860s though the Grange, through the Farmer's Alliances, and eventually through the Populist party.

- Dime-store novels of the era and the Turner Thesis present contrasting views of western settlement and its overall impact on American society.

Time Line

1848: California Gold Rush
1859: Silver Discovered in Comstock, Nevada
1862: Homestead Act, Morrill Land-Grand Act
      Department of Agriculture created by Congress
1867: Founding of the Grange
1869: Transcontinental Railroad completed
1870s: Popularity of *Deadwood Dick,* stories by Bret Harte, and other dime-store novels on the West
1874: Barbed wire invented by Joseph Glidden
1876: Battle of the Little Bighorn
1879: Exoduster movement leaves South for the Great Plains
1880s: Large movement of immigrants westward
1883: "Buffalo Bill's Wild West Show" begins
1886: Beginnings of harsh weather that will help destroy the cattle industry
1887: Dawes Act
1889: Indian territories open for white settlement
1890: Massacre at Wounded Knee
      Wyoming women get the vote
      High point of political influence of the Farmer's Alliances
1893: Beginning of great depression of the 1890s
      Publication of the Turner Thesis
1896: William Jennings Bryan's "Cross of Gold" speech

✔ Review Questions

1. Those farmers who were successful on the Great Plains

   A. came to the West as single men, without families
   B. utilized many farming techniques they had learned in the East
   C. personified the spirit of rugged individualism
   D. relied on the assistance of other settlers around them
   E. personified the image of the yeoman farmer of Thomas Jefferson

(Correct Answer: **D.** Almost every diary of memoir from individuals who lived on the plains noted that rugged individualism was not enough to be successful.)

2. Exodusters were

   A. newly arrived miners in Oregon
   B. Southern blacks who went west to settle
   C. settlers who went to Washington state to be part of the lumbering industry
   D. those who "dusted" or cleaned crops on bonanza farms
   E. immigrants who went west to farm

(Correct Answer: **B.** This group went west to farm in 1879 and modeled their journey after the journey of the Israelites fleeing Egypt to the Promised Land.)

3. The Dawes Act

   A. tried to turn Native Americans into farmers who would farm their own individual plots only
   B. protected Native American land from further encroachment
   C. broke up large Native American reservations into smaller ones
   D. made Ghost Dances illegal
   E. made the further killing of buffalo by Western settlers illegal

(Correct Answer: **A.** The Dawes Act tried to "civilize" Native Americans and destroy their tribal lands.)

4. The organization that expressed the views of farmers to the largest national audience was

   A. the Greenback party
   B. the Populist party
   C. the Grange
   D. the Colored Farmer's National Alliance
   E. the Farmer's Alliances

(Correct Answer: **B.** The Populist party platform was intended to appeal to all workers in society, including those in the city. The policies of the Populist Party were heard nationwide in the 1892 presidential election; however, because of the power of the Democratic party in the South, the Populist presidential candidate received only 1 million votes in the election.)

5. The Turner thesis

   A. agreed with accounts of the West in the dime-store novels of the 1870s concerning the character of western expansion
   B. emphasized the diversity of those who traveled west
   C. takes into account the massacre of Native Americans
   D. notes the impact of western expansion on the American character
   E. emphasized the "hard living" that went on in many western settlements

(Correct Answer: **D.** Turner himself would later revise his thesis based on some of the characteristics of western expansion noted in the other possible answers.)

Chapter 14

America Transformed into the Industrial Giant of the World (1870–1910)

 Immense changes rocked the United States between 1870 and 1910 that transformed the very nature of the American republic. During this period, for the first time in American history, more people lived in urban settings than in rural ones. America began to lose the small town and rural character that had defined the nation since its inception. Many who moved to the cities went to work in factories, helping to turn America into the greatest industrial (and agricultural) producer in the world. It was also during this period that immigrants, many from southern and eastern Europe, began to enter the United States by the millions and further transform the American character. In addition, the presidents during this era were generally weak (with several noticeable exceptions), which put extensive power in the hands of the legislative branch; these presidents were disinclined to exert strong executive action against the trusts and monopolies that were developing at the time.

THE GROWTH OF INDUSTRIAL AMERICA

By 1894 the United States had become the largest manufacturing nation in the world. Compared to industrial growth that had occurred in Europe earlier in the century, the economic growth that took place in America during this period was nearly beyond belief. Massive factories employed very large number of workers. In 1860 nearly one out of every four Americans worked in manufacturing, while by 1900 this number was increased to one out of every two. Radical transformations also took place in the approaches to work taken by former rural dwellers or immigrants who moved to the American city for factory work. Things such as time clocks, scheduled breaks, and the repetition of doing the same tasks over and over made work very different for those who came from rural settings.

The essential characteristics of this <u>Second Industrial Revolution</u> developed because of a combination of new developments in both technology and business organization. Initially, this growth was aided by the lack of governmental control over the affairs of business (laissez-faire capitalism was the dominant economic theory of the era).

THE CHANGING NATURE OF AMERICAN INDUSTRY

The massive industrial growth of this period was largely based on the expansion of <u>heavy industry</u>. Prior to the Civil War, most American production was based on turning out materials that the American consumer would purchase, such as food products and textiles. These products continued to be produced, but during 1870–1910, rapid industrial growth was fueled by the production of steel, machinery, and petroleum products. Most of these products were designed *not* for the consumer, but for those who produced the goods. Heavy industry produced new machinery that a textile mill might install, or a stronger, more durable steel that a railroad line might use for a new stretch of tracks. Industrial expansion during this era spiraled; new machinery introduced in textile mills, for example, fueled a further expansion of textile manufacturing.

Another key component of the Second Industrial Revolution was the development of new and more efficient sources of power. In 1865 the majority of American industries were still dependent on water power. The discovery of <u>anthracite coal</u> (in Pennsylvania, West Virginia, and elsewhere) caused the price of coal to drastically drop and fueled the transformation in many American industries to steam power. By 1890 nearly 70 percent of American industries used steam. After the turn of the century, the inventiveness of Thomas Edison allowed electricity to replace steam as the cheapest and most efficient source of power in American factories.

Industry expanded in this era into geographic regions where it had scarcely existed before. In the <u>New South</u> many former sharecroppers went to work in textile factories, which oftentimes utilized state-of-the-art machinery that had been produced in the North. The American Tobacco Company started to manufacture cigarettes by machine, and the steel mills found in Southern cities such as Birmingham, Alabama, made these cities start to resemble factory cities in the North.

Changes in the Workplace

Production methods changed in virtually every factory in America during this period, as the desire for more efficiently produced goods became paramount. Efficiency experts were utilized by many companies, and most championed the ideas of Frederick W. Taylor, a mechanical engineer who wrote popular treatises on efficiency and scientific management. <u>Taylorism</u> emphasized speed and efficiency in the workplace; factories found that paying workers "by the piece" made them produce more. Workers were timed and factories sometimes redesigned to promote efficiency and greater production. One by-product of Taylorism was the elimination of some workers in the factory as other workers did their jobs "more efficiently."

Part of this move toward efficiency was the beginning of assembly line production methods. The application of Taylorism and the introduction of the assembly line best demonstrate the combination of technology and business organization that fueled much of the economic growth of the era. The Ford Motor Company was first established in 1903, and by 1910, it was producing nearly 12,000 cars per year. Henry Ford's factories first used assembly line production methods in 1913; during that year Ford produced nearly 250,000 automobiles. Similar growth occurred in the chemical and electrical industries as new production methods were introduced.

How did the role of workers in the production process change in this era? Critics charged that the individual worker had merely become "one more cog in the machine"; in an automobile assembly line the worker might, for example, put the left door on a whole series of identical automobiles all day long. The need for skilled craftsmen, so important in pre-industrial America, drastically lessened as a result of the assembly line.

Many factory jobs could now be learned in several hours or less. The result of this on the nature of the workforce was immense. Immigrants with no previous training could perform the simple tasks associated with many industrial jobs. In addition, many women left their previous jobs as domestics to go to work in the textiles mills (many women took clerical jobs in this era as well). Children could also do some of the more menial tasks associated with factory work and be paid a pittance of what adults were making. By 1900 nearly 20 percent of all children between 10 and 15 were employed, many in textile mills and shoe factories. During this period some states began to pass laws regulating child labor, although these were oftentimes difficult to enforce.

Clear differences were present in this period between the pay offered to men and women in most factories. Skilled women factory workers made $5 a week, while unskilled male workers often made $8 per week. Women still preferred factory work to the very time-consuming and low-paying job of being a domestic worker. Some female workers turned to prostitution; there is some evidence that the number of prostitutes increased in industrial cities at the end of the nineteenth century.

Marriage usually ended a woman's work in the factory; doing all of the chores while the husband was away at work was a back-breaking exercise in this era. Some urban married women also added income to the household by doing knitting or sewing for others at home.

THE CONSOLIDATION OF BUSINESSES

John D. Rockefeller made millions through Standard Oil, as did Andrew Carnegie through U.S. Steel. During this period these businessmen and others attempted to further control the industries in which they were invested. Many of these schemes did allow the rich to get richer, with little or no benefit to those working under them.

Some of these organizational schemes were quickly squashed by governmental intervention. Influential stockholders of companies of the same industry would sometimes agree to limit production, set prices, and even share profits. This type of activity was outlawed in 1887 by the **Interstate Commerce Act**. This bill was passed with the intent of regulating the railroads, but it generally was not enforced. The commission in charge of enforcement was made of former railroad executives and others who favored the interests of the railroads.

Another popular method of business organization was the creation of **trusts**, an organizational technique perfected by John D. Rockefeller and Standard Oil. At the time, state laws prohibited one corporation from holding stock in another. However, it was legal to create a trust, by which stockholders in a smaller oil company could be "persuaded" to give control of their shares in that company "in trust" to the board of trustees of Standard Oil. Using this technique, Standard Oil established a **horizontal integration** of the oil industry in the early 1880s, meaning that the board of trustees of Standard Oil also controlled many other oil-producing companies.

Standard Oil expanded in the late 1880s even further by becoming a **holding company**. In 1888 New Jersey passed new legislation allowing businesses incorporated there to own stock in other corporations. Standard Oil stockholders began to buy up shares in other companies as well; under the regulations for a holding company, management of various companies could be joint as well. Standard Oil stockholders became the majority holders in other oil companies, allowing Standard Oil management to run these companies also. By the early 1890s Standard Oil had merged 43 oil-producing companies together under their control and produced nearly 90 percent of all oil in America. Standard Oil also achieved **vertical integration** when the company not only moved to control production but also the marketing and distribution of the finished product. Similar examples of vertical integration were found in many other companies (Gustavus Swift exhibited similar control over the meat-processing industry). Carnegie's steel operation is often cited as the best example of vertical integration in this era.

Those at the very top of the economic pinnacle were able to rationalize their incredible economic successes. American social philosopher William Graham Sumner wrote in this period about **Social Darwinism**, which proclaimed that God had granted power and wealth to those that most deserved it. Believers in Social Darwinism could thus justify any scheme that could bring more money to the Rockefellers and the Carnegies of America, since God had wanted them to have that economic power. Carnegie spoke and wrote about the "**Gospel of Wealth.**" According to this theory, the major role of America's industrialists was to act as the "guardians" of the wealth of America (and *not* to give this wealth out in the form of higher wages for the workers). Carnegie stated that is was the duty of the wealthy to return a large portion of their wealth to the community. To the credit of both Rockefeller and Carnegie, foundations they established have contributed over $650 million to various educational and artistic ventures since the time of their deaths. Observers with a less sympathetic view call the giants of business from this era "robber barons."

THE GROWTH OF LABOR UNIONS

Although craft unions existed in the period before the Civil War, the first major strike in American history was the large strike of railroad workers that began in July 1877. Railroad workers protested layoffs and the reduction of their wages. In various parts of the country, railroad property was destroyed and trains were derailed. In Pittsburgh, Pennsylvania, over 30 strikers were killed by militia forces loyal to the railroad companies. President Hayes finally sent in government troops to restore order and break up the strike, although he felt that steps should be taken to "remove the distress which afflicts laborers."

The major union to emerge from the 1870s was the **Knights of Labor**, which was founded in Philadelphia in 1869. Many earlier unions represented single crafts (shoemakers, for example). The Knights of Labor opened their doors to skilled *and* unskilled workers, and welcomed immigrants, blacks, and women as well. Membership in the Knights of Labor peaked around 750,000 in the mid-1880s. Brochures written by the Knights of Labor proposed a new, cooperative society, where laborers would one day work for themselves and not for their industrial bosses. Unfortunately, this rhetoric failed to impress many bosses, and in several large strikes, ownership refused to even negotiate with representatives of the union, causing it to gradually lose members.

On May 1, 1886, a massive labor rally was held in Chicago, with nearly 100,000 workers turning out to support strikers at the nearby McCormick reaper plant. Chicago authorities were aware of the violent tactics practiced by many European socialists at this time and vowed not to let that happen in Chicago. The next evening a large worker's demonstration took place near **Haymarket Square** in downtown Chicago. Police and militia forces arrived to break up the demonstration. At that moment, a bomb went off. Seven people died and nearly 70 were wounded. Eventually, eight anarchists were convicted of setting off the bomb. To many not involved in labor unions, the events at Haymarket Square hurt the labor movement; the press at the time drew little distinction between "hard-working union men" and "foreign" socialists and anarchists. Police forces in cities across the country also increased their supplies of ammunition, guns, and men in preparation for the next outbreak of "anarchism" that might break out. The Knights of Labor suffered a decline in membership as a result of Haymarket Square.

The **American Federation of Labor** (A.F.L.) was the next major national labor organization to achieve national stature. The A.F.L. was organized by crafts and made up almost exclusively of skilled workers. This helped its image, since in the eyes of the public, most anarchists and other radicals were unskilled workers. The union's first leader was Samuel Gompers. Unlike the idealistic philosophy of the Knights of Labor, the A.F.L. bargained for "bread-and-butter issues" like higher wages and shorter hours. By 1917 the A.F.L. had over 2.5 million members. Although the union used strike tactics on many occasions it strenuously avoided the appearance of being controlled by radicals. Major strikes of era included a 1892 strike against the Carnegie Steel Company in Homestead, Pennsylvania, and a 1894 strike by the American Railway Union against the Pullman Palace Car Company. The American Railway Union was founded by Eugene V. Debs, who would later run for president on the Socialist party ticket.

Miners in the West also were engaged in labor activity, and in late 1905 helped to found the **Industrial Workers of the World** (I.W.W.). In spirit this union was close to the old Knights of Labor, as it attracted both skilled and unskilled workers. Union literature spoke of class conflict, violence, and the desirability of socialism. I.W.W. members were called "Wobblies" and included "Mother" Jones, who organized coal miners, and Big Bill Haywood of the Western Federation of Miners. The union was involved in many strikes, many of them bloody, and was destroyed during World War I when many of its leaders were jailed.

Strikes by all of the unions mentioned in the preceding text clearly advanced the condition of the American worker during this era. Their wages had risen, and the hours they worked were less. However, the limitations of unions in this era must also be noted. The Knights of Labor and the Industrial Workers of the World were the only unions that recruited women, blacks, and immigrants. The A.F.L. vigorously rejected the recruitment of these groups, claiming that their acceptance in the workforce would depress the wages of all. Some women did form their own labor unions; the 1909 strike by the International Ladies Garment Workers Union in New York City was one of the largest strikes of the era.

Industrial bosses were able to scare some workers away from joining unions, and many continually suspected that unions were filled by anarchists and other agitators. The government supported industrial owners on several other occasions by sending in the military to end strikes. Pinkerton guards were also used against strikers. Unions had still not achieved widespread acceptance in this era. Even in 1915 only 12 percent of the workforce was unionized.

AN INCREASED STANDARD OF LIVING?

Many history textbooks place great emphasis on the growth of a **consumer society** in America during this period. These textbooks would note that Americans could now afford things that previously had been luxuries of the upper classes, such as tea and silk stockings. The texts would discuss the fact that average life expectancy increased by over six years between 1900 and 1920, and that things like flush toilets were now present in many houses. The growth of the department store would be emphasized to demonstrate all of the goods that the new consumer could buy.

It should be carefully noted, however, that large segments of American society did not share the newly created wealth found in the pockets and bank accounts of many upper middle-class and upper-class Americans. Many Americans, especially newly arrived immigrants, experienced crushing poverty. Conveniences such as flush toilets were not available in most working-class housing until the late 1920s or 1930s. Wages may have gone up, yet in many parts of the country, increases in living costs were even more profound. Clothing made out of new fabrics and fresh fruits were now available, but with the wages that workers were being paid, actually purchasing any of these goods was absolutely out of the question for the vast majority of workers. For many in the growing middle class, however, families could now not just buy the goods and services that they needed; they could begin to buy merchandise and services that they wanted as well.

THE IMPACT OF IMMIGRATION ON AMERICAN SOCIETY

Immigration patterns shifted dramatically in the late 1880s and 1890s. Before then, most European immigrants coming to the United States came from northern Europe, with large numbers coming from England, Ireland, and Germany. A large segment of these immigrants were English speakers; although assimilation into American society was difficult, the commonality of language made it less so. Starting in the late 1880s, most immigrants arrived from non-English-speaking areas, such as Eastern Europe, Russia, and Italy. Many of these "**new immigrants**" were poorer that those who had arrived in America earlier. This and the language barrier made their assimilation into American society more difficult.

From 1870 to 1920 nearly 28 million immigrants arrived in the United States (peak years for immigration were from 1900 to 1910). Ellis Island opened in 1892, and Europeans desiring to settle in America first had to undergo the physical, psychological, and political testing that was given there. In 1910 Angel Island in San Francisco was completed; this was the West Coast's version of Ellis Island.

Nearly 14,000 Chinese laborers had been recruited to build the transcontinental railroad. Many Chinese avoided racial hostilities by moving to sections of cities like Chinatown in San Francisco. The fear existed that Chinese workers would work for lower wages than "our" workers would, and the Chinese Exclusion Act of 1882 prohibited any new Chinese laborers from entering the country (those who were already here were permitted to stay). After the United States acquired Hawaii in 1898, many Japanese living in Hawaii came to California to work in vegetable and fruit fields there. The Japanese faced many of the same prejudices that the Chinese had faced. In 1906 the Board of Education in San Francisco ruled that separate schools would have to be established for white and Asian students. The 1913 California **Webb Alien Land Law** prohibited Asians who were not citizens from owning land anywhere in the state.

The majority of immigrants on both the West and East Coasts initially settled in coastal cities. Eastern and southern Europeans on the East Coast had come to America to escape oppressive governments, religious persecution, rising taxes, and declining production on their farms. The transformation for many from working in agriculture in Europe to working in a factory in America was massive. To survive, many clung to their old European customs, spoke their native languages at home, lived in neighborhoods dominated by their own ethnic group (thus the development of Chinatown and Little Italy in New York City), became members of mutual benefit associations or other ethnic organizations, or sent their children to religious instead of public schools.

The initial intent of many of these immigrants was to come to America, make money, and then return to their homeland. Some did return, yet those who remained were a crucial component of the economic growth of the era. Eastern and southern Europeans worked in many factories on the East Coast but also provided the manpower for the economic growth of cities such as Milwaukee and Chicago as well. Some immigrants did become involved in agriculture; a small number of Europeans continued on to the mining towns of the West. The one part of the country where few immigrants went was the South; few jobs opened up for them there.

THE TRANSFORMATION OF THE AMERICAN CITY

The construction of new factories and the influx of immigrants from abroad and from the countryside helped to force the radical transformation of many industrial cities in this era. Before the Civil War, cities were relatively small, with most people who lived within the city being able to easily walk to work. Almost all cities had poor sections in them before the Civil War. The rapid influx of poor immigrants turned many of these sections into horribly overcrowded slums.

New methods of transportation aided in the transformation of the industrial city. Elevated trains (first introduced in New York in 1867), cable cars (in San Francisco), electric trolleys, and subways (first found in Boston in 1897) allowed middle- and upper-class citizens to move further and further away from the center of the city. In the early nineteenth century the "best" houses were found in the middle of the city; residents of these houses were now relocating to **suburbia**. Businesses, banks, and offices became located in the business district, usually found in the center of the city. Little housing existed in this part of the city. Located in various sectors surrounding the business district were factories and other centers of manufacturing. Cheap housing for workers usually was located very close to each factory. The upper and lower classes physically lived much further apart in the "modern" cities of the late 1800s than they had earlier in the century.

The conditions of working-class slums are well documented. Many workers lived in "apartments" that were created from residences formerly belonging to middle- and upper-class residents. Room in these buildings were divided and subdivided again so that large numbers of families could live in buildings that formerly housed one family. Tenement buildings were more cheaply constructed and were built to house as many families as possible. Outdoor bathrooms were still the rule in many slum areas. Even those that could receive water inside often emptied waste, human and otherwise, into back alleys (sewage system proved to be woefully inadequate in almost every city). Poverty, disease, and crime were the central elements of life for many living in industrial slums, although in many cities somewhat better conditions were available for workers who were better off. Technology did bring some changes to life even in the slums after the turn of the century, as a few worker residencies started to have gas, electricity, and running water. In the later 1800s cities such as New York also started to develop building codes for all new construction.

Office buildings in many cities became taller during this era. Before the Civil War the tallest buildings in most American cities were four or five stories high. The development of stronger and more durable **Bessemer steel** meant that steel girders could now support taller buildings, and the first elevators began to be installed in buildings in the early 1880s. The first actual "skyscraper" was the building of the Home Insurance Company in Chicago. Finished in 1885 this building was 10 stories high, with four separate elevators taking passengers to the top.

City officials in almost every industrial city realized the necessity of construction and city improvements. After the turn of the century, schools, public buildings, and even sewers began to be built at a rapid rate. However, lack of housing was a major problem that urban planners were unable to solve. Many urban reformers, who will be discussed in a later chapter, had other plans to improve the lives of the urban poor.

POLITICS OF THE GUILDED AGE

Mark Twain coined the term "**The Guilded Age**" to refer to the period between 1875 and 1900. This is not a positive image of the era; it implies a thin layer of gold (symbolizing prosperity) covering all of the problems of the era, including grinding poverty in the time of incredible wealth and political corruption on a wide scale.

The irony of political life in this period was that many Americans were deeply involved in political activity. Large numbers of Americans were involved in party politics; nearly 75 percent of all registered voters voted in the presidential elections of the era, far more than have voted in any recent presidential election. Yet at the same time, much of the political activity at the time was at a superficial level. Few elections of the era had two candidates who differed radically on the issues; most campaigns revolved around different personalities and not around issues. One observer noted that the American politicians of the period were the most "thoroughly ordinary" political leaders in the history of the United States. On top of all this, there was more corruption in the American political system during this period than in any other period of the nineteenth century.

During the 1870s Congress exerted a greater power than the executive branch. This was largely caused by the weak Republican presidents that followed Abraham Lincoln (Andrew Johnson and U.S. Grant). It was during this period that the some reformers began to point out the evils of the **spoils system** to the American public. This system, which had been begun by Andrew Jackson, allowed the victorious party in any election to reward their loyal supporters by giving them government jobs.

The lack of controversy or debate on issues during this period was partially because Republicans and Democrats each had roughly the same amount of support. As a result, neither party could risk alienating or turning away anyone from their party ranks. One way to do this was not to talk about real issues. Republicans support from bankers, industrialists, and farmers was balanced by Democratic support from immigrants (those who could vote), laborers, and farmers (especially from the West). Democrats of this era (as well as Democrats of today) have always made the claim that their party represents "the people."

President Rutherford B. Hayes, the successor to Grant, did make an attempt to reform the spoils system. After he won the election of 1876, Hayes refused to use the spoils system when he named officials for his new administration, and he removed some individuals from government positions who had been appointed to their position by patronage, including Chester A. Arthur in New York, a future president.

What to do about the spoils system was an important issue in the 1880, with Republicans themselves being divided on what to do with it. James Garfield, a congressman from Ohio, suggested that the system be reformed. Garfield was not a strong campaigner but emerged victorious in the presidential election, becoming the fourth consecutive Republican president. Garfield, ironically, was assassinated in July 1881 by a man who was outraged because he was passed over on a job that he thought he should get through the spoils system.

After Garfield's assassination, many major newspapers and some politicians began to call for a thorough reform of the spoils system. Garfield's successor, Chester A. Arthur, urged Congress to pass legislation to that effect. The result was the **Pendleton Civil Service Act**, which went into effect in 1883. This act created a **Civil Service Commission**, which would test applicants and ensure that government jobs were given to those who were qualified to get them. The legislation also stated that government officials couldn't be required to contribute to political campaigns (a practice that had been relatively commonplace). As a result, a **professional bureaucracy** began to be created in both the legislative and executive branches. Aides to cabinet members and congressmen became indispensable to the operations of government. Some at the time suggested that this professional bureaucracy was important because it couldn't be voted out office by the "rabble" who were increasingly being given the vote. As any observer of the American political system knows, however, the reforms of this era did not end corruption as a major influence on the system.

Perhaps the best example of politics focusing on the individual and not the issues was the presidential election of 1884. The regulation of business deserved serious discussion, as did the government's tariff policies (a fiercely debated topic at local political meetings across the nation), yet the campaign largely centered around whether Republican James Blaine had when he was a congressman accepted free railroad stock while voting to support bills favorable to the railroad industry. The second most important issue of the campaign was whether Grover Cleveland had fathered a child before he was married. When all was finished, Cleveland became the first Democrat since 1856 to be elected president.

The issue of tariffs remained a major one throughout the 1880s and into the 1890s, with Eastern business interests leading the charge for higher tariffs. As discussed in the previous chapter, a major depression began in 1893. Millions of Americans lost their jobs. Standard economic and government policy of the time was that it was not the job of the federal government to intervene. A Populist from Ohio named Jacob Coxey led a group of unemployed workers to Washington in 1894 and demanded that the government assist the unemployed of America. **Coxey's Army** did little to affect government policy in Washington, although it did demonstrate the distress felt by unemployed Americans.

The policies of the Populists in the 1890s and William Jennings Bryan and his defeat at the hands of William McKinley were discussed in Chapter 13. McKinley's rout of Bryan in the 1896 election signaled a major shift in American politics. As previously stated, both parties were nearly similar in strength for much of the period discussed in this chapter. The 1896 election ended this. The 1896 election cast the Republicans as a truly national party (Bryan's support was largely sectional). Republicans could claim they were the party of prosperity: Nearly as soon as they were elected, the effects of the depression began to end (a part of this was luck; gold was discovered in parts of Alaska in late 1892, thus increasing the national money supply). Republican domination of politics at the national level filtered down to the state and local levels as well. As a result, many local races were no longer close (in an increasing number Democrats even failed to challenge Republicans in a number of races). One result of this was a striking decrease in political participation and voting by supporters of both major parties. Some historians also argue that William McKinley was the first "modern" president, in that he amassed a large amount of power in the office of the presidency.

Political life in many of the major industrial cities was controlled by **political machines**. These political organizations were designed to keep a certain party, or in many cases a certain individual, in power. Favors, jobs, and in some cases money were promised to voters in return for political support. Many machines used the support of immigrants to remain in power, as newly arrived immigrants were often eager to receive the types of help that political machines could give them. Some machines did make positive reforms in local services and education. The most famous machine existed in New York City, where William Marcy Tweed ("Boss" Tweed) ran New York City through the political club located at **Tammany Hall** beginning in 1870. Tweed and his associates bilked the city treasury out of millions of dollars. The famous political cartoons of

Thomas Nast helped to bring Tweed down and send him to jail, although Tammany Hall ran the politics of New York City for nearly 50 years.

CULTURAL LIFE IN THE GUILDED AGE

There are several literary sources written in the era that expressed strong opinions about the economic changes taking place in society. The Horatio Alger stories published in the era promised that hard work and honesty would oftentimes lead to economic success. Henry George's 1879 book *Progress and Property* was a huge seller; in this book the author advocates a single land tax as a method of greatly improving America by redistributing the wealth.

Several other books present a more critical view of America. *Looking Backward* (1888) by Edward Bellamy was also a very popular book. This book looks ahead to Boston in 2000: In Bellamy's view everyone works hard in efficient factories. A difference, however, was that in Bellamy's view of the future, cooperation between the workers and the bosses has replaced the ruthless capitalism that existed in Bellamy's time.

In 1890 Jacob Riis published *How the Other Half Lives*, a documentary account of slum life in New York City. This book was especially powerful because it also contained photographs he had taken of immigrants and the conditions they lived in. Finally, *The Jungle* (1906) by Upton Sinclair was written as an exposé of the meatpacking industry.

CHAPTER REVIEW

Rapid Review Guide

To achieve the perfect 5, you should be able to explain the following:

- The industrial growth that occurred in the United States during this era made the United States the major industrial producer of the world.

- The industrial growth was largely based on the expansion of heavy industry; the availability of steel was critical to this expansion.

- Taylorism and the assembly line created major changes in the workplace for factory workers.

- Horizontal and vertical integration allowed businesses to expand dramatically during this era; Standard Oil (John D. Rockefeller) and U.S. Steel (Andrew Carnegie) are the best examples of this type of expansion.

- Andrew Carnegie's "Gospel of Wealth" proclaimed it was the duty of the wealthy to return large amounts of their wealth back to the community.

- American workers began to unionize in this era by joining the Knights of Labor, the American Federation of Labor, and the Industrial Workers of the World. Because of intimidation by company bosses and the publicity that came from several unsuccessful strikes, union membership remained low, even into the twentieth century.

- The impact of the "new immigrants" from eastern and southern Europe on American cities and in the workplace was immense.

- The American city became transformed in this era, with new methods of transportation allowing many from the middle and upper class to move to suburbia and still work in the city.

- Political life at the state and city level during this era was dominated by various political machines, although reforms were instituted at the federal level and in some states to create a professional civil service system.

Time Line

1869: Knights of Labor founded in Philadelphia
1870: Beginning of Tammany Hall's control over New York City politics
1879: Publication of *Progress and Prosperity* by Henry George
1881: Assassination of President James Garfield
1882: Chinese Exclusion Act passed by Congress
1883: Pendleton Civil Service Act enacted
1885: Completion of Home Insurance Company Building in Chicago, America's first skyscraper
1886: Haymarket Square demonstration and bombing in Chicago
1887: Interstate Commerce Act enacted
   Major strike of railroad workers; President Hayes sends in government troops to break up strike in Pittsburgh
1888: New Jersey passes legislation allowing holding companies
   Publication of *Looking Backward* by Edward Bellamy
1890: Publication of *How the Other Half Lives* by Jacob Riis
1892: Ellis Island opens to process immigrants on the East Coast
1893: Beginning of major depression in America
1894: March of Coxey's Army on Washington, DC
   United States becomes world's largest manufacturing producer
1896: Decisive victory of Republican William McKinley breaks decades-long deadlock between Democrats and Republicans
   America begins to recover from Great Depression of early 1890s
1897: America's first subway begins regular service in Boston
1901: Assassination of President William McKinley
1903: Ford Motor Company established
1905: Industrial Workers of the World formed
1906: Publication of *The Jungle* by Upton Sinclair
1909: Strike of International Ladies Garment Workers Union in New York City

1910: Angel Island opens to process immigrants on West Coast
Number of American children attending school nears 60 percent
1913: Webb Alien Land Law enacted, prohibiting aliens from owning farmland in California
Ford Motor Company begins to use assembly line techniques; 250,000 automobiles produced

✓ Review Questions

1. The practices championed by Frederick W. Taylor that were championed by many factory owners of the era

    A. made it easier for immigrant workers to assimilate into the American working class
    B. ensured that all workers would receive higher wages and conditions in the factories would improve
    C. emphasized the need for greater efficiency in factory operations
    D. reemphasized the need for extensive training before the worker could do almost any job in the factory
    E. created less profits for factory owners

(Correct Answer: **C.** Taylorism made efficiency in the workplace a science and set the stage for assembly line production techniques.)

2. Many citizens became involved in the political process by actively supporting the Republican and Democratic party for all of the reasons listed *except*

    A. the parades, rallies, and campaigns of the era provided an exciting entry into the American political system
    B. the strength of the two parties was roughly identical in this era, thus creating close and interesting races
    C. the expansion and spread of newspapers in this era made more people aware of political developments
    D. candidates for president for both parties in almost every race of this

era were dynamic and very popular campaigners, thus energizing the forces of both parties
    E. energetic campaign workers were sometimes rewarded with government jobs

(Correct Answer: **D.** Most of the presidential candidates—and presidential winners—of this era were nondescript men, thus allowing much power to go over to the Congress.)

3. An analysis of the march on Washington by "Coxey's Army" in 1894 demonstrates that

    A. large segments of the unemployed in America were willing to become involved politically to protest their situation
    B. all classes in American society were deeply affected by the depression of the early 1890s
    C. the policies of dealing with depression in the 1890s were somewhat similar to policies championed by Herbert Hoover from 1929 to 1932
    D. public opinion had a major effect on government policy in the late 1800s
    E. the march was extremely well covered by the press

(Correct Answer: **C.** The march had little effect on government policy. Coxey's Army was relatively small by the time it got to Washington. Official policy of the time was that it was not the job of the federal government to actively intervene during hard times, a policy similar to that supported by Herbert Hoover in the first years of the Great Depression.)

4. The following statements are true about the new industrial city of the late nineteenth century *except*

    A. the working class lived around the factories, usually somewhat near the center of the city
    B. the factories of the city were almost always found near a source of water, since water power was common
    C. mass transportation allowed workers to travel to various parts of the city, where before they had to walk to work
    D. the central area of the city usually consisted of offices, banks, and insurance buildings
    E. many saloons existed in working-class neighborhoods

(Correct Answer: **B.** By 1890 most American industry had converted to steam power.)

5. Evidence that the standard of living for the working class improved in this era could be found by carefully analyzing all of the following *except*

    A. a comparison of increased wages with increased living costs for factory workers
    B. an analysis of the increased diversity of foods available for purchase by factory workers
    C. a study of former luxuries that were now staples in the homes of some industrial workers
    D. an analysis of the growth of amusement parks, sporting events, and movie theaters in the major cities
    E. a comparison of the wages of most immigrant workers with the wages of workers who remained to work in the "old country"

(Correct Answer: **A.** Many diverse foods were available for purchase by factory workers, but few could afford them. For many workers wages did go up in this period; however, increased living costs oftentimes outstripped higher wages.)

Chapter 15

The Rise of American Imperialism (1890–1913)

 During the 20 years between 1890 and 1910, the United States proved itself to be as powerful as the major European states in every respect. By the turn of the century the United States had already surpassed Germany as the major industrial producer of the world. During this same period the United States was proving that its imperialist aims were as aggressive of those of France, England, and Germany, and that it would vigorously fight to maintain territories that it acquired. There were many constituencies in the United States that opposed American imperialism and many that supported it. American actions in this era, especially in the Philippines, showed that the United States was capable of doing every evil deed abroad that it had criticized various European powers for doing in the previous century.

A PERIOD OF FOREIGN POLICY INACTION

In the years immediately after the Civil War, the United States aggressively sought out new territories to acquire or to economically control. In 1867 the United States purchased Alaska from the Russians. During the same year, the Midway Islands were also annexed, as the United States was also searching for potential bases in the Pacific Ocean.

Beginning in 1871 the Europeans powers began an era of great imperialistic expansion, culminating in the "Scramble for Africa," which left virtually the entire continent colonized by England, France, Germany, or Belgium. The United States did not take part in imperialistic adventures until the 1890s. Several reasons can be cited for this. America was still expanding, but this expansion was still westward; the America frontier did not totally close until the last decade of the century. In addition, rapid industrial growth, urban growth, and a large influx of immigrants kept

America occupied for much of the later nineteenth century. Another factor was that most of the men in power had been veterans of the Civil War or had intimate knowledge of it. These men had little stomach for further warfare, which imperialism was likely to bring.

The results of these factors were obvious. During the 1870s and early 1880s, the American State Department had less than 100 employees. The United States Army and Navy both would have been no match for the military forces of four or five European countries. Virtually no politician spoke of increased imperialistic adventures when campaigning in this era.

A SIGN OF THINGS TO COME: HAWAII

An initial indication that American attitudes toward the use of force abroad was first demonstrated by American actions in Hawaii. American missionaries had first come to Hawaii in the 1820s. The United States was, for obvious reasons, interested in Hawaii's sugar plantations. In 1887 a deal was struck allowing sugar from the islands to be imported into America duty-free. This stimulated the sugar trade in Hawaii. Sugar planters in Hawaii exerted tremendous economic and political power; during that same year they forced King Kalakaua to accept a new constitution that took away some of his political power and put it in their hands.

In 1891 the king died and his sister Queen Liliuokalani replaced her. By this point planters in Hawaii, and some members of the United States Senate, saw the obvious economic advantages of turning Hawaii into a United States protectorate. Queen Liliuokalani vigorously rejected this; her goal was to greatly reduce the influence of foreign countries, especially the United States, in Hawaii. In 1893 pro-American sugar planters, assisted by American marines, overthrew the queen, declared Hawaii to be a republic, and requested Hawaii be annexed by the United States. This takeover was partially a reaction to U.S. tariff policies, which favored domestic producers. If Hawaii was annexed, then planters from Hawaii would be considered domestic producers.

Much debate took place on the floor of the Senate on the proper role of the United States in Hawaii. President Grover Cleveland sent a commission to Hawaii to determine the wishes of the citizens of Hawaii concerning their future. After the commission reported that most people interviewed supported Queen Liliuokalani, Cleveland announced that he was opposed to annexation but recognized the Republic of Hawaii. President McKinley had no such reservations after his election in 1896, stating that it was "**manifest destiny**" that the United States should control Hawaii. The Congress soon approved annexation, largely on the promise that future military bases that could placed in Hawaii could cement America's strategic position in the Pacific.

It also should be noted that American economic interests desired increased involvement in China during this period as well. The possibility of investment in China would cause Secretary of State John Hay to ask European leaders for an "**Open-Door**" policy in China in 1899, which would allow all foreign nations, including the United States, to establish trading relations with China.

THE 1890s: REASONS FOR AMERICAN IMPERIALISM

By the 1890s many American leaders began to have new attitudes toward imperialistic adventures abroad. The reasons for this were also numerous. At the forefront of those pushing for an aggressive American policy abroad were various industrial leaders, who feared that the United States would soon produce more than it could ever consume. New dependent states could prove to be markets for these goods. Some in business also perceived that in the future, industries would need raw materials that could simply not be found in America (rubber and petroleum products, for example). In the future, America would need dependent states to provide these materials.

Other influential Americans stated that it was important for political reasons that America expand. Bases would be needed in the future in the Pacific, many claimed—thus the need to acquire strategic locations in that region. Many of those interested in reviving the American navy also were very interested in imperialistic adventures; the **Naval Act of 1900** authorized the construction of battleships that would be clearly offensive in nature. A major supporter of naval expansion was Captain Alfred T. Mahan, who in 1890 wrote *The Influence of Sea Power upon History*, which stated that to be economically successful America must gain new markets abroad; the navy would have to be expanded to accomplish this.

Other factors accounted for increased American interest abroad in the 1890s. The concepts of **Social Darwinism** were used by supporters of imperialism, as were ideas, many imported from Europe, about the racial superiority of the Anglo-Saxon race. *Our Country,* written in 1885 by Josiah Strong, stated that God has appointed the Anglo-Saxons to be their "brother's keepers." Some Americans believed in Kipling's "**White Man's Burden**" and felt it was their duty to go over and civilize the "inferior races" of African and Asia. This was also the period where American missionaries felt the time was right to Christianize the "heathen" of these regions. Others, including Senator Albert J. Beveridge of Indiana, feared that the American spirit would be sapped by the closing of the frontier and suggested that adventures abroad might help to offset this. It should also be remembered that a new generation of Americans, less affected by the horrors of the Civil War, were now in positions of power in Washington, DC.

THE SPANISH-AMERICAN WAR

Those who wanted American adventure abroad finally got their wish with the **Spanish-American War**. In this "splendid little war," America was able to fight against an insignificant European power with little military clout. The steps leading to this war began in 1868, when Cuban colonists revolted against the Spanish who controlled the island. The Spanish made some efforts to control the efficiency of their operations in Cuba, but generally failed in their promises of allowing more self-government on the island. In 1895 an economic depression, caused by falling sugar and tobacco prices, hit the native population especially hard, and another revolt took place.

American investors, plantation owners, and government officials initially did not support the rebellion. The Spanish sent in a huge force of 150,000 troops and instituted a policy of **reconcentration**, which sent civilians, including women and children, who the Spanish thought might be potential allies of the rebels into heavily guarded camps. Conditions in these camps were appalling; it was estimated that in two years up to 225,000 people died in them.

The Cuban exile community in the United States pressured America to intervene on the side of the rebels, yet both President Cleveland and President McKinley resisted these efforts. Pressure on McKinley to intervene increased when Cuban rebels started to destroy American economic interests in Cuba, such as sugar mills.

American public opinion began to swerve toward intervention in Cuba. It is often pointed out that the American press was more responsible for this than were actual events in Cuba. Several American newspapers practiced the most lurid forms of **yellow journalism** when dealing with events in Cuba. Stories of the rape of Cuban girls by Spanish soldiers and brutal torture and execution of innocent Cuban citizens were standard fare in the *New York World* (published by Joseph Pulitzer) and the *New York Morning Journal* (owned by William Randolph Hearst), both of which were competing for circulation in New York. Both papers sent numerous reporters and illustrators to Cuba, and editors in New York demanded sensationalized stories. Newspapers across the country reprinted the accounts published in these papers. As a result of these stories, **jingoism** developed in America; this combined an intense America nationalism with a desire for adventure abroad.

It became harder for McKinley to resist the calls for intervention in Cuba, especially after the sinking of the **USS *Maine*** on February 15, 1898. The *Maine* had been sent to Havana harbor to protect American interests after violent riots broke out in Cuba in January. During the same month a letter stolen from the Spanish ambassador to Washington, in which he called President McKinley "weak," was published in newspapers across the country, further inflaming public opinion. The sinking of the *Maine* was undoubtedly caused by an explosion on board, yet both New York newspapers in banner headlines called for Americans to "Remember the Maine!" An American commission sent to study the sinking of the *Maine* was never able to conclusively determine why or how the ship was sunk.

The Outbreak of War

Theodore Roosevelt was the Assistant Secretary of the Navy at the time, and a vigorous supporter of an increased American role abroad. On February 25 (without the approval of his boss) he cabled all of the commanders in the Pacific to be ready for immediate combat against the Spanish. When the existence of these cables was discovered, President McKinley ordered the content of all of them to be rescinded, except the one to Admiral George Dewey; McKinley reaffirmed that if war broke out in Cuba, Dewey should attack the Spanish fleet quartered in the Philippines.

The pressure on McKinley to go to war was enormous. It should be noted that at this point both American expansionists and those with humanitarian motives supported American intervention in Cuba. McKinley sent the Spanish a list of demands that had to be met to avoid war. The Spanish agreed to the vast majority of them, yet McKinley finally gave in to pressures at home. On April 11, 1898, he finally sent a message to the Congress stating that he favored American intervention in Cuba. The next day Congress authorized the use of force in Spain.

It is still debated whether American disorganization or Spanish disorganization was more pronounced in the Spanish-American War. American efforts to organize an army to go to Cuba were woefully inefficient. Theodore Roosevelt resigned his position in the Naval Department to lead the "**Rough Riders**" up San Juan Hill in the most famous event of the war; his actual role in this battle has been debated. Americans lost 2500 men in this war, the vast majority from malaria or food poisoning. Only 400 died in battle.

It was the American navy earlier championed by Captain (now Admiral) Mahan that proved decisive in the American victory over the Spanish. In seven hours Admiral Dewey destroyed the Spanish fleet in the Pacific; every ship of the Spanish Atlantic force was also destroyed by the American navy. In the **Treaty of Paris** ending the war, Spain recognized the independence of Cuba and for a payment of $20 million gave the Philippines, Puerto Rico, and Guam over to the United States.

THE ROLE OF AMERICA: PROTECTOR OR OPPRESSOR?

After victory over the Spanish, the United States was placed in a somewhat uncomfortable position. It had criticized Spain for the way it had controlled Cuba, yet many in America did not want Cuba to be totally free either. The dilemma facing Americans after victory was one that would be rethought throughout the twentieth century: how to combine imperialistic intentions with the deep-seated American beliefs in liberty and self-government.

Fearing that America would want to annex Cuba, supporters of Cuban independence in Congress had inserted the **Teller Amendment** in the original congressional bill calling for war against Spain. This amendment stated that America would simply not do that under any circumstances. Nevertheless, President McKinley authorized that the Cubans would be ruled by an American military government (which kept control until 1901). The military government did authorize the Cubans to draft a constitution in 1900 but also insisted that the Cubans agree to all of the provisions of the **Platt Amendment**. This document stated that Cuba could not enter into agreements with other countries without the approval of the United States, that the United States had to right to intervene in Cuban affairs "when necessary," and that America be given two naval bases on the Cuban mainland. The Platt Amendment remained in force in Cuba until the early 1930s.

THE DEBATE OVER THE PHILIPPINES

The debate in America over what to do with the Philippines was a much more intense one. This debate took place on the floor of the Senate and in countless editorial pages across the country. An aggressive policy toward Cuba could be justified, since they were only 90 miles away and seemed important to the United States' position in the Western Hemisphere. Many had second thoughts, however, over controlling the Philippines; the Filipinos seemed a world away, and, after all, were not "like us." In addition, Americans became aware that Filipinos expected that after the Americans helped throw out the Spanish they would then help them achieve independence. What, indeed, should America's role in the Philippines be?

All of the most basic arguments on the merits of imperialism were debated in the aftermath of the Spanish-American War. Didn't the concept of ruling a territory by force violate everything that America stood for? An **Anti-Imperialist League** was formed in 1898 (with Mark Twain and William Jennings Bryan as charter members). The first brochures put out by this organization wondered if America didn't have too many problems at home to be involved abroad, and also expressed the fear that the armies needed for imperialistic adventures abroad might also be used to curb dissent at home.

Others pointed to the huge costs of imperialism and the fear that natives from newly acquired territories might take the jobs (or lower the wages) of American workers. Some pointed out the basic racism involved in American attitudes toward the Filipinos; some Southerners opposed imperialism because they feared it would bring people of the "inferior races" to America in greater numbers.

In the end, those arguing the political, strategic, and economic advantages that control of the Philippines would bring won the national argument. The American frontier *was* closing; wouldn't expansion abroad keep America vital and strong? In addition, religious figures noted that the acquisition of the Philippines would give the Church the opportunity to convert Filipinos to Christianity.

In the end, President McKinley supported American control of the Philippines, stating that if the Americans didn't enter, civil war was likely there. He also proclaimed that the Filipinos were simply "unfit for self-government." The treaty authorizing American control of the Philippines was ratified in February of 1899. It should be noted that American soldiers fought Filipino rebels for the next three years, with nearly 4500 American soldiers killed in this fighting. The American army attacked Filipino rebels with a vengeance; by the end of the insurrection, 200,000 Filipinos had been killed. Many humanitarian groups in America, which had initially enthusiastically supported the Spanish-American War, were appalled. An American commission later criticized the U.S. military for its conduct when dealing with the rebel forces.

CONNECTING THE PACIFIC AND THE ATLANTIC: THE PANAMA CANAL

After the Spanish-American War, most in America and in Europe regarded America as one of the major world powers. Theodore Roosevelt became president after the assassination of President McKinley and, as he had previously demonstrated, favored an aggressive foreign policy. (McKinley was killed during the first year of his second term as president by an anarchist; the next day political boss Mark Hanna lamented "now that damned cowboy is President of the United States".) One of Roosevelt's most cherished goals was the construction of a **Panama Canal,** which would link the Pacific and the Atlantic Oceans. The strategic and economic benefits of such a canal for America at the time were obvious.

A French building company had already acquired the rights to build such a canal in the region of Panama (which was controlled by Colombia). In 1902 the United States bought the rights from the company to construct the land, but this agreement was opposed by the Colombians. A "revolt" was organized in Panama by the French. United States warships sailed off the coast of Panama to help the "rebels." The United States was the first to recognize Panama as an independent country; newly installed Panamanian officials then gave America territory to build a canal. By the terms of the Hay-Bunau-Varilla Treaty of 1904, the United States received permanent rights and sovereignty over a 10-mile-wide area on which they planned to build the canal. In return, Panama was given $10 million. Construction of the canal began shortly afterward.

There was much criticism of American actions in Panama within the United States, but as in the case of the Philippines, the practical benefits of having a canal won out. The canal was finally completed in 1914. American businesses could now ship their goods faster and cheaper, although the acquisition of Panama deepened the suspicion of many in Latin America toward the United States.

THE ROOSEVELT COROLLARY

Theodore Roosevelt's most famous quote was to "speak softly and carry a big stick." In 1904 he also announced the **Roosevelt Corollary** to the Monroe Doctrine to Congress, which stated that the United States had the right to intervene in any country in the Western Hemisphere that did things "harmful to the United States," or if the threat of intervention by countries outside the hemisphere was present. The Roosevelt Corollary strengthened American control over Latin America, justified numerous American interventions in Latin American affairs in the twentieth century, and increased "Yankee go home" sentiment throughout the region. In Santo Domingo (now the Dominican Republic) the government went bankrupt and European countries threatened to intervene to collect their money; under the provisions of the Roosevelt Corollary, Roosevelt organized the American payment of Santo Domingan debt to keep the Europeans out.

In fairness, it should also be noted that Roosevelt won the Nobel Peace Prize for his mediation between the Japanese and the Russians after the Russo-Japanese War of 1904.

William Howard Taft, Roosevelt's successor, was not as aggressive in foreign policy as Roosevelt. He favored "dollars over bullets" and instituted a policy labeled by his critics as "**Dollar Diplomacy**," which stated that American investment abroad would ensure stability and good relations between America and nations abroad. This policy would also be hotly debated throughout the twentieth century.

CHAPTER REVIEW

Rapid Review Guide

To achieve a perfect 5, you should be able to explain the following:

- America became the economic and imperialistic equal of the major European powers by the beginning of the twentieth century.

- The United States acquired territory in the years immediately following the Civil War, but then entered a period where little foreign expansion took place.

- Americans and natives friendly to America increased the economic and political control of Hawaii by the United States, signaling a new trend in foreign policy.

- America desired trade in China; these desires were represented in John Hay's Open-Door policy.

- Economic, political, and strategic motives pushed America to pursue imperialist goals in the 1890s.

- Many in this era also opposed imperialism, often on moral or humanitarian grounds.

- The Spanish-American War allowed American imperialistic impulses to flourish; religious figures also supported imperialism in this era.

- Spanish incompetence and the strength of the American navy were important factors in the American victory in the Spanish-American War.

- America was deeply conflicted but finally decided to annex the Philippines, with three years of fighting between Americans and Filipino rebels to follow.

- The Panama Canal was built by the United States for military, strategic, and economic reasons; its construction began in 1904 and was completed in 1914.

- The Roosevelt Corollary to the Monroe Doctrine increased American control over Latin America.

Time Line

1867: United States purchases Alaska from Russia
      United States annexes Midway Islands
1871: Beginning of European "Scramble for Africa"
1875: Trade agreement between United States and Hawaii signed
1885: Publication of *Our Country* by Josiah Strong; book discusses role of Anglo-Saxons in the world
1890: Captain Alfred T. Mahan's *The Influence of Sea Power upon History* published
1893: Pro-American sugar planters overthrow Queen Liliuokalani in Hawaii
1895: Revolt against Spanish in Cuba; harsh Spanish reaction angers many in United States
1898: Explosion of USS *Maine* in Havana harbor; beginning of Spanish-American War
      Annexation of Hawaii receives final approval from Congress
      Anti-Imperialist League formed
1899: Secretary of State John Hay asks European leaders for an Open-Door policy in China
      First fighting between American army forces and Filipino rebels in Manila
1900: Naval Act of 1900 authorizes construction of offensive warships requested by navy
1901: Assassination of President McKinley; Theodore Roosevelt becomes president
1904: Roosevelt Corollary to Monroe Doctrine announced
      United States begins construction of Panama Canal
1905: Roosevelt mediates conflict between Japan, Russia in Portsmouth, New Hampshire
1914: Completion of the Panama Canal

✓ Review Questions

1. The intent of the Roosevelt Corollary to the Monroe Doctrine was

    A. to prevent European powers from becoming directly involved in affairs of the Western Hemisphere
    B. to allow the United States to intervene in Latin American countries causing "trouble" for the United States
    C. to allow the United States to "assist" countries in the area that demonstrated economic or political instability
    D. to allow the United States to remove "unfriendly governments" in the Western Hemisphere
    E. All of the above

(Correct Answer: **E.** The Roosevelt Corollary allowed the United States to intervene in affairs of Latin American countries under several circumstances, but was also intended to keep the European powers out of Latin America.)

2. Many humanitarians in the United States initially supported the Spanish-American War because

    A. they were appalled at the Spanish policy of reconcentration in Cuba
    B. they were able to ignore editorial comments found in most American newspapers
    C. they were following the lead of the Anti-Imperialist League
    D. they desired to assist the Filipino natives
    E. of American economic interests in Cuba

(Correct Answer: **A.** The Spanish policy of placing civilians in camps horrified many Americans. Most American newspapers initially supported the war as well. Concern for the Filipinos only became an issue during the debate over whether or not the United States should annex the Philippines.)

3. The major criticism that some Americans had concerning the construction of the Panama Canal was that

    A. the canal would force America to have a navy in both the Pacific and the Atlantic
    B. the canal would be outlandishly expensive to build
    C. the tactics that the Americans used to get the rights to build the canal were unsavory at best
    D. a French construction team had agreed to build the canal first
    E. American forces would have to be stationed indefinitely in Panama to guard the canal

(Correct Answer: **C.** The United States acquired the rights to territory to build the canal through the encouragement of a "revolt" by Panamanians against Colombia. The American navy wanted the canal. The French construction team had already been bankrupted by the excessive construction costs of the canal project.)

4. The United States was able to annex Hawaii because

    A. Queen Liliuokalani desired increased American investment in Hawaii
    B. pro-American planters engineered a revolt in Hawaii
    C. American marines had forcibly removed the queen from power
    D. public opinion in Hawaii strongly favored annexation
    E. Hawaii felt threatened by other Pacific powers

(Correct Answer: **B.** Queen Liliuokalani desired decreased American involvement in Hawaii. American marines were involved in the removal of the queen from power, but only in a supporting role. Public opinion in Hawaii supported the queen.)

5. American missionary leaders supported imperialism in this era because

   A. they thought their involvement would temper the excess zeal of other imperialists
   B. they admired the "pureness of spirit" found in the Filipinos and other native groups
   C. religious leaders in Europe favored imperialism
   D. they saw imperialism as an opportunity to convert the "heathen" of newly acquired territories
   E. American presidents, especially Theodore Roosevelt, strongly pressured them to take that stance

(Correct Answer: **D.** Missionary leaders worked in conjunction with other imperialists in this era. Little admiration of the natives was demonstrated by missionary leaders; the possibilities of conversions was the major reason for religious support for imperialism.)

Chapter 16

The Progressive Era (1895–1914)

 In 1896 and 1897 America emerged from the serious depression that had jolted it in the first part of the decade. It remained obvious to many observers that large social and political problems continued to plague American society. The gap between the poorest and richest members of American society continued to widen. Vast numbers of immigrants continued to pour into eastern cities without any meaningful system to support them. Corrupt political machines continued to dominate many American cities. As a result of these and countless other social problems, a group of largely middle-class men and women attempted to reform American society in many meaningful ways. These individuals, called **progressives**, oftentimes blamed capitalism for many of the problems facing America society. Their goal, however, was not to destroy capitalism in any way; it was to make capitalism and the social structures created by it operate more efficiently and more humanely. This reform impulse was a key influence in American political life until the outbreak of World War I in 1914 and was called **progressivism**. Most progressives were either writers or journalists.

THE ORIGINS OF PROGRESSIVISM

It should be emphasized that progressivism was not a unified movement in any way. There was never a unifying agenda or party; many "progressives" eagerly supported one or two progressive reforms without supporting any others. Thus, progressive reforms could be urban or rural, call for more government or less government, and on occasion could even be perceived as being pro-business.

Progressivism has many sources of origin. Books mentioned in Chapter 14 such as *Progress and Poverty* by Henry George and *Looking*

Backward by Edward Bellamy were read by most early progressives. **Taylorism** (also discussed in Chapter 14) influenced many progressives; many felt that the efficiency that Taylor proposed for American industry could also be installed in American government, schools, and even in one's everyday life.

Progressive reforms also shared some of the same critiques of society that American **socialists** were making at the time. Progressives and socialists both were very critical of capitalism and wanted more wealth to get into the hands of the poor working class. However, as stated previously, progressives were interested in reforming the capitalist system, while American socialists wanted to end capitalism (by this point, by the ballot box). It should be noted that many progressive reformers had knowledge of socialism, some attended socialist meetings at some point in their careers, and a few progressives remained socialists throughout their careers. Upton Sinclair, author of *The Jungle,* was both a progressive and a socialist.

Progressivism was also influenced by religious developments of the era. During this era the **Social Gospel** movement flourished; this movement had its origin in Protestant efforts to aid the urban poor. The Social Gospel movement emphasized the elements of Christianity that emphasized the need to struggle for social justice; followers stated that this fight was much more important than the struggle to lead a "good life" on a personal level. Many progressive leaders (such as Jane Adams) had grown up in very religious homes and found in progressive politics a place where they could put their religious beliefs into action. The Social Gospel movement was strictly a Protestant movement.

Finally, progressives were deeply impacted by the **muckrakers**. Newspaper editors discovered that articles that exposed corruption increased circulation, and thus exposés of unethical practices in political life and business life became common in most newspapers. The term muckrakers was used in a negative way by Theodore Roosevelt, but writers using that title exposed much corruption in American society. *The Jungle* by Upton Sinclair attacked the excesses of the meatpacking industry. Ida Tarbell wrote of the corruption she found in the Standard Oil Trust company, while Lincoln Steffens exposed political corruption found in several American cities in *The Shame of the Cities.* Jacob Riis exposed life in the slums in *How the Other Half Lives.* Progressives wanted to act on the evils of society uncovered by the muckrakers.

THE GOALS OF PROGRESSIVES

The fact that many in the progressive movement were from the middle class greatly influenced the goals of progressivism. Progressives wanted to improve the life experienced by members of the lower classes; at the same time most desired that the nature and pace of this improvement be dictated by them and not the workers themselves. Progressives greatly feared the potential for revolution found in socialist and anarchist writings of the era; they proposed a series of gradual reforms. *Progressives, as stated previously, wanted to make existing institutions work better.* Factories, they felt, could be changed so that they would be concerned with the quality of life of their workers; governments could be altered so that they would act as protectors of the lower classes.

It should be noted that progressive goals and programs were not universally popular. Progressive programs for the betterment of the poor oftentimes meant that the government would have more control over their lives; many in the lower class were vehemently opposed to this. In addition, progressives wanted to crack down on urban political machines, which in many cases did much to aid the lives and conditions of the lower classes. As a result, the very people that progressive reforms were designed to help were oftentimes resentful of these reforms.

URBAN REFORMS

Many of the early successes of progressivism were actions taken against urban political machines. Yet again, some reforms supported by progressives put more power in the hands of those machines. Certain "reform mayors," such as Tom Johnson in Cleveland and Mark Fagan in Jersey City, were legitimately interested in improving the living and working conditions of the lower classes and improving education. In cities such as Cleveland, municipal utilities were taken over by the city to provide more efficient service. Some reform mayors also pushed citywide relief programs and established shelters for the homeless.

Other progressive reformers wanted to professionalize the administrations of various cities and to enact measures so that mere "political hacks" could not get municipal jobs. It should be noted that some of these reforms appeared to be antidemocratic in nature. By attacking the system of political machines and ward politics, reformers were attacking a system that had given a degree of assistance and influence to the urban working classes. The new "professionals" who reformers envisioned getting municipals jobs would be almost exclusively from the middle class, the same class as the reformers themselves.

THE PROGRESSIVES AT THE STATE LEVEL

It was at the state level that some of the most important political work of the progressives took place. Governors Robert La Follette from Wisconsin and Hiram Johnson from California introduced reforms in their states that would allow citizens to have a more direct role in the political process. These reforms included the following:

1. The adoption of the Seventeenth Amendment. Finally adopted in 1913, it allowed voters, instead of the state legislatures, to directly elect United States senators.

2. The adoption of the initiative process. This initiative allowed a citizen to propose a new law. If he or she got enough signatures, the proposed law would appear on the next ballot.
3. The adoption of the referendum process. Referendum allowed citizens to vote or a law that is being considered for adoption.
4. The adoption of the recall process, which allowed the voters to remove an elected official from office before his or her term is up.
5. The adoption of the direct primary, which allowed party members to vote for prospective candidates instead of having them hand-chosen by the party boss.

WOMEN AND PROGRESSIVISM

Women played a major role in progressivism from the very beginning. In 1899 Florence Kelley founded the **National Consumers League**, an organization made up largely of women that lobbied at the state and national level for legislation that would protect both women and children at home and in the workplace. Minimum wage laws for women were enacted in various states beginning in 1911; more stringent child labor laws began to be enacted in states one year later.

Women also played a crucial rule in the creation of **settlement houses**. In 1889 Jane Addams and Ellen Gates Starr founded **Hull House** in Chicago, which would become a model for settlement house construction in other cities. Found at Hull House (and at many other centers) were clubs for adults and children, rooms for classes, and a kindergarten. Settlement house workers also gave poor and immigrant women (and their husbands) advice on countless problems that they encountered in the city. Some settlement houses were more successful than others in actually helping lower-class families cope with urban life. Programs at settlement houses were multidimensional, stressing art, music, drama, and dance. Classes in child care, health education, and adult literacy could be found at most settlement houses.

Women differed greatly on how they felt the urban poor could be helped. Some pushed heavily for reforms in the workplace, while others joined organizations such as the **Anti-Saloon League**, whose members felt that alcohol was the major cause for the woes of the lower classes. Still others became deeply involved in the suffrage movement, oftentimes attempting to get lower-class women interested in the vote as well. Women started to get the vote in individual western states beginning with Idaho, Colorado, and Utah in the 1890s. In 1916 Alice Paul founded the radical **National Woman's party**, and Carrie Chapman Catt founded the **National American Woman's Suffrage Association**. Both organizations would be crucial in the final push for women's suffrage after World War I.

In addition, during this era women in public meetings first began to discuss the topic of **feminism**. The word was first used by a group of women meeting in New York City in 1914. Feminists wanted to remove themselves from the restraints that society had placed on them because they were female. A radical feminist of the time was Margaret Sanger, who as a nurse in New York City observed the lack of knowledge that immigrant women had about the reproductive system. Sanger devoted herself to teaching the poor about birth control and opened the first birth control clinic in the United States.

Some laws were passed in the era to protect working women. In _Muller_ v. _Oregon,_ a case that went all the way to the Supreme Court in 1908, it was ruled constitutional to set limits on the number of hours a woman could work. The rationale given for this, which the Court agreed with, was that too much work would interfere with a woman's prime role as a mother.

REFORMING THE WORKPLACE

Horrible events such as the **Triangle Shirtwaist Fire** convinced many progressives to push for reforms of safety and health conditions in factories. Progressives lobbied hard for the creation of accident insurance programs for workers in New York and elsewhere. From 1910 to 1917, many states adopted legislation that would help to protect families of those killed or injured in workplace and mine accidents.

Progressives and labor unions oftentimes did not see eye to eye. However, one issue that some progressives and unions did agree on was the need to restrict further European immigration, especially from southeastern Europe. Immigrants were not union supporters, and increased immigration would cause a larger supply of labor, thus driving down wages. By not bringing in more immigrants that were "unlike ourselves," supporters stated that city life and morale in the workplace would improve. To some, opposing immigration was a progressive reform. More than anything, this demonstrated that "progressivism" meant very different things to different people.

THE SQUARE DEAL OF THEODORE ROOSEVELT

Theodore Roosevelt's ascendancy to the presidency in 1901 after the assassination of William McKinley brought to office a man unafraid to use the power of the government to address the evils of society. In 1902 Roosevelt helped to mediate a strike between the United Mine Workers and the coal companies. Roosevelt stated that the agreement was a "**Square Deal**" for both sides. This term would be used throughout his time in office to emphasize that government intervention could help the plight of ordinary Americans.

Roosevelt was reelected in 1904, and in 1906 Roosevelt supported legislation that was progressive in nature. He supported the Hepburn Act, which gave teeth to the **Interstate Commerce Commission**, designed to further regulate interstate shippers, and the creation of the **Pure Food and Drug Act** and the **Meat Inspection Act**. The writings of many muckrakers, including Upton Sinclair's *The Jungle,* highlighted many of the problems of the food industry addressed in these bills.

Roosevelt also used the federal government to aggressively investigate and prosecute illegal **trusts** and **holding companies** (both described in Chapter 14). The **Sherman Antitrust Act** had been in place since 1890, yet neither President Cleveland or President McKinley had ordered its enforcement on a regular basis. To many Americans it appeared that a small group of Wall Street bankers controlled the entire American economy (this complaint would be echoed many times in the twentieth century). Roosevelt had the Justice Department sue the Northern Securities Company, a holding company that controlled many American railroads, Standard Oil, and the American Tobacco Company. All were partially broken up as a result of these government actions. By the end of his time in office, Roosevelt had taken on 45 major American corporations. It should be emphasized that Theodore Roosevelt was *not* antibusiness; however, he did strongly believe that corporations who abused their power should be punished.

Roosevelt also enacted other measures applauded by progressives. In 1905 he created the **United States Forest Service**, which soon acted to set aside 200 million acres of land for national forests. The **Sixteenth Amendment**, enacted in 1913, authorized the collection of federal income taxes, which could be collected largely from the wealthy (the income of the federal government had been previously collected from tariffs; progressives argued that to pay for them the prices of goods sold to the working classes were artificially high). In the end the "Square Deal" was based on the idea of creating a level playing field. Roosevelt was not against trusts; he opposed trusts that were harmful to the economy. He supported Standard Oil, for example, because of the benefits he said it brought to America.

PROGRESSIVISM UNDER WILLIAM HOWARD TAFT

Many historians regard Taft as the real trustbuster. More antitrust lawsuits went to court when he was president than during the Roosevelt presidency, although some of them had begun during the Roosevelt administration. In the 1908 presidential election, William Howard Taft, Theodore Roosevelt's hand-picked successor, defeated three-time candidate William Jennings Bryan. In the campaign, Bryan continually came across as supporting more progressive measures than Taft did. Taft did promise to follow Roosevelt's progressive legacy, and to some degree, he followed through on this; during his presidency the Sherman Antitrust Act was used against another 95 corporations.

However, Taft never had the personal magnetism that Roosevelt possessed, and totally unlike Roosevelt, he deferred on important issues to the Congress. Taft was influenced by the conservative wing of the Republican party, which opposed additional progressive reforms. His support of the Payne-Adrich Tariff Act of 1909 further angered progressives, who usually viewed tariffs as hurting the lower classes (since to pay for them the prices of goods were usually higher).

Progressives in the Republican party finally took action against Taft after the **Ballinger-Pinchot Affair**. Richard A. Ballinger was Secretary of the Interior under Taft and allowed private business interests to gain access to several million acres of land in Alaska. A close friend of Roosevelt, Gifford Pinchot, headed the Forest Service. When Pinchot protested against Ballinger's actions in front of a congressional committee, Taft proceeded to fire him. Progressives now labeled Taft as being anti-environment.

Progressive Republicans began to campaign against Taft and the "old guard" of pro-business Republicans. In the 1910 congressional primaries, Taft campaigned against several of these progressives. Theodore Roosevelt, just back from an extended trip to Africa, campaigned for a number of these Republican progressives. His speeches called for more progressive reforms, especially in the workplace. Roosevelt called his program for reform the **New Nationalism**. Roosevelt called again and again for a greatly expanded role of the federal government. As a result of the 1920 congressional elections, progressives dominated the United States Senate.

THE 1912 PRESIDENTIAL ELECTION

By early 1912 Theodore Roosevelt decided that the policies of President Taft were not progressive enough and announced he was running for president. The single event that several biographers say pushed Roosevelt to run was the decision of Taft to go after United States Steel because it had purchased Tennessee Coal and Iron back in 1907. Taft knew that Roosevelt had personally approved this deal. As might be expected, Taft's followers controlled the Republican party machinery, thus allowing Taft to easily win the 1912 Republican nomination.

Roosevelt's followers marched out of the Chicago convention site, proclaimed themselves to be the Progressive party, and nominated Roosevelt for president (with California's progressive governor Hiram Johnson as his running mate). This party soon became known as the **Bull Moose party**. Its platform included many progressive causes, including the elimination of child labor, suffrage for women, and an eight-hour workday. Many women supported the Bull Moose party; in several states where women had the vote, women ran for local offices as members of the party.

The beneficiary of the split in the Republican party was the Democratic candidate Woodrow Wilson, governor of New Jersey. Wilson also campaigned as a progressive, although in his platform, called the

New Freedom policy, he also cautioned against big government. Wilson argued that government was wrong to concentrate on regulating big monopolies; instead, government should be trying to break them up. Wilson won the election, but only received 42 percent of the popular vote. Roosevelt received 27 percent and Taft only 23 percent. It should also be noted that Eugene Debs ran as a candidate of the Socialist party and received 6 percent of the votes. The political will of the times is easily shown in this election: The three candidates openly calling for progressive policies (Wilson, Roosevelt, and Debs) received 75 percent of the popular vote.

THE PROGRESSIVE LEGACY OF WOODROW WILSON

Much legislation was enacted under Woodrow Wilson that pleased reformers. The Underwood Tariff Act of 1913 cut tariffs on imported goods. The Clayton Antitrust Act of 1914 was a continuation of the Sherman Antitrust Act, and outlawed certain specific business practices. A key element of this act also helped the labor movement by making strikes and other labor activities legal. In 1914 the Federal Trade Commission was established; the main job of this organization was to uniformly enforce the antitrust laws. Wilson also signed legislation creating the Federal Reserve system, which established 12 district reserve banks and the creation of Federal Reserve notes. This system was designed to protect the American economy against further panics such as had occurred in the early 1890s.

DID PROGRESSIVISM SUCCEED?

Progressives had done much to improve the condition of American cities, the plight of factory workers, the support available for urban immigrants, and the democratic nature of the American political process. However, progressive reforms did much less for migrant farmers and others outside of the city. Many blacks were disappointed that few alliances ever took place between black leaders and progressives; Theodore Roosevelt met twice with Booker T. Washington but other than that did little to help the conditions of blacks during his presidency. Race riots occurred in Springfield, Illinois, in 1908. The anti-black message of D. W. Griffith's 1915 film *Birth of a Nation* was applauded by many; President Wilson stated that the film presented a "truthful" depiction of the Reconstruction era. In 1909 the National Association for the Advancement of Colored People (NAACP) was founded to further the fight of blacks for political equality in America.

The outbreak of World War I in Europe turned the interests of many away from political reform. Only those reformers concerned with women's suffrage relentlessly pursued their cause during the war years.

CHAPTER REVIEW

Rapid Review Guide

To achieve the perfect 5, you should be able to explain the following:

- Political, economic, and social inequities and problems existed in America in the late 1890s, and the Progressive movement developed to attempt to address some of those problems.

- The Progressive movement did not have a unifying set of goals or leaders.

- Progressives shared some of the critiques of American society as the socialists, but wished to reform and not attack the American system.

- Progressive reformers were closely tied to the Social Gospel movement of the Protestant church; progressivism and religious fervor often marched hand in hand.

- Muckraking magazines and newspapers of the era oftentimes created and published the progressive agenda.

- Many progressives were determined to reform city government and the services provided by city government.

- Progressive political reforms included the initiative process, the referendum, recall, and the direct primary.

- Hull House was an example of a settlement house copied by reformers across the country.

- The presidency of Theodore Roosevelt was a high point of progressivism; Roosevelt's "Square Deal" included many progressive measures.

- Progressive policies were sometimes challenged by Roosevelt's successor, William Howard Taft; the advent of World War I blunted the progressive reform impulse for many.

- Progressivism succeeded in achieving some of its goals but fell short in aiding farmers and minorities in America.

Time Line

1879: *Progress and Poverty* by Henry George published
1888: *Looking Backward* by Edward Bellamy published
1889: Formation of National Consumer's league
1890: National American Woman Suffrage Association founded
1901: Theodore Roosevelt becomes president after assassination of William McKinley
  Progressive Robert La Follette elected as governor of Wisconsin
  Progressive Tom Johnson elected as mayor of Cleveland, Ohio

1903: Founding of Women's Trade Union League
1904: *The Shame of the Cities* by Lincoln Steffens published
1905: IWW (Industrial Workers of the World) established
Establishment of United States Forest Service
1906: *The Jungle* by Upton Sinclair published
Meat Inspection Act enacted
Pure Food and Drug Act enacted
1908: William Howard Taft elected president
1909: Foundation of the NAACP
1910: Ballinger-Pinchot controversy
1911: Triangle Shirtwaist Company fire
1912: Progressive party ("Bull Moose party") founded
by Theodore Roosevelt
Woodrow Wilson elected president
Establishment of Industrial Relations Committee
1913: Establishment of Federal Reserve System
Ratification of Sixteenth Amendment, authorizing federal
income tax
Ratification of Seventeenth Amendment, authorizing direct election of senators
1914: Clayton Antitrust Act ratified
Outbreak of World War I in Europe
1915: First showing of D. W. Griffith's film *Birth of a Nation*

✓ REVIEW QUESTIONS

1. Successful reforms initiated by the progressives included all but which of the following:

   A. Governments became more efficient in American cities such as Cleveland
   B. Health and safety conditions improved in some large factories
   C. The conditions of migrant farmers improved to some degree
   D. Some state governments became more democratic with the introduction of measures such as referendum and recall
   E. The federal government began to collect a national income tax.

(Correct Answer: **C.** Progressives did much less for workers in the agricultural sector than they did for factory workers.)

2. Theodore Roosevelt ran for president in 1912 because

   A. the policies of William Howard Taft's administration were almost exclusively antiprogressive
   B. he desired to split the Republican party and give the election to the Democrats
   C. he was appalled by the results of the Ballinger-Pinchot Affair
   D. of the Taft administration's decision to apply the Sherman Antitrust Act to United States Steel
   E. He felt that Taft was not adequately preparing America for potential war with Europe.

(Correct Answer: **D.** The Taft administration enacted many important progressive measures. Roosevelt considered the actions against United States Steel to be a personal affront to him.)

3. American blacks were discouraged by their lack of racial progress during the

Wilson administration. Which of the following is *not* true.

A. The film *Birth of a Nation* presented a positive view of blacks in Reconstruction states after the Civil War.
B. Black and progressive leaders forged tight political bonds during the Wilson administration and battled for many of the same causes.
C. Springfield, Illinois, was one city that demonstrated positive relations between white citizens and newly arrived blacks.
D. Booker T. Washington and Theodore Roosevelt developed close political ties after their two meetings together.
E. All of the above.

(Correct Answer: **E.** D. W. Griffith's film presented a very negative view of blacks during Reconstruction. Progressives and black leaders never worked closely together. Race riots were held in Springfield, Illinois. Theodore Roosevelt met twice with Booker T. Washington but did little to help the conditions of blacks.)

4. Many progressives agreed with socialists that

A. Capitalism had created massive inequality in America

B. the American factory system had to be fundamentally altered
C. labor unions were inherently evil
D. revolutionary tactics were needed to reform the economic and social systems
E. Factory owners were inherently greedy and could not be trusted

(Correct Answer: **A.** Progressives and socialists were both critical of the effects of capitalism in the United States. Progressives, however, were intent on reforming that system.)

5. Which of the following was least likely to be a progressive in this era?

A. A member of the Industrial Workers of the World
B. A member of the Protestant Social Gospel movement
C. A large stockholder in United States Steel
D. A follower of Eugene Debs
E. A member of the Bull Moose party

(Correct Answer: **C.** Progressives were insistent that corporations like U.S. Steel be made to reform. The IWW shared goals with progressives, as did members of the Social Gospel movement and socialist followers of Debs.)

Chapter 17

The United States and World War I

 Students of world or European history can recall the horrific effects that World War I (or the "Great War," as it was then called) had on France, Germany, and other European nations. Trench warfare, poison gas, and U-boats are known about by virtually everyone who has studied the war. Students of United States history should note that the war had a large effect on America as well. Even though America did not enter the war until 1917, the economic benefits of the war were large; many blacks moved north and found jobs during World War I, and during the war women found that they could be more than stenographers. In addition, during World War I America entered the world stage as a major power. Ironically, America seemed reluctant to accept that role in the immediate postwar years; it was only after World War II that America took on that position with assurance.

THE AMERICAN RESPONSE TO THE OUTBREAK OF WAR

The assassination of the Archduke Franz Ferdinand by Bosnian nationalists on June 28, 1914, set off the series of events that would lead to World War I. Tensions between European powers had been building, with almost all of the major powers undergoing rapid military buildup in the years immediately prior to 1914. These conflicts were caused by increasing nationalism throughout Europe, the competition of imperialism, and the complicated system of alliances that wove together the fates of most European nations. When the war actually began in earnest in August 1914, France, Russia, and Great Britain were the major **Allied powers**, while Germany, Austria-Hungary, and Italy made up the **Central powers**.

Many Americans felt deeply connected to the events of World War I, as over one-third of the American population was a first- or second-generation immigrant. President Wilson and others personally supported the cause of the Allied powers, especially when reports of the alleged barbarism of the German soldiers in the battles of 1914 appeared in American newspapers.

On August 4, 1914, President Wilson issued an official proclamation of American neutrality in the war. Even though most Americans were sympathetic to the cause of the Allied powers, economic common sense dictated that America remain neutral; America in 1914 desired to continue to trade with both sides. After English ships interfered with American trade with Germany and German submarines interfered with American trade with England, America issued a series of diplomatic protests.

INCREASING AMERICAN SUPPORT FOR THE ALLIED POWERS

American sympathies and practical considerations dictated that American trade with the Allies increase as the war progressed. By 1916 American trade with the Central powers was down to near zero, whereas trade with the Allied powers had increased nearly 400 percent. Many who traded with Great Britain urged Washington to begin to prepare the United States for eventual war against Germany. A private **National Security League** was founded in late 1914 to instill patriotism in Americans and to psychologically prepare Americans for war. By the summer of 1915, Congress was taking the first steps to prepare the American army for actual combat in Europe. It should also be noted that peace movements existed in many major America cities, with women making up a large part of the membership of these organizations.

It was the actions of German U-boats that angered many Americans and caused them to favor entering the war against the "**Hun**." According to existing international law, if one ship were to sink another, it first had to board the ship before sinking it and offer all on board "safe passage." The advantage a U-boat had was that it glided underwater undetected and fired at other ships without warning.

Americans were outraged when a German U-boat sank a British passenger ship, the **_Lusitania_**, in the Atlantic Ocean on May 7, 1915; 128 Americans on board all perished. President Wilson issued a strong protest, but it should be noted that the ship was carrying weapons on it meant to help the Allied cause (which made it technically legal for the Germans to sink the ship). In addition, Germany had placed advertisements in major American newspapers warning Americans not to travel on the ship that day.

In August the _Arabic,_ another passenger liner, was sunk by the Germans. President Wilson again forcefully protested; in response the Germans issued the "Arabic pledge," in which they promised to stop sinking passenger ships without warning as long as the crews of the ships allowed the Germans to search the ships.

Official American concern about the actions of the U-boats continued. On March 24, 1916, a French ship called the _Sussex_ was attacked by a U-boat; seven Americans on board were badly injured. The United States threatened to entirely cut diplomatic ties with Germany over this incident. In the **Sussex Pledge** the Germans promised to sink no more ships without prior warning. The actions described above all caused public opinion in the United States to increasingly favor military support of the Allied powers.

AMERICA MOVES TOWARD WAR

Woodrow Wilson won the 1916 presidential election over his Republican opponent Charles Evans Hughes, by stating that the Republicans were the party of war. "He kept us out of war" was the popular slogan of Wilson's supporters. This was a promise, however, that Wilson could not keep for long. On January 31, 1917, Germany announced a policy of **unrestricted submarine warfare**, stating that any ship from any country attempting to enter the ports of Allied nations would be sunk. Historians believed that the Germans knew that eventually the United States would enter the war; by beginning this policy at this time, the Germans were gambling that they could win the war before the United States was truly involved. On February 3 Wilson officially broke off American diplomat relations and suggested to Congress that American merchant ships be armed.

American public opinion became increasingly enraged when they heard about the **Zimmermann Telegram**. This was an intercepted message between Arthur Zimmermann, the German foreign ministry, and German officials in Mexico suggesting that when Germany went to war with the United States, the Mexicans should be persuaded to attack the United States. As a reward, the Mexicans would receive Texas, New Mexico, and Arizona after the United States was defeated.

Between March 16 and March 18 three more American ships were sunk by German vessels. On April 2 President Wilson formally asked Congress for a declaration of war; this declaration was enthusiastically passed the following day. Wilson was motivated to declare war by the legitimate danger to American shipping that existed and by his belief that American entry into the war would help to shorten it.

AMERICA ENTERS THE WAR

By the time the Americans entered the war in April of 1917, the English and the French were desperate for American assistance. The Russian army had suffered crushing defeats since 1916, and in March of 1917 the removal of the tsar from power threw into doubt the entire Russian commitment to the war effort. Without Russia in the war, the Germans could place virtually their entire army in the western front.

The initial **American Expeditionary Force** that landed in France in June 1917 under the command of General John J. Pershing consisted of 14,500 men; its main psychological effect was to help boost the morale of the Allies. Volunteers were recruited to serve in the army, but a Selective Service Act was passed in May 1917. Those originally drafted were between 21 and 30; this was later extended to ages 17 and 46.

Both women and blacks were in the armed forces during the war. Some 11,500 women served, primarily as nurses and clerks, and over 400,000 blacks served. Black units were kept segregated and almost always had white officers.

American shipping to Europe became increasingly disrupted by German U-boats after the formal American declaration of war. Starting in May 1917, all American shipping to Europe traveled in a **convoy system**. The navy developed special torpedo boats that were able to destroy submarines. These techniques drastically decreased the damage done by German U-boats and other ships; only two troop transports were sunk from this point onward, and losses suffered by the merchant marine were much less.

THE IMPACT OF THE AMERICAN EXPEDITIONARY FORCE

The size of the American Expeditionary Force (AEF) expanded to over 2 million by November of 1918, and they were definitely needed. Lenin and the Bolsheviks took over in Russia in November of 1917 and pulled the Russians out of the war. With only one front to worry about, by March of 1918 the Germans had almost all of their troops on the western front, and in early June were less than 50 miles from Paris.

American soldiers played a major role in preventing the Germans from taking Paris. The Americans held firm at the **Battle of Chateau-Thierry**, preventing the Germans from crossing the Marne and advancing toward Paris. Americans were also involved in a major offensive against the Germans in July and decisively defeated the Germans at the Battle of St. Mihiel. Over 1 million AEF forces took part in the final **Meuse-Argonne Offensive** of late September 1918, which cut the supply lines of the Germany army and convinced the German general staff that victory was impossible.

The armistice ending the war was signed on November 11, 1918. Nearly 115,000 Americans died in this war, a mere pittance compared to the nearly 8 million European soldiers who died in battle. American military heroes from World War I included American fighter pilot Eddie Rickenbacker and Captain Alvin York, who single-handedly shot 25 German soldiers and captured another 132.

THE HOME FRONT DURING WORLD WAR I

Despite the fact that America was far removed from the physical fighting of World War I, much had to be done to prepare America for the war effort. Americans were encouraged to buy **Liberty Bonds** to support the war; movie stars of the era such as Charlie Chaplin made speeches and short films extolling the virtues of Liberty Bonds.

Poor harvests in 1916 and 1917 made it necessary to regulate food production and consumption during the war years. In August 1917, Congress passed the **Lever Food and Fuel Control Act**; almost immediately the government began to regulate food consumption. The Food Administration was headed by future President Herbert Hoover, who attempted to increase production and decrease consumption. Hoover's approach to problems was centered around voluntary cooperation, as "Wheatless Mondays" and "Meatless Tuesdays" became commonplace. Harvests greatly improved in 1918 and 1919 as well. The introduction of daylight saving time allowed farmers more time in the evenings to work in the fields and also served to save electricity.

Industry was also regulated by the **War Industries Board**, headed by Wall Street financier Bernard Baruch. This board attempted to stimulate production for the war effort by strictly allocating raw materials and by instituting strict production controls. A Fuel Administration also acted to preserve coal and gasoline; "Fuelless Mondays" and "Gasless Sundays" also existed in 1917 and 1918.

Some historians make the point that World War I was actually the high point of **progressivism**. The government regulated the economy in positive ways that could have only been dreamed about in the days of Theodore Roosevelt. Business leaders loudly claimed they were supporting the war effort (many of them were). As a result, the Sherman Antitrust Laws were largely forgotten during World War I.

KEEPING AMERICA PATRIOTIC

Another new agency created in 1917 was the **Committee on Public Information**, headed by George Creel. The job of this agency was to spread anti-German and pro-Allied propaganda through newsreels and lectures, and through the cooperation of the press. Germans were portrayed as beastlike **Huns** wherever possible. Liberty Leagues were established in communities across America; members of these organizations were encouraged to report suspicious actions by anyone (especially foreigners) to their local authorities. George Creel asked newspapers to voluntarily censor themselves and to print only articles that would be helpful to the war effort.

A fine line between patriotism and oppression existed during much of World War I. **The National Security League** convinced Congress to insist on a literacy test for all new immigrants. German language instruction, German music, and even pretzels were banned in some cities. In April 1918 a German-born American citizen was lynched outside of St. Louis; ironically, an investigation found that he had recently attempted to enlist in the American navy.

Most Americans felt they were fighting the war to help the spread of democracy, yet many critics lamented some of the actions taken by the government during the war era. The 1917 **Espionage Act** made it illegal to obstruct the draft process in any way and stated that any material that was sent through the mail that was said to incite treason could be seized. The **Sedition Act** of 1918 stated that it was illegal to criticize the government, the Constitution, the U.S. Army, or the U.S. Navy. Prominent socialist Eugene Debs received a 10-year prison term for speaking against militarism; movie producer Robert Goldstein was even sentenced to 10 years in prison for showing the Americans fighting the British in a Revolutionary War film. Radical labor unions such as the IWW were also harassed during the war years. Over 1000 Americans were found guilty of violations of either the Espionage Act or the Sedition Act.

The war did provide a measure of social mobility for blacks and women. With large numbers of men fighting in Europe and no immigrants entering the country, northern factories needed workers, and encouraged blacks to move north to take factory jobs. This move north was called the **Great Migration**; during the war nearly 600,000 blacks moved north. Many women were able to find jobs on farms or in factories for the very first time during the war. After the war, men would replace them in the labor market and force them to return to the "women's sphere."

WOODROW WILSON AND THE TREATY OF VERSAILLES

The Paris Peace Conference began on January 12, 1919, and had the very difficult task of creating a lasting European peace. The conference was dominated by the "Big Four": the representatives of England, France, Italy (which had switched sides in the middle of the war), and the United States.

Woodrow Wilson was treated as a hero when he arrived in Paris, yet it was obvious in the initial sessions of the peace conference that the leaders of the victorious countries had very different goals. The suffering of England and especially France during the war was horrific; the goals of the French delegation was clearly to punish Germany as much as possible. Woodrow Wilson, on the other hand, came to France supporting his **Fourteen Points**, which called for open peace treaties, freedom of the seas, free trade, arms reduction, a gradual reduction of colonial claims, and some sort of a world organization to ensure peace. Wilson's plan was coolly received in France; the French, as stated previously, were mainly interested in what they could get out of the Germans. It was also coolly received in the United States by those who were opposed to continued American involvement in European affairs.

Wilson's Fourteen Points were largely opposed by the other members of the Big Four. Wilson called for a reduction of colonial claims: England and France had every intention of taking Germany's colonies after the war. When the treaty was finally signed, Wilson got only a fraction of what he initially wanted. Germany was held responsible for the war and was made to pay reparations. The **League of Nations** was created, although initially without Germany and the Bolshevik-led Soviet Union. Wilson believed that this was the most important of the Fourteen Points, so he did not leave Paris totally discouraged.

THE TREATY OF VERSAILLES AND THE UNITED STATES SENATE

Woodrow Wilson had not appointed a Republican member of the Senate to the United States delegation to the Paris Peace Conference. This proved to be a huge political mistake. Wilson returned from Paris, needing Senate confirmation of the Treaty of Versailles. Many Republicans in the Senate had huge reservations about the treaty; all of them centered around American commitment to the League of Nations. A dozen senators were "<u>irreconcilables</u>," opposed to American membership in the League under any circumstances. Another large group, led by Henry Cabot Lodge, were called "<u>reservationists</u>" and wanted restrictions on American membership in the League. Lodge, for example, wanted it stated that the Congress would have to approve any American action on behalf of the League, and that provisions of the Monroe Doctrine remain in place even if the League of Nations opposed them.

To win national support for the Versailles Treaty, Wilson began a national speaking tour on September 3, 1919. On October 2 he suffered a severe stroke and never totally recovered. Lodge stated that he would support passage of the Versailles Treaty with certain reservations; Wilson rejected the reservations, and the treaty never got the two-thirds majority necessary for its passage. Many politicians both at home and abroad urged Wilson to compromise with congressional leaders and to get America into the League of Nations. Wilson was never willing to do this; his chief biographer maintains that his stroke impeded his judgment during this era, and that if he had not had a stroke, a compromise would have been struck. In 1921 the United States formally ended the war with Germany, but the United States never entered the League of Nations.

THE CONSEQUENCES OF AMERICAN ACTIONS AFTER THE WAR

The failure of the United States to join the League of Nations greatly affected European affairs in the succeeding decades. The League of Nations was never the organization it could have been with American involvement. Many European leaders felt that the United States could have been the "honest broker" in the League, and that with U.S. involvement the League could have had more substance. In addition, Europeans expected the United States to be a major player in European and world affairs in the years following the war. Led by the Senate, the United States backed off of the commitment, and entered a period of isolationism that would last through the 1930s. It was only after World War II in 1945 that America finally took the role that many thought it would take in 1920.

CHAPTER REVIEW

Rapid Review Guide

To achieve the perfect 5, you should be able to explain the following:

- World War I greatly impacted the American mind-set and America's role in world affairs; this was the first time that America became directly involved in affairs taking place on the European continent.

- Many American expressed support for the Allied powers from the beginning of the war; German U-boat attacks solidified American support for Britain and France.

- The sinking of the *Lusitania* and the Zimmermann Telegram did much to intensify American anger against Germany.

- Germany's decision to utilize unrestricted submarine warfare caused President Wilson to call for war in 1917; Wilson claimed that this policy violated America's rights as a neutral power.

- The American Expeditionary Force did much to aid the Allied war effort, both militarily and psychologically.

- The federal government did much to mobilize the American population at home for the war effort; Liberty bonds were sold, voluntary rationing took place, and propaganda was used to encourage Americans to oppose the "Hun" however possible.

- Many blacks moved to northern cities to work in factories during World War I; this migration would continue through the 1920s.

- Woodrow Wilson's Fourteen Points met opposition from French and English leaders at the Paris Peace Conference; many of them had to be abandoned to secure the creation of the League of Nations.

- The Treaty of Versailles was opposed by U.S. Senators who felt that America should pursue an isolationist policy after the war. As a result, the treaty was never signed by the United States and the United States never joined the League of Nations.

- Many Europeans leaders expected America to be active as a leader in world affairs after World War I. Instead, America adopted neo-isolationist policies that lasted until America entered World War II.

Time Line

1914: Outbreak of World War I in Europe
Woodrow Wilson officially proclaims American neutrality in World War I
National Security League founded to prepare America for war

1915: Sinking of the *Lusitania* by German U-boat

1916: Germany torpedoes *Sussex,* then promises to warn merchants ships if they are to be attacked

Woodrow Wilson reelected with campaign slogan of "He kept us out of war"

1917: Zimmermann Telegram

Germany declares unrestricted submarine warfare

United States enters World War I, stating that U.S. rights as a neutral had been violated

Russian Revolution; Russian-German peace talks

Conscription begins in United States

War Industries Board formed to create a war economy

Espionage Act passed

American Expeditionary Force lands in France

1918: Military success by American Expeditionary Force at Chateau-Thierry

Sedition Act passed; free speech limited (illegal to criticize government or American military forces)

Wilson announces the Fourteen Points

Armistice ends World War I (November 11)

1919: Paris Peace Conference creates Treaty of Versailles

Race riots in Chicago

Wilson suffers stroke during speaking tour promoting Treaty of Versailles

Senate rejects Treaty of Versailles; United States does not join League of Nations

✓ Review Questions

1. All of the following events prepared America for war against Germany *except*

   A. accounts of the conduct of the "Huns" during military operations reported in many American newspapers
   B. the Sussex Pledge
   C. German policy concerning use of U-boats in 1917
   D. the sinking of the *Lusitania*
   E. The Zimmermann telegram

(Correct Answer: **B.** In the Sussex Pledge the Germans actually promised not to sink American merchant ships without warning. All of the other choices deeply angered many in America. It was reported in American newspapers that German soldiers—"Huns"—ate babies in villages they occupied, although there was no evidence that this had ever actually occurred.)

2. The French were opposed to many of Wilson's Fourteen Points because

   A. they were fundamentally opposed to the creation of a world body such as the League of Nations
   B. they felt that the French and the Italians should formulate the major provisions of the treaty
   C. they were angry that Wilson had insisted that the Germans not take part in the creation of the treaty

D. French diplomats had little respect for Wilson and his American counterparts

E. the Fourteen Points disagreed fundamentally with what the French felt should be contained in the Treaty of Versailles

(Correct Answer: **E.** While Wilson saw the treaty as an opportunity to create a democratic world free of old diplomatic entanglements, the French saw the treaty as an opportunity to punish the Germans in as many ways as possible, as much of the fighting of the war had taken place on French territory.)

3. After America declared war in 1917

A. millions of American men showed up at draft boards across the country to volunteer for the war

B. ration cards were issued to all families

C. camps were set up to detain "troublesome" Americans of German background

D. drills took place in American cities to prepare Americans for a possible attack

E. movie stars and other celebrities helped sell Liberty Bonds to the American public

(Correct Answer: **E.** Charlie Chaplin and others appeared at rallies and encouraged Americans to buy Liberty Bonds. A draft was needed to get enough American soldiers for the war; rationing during World War I was voluntary.)

4. Some critics maintained that the United States had no right to be outraged over the sinking of the *Lusitania* because

A. the *Lusitania* was carrying contraband, which meant that it could legally be sunk

B. the Germans had sunk a passenger ship before

C. the Germans had placed advertisements in American newspapers warning Americans not to travel on the *Lusitania*

D. German U-boat policies were well publicized

E. All of the above

(Correct Answer: **E.** Six months earlier the Germans had sunk the *Arabic*, another passenger liner. Many maintain that the advertisements the Germans put in American newspapers were strong enough warnings that the ship was going to be sunk.)

5. Many senators were opposed to American entry into the League of Nations because

A. they feared that the United States would end up financing the organization

B. they feared the U.S. Army would be sent into action on "League of Nations business" without congressional authorization

C. American opinion polls demonstrated that the American public was almost unanimously opposed to American entry into the League

D. they feared that the Germans and the Russians would dominate the League

E. Warren G. Harding, Wilson's vice president, was a staunch isolationist

(Correct Answer: **B.** A major fear of many influential senators was that American entry into the League would cause Congress to lose its right to right to declare war and approve American military actions. It should be noted that Germany and the Soviet Union were not initially members of the League of Nations.)

Chapter 18

America in the 1920s: The Beginning of Modern America

 During the 1920s tremendous transformations took place in America. Incredible industrial growth created a **consumer economy**, with washing machines, radios, and automobiles available to every household that was willing to pay for these and other products using the installment plan. The continued migration of America from rural areas to the cities finally created a nation in 1925 where the majority lived in urban settings. A **national culture** was created during the 1920s; this was largely caused by the advent of the radio, the massive increase in advertising, and the incredible increase in popularity of motion pictures.

The nationalization (and urbanization) of American culture was resisted by many in small-town and rural America. Many of the cultural conflicts of the 1920s, including battles over Prohibition, evolution, racism, and immigration, were caused by attempts of the America that was "being left behind" to attempt to keep small-town, rural values prominent in American society.

A DECADE OF PROSPERITY

By the middle of the 1920s many of the dire predictions of the effects of capitalism that had been preached by progressives 15 years earlier seemed like no more than ancient history. Business opportunities were plentiful: The prosecution of trusts, which took up much of the Justice Department's time in World War I, were few in the 1920s. New opportunists with capital could challenge corporations like U.S. Steel and make profits doing it. Nevertheless, certain industries, such as the automobile industry, were virtually impossible to crack; by 1929 Ford, General Motors, and Chrysler controlled nearly 85 percent of all auto sales. Socialist predictions that the plight of the workers were getting worse seemed to be negated by statistics published in 1924 stating that industrial workers were making nearly double what they had made 10 years earlier.

Strikes and union activities were plentiful in the two years immediately following the end of World War I, but diminished greatly after that (many factory owners realized that paying their workers a decent wage would make them less likely to listen to speeches made by union "agitators").

By the mid-1920s products made in American factories were available to Americans and also in many European and other world markets. The assembly line of Henry Ford continued to be perfected to the point that by 1925 a **Model T** was being produced in a Ford plant every 24 seconds. During the decade, the ideas of "scientific management" first proposed by Frederick W. Taylor (see Chapter 14) were utilized in businesses and factories across the country. Production was now being done more efficiently; this ultimately lowered the cost of production and the cost to the consumer.

Many other consumer products, such as vacuum cleaners, refrigerators, and: radios, were also churned out by American factories at record rates. Many of the products also were produced by assembly line techniques, and the stream of workers who continued to enter the cities from rural America could get work doing one of the monotonous jobs involved in assembly line production. For the consumer, products that were impossible to even dream about 10 years early could now be purchased with the installment plan. For 36 or 48 "easy" payments, a middle-class family in the 1920s could have an automobile, a refrigerator, *and* a vacuum cleaner. Some economists saw danger in the fact that by 1928 nearly 65 percent of all automobiles were being purchased on credit. Most Americans saw little problem with this, since they could not foresee a time when Americans would be unable to make payments on these goods.

The decade of the 1920s can be certainly seen as the beginning of the **advertising age**. Consumers were warned that if they wanted to live the "good life," they *had* to have the latest model refrigerator or automobile. People living in urban, suburban, and rural areas all saw the same advertisements for products that had been placed in both national and local publications by advertising men. As stated previously, this helped to create a universal national culture: Advertisements showed the farmer in Kansas and the suburbanite in Connecticut that they *had* to have exactly the same product.

REPUBLICAN LEADERSHIP IN THE 1920s

Throughout the 1920s the Republican party was truly dominant at the national level. Both houses of Congress were under Republican control, the three presidents of the decade (Warren G. Harding, Calvin Coolidge, and Herbert Hoover) were all Republicans, and for most of the decade the Supreme Court was dominated by Chief Justice (and ex-president) William Howard Taft. Government policies throughout the decade were almost exclusively pro-business; Republican candidates at all levels during this decade *had* to be acceptable to the business community.

THE PRESIDENCY OF WARREN G. HARDING

Many presidential scholars claim that Warren G. Harding was one of the least qualified men ever nominated for the presidency by a major party in America. Harding, a senator from Ohio, was not even mentioned as a possible candidate before the Republican convention of 1920. Harding finally became the Republican nominee after the party bosses determined that he would be a candidate they could control. He was opposed in the national election by Governor James Cox of Ohio. Harding ran on a platform of low taxes, high tariffs, farmer's assistance, and opposition to the League of Nations.

Where Governor Cox (and his running mate, Assistant Secretary of the Navy Franklin D. Roosevelt) ran a strong and aggressive campaign, Harding was generally content to campaign from own back porch. He ended up winning 61 percent of the national vote. Americans found something they liked in both the message and style of Harding: His message was essentially that it was time to pull back from "schemes" to change the world (the postwar plans of Woodrow Wilson) and "social experiment" (all of the programs of the progressives). Harding's call for a period of "normalcy" struck a chord with Americans and seemed to put the final nail in the coffin of progressivism in American thought.

During the presidency of Harding, efforts were made to prevent America from having any involvement with the League of Nations or any other provision of the Versailles Treaty. One of the outstanding appointments made by Harding was the naming of former Supreme Court Justice Charles Evans Hughes as Secretary of State. Hughes' major accomplishment as Secretary of State took place at the **Washington Conference** of 1921. At this meeting diplomats from the United States, Japan, China, the Netherlands, Belgium, Portugal, France, Great Britain, and Italy met to discuss the possible elimination of further naval development and affairs in China and the rest of Asia. All nine nations agreed to respect the independence of China (and maintaining the Open Door in China), a major goal of American business interests. The United States, Britain, France, Japan, and Italy all agreed to halt the construction of naval vessels (at the time Hughes did not realize that this gave naval superiority in the Pacific to the Japanese).

Another notable appointment by Harding was the naming of Andrew Mellon, the "richest man in America," as Secretary of the Treasury. Mellon firmly believed in the traditional Republican tenant that very low taxes would ultimately encourage business investment and ensure economic prosperity. To do this, Mellon sought to reduce government spending in any way possible, and to reduce taxes, especially for the wealthier business classes. To cut expenses, Harding opposed bonus payments to World War I veterans in 1921; some benefits for veterans were authorized by the Congress. In the Revenue Act of 1921 the administration proposed large reductions in the amounts of taxes that the wealthiest Americans would have to pay (protests from some Republicans from farm states caused these reductions to be less than Mellon desired). In the end, many of Mellon's policies increased the economic pain of the working class while benefiting the rich.

To assist American business interests, Mellon also wanted large tariff increases on imported industrial goods. The **Fordney-McCumber Tariff** of 1922 did increase the tariffs on industrial products. However, to appease Republicans from farm states the largest tariff increases were on imported farm products.

Little was done in the Harding administration to assist organized labor. Many court decisions of the decade took the side of management, including several court decisions that overturned lower-court rulings making child labor illegal. It was clear in the decade that the interests of farmers and the interests of industrial workers were very dissimilar.

THE SCANDALS OF THE HARDING ADMINISTRATION

The Harding administration may have been the most scandal-ridden administration in American political history. No principal whatsoever was involved in these scandals; the participants were only interested in money. There is no knowledge that Harding participated in any way in these scandals; his biggest sin was probably appointing political cronies from his Ohio days to important government positions in his administration and not supervising them.

The scandals of the Harding administration were numerous. Charles Forbes, the director of the Veteran's Bureau, stole or horribly misused nearly $250 million of government money; he was indicted for fraud and bribery concerning government hospital supply contracts. Harding allowed Forbes to go abroad and to resign, although he eventually did go to jail. Attorney General Harry Daugherty had taken bribes from businessmen, bootleggers, and many others. Daugherty failed to go to jail when a hung jury was unable to convict him.

The worst of the scandals was the **Teapot Dome** scandal. Secretary of the Interior Albert Fall maneuvered to have two oil deposits put under the jurisdiction of the Department of the Interior; one of these was a reserve in Wyoming called Teapot Dome. Fall then leased these reserves to private companies and got large sums of money from them for doing it. Fall was convicted and finally went to prison in 1929.

The revelation of these scandals greatly bothered Harding, who died of a stroke on August 2, 1923. He was replaced by his vice president, Calvin Coolidge of Vermont.

THE PRESIDENCY OF CALVIN COOLIDGE

American business leaders could have had no better friend in the White House than Calvin Coolidge. His credo was that "the business of the United States is business." Coolidge did little as president, but this was largely intentional; he was convinced that the major decisions affecting American society should be made by businessmen. Like Harding, Coolidge believed in increased tax cuts for the wealthy and favored policies that would help promote American business.

Several decisions made during Coolidge's presidency demonstrate the administration's thinking. Coolidge proposed that a dam constructed at Muscle Shoals, Alabama, on the Tennessee River by the government during World War I be turned over to private interests; this plan was defeated by the Congress (the dam would become a crucial part of the Tennessee Valley Authority in the 1930s). In the Revenue Act of 1926 large tax cuts were given to the wealthiest members of society. Finally, on the grounds that the government couldn't afford it, Coolidge vetoed payments to World War I veterans (Congress passed the legislation over the president's veto).

THE ELECTION OF 1928

Coolidge announced "I do not choose to run" several months before the 1928 presidential election. The Republicans nominated Secretary of Commerce Herbert Hoover. Hoover was a seemingly perfect candidate for the mood of the era. He was a self-made man, worked his way through Stanford, made his first million in business before he was 40, and had run relief efforts in Belgium and the Commerce Department with tremendous, although unsmiling, efficiency. Hoover's campaign speeches emphasized the achievements of past Republican administrations that had created prosperity and the possibilities for success possible through rugged individualism.

The Democratic candidate was New York Governor Al Smith, an opponent of Prohibition and a Catholic. Many Southern Democrats had obvious suspicions about him; Smith's supporters received their support by promising that the Democratic platform would say nothing about the repeal of Prohibition. The election was a landslide for Hoover, with Smith only winning eight states. Nevertheless, the fact that many people living in the large cities of America voted for Smith showed the divisions that existed in American society in the 1920s.

URBAN VS. RURAL: THE GREAT DIVIDE OF THE 1920s

As stated previously, the 1920s was the decade that the United States, population-wise, became an urban country. Tremendous resentment existed in rural and small-town America against the growing urban mind-set that was increasingly permeating America. Many citizens who did not live in America's cities felt that the values associated with urban life needed to be opposed. From these sentiments came many of the great cultural battles that were at the center of American life in the 1920s.

Many in the North and the South shared resentment against black Americans in the years immediately after World War I. A number of blacks had come North during the war to take factory jobs in urban centers; now that the war was over, many Northerners saw them as competitors for prime industrial employment. In 1919 large race riots took place in Washington, DC, and in many other Northern cities; anti-black riots in Chicago lasted nearly two weeks. Press reports of these riots oftentimes noted the participation of white veterans.

During the postwar years violence against blacks intensified in the South as well. Lynchings increased dramatically in the postwar years; over 70 blacks were lynched in 1919 alone. The response by some blacks was to think of leaving the United States altogether; beginning in 1920 sign-ups began for the **Universal Negro Improvement Association**, headed by Marcus Garvey. Garvey called on blacks to come with him to Africa to create a new empire (with him on the throne). By 1925 nearly half a million people had expressed interest in Garvey's scheme. In the end the Garvey program was a failure, since few blacks actually went to Africa, and many of those that did go ended up returning to the United States. Garvey was later arrested and jailed for fraud, but the fact that his plan attracted so many black supporters demonstrated the plight of black Americans.

The **Ku Klux Klan** grew tremendously during the early 1920s; by 1925 the Klan's membership was over 5 million. Unlike the Klan of the Reconstruction era, membership in the Klan was not entirely from the South, although it *was* almost entirely from rural and small-town America (Indiana was a huge hotbed of Klan activity in the 1920s). Blacks continued to be a target of the Klan, as were other groups who appeared to be "enemies" of the rural way of life, such as Catholics and immigrants. The Klan had tremendous political power in several states, although terror tactics such as lynchings and cross burnings remained a dominant part of Klan activity.

The Klan began to lose its popularity in 1925 with revelations of scandals involving Klan members, including the murder conviction of the leader of the Klan in Indiana. Many historians see the popularity of the Klan in the 1920s as a symbol of the intolerance prominent in much of American society; several see it as an American version of totalitarianism, which took control in Germany, the Soviet Union, and Italy during this period.

Many Americans in the years following World War I were also terrified of Bolshevism. America, to no avail, gave military aid and actual manpower to forces attempting to overthrow Lenin and Bolsheviks in the years immediately following the Russian Revolution of 1917. Much about Bolshevism (soon to be called communism) was in opposition to mainstream American thought. Communism taught that capitalism was evil, and that worker's revolutions would soon break out in highly industrialized countries like the United States. As a result, a **Red Scare** developed in America in 1919. Many historians maintain that Americans were not just opposed to the ideas of communism, but that many Americans began to see everything wrong in American society as a creation of the "Reds."

Beginning in November of 1919 Attorney General Mitchell Palmer carried out raids on the homes and places of employment of suspected radicals. As a result of the **Palmer Raids**, thousands of Americans were arrested, in many cases for no other crime than the fact that they were not born in the United States. Hundreds of former immigrants were sent back to their countries of origin, even though it was never proven (or even in most cases even charged) that they were political radicals. The Red Scare demonstrated the nativism present in American during the period. This was also one of the worst examples in American history of the trampling of the constitutional rights of American citizens.

Nativism probably also accounts for the results of the case of Sacco and Vanzetti. Both were Italian immigrants, and were charged with the murdering of two employees of a shoe company in Massachusetts in 1920. Although there was little evidence against them, they were convicted and finally executed in 1927.

American nativism also was displayed in immigration legislation that was passed in the early 1920s. Many in small-town America blamed the problems of America on the continued inflow of immigrants to the country; pseudoscientific texts published in the first part of the decade claimed that the white Americans were naturally superior to Southern and Eastern Europeans as well as blacks, but warned that these groups had to be carefully controlled to prevent them from attempting to dominate the country.

The Congress passed the **Emergency Quota Act** of 1921, which limited immigration to 3 percent of the number of persons each country had living in the United States in 1910. This act limited the immigration of Eastern and Southern Europeans, and cut immigration in 1922 to roughly 40 percent of its 1921 totals. A real blow to immigration was the **National Origins Act** of 1924. This legislation took that number of immigrants from each foreign country living in the United States in 1890, and stated that immigration to the United States from these countries could now be no more than 2 percent of that; the bill also stated that no more than 150,000 new immigrants could come from outside the Western Hemisphere. In addition, all immigration from Asia was halted. The intent and the effect of this legislation was obvious. Immigration from countries such as Italy and Poland was virtually halted.

Another area where urban and rural/small-town interests clashed was over the issue of Prohibition. Statistics from 1924 stated that in Kansas 95 percent of citizens were obeying the Prohibition law, while in New York state the number obeying was close to 5 percent. For many small-town observers, alcohol, immigrants, and urban life were viewed together as one giant evil. Many small-town preachers spoke of alcohol as an "instrument of the devil" and were outraged that the law was not enforced in places like New York City.

However, the enforcement of Prohibition in a city like New York would have been virtually impossible. Neither the citizenry nor elected officials favored enforcement (it was reported that Warren Harding had a large collection of bootlegged alcohol that he served to guests). **Speakeasies** were frequented by police officers and city officials in many locations; "bathtub gin," some of it good and some of it absolutely atrocious, was also consumed by thousands eager for some form of alcohol during the Prohibition era. Bootlegging of alcohol allowed many famous gangsters of the 1930s to get their feet wet in the world of organized crime; Al Capone in Chicago became the king of the bootleggers, with judges, newspapers, and elected government officials all eventually under his control.

The final area where urban and rural/small-town mind-sets drastically differed was over religion and evolution. Many in small-town America felt vaguely threatened by the changes that science had brought about, and clung to the literal interpretation of the Bible as a defense. William Jennings Bryan and others led the charge against the teachings of Darwin in the postwar years. In 1925, Bryan assisted a group in Tennessee in drafting a bill that would outlaw the teaching of evolution in the state. The American Civil Liberties Union offered to assist any teacher who would challenge this law, and John Scopes of Dayton, Tennessee, volunteered. For several weeks in 1925, the **Scopes Trial** (or "monkey trial") riveted the nation.

One of America's finest lawyers, Clarence Darrow, assisted Scopes, while Bryan was retained to work with prosecutors who wanted to convict Scopes. Scopes was found guilty and fined (this was later overturned on a technicality), but the real drama of the trial was when Darrow questioned Bryan, who took the stand as an "expert on the Bible." Bryan seriously discredited the entire cause of **creationism** when he admitted on the stand that he personally did not take every fact found in the Bible literally.

CULTURE IN THE 1920s

Vast numbers of Americans were attracted to the culture of business that so permeated American life in the 1920s. It was possible, it was felt, that an individual could start with nothing and become a millionaire (a few buying land in Florida and elsewhere did exactly that). It is no surprise that individual heroes were worshipped in the press, on the radio, and on street corners. Sports heroes such as Babe Ruth were perceived as hardly mortal (members of the press had to cover up the excesses found in the personal lives of Ruth and many other heroes). Newspapers delighted in reporting incidents such as those involving Ruth visiting children's hospitals and promising countless home runs for sick children.

Other heroes of the decade included other athletes, such as boxer Jack Dempsey and movie stars Rudolph Valentino, Charlie Chaplin, Clara Bow, and Mary Pickford. No hero, however, was lionized more than Charles Lindbergh after he became the first person to fly across the Atlantic Ocean by himself in 1927. Incredible numbers of songs and newspaper headlines were devoted to Lindbergh for several years after this historic flight.

THE JAZZ AGE

Many Americans rejected the values of business civilization adopted by many in the decade. These people, both men and women, decided that pleasure and private expression were more important than the virtues of Taylorism. Those associated with the **Jazz Age** adopted more open attitudes toward sex, and adopted jazz music as another symbol of their rejection of traditional society. Rural/small-town America (and some in the cities) saw jazz as "the devil's music," as black music, and as a music that helped to promote lewd dancing and sexual contact. For many who went to jazz clubs in Harlem in the early 1920s, these were probably the very reasons they listened to it.

The typical symbol of the Jazz Age was the **flapper**, a young girl with short hair, a short hemline, a cigarette in her hand, and makeup (all of these things were frowned on in rural/small-town America and in pre-World War I urban America). The number of actual flappers in American cities was always relatively small. Many advertisements of the 1920s portrayed women as sex objects; as a result, in the eyes of many Americans, women lost their respected position as moral leaders of the family.

Statistics do show that both sexual promiscuity and the consumption of alcohol increased among the young during this decade. This revolution was greatly aided by the availability of the automobile, which allowed young people to get away from the prying eyes of parents. Margaret Sanger and others promoted the increased availability and usage of birth control during this period. The behavior of flappers and their male counterparts was looked down on by some urban and by almost all rural observers. It should be noted that this "freer" behavior by young people would be drastically reduced by the massive economic difficulties of the Great Depression and World War II, but would again become pronounced in the 1950s (with critics voicing many of the same criticisms as critics had in the 1920s). By the 1950s rock and roll had replaced jazz as the "devil's music."

After the passage of the Nineteenth Amendment in 1920, which gave women the right to vote, many female leaders thought that women would come to have a pronounced role in American political life. Much to their disappointment, this did not occur in the 1920s. Women did not vote in a block "as women." Yet the overall position of women did increase in the decade. Divorces increased throughout the decade, showing that more women (and men) were leaving unhealthy marriage relationships. The number of women working during the decade also increased, although working women were usually single. Restrictions remained, however. Women seldom received the same pay for doing the same work as a man, and women were almost never put into management positions. Most women still worked in clerical jobs, as teachers, or as nurses.

The Rise of Radio and Motion Pictures

As stated previously, as more and more people read newspapers, listened to the radio, and watched movies, a truly universal mass culture was being created. Movie attendance rose incredibly during the 1920s; in 1922 about 35 million people a week saw movies. By 1929 this figure was up to 90 million people per week. In 1927 **_The Jazz Singer_**, staring Al Jolson, became the first "talking" motion picture, a trend that would create new movie stars and ruin the careers of others who had been stars in the silent era.

Nothing created a more national mass culture than did the radio. Station KDKA in Pittsburgh was the first station to get a radio station license in 1920. Radio networks began to form (the National Broadcasting Company being the first in 1926) and brought listeners across the country news, variety shows, and (at first) re-created sporting events.

THE LOST GENERATION

Many novels were written during the 1920s that supported the business culture of the decade. The most famous of these was Bruce Barton's 1925 *The Man Nobody Knows,* which portrayed Christ as a businessman. Most famous novelists of the era, however, wrote of deep feelings of alienation from mainstream American culture. These writers, called by Gertrude Stein members of the "**Lost Generation**," turned their backs on the business culture and the Republican political culture of the era. Some of these writers ended up in Paris, while others congregated in Greenwich Village in New York City.

The goal of these writers seemed to be to attack the notion of America that they had either physically or spiritually left behind. In novels such as *Main Street* and *Babbit,* Sinclair Lewis attacked the materialism and narrow thinking of middle-class business-types in small-town America. Sherwood Anderson's *Winesburg, Ohio* was another novel of alienation in small-town America.

F. Scott Fitzgerald was both a celebrant of the Jazz Age and a brilliant commentator on it; his novel *The Great Gatsby* dissects the characters of typical Jazz Age figures. Ernest Hemingway in works such as *A Farewell to Arms* express a deep dissatisfaction with American values, especially concerning war. Perhaps none was more direct in his criticisms of American society than journalist H. L. Mencken, who called the American people an "ignorant mob" and was especially disdainful of the "booboisie," his term for the American middle class.

It should also be remembered that in the 1920s black cultural expression was being celebrated in a cultural movement called the **Harlem Renaissance**. Writers of this movement, including Langston Hughes and Zora Neale Hurston, wrote of the role of blacks in contemporary American society; the theme of blacks "passing" into the white world and the importance of black expression were common themes among writers of the Harlem Renaissance. Many in the Harlem Renaissance studied African folk art and music and anthropology. The goal of many in the movement was reconciling the notions of being black and being American (and also to reconcile the notions of being black and being intellectual). Jazz was the music of the movement, with Louis Armstrong and Duke Ellington playing this "primitive music" in clubs across Harlem.

When Herbert Hoover was inaugurated in early 1929, America looked to the 1930s with eager anticipation. The stock market was at an all-time high, and Hoover had continually promised during the campaign that the Republican goal was to wipe out poverty once and for all. All of this would make the events that would begin to unfold in the fall of 1929 even more cruel and devastating.

CHAPTER REVIEW

Rapid Review Guide

To achieve the perfect 5, you should be able to explain the following:

- A consumer economy was created in the 1920s on a level unprecedented in American history.

- Advertising, newspapers, radio, and motion pictures provided new forms of entertainment in the 1920s and helped to create a uniform national culture.

- The changes of the 1920s were resisted by many in small-town/rural America, creating many of the cultural conflicts of the decade.

- Assembly line techniques and the ideas of scientific management of Frederick W. Taylor helped to make industrial production in the 1920s quicker and more efficient, ultimately creating cheaper goods.

- Installment buying helped to fuel consumer buying in the 1920s.

- The Republican party controlled the White House, the Congress, and the Supreme Court in the 1920s, generally sponsoring government policies friendly to big business.

- The scandals of the Harding administration were among the worst in history.

- Resentment against blacks existed in both the American South and North in the years after World War I, resulting in race riots in the North and lynchings and the rebirth of the Ku Klux Klan in the South.

- The Red Scare of 1919 and 1920 resulted in the suspension of civil liberties and deportation of hundred of immigrants, the vast majority of which had committed no crime.

- Nativist fears also resulted in restrictive quota legislation passed in the early 1920s.

- Cultural conflicts between urban and rural American also developed over the issues of Prohibition and the teaching of evolution in schools (resulting in the Scopes Trial).

- During the Jazz Age many Americans rejected the prominent business values of the decade and turned to jazz, alcohol, and looser sexual mores for personal fulfillment.

- The flapper was the single most prominent image of the Jazz Age.

- Writers of the Lost Generation expressed extreme disillusionment with American society of the era; writers of the Harlem Renaissance expressed the opinions of American blacks concerning American culture.

Time Line

1917: Race riots in East St. Louis, Missouri
1918: Armistice ending World War I
1919: Race riots in Chicago
Major strikes in Seattle and Boston
Palmer Raids
1920: Warren Harding elected president
First broadcast of radio station KDKA in Pittsburgh
Publication of *Main Street* by Sinclair Lewis
Arrest of Sacco and Vanzetti
Prohibition takes effect
1921: Immigration Quota Law passed
Disarmament conference held
1922: Fordney-McCumber Tariff enacted
Publication of *Babbitt* by Sinclair Lewis
1923: Teapot Dome scandal
Death of Harding; Calvin Coolidge becomes president
Duke Ellington first performs in New York City
1924: Election of Calvin Coolidge
Immigration Quota Law enacted
Ku Klux Klan reaches highest membership in history
Women governors elected in Wyoming and Texas
1925: Publication of *The Man Nobody Knows* by Bruce Barton
Publication of *The Great Gatsby* by F. Scott Fitzgerald
Scopes Trial held in Dayton, Tennessee
1926: Publication of *The Sun Also Rises* by Ernest Hemingway
1927: *The Jazz Singer,* first movie with sound, released
Charles Lindbergh makes New York to Paris flight
Execution of Sacco and Vanzetti
15 millionth car produced by Ford Motor Company
$1.5 billion spent on advertising in United States
Babe Ruth hits 60 home runs
1928: Election of Herbert Hoover
1929: Nearly 30 million Americans have cars
Stock market crash

✓ Review Questions

1. Many in rural/small-town America would support legislation that

   A. increased immigration from Eastern Europe
   B. mandated the teaching of creationism in schools
   C. lessened the penalties for those that sold illegal alcohol
   D. made it harder to deport immigrants who might have "Red" ties
   E. None of the above

(Correct Answer: **B.** All of the other "causes"—more immigration, the lessening of Prohibition, and the lessening of methods to deport potential communists—were vehemently opposed by most in small-town America. They would, however, support the elimination of the teaching of evolution, and the continued teaching of creationism in American schools.)

2. The novel that supported the business philosophy of the 1920s most definitively was

   A. *Main Street*
   B. *The Great Gatsby*
   C. *The Man Nobody Knows*
   D. *Babbitt*
   E. None of the above

(Correct Answer: **C.** All of the other novels are unsympathetic to the world of business—both A and D are by Sinclair Lewis. In *The Man Nobody Knows,* Jesus Christ was portrayed as a businessman.)

3. In 1928 in most Eastern cities one could find

   A. a speakeasy
   B. a continual flow of immigrants from Northern, Southern, and Eastern Europe

   C. large numbers of supporters of the Ku Klux Klan
   D. the first bread lines
   E. a large number of political supporters of William Jennings Bryan

(Correct Answer: **A.** The influx of immigrants had been greatly reduced by immigration legislation passed in the first half of the decade. Supporters of the KKK were largely not city dwellers; the KKK had also lessened in importance by 1928. Bread lines were not found until the beginning of the Great Depression. Few supporters of William Jennings Bryan came from eastern urban centers.)

4. Republican leaders of the 1920s believed all of the following *except*

   A. "the business of government is business"
   B. the government should do as little as possible
   C. labor unions should be strengthened through legislation
   D. taxes for the wealthiest should be reduced
   E. All of the above

(Correct Answer: **C.** All of the other answers are solid beliefs of Republican leaders of the 1920s. Republicans did very little for labor unions in the decade.)

5. The election of Herbert Hoover in 1928 demonstrated all of the following *except*

   A. Americans were attracted to self-made businessmen
   B. most Americans believed that Republican policies had been responsible for the prosperity of the 1920s

C. fewer divisions existed between the urban and rural populations than had existed at the beginning of the decade

D. Prohibition was still a "hot-button issue" for many Americans.

E. All of the above

(Correct Answer: **C.** Hoover's overwhelming election demonstrated the appeal of his business background and the fact that many Americans credited the Republicans for prosperity. The fact that Al Smith was stomped in this election demonstrated that his anti-Prohibition statements definitely hurt him. However, many in urban centers voted for him; this demonstrated that the divisions between urban and rural America were still wide at the end of the decade.)

Chapter 19

The Great Depression and the New Deal

 The era of the Great Depression tested the character of the American nation as no previous crisis period in America had (with the obvious exception of the Civil War). The lives of those who struggled through the Great Depression were inexorably changed. The factions that came together to make up the Democratic party in the 1930s continued to control much of American political life for the next 50 years. The New Deal, Franklin Roosevelt's series of experimental programs designed to tackle the monumental problems of the 1930s, greatly changed the role of the federal government in American society. The political, social, and cultural fabric of America was permanently altered by the events of the 1930s.

THE AMERICAN ECONOMY OF THE 1920s: THE ROOTS OF THE GREAT DEPRESSION

The vast majority of Americans in 1929 foresaw a continuation of the dizzying economic growth that had taken place in most of the decade. In his inauguration speech, newly elected president Herbert Hoover reemphasized his campaign promise that it was the goal of the Republican party to permanently wipe out poverty in America. In early September 1929, the average share of stock on the New York Stock Exchange stood near 350, a gain of nearly 200 points in a little over a year.

However, careful observers of the American economy noticed several disturbing trends that only seemed to be increasing. These included the following:

1. *Agricultural problems.* Farm prices were at a record high during World War I, dropped after the war, and never recovered. Many farmers were unable to pay banks back loans they had acquired to purchase land,

tractors, and other equipment; many farms were foreclosed on and in farm states over 6200 banks were forced to close. Legislation to help farmers had been passed by the Congress, but bills to help the farmers were vetoed by President Coolidge on two occasions.

2. *Installment buying.* As stated in the previous chapter, large numbers of Americans purchased automobiles, refrigerators, vacuum cleaners, and similar household products on credit. Many Americans simply did not have anywhere near enough cash to pay for all they had purchased. The money of many families was tied up making installment payments for three or four big-ticket items; this prevented them from purchasing many other items available for sale. In 1928 and 1929 new goods continued to be produced, but many people could simply not afford to buy them. As a result, layoffs began occurring in some industries as early as 1928.

3. *Uneven division of wealth.* America was wealthy in the 1920s, but this wealth did not extend to all segments of society. The gains made by wealthy Americans in the 1920s far outstripped gains made by the working class. By the time of the stock market crash, the upper 0.2 percent of the population controlled over 40 percent of the nation's savings. On the other hand, over three-quarters of American families made less than $3000 a year. Problems that could develop from this situation were obvious. The bottom three-quarters of families were too poor to purchase much to help the economy to continue to flourish. Furthermore, at the early signs of economic trouble, many of the wealthiest Americans, fearing the worst, curtailed their spending.

4. *The stock market.* There were cases in the late 1920s of ordinary citizens becoming very, very rich by purchasing stock. Some of these people were engaged in **speculation**, meaning that they would invest in something (like the previously mentioned Florida lands) that was very risky, but that they could potentially "make a killing" on. Another common practice in the late 1920s was buying shares of stock **on the margin**. A stockbroker might allow a buyer to purchase stock for only a percentage of what it was worth (commonly as low as 20 percent); the rest could be borrowed from the broker. As long as stock prices continued to rise, investors would have no trouble paying brokers back for these loans. After the stock market crash, brokers wanted payment for these loans. Countless numbers of investors had no way to make these payments.

THE STOCK MARKET CRASH

The prices of stock crested in early September of 1929. The price of stock fell very gradually during most of September and early October. Some investors noted that some factories were beginning to lay workers off; whispers were heard around Wall Street that perhaps the price of stock *was* too high, and that it might be good to sell before prices began to fall.

The first signs of panic occurred on Wednesday, October 23, when in the last hour of trading, the value of a share of stock dropped, on the average, 20 points. On October 24 a massive amount of stock was sold, and prices again fell dramatically. Stockbrokers told nervous investors not to worry; Herbert Hoover announced that the stock market and the economy "is on a sound and prosperous basis."

A group of influential bankers and brokers pooled resources to buy stock, but this was unable to stop the downward trend. Prices fell again on Monday, October 28, and on the following day, Black Tuesday, the bottom fell out of the market. Prices fell by 40 points that day; it is estimated that total losses to investors for the day was over $20 million. Stockbrokers and banks frantically attempted to call in their loans; few investors had the money to pay even a fraction of what they owed.

How the Stock Market Crash Caused the Great Depression

In the weeks immediately following the crash, important figures from the banking world and President Hoover all assured the American people that America was still economically sound, and that the crash was no worse than other stock downturns that had had little long-term effect on the economy. In retrospect, it can be seen that through both direct and indirect means, the stock market crash was a fundamental cause of the Great Depression. As a result of the crash:

1. *Bank closings increased.* As stated previously, many banks in rural America had to close when farmers couldn't repay loans. The exact same thing happened to many city banks after 1929 when investors could not repay their loans. In addition, the news of even a single bank closing had a snowball effect; thousands of people went to banks across the country to withdraw their life savings. Banks did not have this kind of money (it had been given out to investors as loans); soon urban banks began to fail as well. It is estimated that by 1932 approximately 5000 banks fell, with the life savings of over 5 million Americans gone forever

2. *Income fell for industrialists.* Many large industrialists invested heavily in the stock market. They had less available cash, and some started to close or reduce the scale of their factory operations. Workers were laid off or made much less money; as a result, they were able to buy fewer products made in other industrial plants, causing layoffs there as well. By 1933 nearly 25 percent of the labor force was out of work.

3. *Effect on the world.* Many European countries, especially Germany, utilized loans from American banks and investment houses in the 1920s and 1930s to remain viable. When American financial institutions were unable to supply these loans, instability occurred in these countries. Some historians make the argument that, perhaps indirectly,

the American stock market crash opened the door for Hitler to come to power in Germany.

THE SOCIAL IMPACT OF THE GREAT DEPRESSION

Many Americans felt a huge sense of uprootedness in the 1930s. By late 1932 virtually all sectors of American society were affected in some way by the Depression. Both professional men and common laborers lost their jobs. It was not uncommon during the Depression for two people to share a job, or for a man who had lost his job to continue to put his suit on every morning and pretend to go to work, somehow averting the shame he felt for being unemployed. Women and minorities were often the first to lose their jobs, although women in certain "female" occupations (such as domestic work) were almost never uprooted by men. "Respectable" white men were willing to take jobs that had been previously seen as fit only for minorities. Many behaviors of the 1920s, such as buying on credit, were forgotten practices by 1932.

Many private agencies established soup kitchens and emergency shelters in the early 1930s, but many more were needed. Many couples postponed marriage and having children. Those with nowhere in live in cities often ended up in **Hoovervilles**, which were settlements of shacks (made from scrap metal or lumber) usually located on the outskirts of cities. Many unemployed young people, both men and women, took to the road in the 1930s, often traveling in empty railroad cars.

The greatest human suffering of the Depression era might have existed in the **Dust Bowl**. For most of the decade, massive dust storms plagued the residents of Oklahoma, Kansas, Nebraska, Colorado, and Texas; farm production in this area fell drastically for much of the decade. A severe drought was the major cause of the dust storms, although poor farming practices (stripping the soil of any topsoil) also contributed to them. By decade's end nearly 60 percent of all farms in the Dust Bowl were either ruined or abandoned. Many Dust Bowlers traveled to California to get agricultural jobs there, and discovered that if an entire family picked grapes from sunup to sundown, it might barely scrape by. (John Steinbeck's book *The Grapes of Wrath,* as well as the film version, are highly recommended for further study of Dust Bowlers and their move to California, as are the recordings of Woody Guthrie entitled "Dust Bowl Ballads" and the Depression-era photos taken by Dorothea Lange.)

The behavior and attitudes of many who lived through the Depression changed forever. Many would *never* in their lives buy anything on credit; there are countless stories of Depression-era families who insisted on paying for everything, including automobiles, with cash. Depression-era shortages led many in later life to be almost compulsive "savers" of everything and anything imaginable. Many who lived through the Depression and had children in the 1950s were determined to given their kids all that they had been deprived of in the 1930s.

THE HOOVER ADMINISTRATION AND THE DEPRESSION

To state that Herbert Hoover did nothing to stem the effects of the Great Depression is not entirely accurate. Nevertheless, he did believe that this crisis could be solved through **voluntarism**. Hoover urged Americans to donate all they could to charities, and held several conferences with business leaders where he urged them not to reduce wages or lay off workers. When it became obvious that these measures were not enough, public opinion quickly turned against Hoover.

The Hoover administration did take several specific measures to offset the effects of the Depression. Even before the stock market crash, the **Agricultural Marketing Act** created a Federal Farm Board that had the ability to give loans to the agricultural community and buy crops to keep farm prices up. By 1932 there was not enough money to keep this program afloat. In 1930 Congress enacted the **Hawley-Smoot tariff**, which to this day is the highest import tax in the history of the United States. In response, European countries drastically increased their own tariffs as well; some historians maintain that this legislation did little to improve the economy of the United States, but that its effects did much to ensure that the American Depression would be a worldwide one.

Hoover did authorize more money for public works programs, and in 1932, he authorized the creation of the **Reconstruction Finance Corporation**. This agency gave money to banks, who were then authorized to loan this money to businesses and railroads. Another bill authorized loans to banks to prevent them from failing. To many in America, these bills were merely signs that Hoover was only interested in helping those at the top of society and that he cared little about the common person. Hoover vetoed legislation authorizing a federal relief program, although in 1932 he did sign legislation authorizing federal loans to the states; states could then administer relief programs with this money.

The views of those Americans who felt that Hoover was unconcerned about the plight of the common man had their views seemingly confirmed by federal actions against the **Bonus Army** that appeared in Washington in the summer of 1932. This group of nearly 22,000 unemployed World War I vets came to ask the federal government to give them the bonuses that they were supposed to get in 1945 immediately. At Hoover's urging, the Senate rejected legislation authorizing this. Most of the Bonus Army then went home, but a few thousand stayed, living in shacks along the Anacostia River. Hoover ordered them removed; military forces led by Douglas MacArthur used tear gas and cleared the remaining bonus marchers from their camp and burned down the shacks they had been living in.

THE 1932 PRESIDENTIAL ELECTION

The two candidates in the 1932 presidential election could not have been more different in both content and style. In a joyless convention, the Republicans renominated Herbert Hoover. In newsreels seen by Americans across the country, Hoover came across as unsmiling and utterly lacking in warmth. He insisted that his policies would eventually lead America out of the Depression, stating that history demonstrated that lulls in the American economy are always followed by upturns. Hoover warned against "mindless experimentation" in the creation of government policies. It should be noted that Hoover was echoing standard economic and political theory of the era.

Hoover's opponent in the election was the Governor of New York, Franklin Delano Roosevelt. Roosevelt was a man of wealth. After serving as Assistant Secretary of the Navy under Woodrow Wilson, Roosevelt unsuccessfully tried to get the vice presidential nomination in 1920. During the summer of 1921, he came down with polio, which left him unable to walk for the rest of his life. Several of Roosevelt's biographers maintain that the mental and physical anguish caused by his polio made Roosevelt much more sensitive to the sufferings of others.

Franklin Roosevelt married a distant cousin, Eleanor Roosevelt, in 1905. While Franklin spent much of the 1920s attempting to recover from polio in Warm Springs, Georgia, Eleanor became a tireless worker in New York state politics, pushing for governmental reform and better conditions for working women. The role that Eleanor Roosevelt played during the presidency of Franklin Roosevelt cannot be overestimated. FDR (this shortening of his name was done by a reporter in 1932) oftentimes stated that Eleanor served as his "legs," visiting miners, schools, and countless other groups. Eleanor also discussed policy with Roosevelt and continually urged him to do more to offset the effects of the Depression.

As Governor of New York during the first years of the Great Depression, Roosevelt instituted relief programs that became models for others across the country. During his campaign Roosevelt promised "**The New Deal**" for the American people; unlike Hoover, he also promised to experiment to find solutions to America's problems. Roosevelt's broad smile and personal demeanor contrasted drastically with the public image of Herbert Hoover; Americans were convinced that Roosevelt cared (this would be demonstrated during his presidency by the hundreds of letters that Roosevelt and his wife both received during their presidency, asking for things such as small loans, money to pay doctors, and old clothes; it should also be noted that many Americans had a picture of Franklin Roosevelt on display somewhere in their living quarters during the Depression).

The 1932 presidential election was easily won by Roosevelt, who won by over 7 million votes. Hoover's only strength was in the Northeastern states. In addition, the Democrats won control of both houses of Congress. Some had feared (or hoped) that the Depression would radicalize the American working class, yet the socialist candidate for president, Norman Thomas, received considerably less than 1 million votes.

THE FIRST HUNDRED DAYS

Franklin Roosevelt's inauguration speech in 1933 was one of optimism; the most quoted line of this speech is ". . . so first of all let me assert my firm belief that the only thing we have to fear is fear itself." Within a week of taking office, Roosevelt gave the first of his many **fireside chats**. During these radio addresses, Roosevelt spoke to the listening audience as if they were part of his family; Roosevelt would usually explain the immediate problems facing the country in these speeches and outline the reasons for his decided solution.

Roosevelt surrounded himself with an able Cabinet, as well as group of unofficial advisors called Roosevelt's "brain trust." In dealing with the problems of the Depression, Roosevelt urged his advisors to experiment. Some programs thus failed, some were continually reformed, and several conflicted with each other. The key, insisted Roosevelt, was to "do something."

During the first **hundred days** of the Roosevelt administration, countless programs were proposed by the administration and passed by the Congress that attempted to stimulate the American economy and provide relief and jobs. A very popular act, for psychological reasons if nothing else, was the repeal of Prohibition, which was actually voted on by the Congress in February 1933.

Roosevelt's economic advisor told him that his first priority should be the banking system. On March 5, 1933, he officially closed all banks for four days and had the federal government oversee the inspection of all banks. By March 15 most banks were reopened; this cooling-off period gave people a renewed confidence in the banks, and slowly people started putting back into banks instead of taking it out. The Banking Act of 1933 created the **Federal Deposit Insurance Corporation** (FDIC), which insured the bank deposits of individual citizens.

During the hundred days, large amounts of federal money were handed down to local relief agencies, and a Federal Emergency Relief Administration (led by Harry Hopkins) was also established. Efforts were also made to help people find work. Thousands were hired from funds distributed to states by the Public Works Administration; many schools, highways, and hospitals were built under this program.

The **Civilian Conservation Corps** (CCC) was during this period and would eventually employ over 2 1/2 million young men. Under this program forest and conservation programs were undertaken. CCC workers were only paid a small amount (this money was actually sent to their families), but in a period where little work was available, many veterans of CCC programs later perceived the program as a godsend.

Roosevelt considered the bolstering of the industrial sector of the American economy to be a top priority. Falling prices had caused layoffs and the failure of many businesses. The **National Industry Recovery Act** (NIRA) was established to try to stop falling prices in industry. Under this act committees of both owners and union leaders in each industry would meet to set commonly agreed on prices, wages, working hours, and working expectations. Unions and collective bargaining were accepted in industry as a result of the NIRA. Wages in many industries rose as a result of this; the thinking in the creation of the NIRA was that as wages rose, workers would then buy more, stimulating the economy and stopping the fall of industrial prices. The goals of this program were largely not met; as wages rose so did prices. As a result, many workers did not buy more, negating any benefit that rising wages were supposed to have.

Another body created by the NIRA was the National Recovery Administration (NRA), which was supposed to enforce the decisions of the NIRA. The entire process of the NIRA was declared unconstitutional in the 1935 Supreme Court case *Schechter* v. *United States,* although the agency had largely lost its effectiveness by then.

Two other important programs developed during the first hundred days. The **Agricultural Adjustment Administration** (AAA) attempted to stop the sharp decline in farm prices by paying farmers *not* to produce certain crops and livestock. It was hoped that this would cause the prices of these goods to rise. The **Tennessee Valley Authority** authorized the construction of a series of dams that would ultimately provide electricity and flood control to those living in the Tennessee River Valley. Thousands who had not had electricity in their homes now did.

The hundred days and the months that followed it provided some relief to those affected by the Depression, but by no means solved the basic economic problems facing the United States. The 1934 midterm congressional elections showed that most Americans favored FDR's policies, yet even in 1935 some 20 percent of all Americans were still out of work.

THE SECOND NEW DEAL

Many wealthy members of American society were appalled by the actions that Roosevelt took during his first year in office; he was called a traitor to his class, a communist, and far worse. Other elements of Roosevelt's brain trust (as well as his wife Eleanor) were advising Roosevelt to do even more to help the unemployed of America. As a result, the **Second New Deal**, beginning in 1935, included another flurry of legislation.

It was obvious that even more dramatic measures were needed to help farmers; many farms were still being foreclosed on because farmers could not make necessary payments on their land. The **Resettlement Administration**, established in May of 1935, offered loans to small farmers who faced foreclosure. In addition, migrant farmers had not been affected by previous New Deal measures dealing with agriculture; funds to help them find work were included under the Resettlement Administration.

One of the outstanding achievements of the Second New Deal was the creation of the **Works Progress Administration** (WPA). The WPA took people that were on relief and employed them for 30 or 35 hours a week. On average, 2 million people per month were employed by the WPA; by 1941 well over 8 million people had worked for the WPA. WPA workers were usually engaged in construction projects, building schools, hospitals, and roads across the country. In addition, unemployed musicians, artists, and actors were all employed by the WPA. WPA artists painted many of the murals found in public buildings, concerts were given for both urban and rural audiences, and plays were performed for audiences who had never seen one before.

Another important piece of legislation from this period was the **Wagner Act**, which reaffirmed the right of workers to organize and to utilize collective bargaining. These rights had been guaranteed by provision 7a of the NIRA guidelines, but when the NIRA was declared to be unconstitutional, additional legislation protecting workers was needed. The Wagner Act also listed unfair labor practices that were outlawed and established the **National Labor Relations Board** (NLRB) to enforce its provisions.

The most important legislation passed during the Second New Deal was the 1935 **Social Security Act**. The critical provision of this act was the creation of a retirement plan for workers over 65 years old. Both workers and employers paid into this retirement fund; the first payments were scheduled to be made in January 1942. It should be noted that the initial social security legislation did not cover agricultural and domestic workers.

Other provisions of this act established a program that provided unemployment insurance for workers who had lost their jobs; this was paid for by a payroll tax that was imposed on all employers with more than eight workers. The federal government also provided financial support to programs at the state level that provided unemployment insurance. The federal government also gave money to the states to provide aid programs for dependent children, for the blind, and for the physically handicapped.

As stated previously, some Americans were exempt from the provisions of the Social Security Act. Nevertheless, this act fundamentally changed the relationship of the federal government to American citizens. At the root of the Social Security Act was the concept that it was the job of the federal government to take care of those who couldn't take care of themselves. This was a fundamentally new role for the federal government to have, and it justified the worst fears of many opponents of the Roosevelt administration.

THE PRESIDENTIAL ELECTION OF 1936

The 1936 election was the first true national referendum on the presidency of Franklin Roosevelt. In his campaign speeches Roosevelt oftentimes railed against the business class; according to Roosevelt they opposed many of his policies only so they could continue to get rich. The Republicans nominated Governor Alfred Landon of Kansas as their presidential candidate. Landon never actually repudiated the programs of the New Deal, but he stated that a balanced budget and less expensive government programs should be top priorities.

The election was one of the most one-sided in American history. Roosevelt won the electoral college 523 to 8; Landon was only able to carry the states of Maine and Vermont. Roosevelt was able to craft a **New Deal Coalition**, which made the Democrats the majority party in America throughout the rest of the 1930s and all the way into the 1980s.

The fact that white urban dwellers supported the Democrats in large numbers was noted during the 1928 defeat of Smith; whites in the Solid South had largely voted Democratic since the nineteenth century. The two groups that joined the Democratic coalition in this era were labor unions and blacks (this was a dramatic shift, as most blacks had voted Republican since the period of Emancipation). Roosevelt enjoyed support in the agricultural community as well.

OPPONENTS OF FRANKLIN ROOSEVELT AND THE NEW DEAL

Despite the overwhelming electoral success of Franklin Roosevelt, many American vehemently disagreed with his programs. Some wealthy Americans called him a traitor to his class, while some businessmen called him a socialist or a communist. To others, the programs of Roosevelt were perceived as being designed to benefit the business interests of America and never truly addressed the human suffering of the country. Some of these Americans felt that neither the Democratic nor the Republican parties were really concerned with helping the average American, and perceived socialism as the only viable solution. Many idealistic Americans dabbled with socialism in the 1930s; for some the one or two party meetings they attended became career-threatening during the McCarthy era of the 1950s.

One group that thought the New Deal had gone too far was the **American Liberty League**. This group was led by former presidential candidate Al Smith and several very influential business figures, including prominent members of the du Pont family. The membership of this organization was largely relatively wealthy Republicans; they were particularly incensed by the **Revenue Act of 1935**, which considerably increased the tax rate for those making over $50,000. The American Liberty League equated the New Deal with "Bolshevism" in much of their literature.

The majority of those opposing the New Deal felt that it didn't go far enough. Dr. Francis Townsend of California proposed an **Old Age Revolving Pension Plan**; under this plan a national sales tax would pay for a pension of $200 per month for all retired Americans. Townsend maintained that the benefit would be that more and more money would be put into circulation. In 1934 Upton Sinclair, author of *The Jungle,* ran for governor of California on the Democratic ticket and announced his "End Poverty in California" (EPIC) plan. Under this plan California factories and farms would be under state control. Sinclair was defeated by the Republican candidate and was also sabotaged by members of his own party; the Democratic smear campaign against Sinclair was approved of by Franklin Roosevelt.

The two most vicious opponents of the New Deal were Father Charles Coughlin and Louisiana Senator Huey Long. Millions of people listened to Coughlin on the radio. Originally a supporter of Roosevelt, by the mid-1930s he told his listeners that Roosevelt was a "liar" and "the great betrayer." By the late 1930s Coughlin was praising Mussolini and Hitler on his broadcasts, and making increasing anti-Semitic statements. Per orders of the church, Coughlin was pulled off the air during World War II.

As Governor and later Senator from Louisiana, Huey Long instituted many New Deal-type programs in Louisiana, and also developed the most effective and ruthless political machine in the entire South. By 1934 Long felt that Franklin Roosevelt was not committed to doing enough to end the Depression. Long called for a true redistribution of wealth in his "Share the Wealth" program, which would have allowed no American to make over a million dollars a year (the rest would be taken in taxes). From these taxes Long proposed to give every American family $5000 immediately and an annual income of $2000. Long talked of running against Roosevelt in 1936, but was assassinated by the relative of a Louisiana political enemy in 1935.

THE LAST YEARS OF THE NEW DEAL

Franklin Roosevelt was frustrated that the United States Supreme Court had struck down several New Deal programs. In early 1937 he proposed the **Justice Reorganization Bill**, which would have allowed him to appoint an additional Supreme Court justice for every justice over 70 years old (nothing in the Constitution stated that there had to be only nine Supreme Court justices). Roosevelt would have been able to appoint six new judges under this scheme. Roosevelt claimed that the purpose of this plan was to help the older judges with their workload, but many Republicans and Democrats in Congress believed that Roosevelt was altering the balance of power between branches of government just to get his ideas enacted into law. Newspaper editorial writers and cartoonists compared Roosevelt to the dictators of Europe, Hitler and Mussolini. Many Southern Democrats joined with the Republicans to defeat this bill; the aftereffects seriously damaged Roosevelt's relationship with Congress. Ironically, without the bill several justices retired in the next two years, allowing Roosevelt to appoint justices who would approve his programs anyway.

Any hopes that the New Deal was actually ending the Depression were dashed by a fairly large recession that occurred in mid-1937. Once again, factories began major layoffs. Critics of the New Deal blamed Roosevelt's programs for this recession. Many in the administration were worried that the national debt was too high, and urged Roosevelt to cut programs. The WPA was drastically scaled back, putting some that had worked for it out of work. In addition, a part of every worker's salary was now deducted to be put into the Social Security fund; critics charged that this money would have been better utilized if it was actually being spent on goods and services. By 1940 the administration restored some of the cutbacks made to government programs, slightly improving the economy again.

THE EFFECTS OF THE NEW DEAL

The Wagner Act and other New Deal legislation permanently legitimized labor unions and collective bargaining. Some unions became emboldened by the Wagner Act, and several <u>sit-down strikes</u> occurred in the late 1930s. The most famous occurred at the General Motors plant in Flint, Michigan, in January of 1937. Workers refused to leave the plant; by February management had to give in to the worker's demands. Other strikes of the era turned bloody; at a 1937 strike at Republic Steel in Chicago, 10 strikers were killed. Nevertheless, union membership rose dramatically in the 1930s.

Another development was the creation of the **Congress of Industrial Organizations** (CIO). The American Federal of Labor, founded in the 1880s, was made up mostly of skilled workers. The first president of the CIO was John L. Lewis; the goal of this union was to organize and represent unskilled factory and textile workers. By 1938 this organization represented over 4 million workers. CIO members were on the front lines of the strikes mentioned in the previous paragraph.

The burden on women and blacks was great during the New Deal. As men lost their jobs, more and more women were forced to take meager jobs to support their families (despite the fact that women workers were oftentimes criticized for "stealing" the jobs of men). It should be noted that Francis Perkins was the Secretary of Labor during the 1930s; Roosevelt employed a number of women in influential roles during his presidency.

Blacks were especially oppressed during the New Deal. Oftentimes they were the first fired from their factory or business; relief programs in Southern states sometimes excluded blacks from receiving benefits. Lynchings continued in the South throughout the 1930s; Roosevelt never supported an antilynching bill for fear of alienating Southern Democrats. The **Scottsboro Boys** trial received national attention. In 1931 nine black young men were accused of raping two white women on a train. Without any real evidence, eight of the nine were sentenced to die. It is ironic that the American Communist party organized the appeals of the Scottsboro Boys; in the end some of their convictions were overturned.

Nevertheless, blacks did support Franklin Roosevelt, as they felt that he was generally supportive of their cause. Roosevelt did hire blacks for several policy posts in his New Deal administration. Mary McLeod Bethune, founder of the National Council of Negro Women, was appointed in 1936 as Director of the Division of Negro Affairs of the National Youth Administration. Bethune lobbied Roosevelt on the concerns of blacks, and also worked to increase the support of influential black leaders for the New Deal.

NEW DEAL CULTURE

Many authors attempted to capture the human suffering that was so pronounced in the 1930s. Zora Neale Hurston wrote *Their Eyes Were*

Watching God about growing up black in a small Florida town. *Studs Lonigen* by James T. Farrell depicted the lives of the Irish in Chicago. The previously mentioned *The Grapes of Wrath* by John Steinbeck tells the story of Dust Bowlers moving to California for survival, while Erskine Caldwell's *Tobacco Road* describes the suffering of sharecroppers in Georgia. *Gone with the Wind* by Margaret Mitchell offered a romanticized tale of survival from another period of crisis, the Civil War.

Most Americans of the 1930s got their entertainment through radio. Radio in the 1930s offered soap operas, comedies, and dramas. Americans were also offered "high culture" on most radio stations, as symphonic music and operas were standard fare. The response to H. G. Well's dramatization of "War of the Worlds" demonstrated the power of radio in American life.

Going to the movies provided a way for Americans to escape the sufferings of their daily lives; by 1939 nearly 70 percent of all adults went to the movies at least once a week. Lavish sets and dancing in movies such as *The Golddiggers of 1933* allowed people to leave their cares behind, at least for a couple of hours. Shirley Temple charmed millions, and movies such as *Mr. Smith Goes to Washington* showed audiences that in the end, justice would prevail. Promoters attempted to make movie-going itself a special event in the 1930s; theaters were designed to look like palaces, air conditioning was installed, and dishes and other utensils were often given away as theater promotions.

CHAPTER REVIEW

Rapid Review Guide

To achieve the perfect 5, you should be able to explain the following:

- The Great Depression had numerous long-lasting effects on American society.

- Franklin Roosevelt was the first activist president of the twentieth century who used the power of the federal government to help those who could not help themselves.

- The Great Depression's origins lay in economic problems of the late 1920s.

- The 1929 stock market crash was caused by, among others things, speculation on the part of investors and buying stocks "on the margin."

- The stock market crash began to affect the economy almost immediately, and its effects were felt by almost all by 1931.

- Herbert Hoover did act to end the Depression, but believed that voluntary actions by both business and labor would lead America out of its economic difficulties.

- Franklin Roosevelt won the 1932 election by promising "The New Deal" to the American people and by promising to act in a decisive manner.

- Suffering was felt across American society; many in the Dust Bowl were forced to leave their farms.

- During the first hundred days, Roosevelt restored confidence in the banks, established the Civilian Conservation Corps, stabilized farm prices, and attempted to stabilize industry through the National Industrial Recovery Act.

- During the Second New Deal, the WPA was created and the Social Security Act was enacted; this was the most long-lasting piece of legislation from the New Deal.

- Roosevelt was able to craft a political coalition of urban whites, Southerners, union members, and blacks that kept the Democratic party in power through the 1980s.

- The New Deal had opponents from the left who said it didn't do enough to alleviate the effects of the Depression and opponents from the right who said that the New Deal was socialist in nature.

- Roosevelt's 1937 plan to pack the Supreme Court and the recession of 1937 demonstrated that New Deal programs were not entirely successful in ending the Great Depression.

- Many Americans turned to radio and the movies for relief during the Depression.

Time Line

1929: Stock market crash
1930: Hawley-Smoot Tariff enacted
1931: Ford plants in Detroit shut down
     Initial trial of the Scottsboro Boys
1932: Glass-Steagall Banking Act enacted
     Bonus marchers routed from Washington
     Franklin D. Roosevelt elected president
     Huey Long announces "Share Our Wealth" movement
1933: Emergency Banking Relief Act enacted
     Prohibition ends
     Agricultural Adjustment Act enacted
     National Industrial Recovery Act enacted
     Civilian Conservation Corps established
     Tennessee Valley Authority formed
     Public Works Administration established
1934: American unemployment reaches highest point
1935: Beginning of the Second New Deal

Works Progress Administration established
Social Security Act enacted
Wagner Act enacted
Formation of Committee for Industrial Organization (CIO)
1936: Franklin Roosevelt reelected
Sit-down strike against GM begins
1937: Recession of 1937 begins
Roosevelt's plan to expand the Supreme Court defeated
1939: *Gone with the Wind* published
The Grapes of Wrath published

✓ Review Questions

1. Which of the following was *not* a cause of the stock market crash?

   A. Excessive American loans to European countries
   B. Uneven division of wealth
   C. Installment buying
   D. Drop in farm prices
   E. Purchasing of stocks "on the margin"

(Correct Answer: **A.** All of the others were major underlying reasons for the crash. Americans loans to Europe benefited both European countries and American banking houses until the crash.)

2. Wealthy businessmen who objected to the New Deal programs of Franklin Roosevelt claimed that

   A. they unfairly aided the many who did not deserve it
   B. Roosevelt was personally a traitor to his class
   C. New Deal programs smacked of "Bolshevism"
   D. New Deal programs unfairly regulated businesses
   E. All of the above

(Correct Answer: **E.** All of the criticisms listed were heard throughout the 1930s.)

3. The purpose of the Federal Deposit Insurance Corporation (FDIC) was to

   A. ensure that poor Americans had something to fall back on when they retired
   B. inspect the financial transactions of important businesses
   C. insure bank deposits of individual citizens
   D. ensure that businesses were established insurance funds for their workers, as mandated by congressional legislation
   E. increase governmental control over the economy

(Correct Answer: **C.** The FDIC was established after the bank holiday to insure individual accounts in certified banks and to increase confidence in the banking system. Americans began to put money back into banks after its institution.)

4. One group of women who were able to keep their jobs during the Great Depression were

   A. schoolteachers
   B. clerical workers
   C. domestic workers
   D. government employees
   E. professional workers

(Correct Answer: **C.** In the other occupations women were oftentimes fired before men, or had their hours drastically reduced.

Those women who were employed as domestic workers were relatively safe, as this was one occupation that men, as a whole, rejected.)

5. The popularity of Huey Long and Father Coughlin in the mid-1930s demonstrated that

   A. most Americans felt that the New Deal had gone too far in undermining traditional American values
   B. more Americans were turning to religion in the 1930s
   C. most Americans favored truly radical solutions to America's problems
   D. many Americans felt that the government should do more to end the problems associated with the Depression
   E. Franklin Roosevelt was losing the support of large numbers of voters

(Correct Answer: **D.** Many Americans wanted more New Deal-style programs and felt that Roosevelt should have gone even further in his proposed legislation. Many may have listened to Long and Coughlin, but when it came time to vote, cast their ballots for Roosevelt—thus negating answer C. The idea that the New Deal went too far in destroying American capitalism was popular in the business community, but was not widely shared in mainstream America.)

Chapter 20

World War II

 World War II altered the American position in the world and ideology at home more than any other event of the twentieth century. For Americans, World War II was the "good war," and Americans at home assisted the war effort in numerous ways. Orders for planes, jeeps, ships, and numerous other war industries had to be quickly filled; this ended the lingering economic effects of the Great Depression.

After World War I, the United States had been reluctant to take on the role of world leader. As a result of World War II, the United States and the Soviet Union emerged as the two major world powers. During the last months of the war, the United States had the awesome responsibility of being the only country to possess the atomic bomb. Decisions made by the United States at the end of World War II helped to usher in the Cold War and the atomic age.

AMERICAN FOREIGN POLICY IN THE 1930s

As Italy, Germany, and Japan all expanded their empires in the 1930s, most Americans favored a continuation of the policy of **isolationism**. An isolationist group, the **America First Committee**, attracted nearly 820,000 members by 1940. Isolationists believed that it was in America's best interests to stay out of foreign conflicts that did not directly threaten American interests. A congressional committee led by Senator Gerald Nye investigated the origins of America's entry into World War I and found that bankers and arms manufacturers did much to influence America's entry into the war. On a practical level, Americans were consumed with the problems of the Great Depression and were generally unable to focus on overseas problems.

Congressional legislation passed in the period attempted to keep America out of future wars between other powers. The **Neutrality Acts**

of 1935 stated that if countries went to war, the United States would not trade arms of weapons with them for six months; in addition, any non-military goods sold to nations at war would have to be paid for up front and would have to transported in non-American ships (this was called "cash-and-carry").

German expansionism in Europe convinced Franklin Roosevelt that the United States, at some point, would *have* to enter the war on the side of Great Britain (even though public opinion strongly opposed this). On September 1, 1939, Germany invaded Poland, and two days later England and France declared war on Germany. Within three weeks Roosevelt asked Congress to pass the **Neutrality Act of 1939**, which would allow the cash-and-carry sale of arms to countries at war (this legislation was designed to facilitate the sale of American arms to Britain and France). The bill passed on a party-line vote.

News of rapid German advances in Europe began to change American attitudes, with more and more people agreeing with Roosevelt that the best course of action would be to prepare for eventual war. The rapid defeat of France at the hands of the Nazis was stunning to many Americans. In September of 1940 Roosevelt gave Great Britain 50 older American destroyers in return for the rights to build military bases in Bermuda and Newfoundland.

THE PRESIDENTIAL ELECTION OF 1940 AND ITS AFTERMATH

No president in American history had ever served more than two consecutive terms. Just before the Democratic National Convention, Roosevelt quietly stated that if he was nominated, he would accept. Roosevelt was quickly nominated; his Republican opponent was Wendell Wilkie, an ex-Democrat. Roosevelt emerged victorious, but by a smaller margin than in his two previous victories. Most historians say that more Americans voted against Roosevelt was mostly a commentary by the voters on the lingering effects of the Great Depression.

Roosevelt interpreted his victory as a mandate to continue preparations for the eventual U.S. entry into World War II. By early 1941 Roosevelt proposed giving the British aid for the war effort without getting cash in return (it was stated that payment could be made after the war). By the terms of the **Lend-Lease Act**, Congress gave the president the ability to send immediate aid to Britain; Roosevelt immediately authorized nearly $7 billion in aid. As Roosevelt had stated in a 1940 speech, the United States had became an "arsenal of democracy."

In August of 1941 Roosevelt secretly met with British Prime Minister Winston Churchill off the coast of Newfoundland. The two agreed that America would, in all probability, soon be in the war and that the war should be fought for the principles of democracy. Roosevelt and Churchill authorized the publication of their commonly held beliefs in a document called the **Atlantic Charter**. In this document the two leaders proclaimed that they were opposed to territorial expansion for either country, and they were for free trade and self-determination. They also agreed that another world organization would have to be created to replace the League of Nations and that this new world body would have the power to guarantee the "security" of the world. Roosevelt also agreed that the United States would ship lend-lease materials bound for Britain as far as Iceland; this brought the United States one step closer to full support for the Allied cause.

THE ATTACK ON PEARL HARBOR

The Japanese desire to create an Asian empire was the prime motivation behind the Japanese invasion of Manchuria in 1931, Japanese attacks on eastern China in 1937, and the Japanese occupation of much of French Indochina in 1941. As a result of Japanese actions in Southeast Asia, Roosevelt froze all Japanese assets in the United States, cut off the sale of oil to Japan, and closed the Panama Canal to Japanese ships.

From July 1941 until the beginning of December, near-constant negotiations took place between diplomats of Japan and the United States. The Japanese desperately wanted to regain normal trade relations with the United States, but American diplomats insisted that the Japanese leave China first, which the Japanese were unwilling to do. Most Japanese military and civilian leaders were convinced that the Japanese could never achieve their goal of a Pacific empire as long as the United States was active militarily in the region. By December 1 the planning was complete for the Japanese attack on Pearl Harbor.

A few revisionist historians believe that Franklin Roosevelt knew of the impending attack on Pearl Harbor. These historians maintain that Roosevelt was acutely aware that many Americans were still opposed to American entry into war, but that an event such as Pearl Harbor would put the entire country squarely behind the war effort. The vast majority of historians believe that American intelligence knew the Japanese were going to attack somewhere, but didn't know that the attack would be at Pearl Harbor; many in American military intelligence believed the Dutch East Indies would be the next target of the Japanese.

On Sunday morning, December 7, 1941, 190 Japanese warplanes attacked the American Pacific fleet anchored at Pearl Harbor. When the attack was done, 150 American airplanes were destroyed (most on them never left the ground), six battleships were sunk, as were a number of smaller ships, and nearly 2400 Americans were killed. Luckily for the American navy, the aircraft carriers based at Pearl Harbor were out at sea on the morning of the attack.

The next day Roosevelt asked Congress for a declaration of war, stating that December 7 was "a date which will live in infamy." On December 11 Germany and Italy (who had signed a Tripartite Pact with Japan in 1940) declared war on the United States.

AMERICAN ENTERS THE WAR

In September of 1940 the President had authorized the creation of a system for the **conscription** of men into the armed forces; in the months immediately after Pearl Harbor, thousands were drafted and countless others volunteered for service. Soldiers in World War II called themselves "**GIs**"; this referred to the "Government Issued" stamp that appeared on the uniforms, tools, weapons, and everything else the government issued to them. A Council for National Defense had also been created in 1940; this body worked rapidly to convert factories over to war production. Additional legislation was also needed to prepare the country for war. In early 1942 the **General Maximum Price Regulation Act** immediately froze prices and established the rationing system that was in place for most of the war. The **Revenue Act of 1942** greatly expanded the number of Americans who had to pay federal income tax, thus increasing the amount of federal revenue.

America was forced to fight a war in Europe and a war in the Pacific. In the European theater of war, American naval forces first engaged the Germans as they attempted to protect convoys of ships taking critical food and supplies to Great Britain. These convoys were often attacked by German submarines. In this **Battle of the Atlantic** German torpedoes were dreadfully accurate (even though sonar was being used by the Americans). Between January and August of 1942, over 500 ships were sunk by German submarines.

American infantrymen were first involved in actual fighting in North Africa. American and British forces joined to defeat French North Africa in late 1942. American troops also played a role in the battles that eventually forced General Rommel's Africa Korps to surrender in May 1943. American and British soldiers also began a difficult offensive into Sicily and Italy two months later; by June of 1944 Rome had surrendered.

Ever since 1941 the Soviet Union had been the only power to consistently engage the Nazi army (the Soviet Union lost 20 million people in World War II). Stalin had asked on several occasions that a second front be opened in Western Europe; by early 1944 an invasion of France by water was being planned by Dwight D. Eisenhower, commander of all Allied forces (who would become president in 1953).

The D-Day invasion took place on the morning of June 6, 1944. The initial Allied losses on Omaha Beach were staggering, yet the D-Day invasion was the beginning of the end for Nazi Germany. By the end of July over 2 million Allied soldiers were on the ground in France, and the final squeeze of Nazi Germany began. American and British forces liberated French cities and towns as they moved eastward; at the same time Russian troops were rolling westward. By August Paris had been liberated.

The last major German offensive of the war was the **Battle of the Bulge**. Nearly 85,000 American soldiers were killed, wounded, or captured in this battle. The German attack moved the Allied lines back into Belgium, but reinforcement led by General George S. Patton again forced the Germans to retreat. When the German general staff learned that they had not been victorious at the Battle of the Bulge, most admitted that Germany would soon be defeated. American and British bombings did much to destroy several German cities.

Advancing American, British, and German troops were horrified to find concentration camps or the remnants of them. These camps were integral parts of Nazi Germany's **Final Solution** to the "Jewish problem." Between 1941 and 1945 over 6 million Jews were killed in the event now referred to as the **Holocaust**. Historians maintain that if the war continued for another two years, all of European Jewry might have been eliminated. Advancing troops were outraged at what they saw in these camps, and on several occasions shot all of the Nazi guards on the spot. Why the Holocaust occurred, and why it was endorsed by so many Germans, is the subject of hundreds of books and articles in scholarly journals.

Some historians are critical of the diplomatic and military actions of the United States both before and during the Holocaust. During the mid- to late 1930s, the State Department made it very difficult for European Jews to immigrate to the United States; with alarming unemployment figures in the United States because of the Great Depression, American decision makers felt it unwise to admit large numbers of immigrants to the country. Franklin Roosevelt knew of the existence of the concentration camps as early as late 1943, yet chose not to bomb them (which many in the camps say they would have welcomed). Roosevelt maintained that the number one priority of America had to be winning the war.

In March 1945 Allied troops crossed the Rhine River, and met up with advancing Russian troops at the Elbe River on April 25. In fierce fighting the Russians took Berlin. Deep in his bunker, Hitler committed suicide on May 1, and Germany unconditionally surrendered one week later. Celebrations for V-E Day (Victory in Europe Day) were jubilant in London and Paris, but were more restrained in American cities, as the United States still had to deal with the Japanese.

In February of 1945 Roosevelt, Stalin, and Churchill met at the **Yalta Conference**. Franklin Roosevelt had been elected to a fourth term in 1944, but photos reveal him to be very ill at Yalta (he would live only another two months). At Yalta the three leaders made major decisions concerning the structure of postwar Europe. It was agreed that Germany would be split into four zones of occupation (administered by England, France, the United States, and the Soviet Union), and that Berlin, located in the Soviet zone, would also be partitioned. Stalin promised to allow free elections in the Eastern European nations he had freed from Nazi control, and said that the Soviets would join the war against Japan after the surrender of Germany. Many historians consider the decisions made at the Yalta Conference (and the failure of the Soviet Union to totally adhere to them) to be major reasons for the beginning of the Cold War.

Some historians are critical of Franklin Roosevelt for "giving in" to Stalin at Yalta. It should be remembered that at the time of this meeting Roosevelt had only two months to live. In addition, in February 1945 the atomic bomb was not yet a working weapon. American planning for the defeat of Japan was for a full attack on the Japanese mainland; in

Roosevelt's eyes, Soviet participation in this attack was absolutely crucial (in return for this support Roosevelt made concessions to Stalin on Eastern Europe and supported the Soviet acquisition of ports and territories in Korea, Manchuria, and Outer Mongolia). Winston Churchill had strong reservations about the ultimate goals and conduct of Stalin and the Soviet Union at Yalta; these reservations would later intensify, and were articulated by Churchill in his "iron curtain" speech of March 1946.

THE WAR AGAINST JAPAN

In the aftermath of the attack on Pearl Harbor, Japan advanced against British controlled islands and territories in the Pacific. By April of 1942 Hong Kong and Singapore were both in Japanese hands. General Douglas MacArthur controlled a large American and Filipino force in the Philippines. A large Japanese force landed there, and in March MacArthur was forced to abandon his troops and go to Australia. On May 6, 1942, Americans holding out on the Bataan Peninsula were finally forced to surrender. 75,000 American and Filipino prisoners were forced to endure the 60-mile **Bataan Death March**, during which over 10,000 prisoners were executed or died from weakness (it was several years before Washington became aware of this March.

Just two days later the Americans won their first decisive victory at the **Battle of the Coral Sea**. American airplanes launched from aircraft carriers were able to stop the advance of several large Japanese troop transports. Troops on these ships were to be used for an attack on Australia. After this defeat the Japanese could never again mount a planned attack there. American airplanes also played a crucial role in the **Battle of Midway**. This battle took place in early June 1942; in it the Japanese lost 4 aircraft carriers and over 300 planes. Many military historians consider the battle to be the turning point of the Pacific War; after this Japan was never able to launch a major offensive. By mid-1942 American industrial might became more and more of a factor; the Americans could simply produce more airplanes than the Japanese could.

The Japanese were again halted at the **Battle of Guadalcanal**, which began in August of 1942 and continued into the following year. American marines engaged in jungle warfare and even hand-to-hand combat. On many occasions Japanese units would fight nearly until the last man. Beginning in 1943 the Allies instituted a policy of **island-hopping**; by this policy key Japanese strongholds would be attacked by air and sea power as American marines would push on around these strongholds. By late 1944 American bombers were able to reach major Japanese cities, and unleashed massive bombing attacks on them.

By 1944 the war had clearly turned against the Japanese. In late October General MacArthur returned to the Philippine island of Leyte (although the city of Manila was not totally liberated until the following March). The Japanese began to use **kamikaze pilots** in a desperate attempt to destroy Allied ships. Several more bloody battles waited ahead for American forces: America suffered 25,000 casualties at the Battle of Iwo Jima, and another 50,000 at the Battle of Okinawa. After these battles, however, nothing was left to stop an Allied invasion of Japan.

THE DECISION TO DROP THE ATOMIC BOMB

The incredibly bloody battles described in the preceding section greatly concerned military officials who were planning for an invasion of Japan. Japanese resistance to such an attack would have been fanatical. Franklin Roosevelt had suddenly died in late 1945; the new president, Harry Truman, was informed in July 1944 about the atomic bomb. The actual planning for this bomb was the purpose of the **Manhattan Project**, begun in August 1942. Construction of this bomb took place in Los Alamos, New Mexico under the direction of J. Robert Oppenheimer. The bomb was successfully tested in the New Mexico desert on July 16, 1945.

Much debate has taken place over the American decision to drop the atomic bomb on Japanese cities. For Harry Truman this was not a difficult decision. Losses in an invasion of Japan would have been large; Truman later admitted that what had happened at Pearl Harbor and on the Bataan Death March also influenced his decision. Some historians also claim that some in both the State Department and the War Department saw the Soviet Union as the next potential enemy of the United States and wanted to use the atomic bomb to "show them what we had." After the atomic bombs were dropped American public opinion was incredibly supportive of Truman's decision. It should be noted that movies, newsreels, and even comic books made the eventual decision to drop the bomb easier by turning the war against the Japanese into a race war. The Japanese were referred to as "Japs," were portrayed with crude racial stereotypes, and were seen as sneaky and certainly not to be trusted (it is interesting to note that the war against Germany was usually portrayed as a war against "Hitler" or against "the Nazis" and almost never as a war against the German people).

On August 6, 1945, the airplane the **Enola Gay** dropped a bomb on the city of Hiroshima. Over 75,000 were killed in the attack. Three days later another bomb was dropped on Nagasaki. Some historians are especially critical of the dropping of the second bomb; there is evidence that the Japanese were pursuing a surrender through diplomatic circles on the day of the attack. Japan surrendered one day later, and V-J celebrations took place in many American cities the following day.

THE HOME FRONT DURING THE WAR

As previously stated, the federal government took actions even before the war began to prepare the American economy for war. Thousands of American businessmen also went to Washington to take on jobs relating to the war effort. These were called "dollar-a-year" men, as almost all still received their regular salary from wherever they worked.

The demand for workers increased dramatically during the war years, thus increasing wages for workers as well. Union membership increased during the war; unions generally honored "no-strike" agreements that were made in the weeks after Pearl Harbor. Beginning in 1943 some strikes did occur, especially in the coal mines.

The government needed money to finance the war effort. As stated previously, more money was raised by expanding greatly the number of Americans who had to pay income taxes. In addition, America followed a policy begun in World War I and sold **war bonds**.

During both wars various celebrities made public appearances to encourage the public to buy these bonds.

Average Americans were asked to sacrifice much during the war. Goods such as gasoline, rubber, meat, sugar, and butter were rationed during the war; American families kept **ration cards** to determine which of these goods they could still buy during any given period. Recycling was commonplace during the war, and many had to simply do without the goods they desired. Women, for example, were desperate for silk stockings; some took to drawing a line up the back of their legs to make it appear that they had stockings on. City dwellers had to take part in "blackouts," where they would have to lower all shades to make any enemy airplane attacks more difficult. Men and boys both took turns at lookout stations, where the skies were constantly scanned for enemy bombers. Many high schools across the country eliminated vacations during the year; by doing this, school could end early and students could go off and do essential work. Many workers stayed for extra shifts at work, called "victory shifts."

Popular culture also reflected the necessities of war. Many movies during the war were light comedies, designed to keep people's minds off the war. Other movies, such as *Casablanca,* emphasized self-sacrifice and helping the war effort. "White Christmas" (sung by Bing Crosby) was a favorite during the war, evoking nostalgia in both soldiers abroad and those on the home front. Professional baseball continued during the war, but rosters were made up of players that had been classified 4-F by local draft boards (unfit for military service). The All-American Girls' Baseball League was founded in 1943 and also provided a wartime diversion for thousands of fans.

Women also entered the American workforce in large numbers during the war. Many women working in "traditional women's jobs" moved to factory jobs vacated when men went off to fight. The figure of **Rosie the Riveter** symbolized American working women during the war. In the 1930s women were discouraged from working (the argument had been that they would be taking jobs from men); during World War II many posters informed women that it was their patriotic duty to work. Problems remained for women in the workplace, however: For many jobs, even in the defense industry, they were paid less than men. It is also ironic that when the war ended women were encouraged that it was now their "patriotic duty" to return home and become housewives.

DISCRIMINATION DURING THE WAR

Many blacks also took important factory jobs and eagerly signed up for military service. However, discrimination against blacks continued during the war. Black military units were strictly segregated and were oftentimes used for menial chores instead of combat. Some American blacks at home began the **Double V campaign**: This pushed for the defeat of Germany and Japan but also the defeat of racial prejudice. CORE (the Congress for Racial Equality) was founded in 1942, and organized the very first sit-ins and boycotts; these actions would become standard tactics of the civil rights movement in the 1950s and 1960s.

Many on the West Coast feared that the Japanese that lived there were sympathizers or even spies for the Japanese cause (even though many had been born and brought up in the United States). On February 19, 1942, Franklin Roosevelt signed Executive Order 9066, which ordered Japanese-Americans to **internment camps**. American public officials told the Japanese that this was being done for their own protection; however, many Japanese noted when they got to their camps that the guns guarding these relocation centers were pointed inward and never outward. Many businesses and homes were lost by Japanese citizens.

Influential Japanese-Americans were outraged by these actions, and a legal challenge was mounted against the internment camps. In a 1944 decision, *Korematsu* v. *United States,* the Supreme Court ruled that the internment camps were legal, since they were based "on military necessity." In 1988 the United States government formally apologized to those who had been placed in camps and gave each survivor $20,000. It should be noted that American units of soldiers of Japanese descent were created during the war, and that they fought with great bravery in the campaign against Hitler.

CHAPTER REVIEW

Rapid Review Guide

To achieve the perfect 5, you should be able to explain the following:

- War production for World War II pulled America out of the Great Depression.

- World War II turned American into one of the two major world powers.

- America continued to pursue a foreign policy of isolationism throughout the 1930s.

- Lend-lease and other measures by Franklin Roosevelt brought America into the war on the side of England one year before America actually entered the war.

- The Pearl Harbor attack was part of an overall Japanese strategy, and it mobilized American public opinion for war.

- Battles fought by American GIs in Africa, Italy, and Western Europe were crucial in creating a "second front" and important in the eventual defeat of Hitler.

- Decision made at the Yalta Conference did much to influence the postwar world.

- Superior American air and sea power ultimately led to the defeat of the Japanese in the Pacific.

- The decision to drop the atomic bomb was based on the calculations of the human cost of an American invasion of Japan and as retaliation for Japanese actions during the war.

- Americans sacrificed greatly during the war and contributed through rationing, extra work, and the purchase of war bonds to the Allied victory.

- American women contributed greatly to the war effort, especially by taking industrial jobs that had been held by departed soldiers.

- Blacks continued to meet discrimination both in and out of the armed services, as did the Japanese. Japanese citizens from the West Coast were forced to move to internment camps. The America government in 1988 issued a formal apology for these actions.

Time Line

1933: Hitler comes to power in Germany
1935: Neutrality Act of 1935
1938: Hitler annexes Austria, Sudetenland
1939: Nazi-Soviet Pact
       Germany invades Poland/beginning of World War II
1940: Roosevelt reelected for third term
       American Selective Service plan instituted
1941: Lend-lease assistance begins for England
       Japanese attack Pearl Harbor/United States officially enters
   World War II
       Germany declares war on United States
1942: American troops engage in combat in Africa
       Japanese interment camps opened
       Battle of Coral Sea, Battle of Midway
       Casablanca released
1943: Allied armies invade Sicily
       United Mine Workers strike
1944: D-Day Invasion
       Roosevelt defeats Thomas Dewey, elected for fourth term
       Beginning of Battle of the Bulge

1945: Yalta Conference
Concentration camps discovered by Allied forces
FDR dies in Warm Springs, Georgia; Harry Truman becomes president
Germany surrenders unconditionally
Atomic bombs dropped on Hiroshima and Nagasaki
Japan surrenders unconditionally

✓ Review Questions

1. The internment of Japanese-Americans began for all of the reasons listed *except*

    A. large numbers of Japanese lived near Pearl Harbor in Hawaii, and some were suspected of being spies
    B. it was felt that Japanese living in California had divided loyalties when war began
    C. newspapers on the West Coast reported incidents of Japanese-Americans aiding the Japanese military effort
    D. Japanese-Americans needed protection, and the camps would provide it for them
    E. the portrayal of the Japanese in American films and magazines

(Correct Answer: **D.** Although this was the official reason given at the time, the other reasons listed were the actual reasons. California newspapers reported fabricated stories of Japanese-Americans assisting the Japanese war effort.)

2. Which was *not* a reason for the hatred many felt toward the Japanese during the war?

    A. The bombing of Pearl Harbor
    B. The fact that they were physically different in appearance from most Americans
    C. The outrage over the Bataan Death March as soon as Americans first learned of it in late 1941
    D. The portrayal of the Japanese in American films, magazines, and newspapers

(Correct Answer: **C.** The Bataan Death March did not occur until 1942, and most Americans did not know about it until 1945.)

3. Many observers would later be critical of the Yalta Conference for all of the following *except*

    A. at the conference the Soviet Union was given control over more of Germany than the other Allied powers
    B. the Soviet Union did not promise to join the war against Japan immediately
    C. Franklin Roosevelt was near death at the time of the conference
    D. all of the countries liberated by the Soviet Union would remain at least temporarily under Soviet control.

(Correct Answer: **A.** At the conference, the Soviet Union, England, France, and the United States were all to administer parts of Germany; the Soviets did not get more than anyone else. Criticism existed because by the decisions made at Yalta, the Soviet Union joined the war against Japan only days before Japan was defeated. In addition, "temporary" Soviet control over Eastern Europe allowed communist governments to be set up there. Other historians question the decisions Franklin Roosevelt made at Yalta; many wonder if his physical and mental condition were adequate for such a conference.)

4. The United States did little to stop the spread of Hitler and Nazi Germany in the 1930s because

   A. the League of Nations promised to take an active diplomatic and military role beginning in 1935
   B. the United States was much more concerned with diplomatic and political affairs in the Pacific than in Europe in the 1930s
   C. the United States was more interested in solving domestic problems in the 1930s
   D. the findings of the Nye commission did much to sour Americans on future military involvement
   E. C and D above

(Correct Answer: **E.** American policies in the 1930s were largely concerned with solving the problems of the Depression, and the Nye commission reported that arms manufacturers, looking for profits, were largely responsible for pushing America into World War I.)

5. Americans continued to crave diversions during World War II and went in large numbers to see all but which of the following:

   A. Auto racing
   B. Professional baseball
   C. Movies
   D. Big band concerts

(Correct Answer **A.** Because of shortages of gasoline and rubber for tires, auto racing was almost totally eliminated for much of the war.)

Chapter 21

The Origins of the Cold War (1945–1960)

 Winning the **Cold War** was the central goal of the United States from 1945 all the way until the fall of communism in 1990 to 1991. Almost all domestic and foreign policy decisions made in this era related in some way to American efforts to defeat the Soviet Union and their allies. A large part of the success of many sectors of the American economy in the post-World War II era was related to defense and defense-related contracts. Some) politicians lost their careers in this era if they were perceived to be "soft on communism."

Exactly whose fault was the Cold War? Initially hundreds of books and articles have been written about that very subject. American historians assigned blame to the Soviet Union for aggressive actions on their part in the period immediately following the end of World War II. "**Revisionist**" American historians have claimed that the Soviets were forced into these actions by the perceived aggressiveness of the United States and its allies. What actually happened in those years immediately following World War II is the subject of this chapter.

THE FIRST CRACKS IN THE ALLIANCE: 1945

The alliance that proved victorious in World War II began to show strains even before the end of the war. In the preceding chapter it was mentioned that tough decisions were made at the **Yalta Conference**, including allowing elections in Eastern European nations. Stalin was especially reluctant to allow free elections in Poland; as Hitler demonstrated, it provided a perfect invasion route into Soviet territory.

The United States would be somewhat handicapped diplomatically by the death of Franklin Roosevelt in April 1945. Roosevelt had excellent personal relations with Winston Churchill and felt that he could at least "understand" Stalin. When Harry Truman took over the presidency, he has little experience in foreign affairs, and Roosevelt had met with him only several times, sharing little about the appropriate way to deal with America's wartime allies.

Truman met Soviet diplomats for the first time at the initial session of the United Nations, which was held in San Francisco two weeks after he took over as president. His first face-to-face meeting with Stalin took place at the **Potsdam Conference**, held at the end of July in 1945. Truman, Stalin, and Clement Atlee (who had just replaced Churchill as Prime Minster) represented the United States, the Soviet Union, and Great Britain at this meeting. Again, the future of Eastern Europe was discussed. It was also decided to hold war-crimes trials for top Nazi leaders (the most famous of these would be known as the Nuremberg Trials). At this meeting Truman announced to Stalin the existence of the atomic bomb (ironically, Stalin had learned of it some two weeks earlier from Soviet spies in the United States).

Great philosophical differences between the two sides were apparent at this meeting also explored at this meeting. Truman expressed the view that free elections should be held in all Eastern European countries. Stalin, on the other hand, expressed the desire to have Eastern European **satellite countries**, which would act as buffers to potential future invasions of the Soviet Union.

THE IRON CURTAIN

During 1946 and 1947 the Soviet Union tightened its hold on Eastern Europe (Romania, Hungary, Bulgaria, and Poland, Czechoslovakia, and East Germany). Promised elections in Europe did not actually take place for two years. In some cases communists backed by Stalin forced noncommunists who had been freely elected out of office.

In March 1946 Winston Churchill made a speech at a college in Fulton, Missouri, where he noted that the Soviet Union had established an **iron curtain** that divided the Soviet Union and its Eastern European satellites from the independent countries of Europe. This speech is often viewed as the symbolic beginning of the Cold War.

Another key document from this era was written by American diplomat and expert in Soviet affairs George F. Kennan. Kennan wrote an anonymous article in *Foreign Affairs* magazine in July 1947 (the author was only identified at "Mr. X"), stating his opinion that Soviet policy makers were deeply committed to the destruction of America and the American way of life. The article maintained that the USSR felt threatened by the United States and felt that it had to expand for self-preservation. Kennan stated that a long-range and long-term **containment policy** to stop communism was needed. According to Kennan, if communism could be contained, it would eventually crumble under its own weight. The policy of containment was central to most American policy toward the Soviet Union for the next 45 years.

If President Truman was looking for an opportunity to apply the containment policy, opportunities soon presented themselves in Turkey and

Greece. The Soviets desperately desired to control the Dardanelles Strait; this Turkish controlled area would allow Soviet ships to go from the Black Sea into the Mediterranean. In addition, communists were threatening the existing government in Greece. In February 1947, the British (still suffering severe economic aftershocks from World War II) stated that could no longer financially assist the Turkish and Greek governments, and suggested that the United States step in (some historians maintain that this symbolically ended Great Britain's great power status and demonstrated that now the United States was one of the two major players on the world stage). In March 1947, the president announced the **Truman Doctrine**, which stated that it would become the stated duty of the United States to assist all democratic nations of the world who resisted communism. Congress authorized $400 million in aid for Greece and Turkey. The policies outlined in the Truman Doctrine and in George Kennan's article can be found embedded in American foreign policy all the way through the 1980s.

THE MARSHALL PLAN

Most Americans applauded Truman's decision to help countries resisting communism. Others wanted to see a much larger American role in Europe in the postwar era. Several observers stated that Hitler was able to rise to power because of the lack of stability in both the German government and economy in the era following World War I, and that such a situation should never be allowed to develop again.

Many felt that it was the duty of the United States to rebuild the devastated countries of Europe after World War II; it was felt that in the long run this would bring both political and economic benefits to the Western world.

By the terms of the **Marshall Plan** the United States provided nearly $12 billion in economic aid to help rebuild Europe. This assistance was of a strictly nonmilitary nature, and was designed, in large measure, to prevent Western Europe from falling into economic collapse. Seventeen Western European nations received aid under the Marshall Plan; several of them became valuable trading partners of the United States by the early part of the 1950s. The Soviet Union was invited to apply for aid from the Marshall Plan. Stalin refused and ordered the Soviet satellite countries to do so as well.

BERLIN: THE FIRST COLD WAR CRISIS

In 1948 the Americans, French, and British announced that they were to combine their areas of occupation in German and create the Federal Republic of Germany. West Berlin (located within the eastern zone of Germany) was supposed to join this Federal Republic. Berlin was already a "problem city" for communist authorities: Many residents of East Berlin (and other residents of Eastern Europe) escaped communism by passing from East Berlin to West Berlin.

In June 1948, Soviet and East German military units blocked off transportation by road into West Berlin. Historians of Soviet foreign policy note that this was the first real test by Stalin of Western Cold War resolve. Truman authorized the institution of the **Berlin Airlift**; for nearly 15 months, American and British pilots flew in enough food and supplies for West Berlin to survive. The Americans and British achieved at least a public relations victory when Stalin ordered the lifting of the blockade in May 1949. Shortly afterward, the French, English, and American zones of occupation were joined together into "West Germany," and the Americans stationed troops there to guard against further Soviet actions.

One month earlier the United States, Canada, and 10 Western European countries announced the formation of **NATO** (North Atlantic Treaty Organization). The main provision of the NATO treaty was that an attack on one signatory nation would be considered an attack on all of them. The NATO treaty placed America squarely in the middle of European affairs for the foreseeable future. NATO would expand in the early 1950s, and in 1955 as a response to NATO, the Soviet Union and its satellite countries created the **Warsaw Pact**.

1949: A PIVOTAL YEAR IN THE COLD WAR

In 1949 two events occurred that rocked American postwar confidence. In September the Soviets announced that they had exploded an atomic bomb. The potential threat of nuclear annihilation was an underlying fear for many Americans throughout the 1950s. Truman quickly gave authorization for American scientists to begin work on the **hydrogen bomb,** a bomb much more powerful than the atomic bombs dropped on Hiroshima and Nagasaki.

An equally horrifying event occurred shortly after the successful Soviet atomic test. Since 1945 the United States had been major financial backers of Nationalist China, led by Chiang Kai-shek. Communist guerrilla forces under Mao Tse-tung was able to capture much of the Chinese countryside. In 1949 Mao's forces captured Peking, the capital city. The People's Republic of China was established by Mao. Nationalist forces were forced to flee to Formosa (now Taiwan). From Formosa Chiang Kai-shek and the Nationalists maintained that they were the "true" government of China, and continued to receive a very sizable aid package from the United States. The question of "who lost China" would be repeatedly asked over the next 10 years in the United States, usually to attack the president, Harry Truman, and the Democratic party, who were in power when Nationalist China fell.

THE COLD WAR AT HOME

During 1949 and 1950 many Americans felt a sense that the tides of the Cold War were somehow shifting over in favor of the Soviet Union. Many felt that the Soviet Union could never do this alone, and that they *had* to have large number of spies within the United States helping them. Thus, under President Truman and later under President Eisenhower, there was a tremendous effort made to rid the United States of a perceived internal "communist menace." As stated in Chapter 19, on the Depression, many idealists had dabbled in communism in the 1930s; this "dabbling" would now come back to haunt them.

The Truman administration began by jailing the leaders of the American Communist party under the provisions of the 1940 **Smith Act**. This document stated that it was illegal to advocate the overthrow by force of the American government. When some Republicans claimed that the Truman administration was "soft on communism," Truman ordered the creation of a **Loyalty Review Board**, which eventually had the legal jurisdiction to investigate both new and experienced federal workers. Three or four million federal workers were examined by the board; as a result of these investigations, slightly over 100 workers were removed from their jobs. Investigations revealed that some of those investigated were homosexuals, who were oftentimes hounded out of office as well.

While the Truman administration was investigating the executive branch of government, the Congress decided to investigate communists in the government and in the entertainment industry. The congressional committee overseeing these investigations was **HUAC** (the House Un-American Activities Committee). In 1947 HUAC began to investigate the movie industry in earnest. Committee investigators relentlessly pursued actors, directors, and writers who had attended Communist party meetings in the past. Directors of movies made during World War II that cast the Soviet Union in a favorable light (such as *Mission to Moscow* and *North Star*) were brought in for questioning. Dozens of writers, actors, and directors were called in to testify about their political orientation. The Hollywood Ten was an influential group of writers and directors who refused to answer questions posed to them by members of HUAC in an open congressional session. Members of the Hollywood Ten were all sentenced to jail time.

The effects on Hollywood were major. Some Hollywood movies of the late 1940s dealt directly with the problems of society (such as *The Best Years of their Lives*). As a result of pressure from HUAC, Hollywood movies became much more tame. In addition, a **blacklist** was made of actors, directors, and writers who were potentially communist and whom the major studios should *not* hire. Many Hollywood careers were ruined by the blacklist; some writers wrote under false names or had "fronts" turn in their screenplays for them. Some of those blacklisted were unable to get work until the early 1960s.

On the senate side, Senator Pat McCarran sponsored several bills to "stop the spread of communism" in the United States. The **McCarran Internal Security Act** was enacted in 1950; under this bill all communist or communist-front organizations had to register with the government, and members of these organizations could not work in any job related to the national defense. The **McCarran-Walter Act** of 1952 greatly limited immigration from Asia and Eastern Europe; this would hopefully limit the "influx of communism" into the United States. President Truman vetoed both of these bills, but Congress passed both of them over the president's veto.

Were There Spies in America?

The trials of Alger Hiss and the Rosenbergs indicated to many Americans that there just might be communist spies infiltrating America. In 1948 HUAC began an investigation of Hiss, a former official in the State Department and an advisor to Franklin Roosevelt at the Yalta Conference. An editor of Time magazine, Whitaker Chambers had previously been a communist and testified to HUAC that Hiss had been a communist too. After several trials Hiss was finally convicted for perjury and spent four years in jail. To this day, the guilt or innocence of Alger Hiss is still debated.

In 1950 Julius and Ethel Rosenberg were charged with passing atomic secrets to the Soviet Union. The government had much more evidence on Julius than on his wife, but they were both found guilty of espionage in 1952 and executed. Considerable debate has also taken place on the guilt of the Rosenbergs, although materials released from the Soviet archives after the fall of communism strongly implicated Ethel.

THE HEATING OF THE COLD WAR: KOREA

After World War II Korea was divided into a communist North Korea and a noncommunist and pro-American South Korea divided along the **38th parallel**. In late June of 1950 North Korea invaded the south. The Security Council of the United Nations voted to send in a peacekeeping force (the Soviet Union was protesting the U.N.'s decision not to allow communist China in as a member and failed to attend the Security Council session when this was discussed). Douglas MacArthur was appointed to lead the United Nations forces, and the **Korean War** began.

U.N. forces under MacArthur drove northward into North Korea. In late November forces from communist China forced MacArthur's troops to retreat, yet by March 1951 his troops were on the offensive again. MacArthur was very critical of President Truman's handling of the war, demanding a greatly intensified bombing campaign and suggesting that Truman order the Nationalist Chinese to attack the Chinese mainland. In April 1951 Truman finally fired MacArthur for insubordination. Armistice talks to end the war dragged on for nearly two years; in the end it was decided to divide North and South Korea along the 38th parallel (along virtually the same line that divided them before the war!). More than 57,000 Americans died in this "forgotten war."

THE RISE OF McCARTHYISM

The seeming American inability to decisively defeat communism both abroad and at home led to the meteoric rise of Senator Joseph McCarthy of Wisconsin. In a speech in Wheeling, West Virginia, on February 9, 1950, McCarthy announced that he had a list of 205 known communists that were working in the State Department. McCarthy's list was sometimes longer and sometimes smaller, and oftentimes also included prominent diplomats, scholars, and Defense Department and military figures. McCarthyism was the ruthless searching out for communists in the government that took place in this period, largely without any real evidence.

For four years, McCarthy reigned supreme in Washington, with few in power or in the news media being willing to challenge him. McCarthy offered a simple reason why the United States was not conclusively winning the Cold War: because of communists in the government. The Republican party was a semireluctant supporter of McCarthy in this era; Republicans realized that the issue of communism was getting them votes. McCarthy even accused Harry Truman and former Secretary of State Marshall of being "unconscious" agents of the communist conspiracy.

In March of 1954 McCarthy claimed in a lengthy speech that the United States Army was full of communists as well. It was at this point that McCarthy began to run into major opposition; Republican President Eisenhower (a former general) stated privately that it was definitely time for McCarthy to be stopped. Tensions between the Army and McCarthy increased when it was announced that McCarthy had asked for special privileges for an aide of his that had been drafted.

The Army-McCarthy Hearings appeared on network television, and thousands found themselves riveted to them on a daily basis. Over the course of the hearings, it was discovered that McCarthy *had* asked for special favors for his aide, had doctored photographs, and had used bullying tactics on a regular basis. The end was clearly in sight for McCarthy when Joseph Welch, attorney for the Army, received loud applause when he asked McCarthy if he had any "sense of decency" and when reporter Edwin R. Murrow went on CBS News with a negative report about McCarthy and his tactics. In late 1954 McCarthy was formally censured by the Senate. His power gone, McCarthy died only three years later. The McCarthy era is now remembered as one where attack by innuendo was common and where during the investigations to "get at the truth" about communism the civil rights of many were violated.

THE COLD WAR POLICIES OF PRESIDENT EISENHOWER

Foreign policy decisions of the Eisenhower administration were often crafted by the Secretary of State, John Foster Dulles. Dulles felt that the policy of containment was not nearly aggressive enough; instead of merely containment, Dulles often spoke of "massive retaliation" against communist advances anywhere in the world. Dulles also spoke of the need to use nuclear weapons if necessary. At one press conference, Dulles stated that instead of containing communism, the goal of the United States should be to "make communism retreat" whenever and wherever possible.

Eisenhower hoped that the death of Stalin in 1953 would allow a "new understanding" between the United States and the Soviet Union. In some ways Nikita Khrushchev was different from Stalin, speaking about the possibilities of "peaceful coexistence" with the United States. However, when Hungary revolted in 1956, Khrushchev ordered this to be brutally stopped by the Soviet army.

The fate of the Hungarian leader Irme Nagy was sealed when the United States failed to assist the anti-Soviet rebellion of his government. Despite the tough talk of John Foster Dulles, who had boldly proclaimed that the United States would come to the aid of any in Eastern Europe who wanted to "liberate" themselves from communism, it was determined that U.S. forces could not be used to help the Hungarian rebels (despite the fact that the CIA operatives in Hungary had promised Nagy this aid), because this might provoke war with the Soviets. Eisenhower was also reluctant to get militarily involved in Southeast Asia, even though he believed in the **domino theory**, which proclaimed that if one country in Southeast Asia fell to the communists, others would follow. In 1954 French forces in Vietnam were being overrun by nationalist forces under the control of Ho Chi Minh. The French desperately asked for aid. Despite segments of the American military who pushed for assisting the French, Eisenhower ultimately refused.

As a result, the French were finally defeated at the **Battle of Dien Bien Phu**. After they left, an international conference took place and the **Geneva Accords** established a North Vietnam under the control of Ho Chi Minh and a South Vietnam under the control of the Emperor, Bao Dai. From the beginning, the United States supplied military aid to South Vietnam. By the terms of the Geneva Accords, a national election was scheduled for 1956 on the potential unification of the entire country. However, a coup in South Vietnam overthrew the emperor and sabotaged the election plans. Nevertheless, the United States continued to support South Vietnam.

Cold War tensions also increased during the Eisenhower administration because of events in the Middle East. After Israel was declared independent in 1948, it was supported by the Americans, while the Arabs opposing Israel were supported by the Soviet Union. In 1953 the Central Intelligence Agency carried out a plan that brought the pro-American Shah of Iran back into power.

The major Middle Eastern crisis during the era was the Suez Canal Crisis. The United States had helped Egyptian leader Colonel Gamal Abdul Nasser build the Aswan Dam. The Egyptians wanted to purchase arms from the United States as well. When the Americans refused, the Egyptians went to the Soviets with the same request. When the United States (and Great Britain), in response, totally cut off all loans to Egypt, Nasser nationalized the British-owned Suez Canal. The British and the French attacked Egypt. In response to Soviet threats that they might join the conflict on the side of the Egyptians, the Americans got the British and French to retreat from Egypt.

Eisenhower and Dulles desperately wanted to prevent the spread of communism in the Middle East. In January 1957, the **Eisenhower Doctrine** was formally unveiled, which stated that Americans arms would be used in the region to prevent communist aggression. The Americans invoked the Eisenhower Doctrine when they landed troops in Beirut, Lebanon, in mid-1958 to put down a rebellion against the government.

The Americans were equally concerned with the spread of communism in Latin America, where America had numerous economic interests. A defensive alliance of most nations of the Western Hemisphere was signed as the **Rio Pact** in 1947. Critics would argue that the United States was never shy about throwing its weight around in the region. In 1954 the CIA helped orchestrate the overthrow of the president of Guatemala on the grounds that his administration was too friendly with the Soviet Union; during this coup, property that had been seized from American businesses was restored to American hands.

In 1959 Fidel Castro orchestrated the removal of dictator Fulgencio Batista from power. Castro soon seized American businesses located in Cuba and began trade negotiations with the Soviet Union. Thus, beginning in late 1960, the United States cut off trade with Cuba, and eventually cut off diplomatic relations with the island (a situation that still exists today).

A DANGEROUS ARMS BUILDUP

During the Eisenhower administration both the United States and the Soviet Union built up their nuclear arsenals to dangerously high levels. By August of 1953 both countries had exploded hydrogen bombs, which made the bomb used at Hiroshima looked primitive in comparison. Both countries carried out nuclear tests, although in 1958 Eisenhower and Khrushchev both agreed to suspend further atomic tests in the atmosphere.

The Soviets concentrated on building up their missile capabilities in this period, causing some Americans to fear that they were falling behind, and that a "missile gap" was developing. The startling fact that the Soviets might be ahead in technology was demonstrated by their 1957 launching of **Sputnik**, the first man-made satellite that could orbit the earth. Americans were shocked as they could look up in the sky and see the satellite whiz by (in the next two years many American high schools and colleges increased the number of math and science courses students had to take so that Americans could "keep up" with the Soviets). Even more troubling was the fact that American tests to create a man-made satellite had all failed.

A final humiliation for the United States came in May of 1960, when the Russians shot down an American **U-2** spy plane. The pilot, Francis Gary Powers, was captured and taken prisoner by Soviet forces. For several days the Americans refused to admit that an American plane had even been shot down; Eisenhower eventually took full responsibility for the incident.

Toward the end of his term in office, Eisenhower warned of the extreme challenge to peace posed by the massive "military-industrial complex" that existed in America in the 1950s. The size of the military-industrial complex would certainly not decline in the 1960s.

CHAPTER REVIEW

Rapid Review Guide

To achieve the perfect 5, you should be able to explain the following:

- Winning the Cold War was the central goal of American policy for 45 years.

- The economic impact of the Cold War on American industry was enormous; many plants continued making military hardware throughout the Cold War era.

- The debate over who "started" the Cold War has occupied the minds of historians since 1945.

- Decisions made at the Yalta and Potsdam Conferences ushered in Cold War tensions between the World War II victors.

- The concept of the "iron curtain" was first articulated by Winston Churchill in 1946.

- The American strategy of containment motivated many foreign policy decisions in the Cold War era.

- The Truman Doctrine, the Marshall Plan, and NATO united America and Western Europe both militarily and economically against the Soviet Union and its satellites.

- America's resolve to oppose communism was tested during the Berlin Crisis and the Korean War.

- 1949 was a critical year in the Cold War, as the Soviet Union got the atomic bomb and mainland China turned communist.

- Some Americans feared that communists had infiltrated the American government and the entertainment industry; investigations by the House Un-American Activities Committee and Senator Joseph McCarthy were dedicated to "rooting out" communists in America.

- Under President Dwight Eisenhower, Secretary of State John Foster Dulles formulated an aggressive foreign policy that would not just contain communism by also attempt to roll communism back whenever possible.

- During the Eisenhower administration, crises in Southeast Asia, the Middle East, and Latin America further tested American resolve.

- Both the Soviet Union and the United States built up their nuclear arsenals to dangerous levels in this era.

Time Line

1945: Yalta Conference
　　　Harry Truman becomes president
　　　Potsdam Conference
1946: Winston Churchill gives "Iron Curtain" speech
　　　Article by George Kennan on containment
1947: HUAC begins probe into movie industry
　　　Introduction of Federal Employee Loyalty program
　　　President Truman articulates Truman Doctrine
1948: Berlin Airlift
　　　Implementation of Marshall Plan
　　　Creation of nation of Israel
　　　Alger Hiss implicated as a communist
1949: NATO established
　　　Soviet Union successfully tests atomic bomb
　　　Mainland China turns communist
1950: Joseph McCarthy gives speech on communists in the
　State Department
　　　Alger Hiss convicted of perjury
　　　McCarran Internal Security Act enacted
　　　Beginning of Korean War
1952: Dwight Eisenhower elected president
1953: CIA orchestrates return of Shah of Iran to power
　　　Death of Joseph Stalin
　　　Execution of the Rosenbergs
1954: Army-McCarthy hearings
　　　Government in Guatemala overthrown
　　　French defeated at Dien Bien Phu
　　　Geneva Conference
1955: Creation of the Warsaw Pact
1956: Hungarian Revolt suppressed by Soviet Union
　　　Suez crisis
1957: *Sputnik* launched by Soviet Union
1959: Castro comes to power in Cuba; United States halts trade
　with Cuba
1960: U-2 Incident
　　　John Kennedy elected president

✓ Review Questions

1. The Army-McCarthy hearings proved

  A. that a number of communists were serving in the United States Army

  B. that Americans were largely uninterested in the issue of communism

  C. that Eisenhower would support McCarthy at any cost

  D. that McCarthy had little proof for his claims

  E. the massive popularity of Joseph McCarthy

(Correct Answer: **D.** The hearings did much to discredit McCarthy. By this point Eisenhower had broken from McCarthy, and many Americans watched these hearing from beginning to end.)

2. The policy of containment stated that

   A. it would be possible for the United States and the Soviet Union to coexist over a long period of time
   B. America should go out and attempt to dislodge communist leaders where ever possible
   C. America should hold firm against communist encroachment in all parts of the world
   D. America should not hesitate to use atomic weapons against the Soviet Union
   E. the United States should depend on its Western European allies for help against the Soviet Union

(Correct Answer: **C.** Containment emphasized stopping communism whenever it attempted to expand; containment did not emphasize attacking communism where it already existed.)

3. America was especially interested in stopping communist expansion in Latin America because

   A. the United States had many economic interests in the region
   B. both Presidents Truman and Eisenhower were close to many of the Latin American leaders
   C. the Soviet Union expressed a special interest in expanding in this region
   D. the CIA had repeatedly failed in operations in Latin America in the past
   E. political leaders were attempting to gain support from voters of Hispanic origin in the United States

(Correct Answer: **A.** The United States had factories in and active trade relationships with many Latin American countries, and feared that communism would destroy American economic interests in the region. The CIA had actually been quite successful in their operations in the region in the past—witness their role in Guatemala.)

4. When HUAC began their investigation of the movie industry they looked with suspicion at writers, actors, and directors who

   A. attended Communist party meetings in the 1930s
   B. wrote or appeared in movies that were critical of the "American way of life"
   C. wrote or appeared in World War II-era films that were sympathetic to the Soviet Union
   D. invoked the Fifth Amendment when testifying before HUAC
   E. All of the above

(Correct Answer: **E.** As a result of the HUAC hearings, the American movie industry changed dramatically.)

5. Republicans claimed that the Democrats were "soft on communism" for all of the following reasons *except*

   A. during the Truman administration mainland China had gone communist
   B. Alger Hiss was an advisor to Franklin Roosevelt at Yalta
   C. the Truman administration failed to establish a system to check on the possibility of communists working for the federal government
   D. decisions made by Roosevelt and Truman at the end of World War II made it easier for the Soviet Union to control Eastern Europe
   E. there were perceived communists in the State Department during the Truman administration

(Correct Answer: **C.** All of the other four were used by Republicans to say that the Democrats were indeed "soft on communism." Truman instituted a Loyalty Review Board to verify that nearly 4 million federal workers were "true Americans.")

Chapter 22

The 1950s: Prosperity and Anxiety

 There are two widely contrasting contemporary perspectives of the 1950s. For social critics who deride the political and cultural revolutionary movements of the 1960s, the 1950s serves as a period of stability and "normalcy" before the "evils" of the 1960s ("sex, drugs, and rock and roll") set in. To others, the 1950s was not a period of placid normality, but was a period where the roots of the ferment of the 1960s began to grow. From both perspectives, the 1950s is a critical decade for historical study. Both sides would agree that most people in the 1950s valued stability. After the tremendous unrest of the Great Depression and World War II, many Americans looked forward to a period free from political unrest. The key conflict of the 1950s was the conformity desired by most American versus the stirrings of individualism and rebellion found in the writers of the Beat Generation, singers like Elvis Presley, and other cultural rebels of the decade.

ECONOMIC GROWTH AND PROSPERITY

Some economists feared that the ending of World War II would lead to economic recession. Instead, the American economy enjoyed tremendous growth in period between 1945 and 1960. In 1945 the American Gross National Product (GNP) stood at just over $200 billion; by 1960 the GNP had grown to over $500 dollars.

A significant reason for this growth was the ever-growing spending on defense during the Cold War era. The "military-industrial complex" (a term coined by Dwight D. Eisenhower) was responsible for billions of dollars of new spending during the 1950s (and far beyond). Millions were spent on technological research throughout the era.

Other significant factors were responsible for the economic growth of the era. Consumers had accumulated significant amounts of cash during World War II, but had little to spend it on, as the production of consumer goods was not emphasized in the war era. With the war over, consumers wanted to spend. Credit cards were available to consumers for the first time; Diner's Club cards were issued for the first time in 1950. Two industries that benefited from this were the automobile industry and the housing industry.

Many American households had never owned a new automobile since the 1920s, and in the postwar era, demand for cars was at a record high. If consumers needed assistance in deciding on which automobile to buy, they could receive assistance from the advertisers who were working for the various automobile companies (advertising reached levels in the 1950s equal to the 1920s). As the 1950s wore on, consumers could buy cars with bigger and bigger fins and fancier and fancier interiors. President Eisenhower and Congress encouraged America's reliance on the automobile when they enacted legislation authorizing the massive buildup of the interstate highway system (at the expense of the construction of an effective mass transit system). The highway system was a by-product of national defense plans of the Cold War; planners thought they would be ideal for troop movements and that airplanes could easily land on the straight sections of them.

The other industry that experienced significant growth in the postwar era was the housing construction business. There was a dire shortage of available housing in the immediate postwar era; in many cities two families living in an apartment designed for one was commonplace. Housing was rapidly built in the postwar era, and the demand was insatiable. The **GI Bill** of 1944 authorized low-interest mortgage loans for ex-servicemen (as well as subsidies for education).

William Levitt helped ease the housing crises when he built his initial group of dwellings in Levittown, New York. Several other **Levittowns** were constructed; homes were prefabricated, were built using virtual assembly line practices, and all looked remarkably the same. Nevertheless, William Levitt and developers like him began the move to the suburbs, the most significant population shift of the postwar era.

The economy was also spurred by the mass of appliances desired by consumers for their new homes in the suburbs. Refrigerators, television, washing machines, and countless other appliances were found in suburban households; advertising helped to ensure that the same refrigerator and television would be found in homes across the nation. Economist John Kenneth Galbraith noted that during the 1950s America had become an "**affluent society**". It should be noted, however, that even though the economy of the era enjoyed tremendous growth, the wages of many workers lagged behind spiraling prices. For many workers real income declined; this led to labor unrest in the postwar era.

POLITICAL DEVELOPMENTS OF THE POSTWAR ERA

It would have been difficult for anyone to follow Franklin Roosevelt as president, and Harry Truman, in the opinion of many, definitely suffered in comparison. Although Truman stated that "the buck stops here" when decisions were made, many critics felt that he had no consistent set of beliefs to guide him as he decided policy. Truman was considered anti-union by much of organized labor, yet he vetoed a key piece of legislation designed to take power away from labor unions. There were many strikes in 1946 and 1947, and in 1947 the **Taft-Hartley Act** was passed by the Congress over the president's veto (several biographers claim that Truman's veto was primarily symbolic and was done for political reasons). This bill stated that if any strike affected the health and safety of the country, the president could call for a 80-day cooling-off period, during which negotiations could take place and workers would go back to work, that the union contributions of individuals could not be used in federal elections, and that union leaders had to officially declare they were not communists. Unions were furious at these and other restrictions the bill imposed on them.

Truman declared a **Fair Deal policy**, in which he tried to expand the principles of the New Deal. Included in Truman's Fair Deal were plans for national health care and civil rights legislation; Truman also wanted to repeal the Taft-Hartley Act and increase government spending for public housing and education. In early 1948 he sent a civil rights bill to Congress (the first civil rights bill sent to Congress by a president since the Reconstruction). Nevertheless, Truman's popularity in early 1948 was low. Republicans rallied behind second-time candidate Thomas Dewey (who had been defeated by Franklin Roosevelt in 1944) and felt that victory would be theirs. Truman's chances seemed especially dim when Strom Thurmond also ran as a Dixiecrat candidate (in opposition to a civil rights plank in the 1948 Democratic Platform) and Henry Wallace, Truman's Secretary of Commerce, ran as a progressive. The highlight of Truman's political career was his eventual victory over Dewey; Truman's success is attributed to the fact that he campaigned more against the "do-nothing" Republican Congress than he did against Dewey. Truman could never capitalize on his 1948 victory; in the years after this victory, charges of being "soft on communism" plagued the administration.

Truman decided not to seek reelection in 1952, and former general Dwight D. Eisenhower defeated Adlai Stevenson in the general election. As president, Eisenhower saw his role as a crafter of compromise, and not as a creator of new policies. He tried to oversee a scaling back of government programs (some of these cutbacks were later rescinded) and a shift of power to the courts and to the Congress. Eisenhower also shifted much of the power traditionally held by the president to his Cabinet and other advisors. He was similar to the Republican presidents of the 1920s in that he was extremely friendly to business interests; most members of his Cabinet were businessmen. At many levels, Dwight Eisenhower was the perfect president for the 1950s.

Eisenhower's vice president was Richard Nixon, a former member of the House of Representatives and U.S. Senate from California. Nixon had first made a political name for himself in the Alger Hiss case, and his role in the 1952 campaign was largely as an anticommunist hatchet man.

Many men felt dissatisfaction with their lives in the postwar years. Many who had served in the "good war," World War II, found it difficult to return to civilian life. Many felt civilian jobs to be largely unrewarding; as the book and film ***The Man in the Gray Flannel Suit*** emphasized, a man who had fought in combat in World War II might find a 9-to-5 job in an office utterly unrewarding. Many men took on hunting and fishing as hobbies; here they could at least symbolically duplicate the war experience. For men the most popular magazines of the 1950s were *Field and Stream* and Hugh Hefner's *Playboy*.

Women felt equal frustration during this era. Many continued to work; yet women's magazines and other publications carried the clear message that now it was the woman's patriotic duty to return to the home and remain a housewife. Doris Day was the star of many films of decade; she had a "girl-next-door" type of appeal, which was attractive to many women and men of the period. College women saw college as an avenue to meet potential husbands; many dropped out immediately after finding one. Many women *did* find fulfillment as mothers and by doing volunteer work in the community. Yet to others, family life was terribly unsatisfying. Women who felt dissatisfaction with their role in suburban life were routinely told by their doctors that they were neurotics; the sale of tranquilizers to women skyrocketed. Many, many suburban women experienced discontent with their lives in the 1950s and early 1960s. Betty Friedan in ***The Feminine Mystique*** maintained that the lack of fulfillment experienced by many housewives was the genesis of the feminist revolution of the 1960s. Friedan would found NOW (National Organization for Women) in 1966.

Stereotypically, 1950s teenagers were seen as the "silent generation," interested in only hot rod cars, school mixers, and panty raids. There is a great deal of truth to this characterization. Teenagers in this era were the first teen generation to be targeted by advertisers; many teens wore the same styles and had similar tastes as a result. Adults spent a great deal of time in ensuring that teenagers did nothing in any way rebellious. Educational films in schools taught students to obey authority, to fit in with the group, to control one's emotions, and to not even think about sex. Popular television shows of the era such as *Ozzie and Harriet* showed young people who acted in exactly that manner.

However, there was a youth rebellion in the 1950s. A few brave students would show it in their attitude and attire, using the main character played by James Dean in ***Rebel Without a Cause*** or Marlon Brando in *The Wild One* as models. Jackson Pollock and other artists were also at the vanguard of another form of cultural rebellion; the significance of their giant "abstract expressionist" painting moved the center of the art world to New York City. Other young people would attempt to copy the writings and attitudes of the **Beat Generation**, a group of writers and artists who rejected an American society obsessed with the atomic bomb and with material culture. In rejecting conventional society, many Beats and their followers enjoyed jazz and drugs, and studied Eastern religious thought. Key works of the Beats include Jack Kerouac's *On the Road,* in which the main characters travel simply for the joy of traveling, and *Howl,* a poem by Allen Ginsberg that outlines in graphic detail the evils of modern society and what that society does to those attempting to live decent lives in it. It should be emphasized that few young people were actual members of the Beat Generation; a larger number went to coffee-houses, dabbled in writing poetry, and sympathized with the plight of Holden Caufield in *Catcher in the Rye.*

The main form of 1950s rebellion for young people was through rock and roll. To many adults, rock and roll was immoral, was the "devil's music," and caused juvenile delinquency; a few even charged that it was sent to America by the communists as part of their plot to conquer the United States. Nevertheless, those who listened and danced to rock and roll were, at some level, rejecting the core values of 1950s America. Young people were told to "control their emotions"; it was very hard to do that when listening to "Good Golly Miss Molly" sung by Little Richard.

The connection in the minds of many adults between rock and roll and blackness accounts for the reaction of many to Elvis Presley. To many, Elvis was very, very dangerous: He covered many black songs, and exuded sex during his live and television performances. For many who feared rock and roll, the best thing that could have possibly happened was when Elvis went into the army in 1958. By the end of the decade, rock had lost much of the ferocity it possessed in 1956 to 1957.

The legacy of the cultural rebels of the 1950s would certainly have tremendous influence in the 1960s. The behavior of members of Beat Generation would be copied by the hippies. In addition, the rules that were so carefully taught to 1950s teenagers would be very intentionally broken by many teens in the 1960s.

CHAPTER REVIEW

Rapid Review Guide

To achieve the perfect 5, you should be able to explain that

- The 1950s is viewed by some as a decade of complacency and by others as a decade of growing ferment.

- Large-scale economic growth continued throughout the 1950s, spurred by Cold War defense needs, automobile sales, housing sales, and the sale of appliances.

- The advertising industry did much to shape consumer desires in the 1950s.

- The GI Bill gave many veterans low-income mortgages and the possibility of a college education after World War II.

- Many families moved to suburbia in the 1950s; critics maintained that this increased the conformity of American society.

- During the baby boom the birthrate drastically increased; the baby boom lasted from 1945 to 1962.

- Presidents Truman and Eisenhower were both dwarfed by the memory of the personality and the policies of Franklin Roosevelt.

- Jackie Robinson did much to advance the cause of rights in the postwar era.

- *Brown* v. *Board of Education* was a tremendous victory for those pushing for school integration in the 1950s.

- The Montgomery bus boycott and the events at Central High School in Little Rock, Arkansas, demonstrated the techniques that would prove to be successful in defeating segregation.

- Many men and many women felt great frustration with suburban family life of the 1950s.

- 1950s teenagers are often called the "silent generation," although James Dean, the Beat generation of writers, and Elvis Presley all attracted followers among young people who did rebel in the 1950s.

Time Line

1944: GI Bill enacted
1947: Taft-Hartley Act enacted
       Jackie Robinson first plays for Brooklyn Dodgers
1948: Truman elected president in stunning upset
       Truman orders desegregation of armed forces
1950: Diner's Club credit card offered
1951: Publication of *Catcher in the Rye* by J. D. Salinger
1952: Dwight D. Eisenhower elected president
1953: Defense budget at $47 billion dollars
       Allen Freed begins to play rock and roll on the radio in
Cleveland, Ohio
1954: *Brown* v. *Board of Education* Supreme Court decision
1955: First McDonald's opens
       Rebel Without a Cause released
       Bus boycott in Montgomery, Alabama
1956: Interstate Highway Act enacted
       Majority of U.S. workers hold white-collar jobs
       Howl by Allen Ginsberg first read
1957: Baby boom peaks
       Publication of *On the Road* by Jack Kerouac
       Resistance to school integration in Little Rock, Arkansas
1960: Three-quarters of all American homes have a TV set

✓ Review Questions

1. Consumer spending increased in the 1950s because of all of the following *except*

   A. many Americans were once again purchasing stock
   B. many Americans were buying appliances for their homes
   C. many families were buying automobiles
   D. many Americans were buying homes
   E. advertising had a major impact on the American consumer

(Correct Answer: **A.** Americans were buying consumer goods in the postwar era. Many had money but not goods to buy in World War II. The purchase of stock would become pronounced only after this post-World War II buying spree ended.)

2. The policies of the presidency of Dwight D. Eisenhower are most similar to the policies of the presidency of

   A. Franklin Roosevelt
   B. William Howard Taft
   C. Calvin Coolidge
   D. Theodore Roosevelt
   E. Woodrow Wilson

(Correct Answer: **C.** Although each was somewhat different in style, Coolidge and Eisenhower were both friends of big business, believed in a balanced budget, and believed in a smaller role for the federal government and the presidency.)

3. How did their experiences in the Great Depression and World War II affect the generation who began to raise families in the postwar era?

   A. They turned inward to family for comfort.
   B. They were likely to want to give their children many of the things they had not been able to have.
   C. Interested in consumer goods, they would be likely to buy many things on credit.
   D. A and B above.
   E. All of the above.

(Correct Answer: **D.** Many of those who lived through the Depression were never comfortable with the idea of buying on credit; some never got credit cards at any point in their lives. Some historians say that this generation of parents spoiled their children, forming the expectations that some of these children would have as young adults in the 1960s.)

4. The most important impact of television on viewers of the early 1950s was that

   A. it provided them with comedies that allowed them to forget the difficult years of the 1950s
   B. it allowed them to receive the latest news of the day
   C. it imposed a sense of conformity on American society
   D. it fostered a growing youth culture
   E. it allowed viewers to view the realities of communism in the Soviet Union

(Correct Answer: **C.** TV viewers could get comedies and news on the radio. There was little on television in the early 1950s that specifically appealed to youth.)

5. Many Americans were especially fearful of rock and roll in the 1950s because

   A. many of the musicians who played it were black
   B. Elvis Presley and many of the early performers of rock and roll came from a decidedly lower-class background
   C. Elvis Presley and many other early rock and roll performers came from the American South
   D. the messages found in early rock and roll supported communism
   E. young people were buying fewer albums by established stars

(Correct Answer: **A.** Elvis, Carl Perkins, Jerry Lee Lewis, and others were of lower-class backgrounds and were from the South, but the main objection to rock and roll was its connection to black culture—for instance, Fats Domino, Chuck Berry, and Little Richard. No known early rock and roll song supported communism.)

Chapter 23

America in an Era of Turmoil (1960–1975)

 Like the 1950s, the decade of the 1960s is perceived very differently by historians and social critics. Some perceive the changes of the 1960s as a very refreshing antidote to the suffocating conformity of the 1950s. Other observers see the revolts of the 1960s as self-indulgent, harmful to America, and the seed of much that is wrong with the United States today. All would agree that conflicts over civil rights and the Vietnam War greatly influenced virtually every major political figure and many ordinary citizens of the 1960s.

THE 1960 PRESIDENTIAL ELECTION

Many Americans perceived the election of John Kennedy over Richard Nixon in 1960 as the beginning of a new age for America. His statement during his inauguration speech "Ask not what your country can do for you—ask what you can do for your country" is remembered by millions today. At age 43, Kennedy appeared young and vigorous (especially when flanked by his wife, Jacqueline). Kennedy was the son of a former ambassador to Britain and had served as a congressman and senator from Massachusetts. He was also a Roman Catholic.

Some voters considered Richard Nixon to be "too tied to the past"; as previously mentioned, he was the vice president under Dwight D. Eisenhower. Historians note that this was the first election greatly affected by television; in four presidential debates Nixon appeared nervous and tired. Ironically, those who heard the debates on the radio didn't feel that Nixon lost them. Some historians argue that the television image projected by Nixon actually cost him the election. The 1960 popular vote was one of the closest in history; Nixon lost by only 120,000 votes (out of nearly 34 million votes cast).

DOMESTIC POLICIES UNDER KENNEDY AND JOHNSON

Early in his administration John Kennedy stated that America was on the brink of entering into a **New Frontier**. The press from this point on dubbed his domestic policies "New Frontier" policies. Kennedy had plans to stimulate the economy and to seriously attack poverty in America (*The Other America* by Michael Harrington was published in 1962; this book outlined the plight of America's poor and had a great effect on Kennedy and his circle). Kennedy supported several important domestic programs, including a Medicare program (later approved during the administration of Lyndon Johnson) and substantial federal aid to education and to urban renewal.

Very little of Kennedy's domestic agenda was adopted by Congress. His plans to cut taxes and to increase spending on education never even got out of congressional committee. One of Kennedy's domestic successes was to convince Congress to raise the minimum wage from $1.00 per hour to $1.25. Kennedy also established a Peace Corps program, in which young men and women volunteered to help residents in developing countries around the world.

One program that was considered a top priority by both Kennedy and Congress was the space program. Kennedy was barely in office when Soviet cosmonaut Yuri Gagarin became the first human to travel in space. In early May America put its first man in space (Alan Shepard), and in February 1962 John Glenn (later a United States Senator) became the first American astronaut to orbit the earth. During this era Kennedy also made the bold promise that America would land a man on the moon by the end of the 1960s.

The New Frontier programs ended permanently when John Kennedy was assassinated in Dallas, Texas, on November 22, 1963. Kennedy was in Texas to heal wounds in the local Democratic party and to rally support for the 1964 presidential election. Kennedy was riding in a motorcade through downtown Dallas when he was killed. An ex-marine named Lee Harvey Oswald was arrested and charged with Kennedy's death. Oswald never went to trial because he was shot and killed by a Dallas nightclub owner, Jack Ruby, two days later. The **Warren Commission** was formed to investigate the assassination; the report of this committee firmly supported those who said that Oswald acted alone. To this day there are those who maintain that a conspiracy was responsible for Kennedy's death.

Vice President Lyndon Johnson was sworn into office shortly after Kennedy's assassination. In the year after Kennedy's death, Johnson was able to get much of Kennedy's domestic policy plans through Congress. Johnson had been the Senate majority leader before becoming vice president, and in early 1964 was easily able to maneuver the previously rejected Kennedy tax cut through Congress.

Johnson ran for reelection against Senator Barry Goldwater in the 1964 presidential election. Goldwater was a conservative from Arizona who was too far to the right for mainstream America to accept. He spoke of using nuclear weapons in Vietnam and famously stated that "extremism in the defense of liberty is no vice." Lyndon Johnson won nearly 62 percent of the popular vote and was able to institute his own economic plans in 1965; in a speech early in that year, Johnson stated that his goal was to create a **Great Society** in America.

In speech after speech Johnson stated that it would be possible to truly end poverty in America. The Department of Housing and Urban Affairs was created as a Cabinet-level department. In 1964 Johnson had begun the **VISTA** program, which organized volunteers who worked in the poorest communities of the United States. In 1965, Congress passed Johnson's Housing and Urban Development Act, which organized the building of nearly 250,000 new housing units in America's cities and authorized over $3 billion for further urban development. Johnson's major initiatives in education authorized grants to help schools in the poorest sections of America and established **Head Start**, a program to help disadvantaged preschool students. In 1965 Johnson established a **Medicare** system, which provided hospital insurance and medical coverage for America's senior citizens, and Medicaid, which assisted Americans of any age who could not afford health insurance.

The Great Society programs of Lyndon Johnson positively impacted the lives of thousands of Americans, but frustration set in when it appeared that large amounts of poverty remained in America. In addition, the cost of Great Society programs put a strain on American taxpayers (some of whom resented the fact that their taxes were going to help poor people). However, it should be noted that the number of those living in poverty was cut by at least 40 percent by Great Society programs. Many of these programs ended up being reduced or eliminated because of the expenses of America's war in Vietnam.

THE STRUGGLE OF BLACK AMERICANS: FROM NONVIOLENCE TO BLACK POWER

As was noted in the previous chapter, Martin Luther King, Jr. emerged as a key leader of the civil rights movement during the Montgomery, Alabama bus boycott. King and other Southern clergymen founded the Southern Christian Leadership Conference (SCLC), which taught that civil rights could be achieved through nonviolent protest. SCLC leaders taught that violence could never be utilized to achieve their goals, no matter what the circumstance.

Many younger blacks were eager for the fight for civil rights to develop at a quicker pace. In 1960 the Student Nonviolent Coordinating Committee (SNCC) was formed; its leaders were not ministers, and they demanded immediate, not gradual, change. During the first years of its existence, SNCC attracted both black and white members; many of the whites were college students from Northern universities.

An effective technique utilized by the civil rights movement in the early 1960s was the <u>sit-in</u>. Blacks were not allowed to eat at the lunch counters of many Southern stores, even though blacks could buy merchandise at these stores. Black and white civil rights workers would sit down at these lunch counters; when they were denied service, they continued to sit there (preventing other paying customers from taking their spaces). Picketers would oftentimes march outside the store in question. Those participating in sit-ins received tremendous verbal and physical harassment from other whites, yet the tactic of the sit-in helped to integrate dozens of Southern establishments in the first several years of the 1960s.

In May 1961 the Congress for Racial Equality sponsored the <u>**Freedom Rides**</u>. During the previous year the Supreme Court had ruled that bus stations and waiting rooms in these stations had to be integrated. On the Freedom Rides, both black and white volunteers started in Washington and were determined to ride through the South to see if cities had complied with the Supreme Court legislation. In Anniston, Alabama, a white mob greeted the bus, beating many of the freedom riders and burning the bus. Freedom rides continued throughout the summer; almost all riders experienced some violence or were arrested.

The Freedom Rides introduced an important influence into the civil rights struggle in the South: the public opinion of the rest of the country. Many Americans were horrified at the violence they witnessed; many called their representatives in Congress to urge that the federal government do more to support the freedom riders. By the end of the summer, marshals from the Justice Department were in every city the Freedom Ride buses passed through to ensure a lack of violence.

Under Attorney General Robert Kennedy the federal government became much more involved in enforcing federal civil rights guidelines and court rulings. In September of 1962 President Kennedy nationalized the Alabama National Guard and sent in federal marshals to suppress protesters and allow James Meredith to be the first black to take classes at the University of Mississippi. In Birmingham, Alabama, city officials turned fire hoses and trained dogs on civil rights protesters; the broadcast of these events to the entire nation again created a widespread outrage against those in the South who were opposing court-ordered integration.

President Kennedy went very slowly on civil rights issues, but in the summer of 1963, he presented to Congress a wide-ranging civil rights bill that would have withheld large amounts of federal funding from states that continued to practice segregation. To muster support for this bill, civil rights leaders organized the August 28, 1963 <u>**March on Washington**</u>. More than 200,000 people showed up to protest for civil rights legislation; it was at this rally that Martin Luther King made his very famous "I have a dream" speech.

In 1964 Lyndon Johnson presented to Congress the most wide-ranging civil rights bill since Reconstruction. The <u>**Civil Rights Act of 1964**</u> stated that the same standards had to be used to register white and black voters, that racial discrimination could not be used by employers to hire workers, that discrimination was illegal in all public locations, and that an

Equal Employment Opportunity Commission would be created. The Voting Rights Act of 1965 outlawed measures such as literacy tests, which had been used to prevent blacks from voting. Passage of this bill was aided by the public sentiment that followed the revelation that three civil rights workers had been killed the previous summer while attempting to register voters in Mississippi. Television reports of violence against civil rights workers, such as was seen during Martin Luther King's march in Selma, Alabama, in 1965, convinced many Americans that additional civil rights legislation was necessary.

Many blacks who lived in poverty in Northern cities believed that the civil rights movement was doing little or nothing for them. In August 1965 riots broke out in the Watts section of Los Angeles; Chicago, Newark, and Detroit soon experienced similar riots. The **Kerner Commission** was authorized to investigate the cause of these riots, and stated that black poverty and the lack of hope in the black urban communities were the major causes of these disturbances. The Kerner Commission reported that two societies existed in America, one white and rich, and the other poor and black.

One group that preached opposition to integration was the **Nation of Islam**. This organization (also called the Black Muslims) preached that it was to the benefit of white society to keep blacks poor and in ghettoes, and that for blacks to improve their position they would have to do it themselves. Malcolm X would become the most famous representative of this group, preaching **black nationalism**. Eventually Malcolm X rejected the more extreme concepts of the Nation of Islam, and he was killed in February 1965.

The ideas of black nationalism exerted a great deal of influence on many of the younger members of SNCC. One, Stokely Carmichael, began to urge blacks to take up arms to defend themselves against whites; Carmichael also orchestrated the removal of all whites from SNCC. In addition, Carmichael began to urge SNCC members to support **black power**; this concept stated that blacks should have pride in their history and their heritage, and that blacks should create their own society apart from the all-controlling white society.

The most visible group supporting black power were the **Black Panthers**. This San Francisco group, founded by Bobby Seale and Huey Newton, had a militarist image. Several members died after vicious gun battles with police. At the same time, the Black Panthers set up programs that gave food to the poorest members of San Francisco's black population and established schools to teach black history and culture to the children in the community. However, the image of this organization was greatly damaged by its violent reputation.

THE RISE OF FEMINISM

Another group that fought for additional freedoms in the 1960s were women. As discussed in the previous chapter, many women felt extreme frustration with their lives in the 1950s. Some college-aged women were active in the civil rights movement in the early 1960s, but oftentimes felt frustrated when they were always the ones asked to make the coffee or do the typing.

In the mid-1960s even women in suburbia began to notice that the frustrations they had were shared by many of the women living around them. Women's support groups became common on both college campuses and in suburban communities. A pivotal book that helped bolster this growing **feminist** movement was *The Feminine Mystique* by Betty Friedan.

In 1966 NOW (**National Organization for Women**) was founded by Friedan. NOW was a decidedly middle-class organization and was dedicated to getting equal pay for women at work and to ending images in the media that objectified women. In 1972 Gloria Steinem founded the feminist magazine *Ms*. The key Supreme Court decision of the era concerning women was the 1973 *Roe v. Wade* ruling, which, with some restrictions, legalized abortion. Many feminists pushed for the passage of an Equal Rights Amendment, but this amendment was never ratified by enough states to become part of the Constitution.

Other groups protested for equal rights during this period. The **American Indian Movement** (AIM) wanted Native Americans to be knowledgeable about their heritage, and also influenced various tribes to mount legal battles to get back land that had been illegally taken from them. A standoff between AIM members and government authorities took place at Wounded Knee, South Dakota, in 1973; as a result, legislation passed in the 1970s gave Native Americans more autonomy in tribal matters.

Latino groups also began to protest for rights in this era. A large number of Latinos were employed as migrant farm workers in California; Cesar Chavez organized the **United Farm Workers** against farmers (especially grape growers) in California. Environmental groups also became active in this era. *Silent Spring* by Rachel Carson came out in 1962 and warned about the dangers of DDT. Many also protested throughout the decade against the dangers of nuclear power.

THE COLD WAR IN THE 1960s

Cold War tensions and fears continued to dominate in the early 1960s. The fear of the bomb continued unabated; movies such as *Fail-Safe* and *Dr. Strangelove* explored a world where an "accident" with the bomb might occur. Both the United States and the Soviet Union openly tested nuclear weapons during 1961 and 1962.

A plan to liberate Cuba from Castro had actually been formulated during the Eisenhower administration; by this plan the CIA would train Cubans living in America to invade Cuba, and the United States would provide air cover. This operation, called the **Bay of Pigs**, took place in April 1961 and was a complete fiasco, with virtually the entire invasion force killed or captured by Castro's forces. The Bay of Pigs was a major embarrassment for the Kennedy administration in their first months in office.

In Berlin, refugees from the East continued to try to escape to West Berlin on a daily basis; in August of 1961 the East Germans and the Soviets constructed the concrete **Berlin Wall**, dividing the two halves of the city. The issue that almost brought the world to World War III was not in Europe, however; it was in Cuba. In mid-October of 1962 American reconnaissance flights over Cuba indicated Soviet-made missile sights under construction. In the **Cuban Missile Crisis** President Kennedy established a naval blockade of Cuba and told Soviet leader Nikita Khrushchev to remove the missiles from Cuba. Khrushchev backed down and removed the missiles, averting the potential of world war. It is known now that if American forces had landed in Cuba, Soviet authorities were seriously contemplating the use of tactical nuclear weapons against them. Luckily, effective diplomacy prevented the outbreak of a potentially catastrophic crisis. Shortly afterward the United States and the Soviet Union signed a Limited Test Ban Treaty, and a "hot line" was installed, connecting the White House and the Kremlin so that future crises could be dealt with quickly.

THE VIETNAM WAR AND ITS IMPACT ON AMERICAN SOCIETY

Since the 1950s the United States had supported noncommunist South Vietnam against the North, led by communist and nationalist Ho Chi Minh. The South Vietnamese government also had to fight the **Vietcong**, communist guerrillas who lived in South Vietnam but supported the North. During the Kennedy administration the number of American advisors in Vietnam increased. American officials became increasingly suspicious of the effectiveness of South Vietnamese president Diem; in the fall of 1963 these officials supported (or orchestrated, depending on which historian you read) the assassination of Diem.

Shortly after becoming president, Lyndon Johnson decided that to achieve victory, the war in Vietnam had to be intensified. In August 1964, Johnson announced to the nation that light North Vietnamese gunboats had fired on American destroyers in the Gulf of Tonkin, which is in international waters. Some historians are skeptical that these events ever took place. Nevertheless, Congress passed the **Gulf of Tonkin** Resolution, which gave the president the power to "prevent further aggression" in Vietnam; this resolution allowed the president to control the war without the necessity of consulting Congress.

Throughout 1965, 1966, and 1967, America continued to increase its commitment in Vietnam; by early 1968 nearly 540,000 American soldiers were stationed in Vietnam. Beginning in 1965 bombing campaigns against North Vietnam became commonplace. American soldiers in Vietnam became increasingly frustrated by the jungle tactics used by their enemies, by the fact that one's friend by day might be one's enemy by night, and by the seeming lack of effectiveness of the South Vietnamese army.

A key battle of the war was the **Tet Offensive**, which began on January 30, 1968. During the first day of the Vietnamese new year, the Vietcong initiated major offensives in cities across South Vietnam. Saigon, the capital, was even attacked, and for several hours the Vietcong held the American embassy. In the end, the Vietcong and North Vietnamese suffered major losses as a result of the Tet Offensive. Nevertheless, this was the battle that began to conclusively turn American public opinion against the war. The sights on television of American forces trying to recapture their own embassy back certainly made many question the idea that "victory was just around the corner," which is what was being told to the American people by military and civilian officials.

The Vietnam War drove Lyndon Johnson from the White House. Diaries of several in Johnson's inner circle show that he was consumed by the war. In February 1968 Johnson began his reelection bid by taking on Senator Eugene McCarthy of Minnesota, who was running on a peace ticket, in the New Hampshire presidential primary. Johnson won, but got only 48 percent of the total votes to 42 percent for McCarthy. Johnson considered this a humiliation, and one month later pulled out of the presidential race. Johnson endorsed Vice President Hubert Humphrey for president. By this point Robert Kennedy had also announced his candidacy.

Throughout 1968 support for the Vietnam War continued to fade in America. The Republican candidate for president, Richard Nixon, gained support when he proclaimed that he had a "secret plan" to end the war. Reports of the brutality of the war also shocked many Americans. Many were disturbed to find that Americans were using **napalm**, a substance that sticks to the skin and burns, on civilian villages. The story of the 1968 **My Lai Massacre**, where nearly 200 Vietnamese women, children, and elderly men were murdered by American soldiers, horrified many Americans. Some Americans began to wonder what the United States was doing in Vietnam, and what the war was doing to the United States.

The student protest movement also began to furiously campaign against the war. Student activists had previously been active in the civil rights movement. In 1960 the **Students for a Democratic Society** (SDS) organization was formed. The ***Port Huron Statement*** was the founding document of this organization, and called for a less materialistic society that encouraged "participatory democracy." SDS would become one of the major student organizations opposing the war.

The **Free Speech Movement** had grown at the University of California at Berkeley in 1964 when school officials refused to allow political materials to be distributed on campus. Campus buildings were occupied, as students demanded college courses more relevant to their lives. Tactics used by Berkeley students were copied by students at colleges across the country.

The Vietnam War greatly expanded the student protest movement in America. Many students were passionately opposed to the war on moral grounds; to be fair, others were part of the movement because they didn't want to be drafted. Television pictures of young men burning their draft cards were commonplace. Antiwar demonstrations that had attracted a few hundred people in 1964 were now attracting thousands; a 1967 antiwar rally drew 500,000 people to Central Park in New York.

1968 saw the protests grow, both in numbers and in intensity. Events of 1968 convinced many young people that getting involved in mainstream politics (as Eugene McCarthy had tried to get them to do) was fruitless. Martin Luther King and Robert Kennedy were killed in the spring of that year; to many, that left the presidential race between two representatives of the old guard, Richard Nixon and Hubert Humphrey. What, many students asked, was the point of even getting involved in politics if candidates like that were the end result? In the spring of 1968 major protests broke out at Columbia University; in August as protesters chanted "the whole world is watching," Chicago police officers brutally beat students and others who had shown up to protest at the Democratic National Convention. By 1969 disputes over how much violence is acceptable began to tear SDS apart as well.

Another group of revolutionaries in the 1960s rejected political involvement and supported cultural revolution instead. Members of the **counterculture** rejected America and its values as much as antiwar protesters did, but believed that personal revolution was most vital. These "hippies," or countercultural rebels, often had little to do with members of SDS; the revolution of the hippies consisted of growing one's hair long, listening to the "right" music, and partaking of psychedelic drugs. Timothy Leary and other proponents of LSD implored young people to "tune in, turn on, and drop out." Sexual freedom was also commonplace in the counterculture. A birth control pill had been approved by the federal government in 1960; a button worn by many in the 1960s stated "If It Feels Good, Do It!" The Mecca for many of these rebels in 1967 was San Francisco, where the music and lifestyle of groups such as the Grateful Dead personified the counterculture of the 1960s. The **Woodstock Music Festival** of 1969 was the most outward manifestation of the "peace and love" rebels of the 1960s. For members of the counterculture, personal rebellion was a much more valid form of rebellion than political rebellion; it should be remembered that Pete Townshend of "The Who" threw radical political organizer Abbie Hoffman off the stage at Woodstock.

Richard Nixon was elected in November of 1968, and soon announced his policy of **Vietnamization** of the war, which consisted of training the South Vietnamese army and gradually pulling American forces out. By 1972 American forces in Vietnam only numbered 24,000 (as the numbers of soldiers in Vietnam lessened, so did the antiwar protests). In April of 1970, however, Nixon announced that to support the South Vietnamese government, massive bombing of the North was needed and that the war needed to be extended into Cambodia to wipe out communist bases there. Colleges campuses across the country, for one last time, joined together in massive protest. At **Kent State University** four students were killed by National Guardsmen who opened fire on the protesters; two students were killed at Jackson State University in Mississippi. American public opinion at this point was deeply divided on the war; two days after Kent State nearly 100,000 construction workers marched in New York City for the war.

In 1971 the **<u>Pentagon Papers</u>** were leaked by a former Department of Defense employee, Daniel Ellsburg. The Pentagon Papers revealed that the government had deceived the American public and the Congress about Vietnam as early as 1964. By this point, most Americans awaited the end of American involvement in the war.

American was involved in negotiations with the North Vietnamese in Paris. Negotiations intensified in December 1972 when President Nixon ordered the heaviest bombing of the war against North Vietnam. In January 1973 it was announced that American forces would leave Vietnam in 60 days, that all American prisoners would be returned, and that the boundary between North and South Vietnam would be respected. On March 29, 1973, the last American soldiers left Vietnam; 60,000 Americans had died there. On April 30, 1975, the North Vietnamese captured Saigon, the capital of South Vietnam, ending the Vietnam War. The last Americans had left the country one day earlier.

CHAPTER REVIEW

Rapid Review Guide

To achieve the perfect 5, you should be able to explain the following:

- The events that dramatically altered America including protests and cultural rebellion in the 1960s are seen by some in a positive light and others in a negative light.

- John Kennedy projected a new image of presidential leadership, although few of his domestic programs were actually passed by Congress.

- The Cuban Missile Crisis was the critical foreign policy crisis of the Kennedy administration, and may have brought the world close to world war.

- After Kennedy's death Lyndon Johnson was able to get Congress to pass his Great Society domestic programs, which included Head Start and Medicare.

- Nonviolence remained the major tactic of the civil rights movement throughout the 1960s, although some black leaders began to advocate "black power."

- Women strove to achieve equal rights in the 1960s through the National Organization for Women and consciousness-raising groups.

- Lyndon Johnson determined early in his presidency that an escalation in the war in Vietnam would be necessary, and more materials and men went to Vietnam from 1965–1968.

- The military in Vietnam was frustrated by the military tactics of the enemy and by faltering support at home.

- The Tet Offensive did much to turn American public opinion against the war.

- Student protesters held increasingly large demonstrations against the war; SDS was the main organization of student activists.

- Members of the counterculture advocated a personal and not a political rebellion in this era.

- Richard Nixon removed American troops from Vietnam through the policy of Vietnamization; the South Vietnamese government fell two years after American troops departed.

Time Line

1960: John Kennedy elected president
Sit-ins beginning
Students for a Democratic Society (SDS) formed
Student Nonviolent Coordinating Committee (SNCC) formed
1961: Freedom Rides
Bay of Pigs invasion
Construction of Berlin Wall
First American travels in space
1962: James Merideth enters University of Mississippi
SDS issues *Port Huron Statement*
Silent Spring by Rachel Carson published
Cuban Missile Crisis
The Other America by Michael Harrington published
1963: John Kennedy assassinated; Lyndon Johnson becomes president
Civil rights march on Washington
The Feminine Mystique by Betty Friedan published
President Diem ousted in South Vietnam
1964: Beginning of Johnson's War on Poverty programs
Civil Rights Act enacted
Free Speech Movement at Berkeley begins
Tonkin Gulf Resolution
Johnson reelected
1965: Elementary and Secondary Education Act passed
Johnson sends more troops to Vietnam
Voting Rights Act passed
Murder of Malcolm X
Watts riots burn section of Los Angeles
1966: Stokely Carmichael calls for "black power"
Formation of Black Panther party
Formation of National Organization for Women (NOW)
1967: Riots in many American cities
Antiwar demonstrations intensify

1968: Martin Luther King assassinated
Robert Kennedy assassinated
Student protests at Columbia University
Battle between police and protesters at Democratic
National Convention
Richard Nixon elected president
American Indian Movement (AIM) founded
Tet Offensive
My Lai Massacre
1969: Woodstock Music Festival
1970: United States invades Cambodia
Killings at Kent State, Jackson State
1971: *Pentagon Papers* published by the *New York Times*
1972: Nixon reelected
1973: Vietnam cease-fire announced; American troops leave Vietnam
Roe v. *Wade* decision
1975: South Vietnam falls to North Vietnam, ending the Vietnam War

✓ Review Questions

1. The initial fate of the Freedom Riders demonstrated that

   A. Southerners had largely accepted Northern orders to integrate bus stations and other public facilities
   B. state governments were at the forefront in the enforcement of civil rights laws
   C. television news broadcasts had a powerful hold on the American public
   D. by 1961 the federal government was committed to vigorously protecting the civil rights of all citizens
   E. some Southern governors were beginning to moderate their positions

(Correct Answer: **C.** The images of burned buses and beaten freedom riders horrified many Americans. At this point neither the federal or state governments protected the rights of freedom riders.)

2. The Tet Offensive demonstrated that

   A. American forces were fairly close to a decisive victory in Vietnam
   B. military and civilian officials had been less than candid with the American people on the progress of the war
   C. the Vietcong could defeat American soldiers in the battlefield
   D. cooperation between Americans and the South Vietnamese army was improving
   E. despite much criticism, the policies of General Westmoreland were proving to be effective

(Correct Answer: **B.** The Tet Offensive was a military defeat for the Vietcong. However, it did prove that victory was not "around the corner," which is what many military officials were publicly claiming.)

3. The membership rolls of Students for a Democratic Society were at an all-time high when

A. the struggles of the civil rights movement in the South were shown on national television
B. Nixon invaded Cambodia
C. Nixon intensified the bombing to its highest levels of the war in 1972
D. more young men were being sent to Vietnam between 1965 and 1967
E. the organization began to plan violent acts against the government

(Correct Answer: **D.** By the time of the invasion of Cambodia and the massive bombing at the end of the war, SDS had split into factions. The civil rights movement attracted a relatively small number of new members to SDS.)

4. Some Northern blacks were attracted to the call for "black power" for all of the following reasons *except*

   A. Martin Luther King and others in the civil rights movement seemed more interested in improving the position of Southern blacks
   B. ghetto sections of Northern cities remained poor, and many residents there felt little hope
   C. Malcolm X and Stokely Carmichael evoked powerful images of black pride

D. vast numbers of Northern blacks had joined the Nation of Islam
E. economic despair still gripped many blacks living in Northern cities

(Correct Answer: **D.** All of the other reasons caused some Northern blacks to abandon Martin Luther King's call for integration. Only a small proportion of blacks ever joined the Nation of Islam.)

5. Highlights for feminist leaders of this era included all of the following *except*

   A. the founding of *Ms.*
   B. the formation of NOW
   C. the drive for passage of the Equal Rights Amendment
   D. the increased awareness of "women's issues" in society
   E. the publication of *The Feminine Mystique*

(Correct Answer: **C.** After a long struggle, the drive to get the ERA in the Constitution was finally abandoned when it became obvious that not enough state legislatures would ever pass it.)

Chapter 24

America from 1968 to 1988: Decline and Rebirth

 Some historians claim that the accomplishments of the presidency of Richard Nixon are oftentimes overlooked. Nixon opened diplomatic relations with China, improved relations with the Soviet Union, and began to break the Democratic stranglehold on politics in the South that had existed since the New Deal. Despite these developments, Richard Nixon will always be associated with the Watergate scandal. Watergate began a period where faith in the national government sharply declined; this lasted through the presidencies of Gerald Ford and Jimmy Carter. With the election of Ronald Reagan, many Americans began to "have faith in America again." Just as Nixon began a new relationship with China, under Reagan, America entered into a more positive relationship with its formal rival, the Soviet Union.

THE PRESIDENCY OF RICHARD NIXON

Richard Nixon's election to the presidency in 1968 capped one of the greatest comeback stories in American political history. Nixon's political obituary had been written after successive defeats in 1960 (when he was defeated by John Kennedy for the presidency) and in 1962 (after being defeated by Pat Brown for governor of California; he informed the press on election night that "you won't have Nixon to kick around anymore," as he was resigning from politics).

Nixon was one of the most interesting men to be elected to the presidency in the twentieth century. He was never comfortable with large groups of people, and even in staged photo events sometimes appeared uncomfortable and out of place (such as the time he was pictured walking "informally" along the beach in dress shoes). Nixon was convinced that large numbers of the news media and many members of the Congress were his enemies. He relied on a small group of close-knit advisors, including H. R. Haldeman, his Chief of Staff, and John Ehrlichman, his Advisor for Domestic Affairs.

Nixon's Domestic Policies

As mentioned in the previous chapter, the Vietnam War took up large amounts of Nixon's time and energies. However, other potentially crucial crises also existed. As Nixon entered office in 1969, inflation was growing rapidly, unemployment was rising, the gross national product was experiencing a lack of growth, and the United States had a rather substantial trade deficit. Some of these economic problems can be attributed to the administration of Lyndon Johnson; paying for Great Society programs and the Vietnam War at the same time created serious strains on the federal budget.

At first, Nixon tried to cut government spending and raising taxes; this policy only worsened the economy. The president then imposed a 90-day freeze on prices and wages; after these measures he also established mandatory guidelines for wage and price increases. By 1971 Nixon also directed that a program of **deficit spending** begin. This was somewhat similar to the approach utilized by Franklin Roosevelt in attacking the economic problems of the Great Depression.

The "Southern Strategy" of Richard Nixon

Southern whites had voted firmly Democratic since the Reconstruction era. In the 1968 presidential election cracks in this relationship between the Democratic party and the South began to show. George Wallace, former governor of Alabama, broke from the party and in 1968 ran for president as a candidate of the American Independence Party. He picked up 13.5 percent of the popular vote (a large percentage of these from the South); this aided Richard Nixon in his victory over Hubert Humphrey.

Richard Nixon decided to take decisive measures to appeal to these Southern whites and win them over to the Republican party. Nixon's "**Southern Strategy**" included delaying school desegregation plans (that had been ordered by a federal court) in Mississippi and attempting to block an extension of the Voting Rights Act of 1965. Nixon also attempted to block school integration by busing after the Supreme Court had endorsed busing as a method to achieve integration. Under Nixon the Supreme Court also became much more conservative, especially with Warren Burger as the new Chief Justice (nevertheless, it should be remembered that in _Roe v. Wade_ this court outlawed state legislation opposing abortion).

Nixon's Foreign Policy

The greatest achievements of the Nixon presidency were undoubtedly in the area of foreign affairs. In formulating foreign policy, Nixon was aided by former Harvard professor Henry Kissinger, his National Security Advisor and beginning in 1973 his Secretary of State. Kissinger had conducted many of the negotiations with the North Vietnamese that allowed American troops to leave Vietnam in 1973. Nixon greatly trusted the judgment of Kissinger on foreign policy affairs.

Nixon's greatest accomplishments included better relationships with both the Soviet Union and China. Nixon had been a fierce anticommunist in the 1950s, but during his first term in office, he instituted a policy of "**détente**" with the Soviet Union. The reduced tensions that this policy created were a welcome relief from the fierce anticommunist rhetoric that had existed through most of the Kennedy and Johnson administrations.

In addition, Nixon realized the foolishness of continued **nuclear proliferation**. He visited the Soviet Union in 1972 and, during discussions with Soviet Premier Leonid Brezhnev, agreed to halt the continued buildup of nuclear weapons. The **SALT I** treaty (Strategic Arms Limitation Talks) was historic, as for the first time the two superpowers agreed not to produce any more nuclear ballistic missiles and to reduce their arsenals of antiballistic missiles to 200 per side.

A journey that Nixon took earlier in 1972 was even more significant. During much of the 1950s and 1960s Nixon spoke about the need to support Nationalist China (who lived on the island of Taiwan) and the need to be vigilant against the expansion of "Red" China (who controlled the Chinese mainland). Henry Kissinger was an admirer of **realpolitik** and convinced Nixon that a new approach to Communist China was necessary. Kissinger maintained that it was foolish to think that the Communist Chinese would ever be overthrown, and that it would be to America's advantage to recognize that fact. In addition, Nixon felt that a friendlier China could be used as a wedge to get future concessions from the Soviet Union.

In February 1972, Nixon and Kissinger made a historic trip to Communist China. Meetings were held with Chinese leader Mao Tse-tung and other officials. At these meetings it was decided that trade talks between the two countries would begin, and that cultural exchanges would start almost immediately. Most importantly, Nixon agreed to support the admission of Communist China to the United Nations (going against what had been traditional U.S. policy for the entire Cold War period).

THE WATERGATE AFFAIR

As a result of his foreign policy successes, Nixon's ratings in public opinion polls were extremely high as the presidential election of 1972 approached. Nixon's opponent was Democrat George McGovern, who campaigned for a faster pullout from Vietnam. Nixon's victory in 1972 was truly staggering; in the Electoral College he won 521 to 17.

The one-sided nature of the 1972 election makes the desires of Richard Nixon and his campaign associates for the events leading up to the **Watergate Affair** difficult to understand. Nixon's paranoid view of the American political system colored the decisions that he and his aids made in the months leading up to the 1972 campaign. In 1971 Nixon created an "**enemies list**" and suggested various forms of harassment that could be used on everyone on the list (wiretaps, investigating income tax records, etc.). On this list were politicians (Senator Edward Kennedy), newsmen (Daniel Schorr of CBS News), and even sports personalities (New York Jets quarterback Joe Namath).

After the Pentagon Papers were released in the spring of 1971 by Daniel Ellsburg, a former employee of the State Department, a special unit to "plug" leaks was formed by the White House. This unit was known as the **Plumbers**, and included Howard Hunt, a former member of the CIA, and Gordon Liddy, a former agent of the FBI. One of the first actions of the Plumbers was to break into Daniel Ellsburg's psychiatrist's office to try to find incriminating information about Ellsburg. Other aides working for CREEP (the Committee to Reelect the President) performed various "dirty tricks" on political opponents. In the 1972 Democratic primaries, CREEP operatives on two occasions ordered 200 pizzas delivered to a opposing campaign office unannounced, "canceled" political rallies for opponents without the opponents knowing it, and with no basis whatsoever, charged that Democratic Senator Edmund Muskie had made negative remarks about French Canadians living in New Hampshire.

On the night of June 16, 1972, James McCord, an assistant in the office of security of CREEP, led four other men into Democratic National Committee headquarters at the Watergate Hotel in Washington, DC. The goal of this group was to photocopy important files and to install electronic surveillance devices in the Democratic offices. The five were caught and arrested; money they had on their person could be traced back to CREEP. This is the beginning of the chain of events that came to be called **Watergate** or the Watergate scandal.

Five days later Nixon became part of the illegal cover-up of the Watergate break-in. On that day he publicly announced that the White House had absolutely nothing to do with the break-in. More importantly, on the same day Nixon contacted friendly CIA officials and tried to convince them to call the FBI and tell the FBI to cease its investigation of Watergate. This was the first illegal action taken by Nixon in the Watergate Affair.

In the months before the 1972 presidential election, "hush money" was paid to the Watergate burglars and several officials of CREEP committed perjury by denying under oath that Nixon had any knowledge of the break-in.

The Watergate story most assuredly would have died if not for the efforts of reporters Carl Bernstein and Bob Woodward of the *Washington Post*. Despite threats from the White House and other political operatives, the two reporters continued to follow the story. They were aided by a secret source named "Deep Throat," who provided them valuable background information about the case.

James McCord and the other Watergate burglars were found guilty in their January 1973 trial; no mention of White House involvement was made by any of the defendants. It later became known that Nixon personally approved the payment of hush money to one of the defendants during the trial. In February the Senate Select Committee on Presidential Campaign Activities began to investigate the Watergate Affair. During these hearing White House attorney John Dean testified that Nixon was involved in the cover-up and another aide revealed the existence of a taping system in the Oval Office that recorded all conversations held by the President. H. R. Haldeman, John Ehrlichman, and Attorney General Richard Kleindienst all resigned in an attempt to save the presidency of Richard Nixon. Nixon's public approval ratings began to fall.

In an effort to quell the firestorm building around him, Nixon appointed a **special prosecutor** to investigate the Watergate Affair. Almost immediately after being appointed, Archibald Cox demanded that the White House hand over the tapes of all taped conversations.

After losing a court argument that the tapes should be exclusive property of the president, Nixon ordered the new Attorney General to fire Cox. Richardson refused, as did his assistant, William Ruckelhaus, and both resigned. Solicitor General Robert Bork (who would later be an unsuccessful Supreme Court nominee) finally fired Cox. All of these events took place on October 20, 1973, and are referred to as the "**Saturday Night Massacre**."

After these events the president's approval rating dipped dramatically. The Judiciary Committee of the House of Representatives began to discuss the formal procedures for impeaching a president. Nixon turned over heavily edited transcripts of most of the tapes to Leon Jaworski, Cox's replacement; many of the vulgar comments made by Nixon on the tapes shocked both opponents and supporters. Also during this period it was revealed that Spiro Agnew, Nixon's vice president, had taken bribes as an elected official in Maryland before he was vice president. Agnew resigned in October of 1973, and it was two months before his appointed successor, Congressman Gerald Ford of Michigan, was approved as the new vice president.

During the following months the calls for Nixon's resignation increased. In April 1974, Nixon released more, but not all, of the tapes requested by the special prosecutor. In July the House Judiciary Committee formally approved three articles of impeachment, stating that the president had ignored their subpoenas, had misused presidential power, and had obstructed justice. Debate was to begin in the full House on impeachment; Nixon's supporters admitted that Nixon would have been impeached.

Before House hearings could begin, the White House finally complied with a Supreme Court order to release all remaining tapes. One had an 18½-minute gap on in; another was the "smoking gun" that Nixon's opponents had been looking for. Nixon had always denied that he had known about the cover-up, yet a tape made one week after the break-in demonstrated that Nixon was actually participating in the cover-up at that point.

With no support left, Nixon finally resigned on August 9, 1974. Gerald Ford took over as president and announced that "our long national nightmare is over." In retrospect, the Watergate Affair was one of the low points of American political history in the twentieth century, rivaled only by the scandals of the presidency of Warren G. Harding.

THE PRESIDENCY OF GERALD FORD

As described previously, Gerald Ford came to the presidency under the worst of circumstances. To his advantage, he was incredibly well liked in Washington and totally free of any hint of scandal. However, during his time in office, Ford seemed to lack a grand "plan" for what he wanted to accomplish. Several historians note that Ford's presidency was doomed from September 8, 1974, when he pardoned Richard Nixon for any crimes that he might have committed. This soured many Americans on Ford; his later explanation was that up until that point virtually his entire time in office was spent dealing with Watergate-related affairs, and that the only way to move past that was to pardon the former president. The public expressed their opinion in the fall congressional elections, when many Democrats were swept into office.

Ford became the second American president to visit China, and the first to visit Japan. It should be remembered it was during the Ford administration that South Vietnam fell to the North Vietnamese and the Vietcong. The last American troops had left in 1973; by 1975 the North Vietnamese army began to occupy several major South Vietnamese cities. Ford toyed with the idea of sending in troops to aid the South Vietnamese, but ended up asking Congress for a major aid package for South Vietnam. By this point the vast majority of Americans wanted nothing to do with the situation in Southeast Asia, and Congress defeated Ford's request. In late April the North Vietnamese were closing in on Saigon; some of the most gripping photographs of the era were photos of American helicopters evacuating Americans and Vietnamese who had worked for them from the roof of the American embassy in Saigon one day before the city was captured by the North Vietnamese.

The major problem that Ford's presidency faced was the economy. The American economy had always suffered from either unemployment or inflation; during the Ford administration the economy suffered from both. This economic situation was termed **stagflation**. Critics of Ford claimed that his tactics were no different than those of Herbert Hoover, as he tried to restore confidence in the economy by asking people to wear "WIN" buttons ("Whip Inflation Now") and to voluntarily spend less to lessen the effects of inflation. Ford pushed for tax cuts and for less government spending; despite these various approaches, by 1975 unemployment in America stood near 10 percent and inflation remained a problem. On several occasions Ford fell or tripped in public settings, which did not improve the image of the presidency.

In the race for the Republican presidential nomination, in 1976 President Ford was able to fend off the campaign of former Governor of California and actor Ronald Reagan. In the election Ford faced the former Governor of Georgia, Jimmy Carter. During the campaign Carter continually stressed that he would be an outsider in Washington, and not tied to any of the messes that had gone on in Washington since 1968; to many in a post-Watergate America, this message sold perfectly. In addition, Ford did not help himself in the campaign by making several misstatements, such as claiming in one debate that Eastern Europe was not controlled by the Soviet Union. Carter won the presidency by a fairly narrow margin by keeping the New Deal Democratic coalition together. Some Southerners who had voted for Nixon in 1968 and 1972 returned to vote Democrat in 1976 because of Carter's Southern roots.

THE PRESIDENCY OF JIMMY CARTER

Jimmy Carter discovered that coming into the presidency as an outsider has some advantages but also some definite drawbacks. One of the weaknesses of the Carter presidency was his inability to find "insiders" in Congress that he could successfully work with to get legislation passed. Carter hired many women and minorities for his White House staff and did away with some of the pomp and circumstance traditionally associated with the presidency (he sometimes wore sweaters when giving addresses to the nation). To Carter's critics, these were signs that he was not really up to the responsibilities of the presidency.

Domestic problems continued to exist in the Carter presidency. Unemployment and inflation remained as major problems. As Ford had done, Carter asked the American people to voluntarily refrain from spending and excessive energy use to bring down inflation. He then tried to cut government spending to cool the economy, and angered many liberal Democrats by cutting social programs. Another approached tried by the administration was to have the Federal Reserve Board tighten the money supply, hoping this would stop inflation; the resulting high interest rates served to depress the economy. Unfortunately, none of these policies worked, and confidence in Carter's abilities to solve economic problems began to wane; by the end of his term, unemployment still stood near 8 percent, with inflation over 12 percent.

Other domestic measures undertaken by Carter included the granting of amnesty to those who had left America to avoid the draft during the Vietnam era and measures for the federal cleanup of chemical waste dumps. Pressures from **OPEC** drove the price of gasoline higher during the Carter presidency; in 1978 the National Energy Act passed, which taxed cars that were not energy efficient and deregulated the prices of domestic oil and gasoline. During the Carter administration a Cabinet-level Department of Energy was created.

In foreign policy, Carter's early speeches stated that the goal of America should be the spreading of basic human rights around the world. Critics maintained that Carter's idealism blinded him to the real interests of America at the time. Conservatives were very critical of his treaty that gave the Panama Canal back to Panama (this would not actually take place until 1999). Critics also attacked his decision to officially recognize the People's Republic of China as the government of China (thus reducing America's support of Taiwan) and his continued negotiations with the Soviets to limit nuclear weapons (critics stated that America's military might should not be limited). Conservatives were cheered by his response to the 1979 Soviet invasion of Afghanistan. Carter cut aid programs to the Soviet Union and refused to allow the athletes to compete in the 1980 Moscow Summer Olympics.

One of the high points of the Carter presidency was the September 1978 negotiations between Menachem Begin of Israel and Anwar Sadat of Egypt that produced the **Camp David Accords**. These negotiations were mediated by Carter; as a result of these talks, Israel promised to return occupied land to Egypt in return for official recognition of Israel's right to exist by Egypt. Carter was unable to negotiate a solution to the problem of Palestinian refugees (a problem that still exists today).

The nadir of the Carter presidency was the **Iranian Hostage Crisis**. Iran had been governed by the repressive Shah of Iran, who was propped up by arms and economic aid from the United States. In 1978 a revolution of fundamentalist Muslims forced the Shah to leave the country; the Ayatollah Khomeini, a fundamentalist Muslim leader, became leader of Iran. In October 1979, the exiled Shah was suffering from cancer, and Carter allowed him into the United States for treatment. This outraged the Iranians; on November 4 protesters stoned and then seized the American embassy in Tehran, Iran, taking 66 Americans who worked there hostage.

The Americans were kept hostage for 444 days. Some were kept in solitary confinement, while others were not; most were moved around on a regular basis to discourage rescue attempts. Carter tried various attempts to win the release of the hostages, including freezing Iranian assets in America, stopping trade with Iran, and negotiating through third parties. A 1980 attempt to rescue the hostages ended in a military embarrassment when helicopters sent to rescue them either crashed or could not fly because of heavy sand. Carter had been criticized for being ineffectual on domestic programs; as the hostage crisis wore on, he increasingly was seen as ineffectual in the diplomatic sphere as well. The hostages were finally released in January 1981, but only after Carter had left office and Ronald Reagan was sworn in as president.

THE ELECTION OF 1980

Carter was able to win the 1980 Democratic nomination for president over a challenge from Edward Kennedy. Ronald Reagan, portraying himself as the spokesperson for the conservatives of America, won the Republican nomination. Carter was forced to campaign on his record, which was a very difficult thing to do. Reagan promised while campaigning to build up the military; at the same time he promised to cut taxes. He promised strong leadership from Washington and also pledged to take power from Washington and give it to the states. Reagan also pledged support for a renewed emphasis on family and patriotism. Reagan won the election by a decisive margin.

The 1980 election was the first totally successful assault on the New Deal Democratic coalition. Social issues of the era, such as the increasing rights of women, sexual freedom, and **affirmative action**, drew many blue-collar workers away from the Democrats and into the Republican camp. (Conservatives successfully convinced many Americans that the Democrats were the cause of the declining image of America abroad and the reason for the decline in traditional morality at home.) Members of the **religious right** supported the Republicans in large numbers (and would continue this pattern in elections that followed). Many Southerners saw the Republicans and Reagan representing their interests more than Jimmy Carter; others perceived Carter to be "soft on communism." As a result of these factors, the **New Right** had become a major force in American politics; besides electing Reagan, they had also pushed the Republicans to the majority in the Senate in 1980.

THE PRESIDENCY OF RONALD REAGAN

Admirers and detractors of Ronald Reagan both agree that he was a true master of politics (Bill Clinton studied the techniques Reagan used to achieve political success). Reagan used his previously honed skills as an actor to set the right tone and present the right messages at meetings and speeches throughout his presidency. Reagan also used his staff well; on many occasions he would set the general policy and allow staff people to set up the details.

Upon becoming president Reagan instituted traditional conservative economic practices. In 1981 federal taxes were cut by 5 percent, and then cut by another 10 percent in 1982 and 1983. Reagan and his economic staff believed in "**supply-side economics**," which stated that if by cutting taxes you put more money in the hands of wealthy Americans, they would invest it in the economy, thus creating more jobs and additional growth (and eventually additional tax revenue). Capital gains taxes were reduced, also with the intent of encouraging investment.

Political battle lines were drawn early in the Reagan administration. As a result of the tax cuts, the government was taking in less money, causing many domestic programs to be cut, including aid to education, to urban housing programs, and to the arts and the humanities. Liberals were outraged over the fact that at the same time social programs were being cut, Reagan increased the defense budget by nearly $13 billion. Reagan also pushed for funding for a Strategic Defense Initiative (SDI; nicknamed "Star Wars") program. As envisioned, this system could shoot down enemy missiles from outer space. Reagan also pushed to give more power back to the states at the expense of the federal government. Reagan called this plan the **New Federalism**. Under this program, how federal money was spent by states was determined by the states and not by the federal government.

During the Reagan administration the policy of deregulation was intensified; industries such as the energy industry and the transportation industry were freed from "cumbersome" regulations imposed by previous administrations (supporters of these regulations would maintain that they were in the interest of the consumers). In addition, funding for the Environmental Protection Agency was greatly reduced during the Reagan presidency. Many perceived the Reagan administration to be anti-union as well; in 1981 the government actively destroyed the union for the air traffic controllers, and striking controllers were fired.

In response to the perceived foreign policy weakness of America in the Carter years, Reagan worked hard to build up America's image in the world. On a small scale, the American army successfully invaded the island of Grenada in 1983. On a much larger scale, Reagan ended the friendlier relations between the United States and the Soviet Union of the détente era. He put new cruise missiles in Europe and referred to the Soviet Union as the "evil empire." Reagan's harsh rhetoric won him much support in the United States. Reagan's popularity also had gone up after the attempt on his life by John Hinckley in 1981.

Reagan ran for reelection in 1984 against Walter Mondale (Mondale's running mate was Geraldine Ferraro, a congresswoman from New York). Mondale criticized Reagan on economic issues; the supply-side approach had not produced as much growth, and as much income from taxes, as its proponents had said it would. However, Reagan's tough Cold War rhetoric and support of conservative social issues allowed him to continue to break up the Democratic New Deal coalition; Reagan got nearly 60 percent of the popular vote in 1984. Critics who said that the major beneficiaries of Reagan's economic policies were the very rich were still very much in the minority.

Reagan continued to practice conservative policies during his second term. The **Tax Reform Act of 1986** dramatically reduced federal tax rates; the tax the wealthiest Americans had to pay on their income, for example, was reduced from 50 percent to 28 percent. In 1986 and 1987 both unemployment and inflation declined. Under Reagan the Supreme Court also became more conservative, as William Rehnquist became Chief Justice and Antonin Scalia was one of the new justices on the court. Reagan also nominated Sandra Day O'Connor to be the first woman to serve on the Supreme Court. Most women's groups, however, strongly disapproved of the Reagan administration, citing actions such as efforts during Reagan's second term to cut food stamps and the federal school lunch program.

During Reagan's second term, serious economic problems also developed. On October 19, 1987, known as "Back Monday" the average price for a share of stock fell nearly 20 percent. During Reagan's second term, federal government deficits grew drastically; this occurred because less income was coming into the government because of the previously-enacted tax cuts and because of a large increase in defense spending. In addition, for the first time since World War I the United States began to import more than it exported.

Nevertheless, Reagan's foreign policy remained incredibly popular. In April of 1986 the United States bombed Libyan air bases after Muammar al-Qadhafi, the leader of Libya, ordered Libyan gunboats to challenge American ships sailing close to Libya. Reagan and the new leader of the Soviet Union, Mikhail Gorbachev, established a close personal relationship and held meaningful negotiations on the reduction of nuclear weapons. Reagan also supported anticommunist forces fighting in Nicaragua and El Salvador.

Many critics of Reagan had claimed since 1980 that he was unaware of what was being done by others working for him. This view seemed to be validated by the **Iran-Contra Affair** of 1986 and 1987. Apparently without the knowledge of the president, National Security Advisor John Poindexter, Lieutenant Colonel Oliver North, and several others devised a "arms for hostages plan." By this plan the United States sold arms to Iran, hoping that they could use their influence to help free American hostages held in Lebanon. The problem with this plan was that at this point America had an official trade embargo with Iran and had gotten several European countries to support this. The money for this sale was to be used to fund anticommunist fighters in Nicaragua, called the "contras." Again, a problem existed: Congress had passed legislation carefully regulating how much funding could go to the contras. Congressional and legal hearings were held on the Iran-Contra Affair, as a result, nearly a dozen officials of the Reagan administration being forced to resign.

Many Americans felt (and continue to feel) that the political hero of the modern era was Ronald Reagan. Many supporters felt he restored pride to America, stood up to our enemies abroad, restored the economy of America, and reasserted "traditional" American values. Critics of Reagan maintain that the economic policies of the Reagan administration only benefited the wealthiest Americans; they point out that the gap between the richest Americans and the poorest Americans dramatically increased under Reagan, with the real income of middle- and lower-class Americans actually receding. Critics stated that Iran-Contra proved the fact that Reagan was dangerously out of touch on many policy decisions. Nevertheless, Reagan's vice president, George Bush, would certainly have a tough act to follow as he ran for president on his own in 1988.

CHAPTER REVIEW

Rapid Review

To achieve the perfect 5, you should be able to explain the following:

- One of the low points of American political life in the twentieth century was the Watergate Affair.

- Richard Nixon's greatest accomplishments were in the field of foreign policy, as he crafted new relationships with both China and the Soviet Union.

- The Watergate Affair developed from the paranoid view of American politics held by Richard Nixon and several of his top aides.

- Gerald Ford's presidency was tainted from the beginning by his pardoning of Richard Nixon.

- Ford faced huge economic problems as president; during his presidency America suffered from both inflation and unemployment.

- Jimmy Carter and many politicians of the post-Watergate era emerged victorious by campaigning as outsiders.

- President Carter's outsider status hurt him, especially in terms of getting legislation passed in Congress.

- Carter demonstrated his diplomatic skills by forging the Camp David Accords; he was unable to negotiate a release of the American hostages in Iran, and this may have cost him the presidency.

- Ronald Reagan was elected as a conservative and restored the pride of many Americans in America.

- Reagan practiced "supply-side" economics, which benefited the American economy but which also helped to create large deficits.

- Under Reagan the gap between the wealthiest Americans and the poorest Americans increased.

- Reagan reinstituted Cold War rhetoric but later created cordial relations with leaders of the Soviet Union.

- Reagan's lack of direct control over the implementation of presidential policies was demonstrated by the Iran-Contra Affair.

- The legacy of Ronald Reagan is a large one.

Time Line

1968: Richard Nixon elected president
1971: Nixon imposes wage and price controls
        Pentagon Papers released
1972: Nixon visits China and Soviet Union
        Nixon reelected
        SALT I signed
        Watergate break-in
1973: Watergate hearings in Congress
        Spiro Agnew resigns as vice president
        "Saturday Night Massacre"
1974: Inflation peaks at 11 percent
        Nixon resigns; Gerald Ford becomes president
        Ford pardons Richard Nixon
        WIN economic program introduced
1975: South Vietnam falls to North Vietnam, ending Vietnam War
1976: Jimmy Carter elected president

1977: Carter signs Panama Canal treaty
      Carter issues Vietnam-era draft amnesty
1978: Camp David Accords
1979: Americans taken hostage in Iran
1980: Ronald Reagan elected president
1981–1982: Major recession
      Assassination attempt on Reagan
1981–1983: Major tax cuts instituted
1983: Reagan proposes "Star Wars"
      Americans victorious in Grenada
1984: Reagan reelected
1985: Gorbachev assumes power in Soviet Union
1986: Additional tax reform measures passed
      Iran-Contra Affair
      "Black Monday"
1988: George Bush elected president

✓ Review Questions

1. What tactic was *not* used by supporters of Richard Nixon in the 1972 presidential campaign?

   A. Breaking into private offices
   B. Reviewing income tax records of suspected "enemies"
   C. Falsifying war records of opposing presidential candidates
   D. Attempting to halt official investigations of actions of campaign officials
   E. Planting false stories about opposing candidates in the press

(Answer: **C**. Of all of the "dirty tricks" practiced by the Republicans in 1972, this was not one of them.)

2. According to supply-side economics, when wealthy Americans received tax cuts, they would precede to do all but which of the following:

   A. Invest heavily in the economy
   B. Open new factories
   C. Purchase stocks
   D. Increase their savings dramatically
   E. Buy more consumer goods

(Answer: **D**. The key to supply-side economics is that when tax cuts give individuals large amounts of money, they will turn and reinvest that money in the economy.)

3. Which of the following did *not* help create the deficits of the second term of the Reagan years?

   A. Reduction of federal tax rates
   B. Desperately needed increases in funding for education
   C. Increases in military spending
   D. The SDI program
   E. Changes in the tax code that favored wealthier Americans

(Answer **B**. Even though education advocates were saying that funding had to be drastically increased in many urban school districts, funding for education declined during the Reagan era.)

4. Critics of Ronald Reagan would most emphasize

   A. the relationship between Reagan and Mikhail Gorbachev in 1987 and 1988

B. the effects of the 1981–1983 tax cuts

C. the U.S. response to threats from Libya

D. the effects of Reagan's economic policies on the middle and lower classes

E. his public image and political skills

(Answer: **D.** The 1981 to 1983 tax cuts did help bring down inflation; at this same time employment possibilities increased. Compared to the wealthiest Americans, the middle and lower classes experienced little benefit from Reagan's economic policies, especially from the tax cuts of the second term.)

5. Gerald Ford's WIN program demonstrated to many Americans that Ford

A. had no real grasp of economic issues

B. had the uncanny knack of knowing how to inspire the American public

C. was still under the shadow of Richard Nixon

D. understood sophisticated foreign policy issues

E. was a supporter of supply-side economics

(Correct Answer: **A.** Many Americans saw the WIN program as a public relations gimmick, demonstrating that Ford did not truly understand the economic problems of America; many equated WIN to some of the public pronouncements of Herbert Hoover in 1930 and 1931.)

Chapter 25

America from 1988 to 2000: Prosperity and a New World Order

For much of the post-World War II era, the popularity of a president was largely determined by his success in foreign policy and in handling foreign crises. With the ending of the Cold War at the end of the 1980s, skills in handling domestic issues became equally important for presidents and their staffs. Presidents Bush (I) and Clinton are perfect examples of this: Bush's popularity was sky-high after his Desert Storm victory, yet he ended up being defeated by Bill Clinton largely because of economic problems that developed in the closing years of his term. Despite a mountain of personal and ethical issues that surrounded him, President Clinton was able to keep high approval ratings because of a continuing successful economy.

THE 1988 ELECTION

Republican advertisements in 1988 touted George Bush as "the most qualified man of our times" to be president. Bush has served as a congressman, as the American ambassador to the United Nations, and as the director of the CIA. The **New Right** had never been entirely comfortable with Bush during his eight years as Reagan's vice president; to appease them, he nominated Senator Dan Quayle, a staunch conservative, as his vice presidential nominee.

The Democrats nominated Massachusetts Governor Michael Dukakis as their candidate. Dukakis campaigned on his experience as a governor, touting the "Massachusetts miracle" that had pulled the state out of its economic doldrums. Televisions during the 1988 campaign were glutted with negative advertisements, the most notable being one that linked Dukakis to Willie Horton, a black man who raped a woman while taking advantage of a furlough program established in Massachusetts by the

Governor. Bush won the election rather handily, despite being behind Dukakis in early polls.

THE PRESIDENCY OF GEORGE BUSH

Conservative suspicions of Bush increased during the first months of this presidency. Many considered his stated desires for a "kinder, gentler America" to be efforts to distance himself from the social policies of former-president Reagan. Bush's major domestic problem was an ever-growing federal deficit. To broker a deal with Congress to lower the deficit, Bush broke his campaign promise of "no new taxes" and in 1990 signed a bill authorizing tax increases. Many conservatives never forgave him for his decision. During Bush's term, few substantive domestic programs were instituted; some commentators complained of the **gridlock** created by a Republican president and a Democratic congress.

During the presidency of George Bush, the 45-year-old Cold War ended. In late 1988 Soviet leader Mikhail Gorbachev admitted to Communist party leaders that the incredible amount of the Soviet economy that was devoted to military spending and to "protecting" the satellite countries was preventing economic growth of any type from taking place. In 1989 the Soviets began to withdraw support from the satellite states; many in Moscow naively believed that communist leaders in the satellite states could remain in power without being propped up by the Soviet Union. In Poland, Solidarity, the noncommunist labor party, removed the communist government from power; throughout late 1989 communists were removed from power in all of the satellite nations. Many of the republics of the Soviet Union also desired independence. In December of 1991 Russian President Boris Yeltsin announced the abolition of the Soviet Union and the creation of 11 independent republics.

A large amount of American aid was pumped into Russia and the other Eastern European states. American academics rushed to Moscow and other major centers in the region, explaining to leaders how capitalism could be introduced in the shortest amount of time. This transition proved much more difficult than many would have ever believed; as this volume is being written, this process is still not completed in Russia and Eastern Europe.

American aid was also sent to help several of the former Soviet republics dismantle the nuclear missiles that had been placed there in the Cold War era. The meaning of the Cold War is still being debated by academics; whether the United States won the Cold War or whether the Soviet Union lost it is still a topic of numerous books and historical papers.

The central crisis of the Bush presidency began on August 2, 1990, when the army of Iraq invaded Kuwait. Fears that Saddam Hussein's next target would be Saudi Arabia, the largest importer of oil to the United States, pushed the United States into action. Almost immediately, in **Operation "Desert Shield"** large numbers of American troops were sent to protect Saudi Arabia.

Encouraged by the United States, members states of the United Nations condemned the Iraqi aggression and authorized the creation of a multinational military force to remove Saddam Hussein from Kuwait. The high point of the Bush presidency was the personal diplomacy undertaken by the presidency to get almost all of the states of the Middle East to support military action against Iraq. On February 24, 1991, a ground offensive, termed **Operation "Desert Storm,"** was instituted against Iraq. Iraqi casualties were over 40,000, while the Americans (who made up most of the troops of the UN international force) lost 150 soldiers in battle. Iraqi soldiers surrendered by the hundreds as they retreated from Kuwait. In a decision that would later be questioned, American forces did not move into Iraq and force Saddam Hussein from power. It should be noted that was *not* part of the United Nations mandate, and such an action would have definitely created division in the Middle Eastern coalition so carefully crafted by Bush.

Bush's popularity was at an all time high after Desert Storm. However, problems soon arose that his administration seemed incapable of solving. A recession and continued economic difficulties hit the United States in early 1992. In addition, the end of the Cold War brought new difficulties in several states formerly controlled by the Soviet Union. In the former Yugoslavia, Serbs began to practice "ethnic cleansing" against Bosnian Muslims. Critics of Bush claimed that he lacked any "vision" of what the role of the United States should be in a post-Cold War world.

THE 1992 ELECTION

George Bush and Bill Clinton ran against each other in 1992. The buzz-word of politics in 1992 was "change," and both candidates claimed they were prepared to offer it. At the 1992 Republican National Convention speakers of the New Right spoke about the need for "family values" and that a "religious war" against the Democrats was needed.

The former governor of Arkansas, Bill Clinton had the political sense to realize that Americans in the early 1990s were interested in economic rather than social issues, and pledged that as president he would overhaul the health care system and work for the preservation of the Social Security system. Clinton campaigned as a **"New Democrat,"** stating that he was not another typical big-spending advocate of big government. During his presidency Clinton on occasion took Republican concepts and claimed them as his own; right-wing critics such as Rush Limbaugh maintained that he would say or do anything if it meant his position would be improved in the polls.

In the 1990s politicians were under more intense scrutiny than ever. Twenty-four-hour cable news networks needed a continuous input of news; political Web sites and talk radio hosts offered up mountains of political information (with no real need to prove any of it). Bill Clinton was a special target of the conservative press during the 1992 campaign and throughout his presidency; he was the first baby boomer president and had taken part in antiwar demonstrations while he was a graduate student in England. Many also resented his wife, Hillary Rodham Clinton, who maintained that if her husband was elected, she would not sit around the White House and "bake cookies."

A third candidate in the 1992 race was Texas multibillionaire Ross Perot. Perot spent a lot of money on campaign ads, complaining in these ads about how the politicians in Washington were beholden only to special interests, and that if elected he would bring "common sense" back to the White House. However, the charts depicting the American economy that he used on his advertisements were understood by few people.

Clinton won the 1992 election fairly easily. Many from the New Deal Democratic coalition that had deserted the Democrats for Reagan came back to vote for Clinton in 1992. Bush appeared oddly out of touch at several points during the campaign; at one point he was caught looking at his watch in the middle of a presidential debate. Nearly 19 million Americans supported Perot; analysts maintain that the support for Perot hurt Bush more than it did Clinton.

THE PRESIDENCY OF BILL CLINTON

From the beginning Clinton strove to create an administration different than the one that had preceded it. He appointed minorities and women to his Cabinet. During his first term there were several legislative successes, such as the Brady bill, which created a waiting period for handgun purchases and the 1994 Anti-Crime bill, which provided federal funds to hire more policemen. However, several of issues Clinton attempted to tackle during his first term drew the ire of many. His attempt to legislate the proper status of gays in the military caused many in all branches of the military service to distrust him. His attempt to legislate a national health insurance plan was defeated by a combination of effective lobbying by the American Medical Association and intense advertising paid for by the health care industry. In addition, the fact that Hillary Rodham Clinton was actively involved in the formulation of health care policy caused debate over the proper role of a First Lady.

Many also began to question the Clintons concerning their financial dealings. Investments in a failed savings and loan company and in a land development called "**Whitewater**" caused much controversy; in August of 1994 Kenneth Starr became the independent counsel in charge of investigating the Whitewater Affair. Many Clinton supporters felt that Starr moved too vigorously and was out to "get" the Clintons.

The 1994 Congressional elections appeared to be a sweeping rejection of the presidency of Bill Clinton. Republicans, led by new Speaker of the House Newt Gingrich, supported the **Contract with America**, and promised to get rid of many social programs long supported by liberals. Republicans soon learned that the political skills of Bill Clinton were formidable, however. In an attempt to lessen the size of the federal government, there were brief shutdowns of the federal government in 1995 and

1996; on each occasion public opinion polls stated that the American public strongly sided with the president in his argument that all of this was the fault of the Republicans.

Clinton's popularity rose further as the economy improved steadily in 1995 and 1996. The values of stocks rose, economic growth continued at a steady rate, and inflation remained low (many credited Alan Greenspan, chairman of the Federal Reserve, for his ability to skillfully maneuver interest rates to keep inflation low and growth high).

Clinton's role as a "New Democrat" was again demonstrated when he supported passage of the Personal Responsibility and Work Opportunity Reconciliation Act of 1996. This legislation more carefully regulated the welfare system, cut the food stamp program, and gave the power to the states to organize their own "welfare-to-work" programs. This program, which ended "welfare as we know it," was hailed by Clinton supporters as a sign of his pragmatism; many liberals were appalled that he so easily "sold them out."

In foreign policy Clinton faced some of the same criticisms that Bush had: Many claimed that the United States still did not have a post-Cold War foreign policy "focus." Many debated the appropriate role for the U.S. military. A humanitarian mission to Somalia led to the death of 18 American soldiers in 1992. The U.S. military was sent in to restore the government of Jean-Bertrand Aristide in Haiti; Clinton also supported NATO air and military efforts to protect Muslims from the "ethnic cleansing" policies of President Slobodan Milosevic of Serbia. Americans remain as peacekeepers in Bosnia to this day.

President Clinton also favored the continued **globalization** of the economy, which included the lowering of tariffs and the expansion of global markets. Clinton worked with many Republicans to secure the passage of **NAFTA** (North American Free Trade Agreement) in Congress. The goal of NAFTA was to gradually remove all trade barriers between the United States, Canada, and Mexico. As with welfare reform, a segment of the traditional Democratic base was infuriated by one of Clinton's policies: In this case it was the labor unions who felt betrayed.

In 2000 Clinton unsuccessfully attempted to broker a peace between the Palestinians and Israel. He increasingly became aware of the threats of fundamentalist Muslims against the United States. In 1993 bombings took place at the World Trade Center in New York City; American embassies were bombed in Tanzania and Kenya in 1998, and a United States naval ship docked in Yemen was bombed in 2000. Clinton attempted several bombing missions in response to these terrorist attacks, and in one instance came fairly close to killing Osama bin Laden, leader of the Al-Qaeda terrorist network.

Campaigning on the continued strength of the American economy, Clinton became the first Democrat since Franklin Roosevelt to win back-to-back terms when he defeated long-time Senator Robert Dole of Kansas in the 1996 presidential election. Early in Clinton's second term the era of gridlock appeared to be over, as both parties joined in passing legislation to reduce the federal budget. Yet it was the Whitewater Affair that consumed the most political energy in Washington during the last years of Clinton's second term.

As was stated previously, Kenneth Starr and the Whitewater investigation was originally charged with analyzing the financial dealings of the Clintons in Arkansas. However, the investigation soon delved into other areas of the president's life. It was revealed that he had an affair with a White House intern, Monica Lewinsky. Clinton boldly proclaimed on television that he had never had "an affair with that woman." In a lawsuit brought against the president by Paula Jones (for alleged sexual harassment when Clinton was governor of Arkansas), Clinton denied, under oath, having an affair with Lewinsky. Physical evidence obtained from Lewinsky seemed to prove otherwise. Talk show hosts and other opponents stated that the case had long gone beyond merely the matter of the president having an affair; he had actually lied under oath about it.

Clinton's approval ratings remained high throughout his second term; his approval was especially strong in black districts across the country. In the 1996 congressional elections the Republicans lost five seats in the House of Representatives. Congressional calls for impeachment began; others wondered whether the actions of the president were actually the "high crimes and misdemeanors" the Constitution stated were grounds for impeachment. On December 19, 1998, the House of Representatives passed two articles of impeachment (obstruction of justice and perjury), thus preparing the way for a trial in the Senate. Two-thirds of the Senators had to vote for an article of impeachment in order to remove him from office. Senate voting took place on February 12, 1999; neither article of impeachment even got a majority. Many Clinton supporters that spoke during the congressional proceedings noted that despite millions of dollars being spent and years of investigation, the Special Prosecutor was unable to uncover any illegal actions by the president or his wife. After the hearings, several of the president's most vocal adversaries became politically discredited. Popular support for the president remained high, and economic prosperity and expansion continued.

THE 2000 PRESIDENTIAL ELECTION

Excitement for the candidates in the 2000 presidential election was very low. The Democrats nominated Al Gore, Clinton's vice president, who often appeared wooden when giving speeches and stirred little emotion, even among long-time Democrats. George W. Bush, son of the former president, was the Republican nominee; in several early interviews he appeared to lack the knowledge of critical issues that might be expected of a presidential candidate. Ralph Nader ran as a candidate of the Green Party.

When the final results were tabulated, Al Gore actually received some 500,000 votes more than Bush (Nader received less than 3 million votes). However, Gore surprisingly lost his home state of Tennessee, and the winner in the Electoral College would be the winner of the popular vote in Florida. Several recounts were held there, with Bush holding on to a tiny lead. Blacks in several parts of Florida (who voted heavily for Gore) complained that in several parts of the state they had been prevented from voting. Further recounts were planned in contested counties. By a 5-to-4 vote on February 9, 2001, the Supreme Court of the United States temporarily halted all recounts. On February 12 the court ruled, again by a 5-to-4 margin, that recounts in contested counties only was a violation of the Constitution, thus securing the election of George W. Bush. In the first months of his presidency, Bush concentrated much of his effort on domestic affairs; the events of September 11, 2001, would dramatically change the course of his presidency.

CHAPTER REVIEW

Rapid Review

To achieve the perfect 5, you should be able to explain the following:

- The ability to manage domestic issues were critical for a president's political success in the post–Cold War era.

- George Bush alienated many conservatives, especially when he broke his "no new taxes" pledge.

- The end of the Cold War can be attributed to American policy decisions and to weaknesses in the infrastructure of the Soviet Union.

- George Bush skillfully managed the "Desert Storm" operation against Iraq.

- Bill Clinton presented himself as a "New Democrat" and concerned with economic issues in the 1992 presidential campaign; these were important factors in his victory.

- Clinton's failure on national health insurance helped pave the way for large Republican gains in the 1994 congressional elections.

- Clinton and Newt Gingrich were formidable opponents in the budget battles of the mid-1990s.

- The Whitewater Affair and investigations of the personal life of Bill Clinton were the defining political events of the second term of Clinton's presidency.

- George W. Bush's election demonstrated the difficulties of arriving at a "final tally" in any election and was finally secured by the intervention of the United States Supreme Court.

Time Line

1988: George Bush elected president
Solidarity replaces communist government in Poland
1989: Berlin wall opened, communist governments fall in Eastern Europe
1991: Persian Gulf War
Breakup of the Soviet Union
Beginnings of economic recession
1992: Election of Bill Clinton
American troops killed in Somalia
1993: NAFTA ratified by Senate
Terrorist bombings at World Trade Center
1994: Republicans sweep congressional elections
U.S. military enters Haiti
Kenneth Starr becomes Whitewater independent counsel
1996: Clinton reelected
1998: Federal budget surplus announced
Articles of impeachment passed in House of Representatives
1999: Clinton acquitted in impeachment trial in U.S. Senate
2000: George W. Bush elected president

✓ Review Questions

1. A defining characteristic of the Clinton presidency was his

   A. strict adherence to traditional Democratic values
   B. pragmatic policy making
   C. close alliance with liberals in the Democratic party
   D. unprecedented alliance with labor unions
   E. ability to work closely with fundamentalist religious groups

(Correct Answer: **B.** In claiming to be a "New Democrat," Clinton sometimes adopted traditional Republican ideas as his own. To many critics, the pragmatism of the Clinton White House masked a lack of core values that the president truly believed in.)

2. George Bush alienated many conservative Republicans by

   A. appointing the relatively inexperienced Dan Quayle as vice president
   B. continuing to urge the tearing down of the Berlin Wall
   C. signing the 1990 agreement with the Democrats to reduce the deficit
   D. pursuing policies against Iraq
   E. approving the Willie Horton campaign advertisement in 1988

(Correct Answer: **C.** This was the agreement where Bush broke his "no new taxes" pledge and broke with traditional Republican policy.)

3. Critics accused Bush of lacking "vision" because

   A. he failed to articulate a successful policy to end the economic deficit
   B. he failed to remove Saddam Hussein from power

C. he failed to broker peace between the Palestinians and Egypt
D. he failed to sign an arms treaty with Mikhail Gorbachev
E. he failed to explain his perception of America's role in the post-Cold War world

(Correct Answer: **E.** Several historians state that a weakness of both Bush and Clinton was that they were unable to articulate a coherent post-Cold War foreign policy.)

4. All of the following were reasons for the end of the Cold War *except*

   A. the United States military buildup under Ronald Reagan
   B. the fact that many producers of military weaponry in the United States did not want to continue to produce this weaponry
   C. the weaknesses of the Soviet economy
   D. the Cold War rhetoric of both Ronald Reagan and George Bush
   E. the tremendous costs to the Soviet Union of continuing to control the satellite countries

(Correct Answer: **B.** Most manufacturers had no desire to stop producing weaponry for the Cold War. When the Cold War finally ended, many of these companies were forced to lay off workers, and some that could not diversify were forced to close.)

5. Bill Clinton was a formidable political opponent for the Republicans for all of the following reasons *except*

   A. his ability to eventually win over former Republicans of the New Right
   B. his support in the black community
   C. his ability to take Republican positions and make them appear to be his own
   D. his ability to withstand political scandal
   E. his ability to stake out moderate positions, thus gaining support from both Democrats and Republicans

(Correct Answer: **A.** The New Right was the group that came to despise Bill Clinton the most. Members of the New Right interested in social issues were among Clinton's most passionate detractors during the Whitewater Affair.)

PART IV

DEVELOPING CONFIDENCE BY TAKING PRACTICE EXAMINATIONS

Practice Exam 1

Answer Sheet For Multiple-Choice Questions

1. _____	21. _____	41. _____	61. _____
2. _____	22. _____	42. _____	62. _____
3. _____	23. _____	43. _____	63. _____
4. _____	24. _____	44. _____	64. _____
5. _____	25. _____	45. _____	65. _____
6. _____	26. _____	46. _____	66. _____
7. _____	27. _____	47. _____	67. _____
8. _____	28. _____	48. _____	68. _____
9. _____	29. _____	49. _____	69. _____
10. _____	30. _____	50. _____	70. _____
11. _____	31. _____	51. _____	71. _____
12. _____	32. _____	52. _____	72. _____
13. _____	33. _____	53. _____	73. _____
14. _____	34. _____	54. _____	74. _____
15. _____	35. _____	55. _____	75. _____
16. _____	36. _____	56. _____	76. _____
17. _____	37. _____	57. _____	77. _____
18. _____	38. _____	58. _____	78. _____
19. _____	39. _____	59. _____	79. _____
20. _____	40. _____	60. _____	80. _____

PRACTICE EXAM 1
AP U.S. HISTORY

Section I

Time—55 minutes

80 questions

Directions: Each of the questions or incomplete statements below is followed by five suggested answers or completions. Select the one that is best in each case and write your answer neatly on the answer sheet.

1. The headright system

    A. enabled wealthy property owners to acquire more land by paying the passage of indentured servants
    B. gave farmers in New England a greater share of the town commons for each head of cattle they raised
    C. placed restrictions on the mobility of slaves in colonial Virginia
    D. outlawed capital punishment for most criminal offenses in British North America
    E. made women in colonial New England subordinate to men in all legal matters

2. The Eisenhower Doctrine attempted to

    A. improve relations with Latin American countries
    B. undermine the government of Fidel Castro
    C. arrest the spread of communism in the Middle East
    D. funnel millions of dollars of business investments into Africa and Asia
    E. lower international tariffs

3. "Abolish slavery in all its forms and aspects, advocate universal emancipation, exalt the standard of public morality, and promote the moral and intellectual improvement of the colored people, and hasten the day of freedom to the Three Millions of our enslaved fellow countrymen."

    The preceding quotation comes from the masthead of the abolitionist newspaper *The North Star*. Its founder was

    A. William Lloyd Garrison
    B. Frederick Douglass
    C. Phyllis Wheatley
    D. Harriet Tubman
    E. Angelina Grimke

4. Demonstrating a significant shift in government policy toward organized labor, which of the following presidents sided with anthracite coal miners in their strike against mine owners?

    A. Grover Cleveland
    B. Woodrow Wilson
    C. William H. Taft
    D. Theodore Roosevelt
    E. Benjamin Harrison

5. Which of the following was a women's rights advocate who published *The Feminine Mystique* in 1963?

    A. Phyllis Schlafly
    B. Geraldine Ferraro
    C. Shirley Chisolm
    D. Gloria Steinem
    E. Betty Friedan

6. Which of the following best explains why President Andrew Jackson resisted annexing Texas during his administration?

   A. He feared that annexation would strengthen the Whig party.
   B. He knew annexation would lead to war with France, which possessed land along the Texas border.
   C. He believed that the addition of another agricultural state would hurt the developing commercial economy.
   D. He had consistently opposed westward expansion.
   E. He feared that debates over annexation would exacerbate sectional strife.

7. The Nineteenth Amendment achieved one of the goals of the Progressives by

   A. granting women the right to vote
   B. establishing Prohibition
   C. providing for the direct election of senators
   D. ensuring citizenship rights for African-Americans
   E. establishing term limits for elected officials

8. Which of the following statements best captures public sentiment about the Great Railroad Strike of 1877?

   A. The strike only affected people along the Pacific Coast and thus only met with regional opposition.
   B. The American public sided with the African-American sleeping car porters.
   C. Applauding the intervention of President Theodore Roosevelt, the American people sided with the railway workers' union throughout the strike.
   D. Public opinion shifted from sympathy to condemnation as

people blamed the strikers for looting and violence.
   E. Rendered apathetic by their belief in "laissez-faire," the American public expressed no opinion on the strike.

9. The *Chesapeake* Incident (1807) involved

   A. the sinking of an British ship off the coast of Maryland
   B. an Anglo-American conflict over the issue of impressment
   C. an investigation of illegal smuggling of slaves into the United States
   D. the seizure of an American merchant ship by the French navy in the English Channel
   E. an attack by the Iroquois on an American fort near the Great Lakes

10. During the Civil War, the Peninsular Campaign (1862) revealed

   A. Ulysses S. Grant's determination to destroy Robert E. Lee's Army of Northern Virginia
   B. Henry Halleck's jealousy of Grant's success on the battlefield
   C. George McClellan's tentativeness
   D. William T. Sherman's application of "total warfare"
   E. the Confederate resolve to keep New Orleans and Vicksburg from falling under Union control

11. Which of the following methods of colonial resistance achieved the greatest success in reversing Parliamentary legislation before the Revolutionary War?

   A. Petitions to King George III
   B. The Sons of Liberty
   C. Boycotts of British goods
   D. The intercession of colonial governors
   E. Contradictory legislation passed by the colonial assemblies

12. The "Saturday Night Massacre" refers to

    A. the death of four students at Kent State in 1970
    B. President Hoover's attempt to remove the Bonus Marchers from Washington, DC in 1932
    C. the assassination of President John F. Kennedy
    D. the clash between civil rights marchers and the Alabama state police on the Edmund Pettus Bridge
    E. President Richard Nixon's attempts to remove special prosecutor Archibald Cox from the Watergate investigation

13. The Dred Scott decision

    A. undermined the authority of Congress to limit the expansion of slavery into the territories
    B. overturned the Fugitive Slave Law
    C. emphasized the supremacy of civilian courts in response to President Lincoln's suspension of habeas corpus in Maryland
    D. silenced the abolitionist press by limiting the proliferation of anti-slavery newspapers in the South
    E. expanded Congress's naturalization powers

14. As governor of the state of Wisconsin, which of the following instituted Progressive reforms such as the initiative, referendum, and state income tax?

    A. Charles Evans Hughes
    B. Woodrow Wilson
    C. Eugene Debs
    D. Hiram Johnson
    E. Robert La Follette

15. The Constitution provided for both the federal government and the states to share the power to

    A. coin money
    B. regulate interstate commerce
    C. establish post offices
    D. control the state militias
    E. admit new states

16. Which of the following statements best describes Chief Justice Roger B. Taney's decision in *Charles River Bridge* v. *Warren Bridge* (1837)?

    A. Taney overturned John Marshall's decision in *McCulloch* v. *Maryland*.
    B. Taney expanded economic opportunity and the powers of a state government.
    C. Taney supported Jackson's opposition to using federal funds on internal improvements.
    D. Taney granted the Charles River Bridge Company exclusive rights to control toll bridges into Boston.
    E. Taney rejected the principle of nullification.

17. At the turn of the nineteenth century, the emergence of Wild West shows and vaudeville demonstrated

    A. an effort by wealthy Americans to recapture a mythic past
    B. the rejection of the early movie industry
    C. a declining emphasis on outdoor recreation
    D. the growing importance of popular culture
    E. a popularization of immigrant traditions brought to the United States

18. Which of the following presidents sent federal troops to Little Rock, Arkansas, when Governor Orval Faubus attempted to stop the integration of Central High School?

    A. Harry S Truman
    B. John F. Kennedy
    C. Dwight D. Eisenhower

D. Lyndon B. Johnson
E. Richard M. Nixon

19. Which of the following technological innovations contributed the most to the economic development of the United States during the first four decades of the nineteenth century?

A. Cotton gin
B. Rubber
C. Chilled steel plow
D. Electricity
E. Barbed wire

20. Which of the following statements best supports Charles Beard's interpretation of the Constitution?

A. The authors of the Constitution emphasized libertarian over conservative interests.
B. The Constitution reflected the interests of the upper class of American society.
C. The authors of the Constitution remained deliberately vague on the issue of slavery.
D. The Constitution reflected the local or regional interests of the signers.
E. The Constitution captured a broad consensus of American society.

21. Which of the following statements best summarizes Abraham Lincoln's views on John Brown's raid at Harper's Ferry in 1859?

A. He distanced his party from Brown and his followers.
B. He criticized Southerners who wanted to execute Brown.
C. He supported Brown as a fellow Republican.
D. He supported Brown's method but not his goal.
E. He praised Brown's goal but criticized his failure to motivate more slaves to join him.

22. "Stagflation," an economic problem characterized by high inflation at a time of slow economic growth, plagued the administration of

A. Dwight D. Eisenhower
B. Richard M. Nixon
C. Franklin D. Roosevelt
D. Harry S Truman
E. Ronald Reagan

23. In an effort to thwart Progressive state legislation, the Supreme Court reinterpreted

A. its original ruling in *Plessy* v. *Ferguson*
B. the theory of Social Darwinism
C. its earliest antitrust suit in the *E. C. Knight* v. *United States* case
D. the property clause of the Sixteenth Amendment
E. the "due-process" clause of the Fourteenth Amendment.

24. Which of the following best describes the Hartford Convention?

A. It expressed Southern concerns over the Fugitive Slave Act.
B. It established the foundations of the Whig party.
C. It produced a series of non-importation agreements among Britain's North American colonies.
D. It led to the demise of the Federalists.
E. It nominated Andrew Jackson for president.

25. Medicaid provided

A. medical insurance for the elderly
B. medical relief under the Marshall Plan
C. medical insurance for the impoverished
D. a regulatory agency of the health profession
E. a medical corps for soldiers during the Vietnam War

26. During the first half of the nineteenth century, the expansion of suffrage increased popular interest in presidential elections. Partisan politics often shifted the voters' attention from issues to images. The "log cabin, hard cider" campaign helped which candidate win the presidency?

    A. James Monroe in 1820
    B. John Quincy Adams in 1824
    C. Andrew Jackson in 1828
    D. William Henry Harrison in 1840
    E. James K. Polk in 1844

27. McCarthyism spawned a hysteria that swept over the nation during the early Cold War. Accusations of links to Communism ruined numerous people and their careers. The decline of Joe McCarthy came after his televised hearings with

    A. the House Un-American Activities Committee
    B. the Army
    C. Edward R. Murrow
    D. the State Department
    E. the FBI

28. All of the following statements about President Thomas Jefferson's administration are true *except*

    A. Jefferson waged an undeclared war on the Barbary pirates
    B. Jefferson sought to influence the conviction of Aaron Burr for treason
    C. Jefferson kept in place many Federalist economic policies
    D. Jefferson moved to cut government expenditures
    E. Jefferson consistently acted as strict constructionist

29. In 1676, Bacon's Rebellion signaled that

    A. colonial taxes fell more heavily on eastern counties than western counties

    B. Nathaniel Bacon's extremist views were only supported by the younger sons of Virginia's wealthy planters
    C. supposedly docile, loyal slaves could, in fact, turn on their masters
    D. colonial governors struggled to contain domestic unrest
    E. excise taxes on whiskey were unpopular with western farmers

30. Although criticized by 1960s conservatives, the Supreme Court case of *Gideon* v. *Wainwright* ensured that those accused of crimes

    A. were informed of the specific charges drawn against them
    B. were entitled to a lawyer even if they could not afford one
    C. had the right to remain silent
    D. did not have to testify against family members
    E. were protect against illegal "searches and seizures"

31. The paintings of Charles Willson Peale and Gilbert Stuart

    A. represent the emerging nationalism of the post-Revolutionary era
    B. reflected the sentiments of the Transcendentalists of the 1840s
    C. were connected to the Ashcan school of painting
    D. were sponsored by the Works Progress Administration (WPA)
    E. focused upon classical rather than modern themes

32. In response to the sinking of the USS *Panay* and three American commercial vessels in 1937, the American public urged President Franklin Roosevelt to

    A. impose economic sanctions on Japan
    B. declare war on Germany
    C. withdraw American ships from China

D. prohibit the sale of arms and munitions to belligerent nations

E. extend Lend-Lease to the Soviet Union

33. Which of the following statements best expresses the outcome of the French and Indian War (1754 to 1763)?

A. It restored a balance of power between the French, British, and Native tribes of North America.

B. It ended Indian resistance to white expansion east of the Mississippi River.

C. It opened the trans-Appalachia west to American trade.

D. It demonstrated the political unity of Britain's North American colonies.

E. It forced Great Britain to reevaluate the administration of its colonial affairs.

34. Jane Addams was significant for

A. voting against a congressional declaration of war in 1917

B. writing the book *Silent Spring,* which raised concerns about the pollution of American waters

C. founding Hull House, a settlement house in Chicago

D. establishing the National Organization of Women

E. helping organize the Populist party in Kansas

35. In order to limit opposition to his liberal domestic programs, which of the following presidents attempted to expand the size of the Supreme Court from 9 to 12 justices?

A. Theodore Roosevelt
B. Woodrow Wilson
C. Harry S Truman
D. Franklin D. Roosevelt
E. John F. Kennedy

36. As settlers from various nations arrived in North America, they interacted differently with the native tribes. A major difference between French and British settlers was that

A. French treated natives with more respect and intermarried with some tribes

B. the French fur traders waged more bloody wars with native tribes before 1720

C. British settlers were less interested in establishing permanent settlements

D. only the French attempted to convert the natives

E. the French outnumbered the British before 1754

37. Which of the following individuals founded Standard Oil Trust, which dominated the oil refining industry in the late nineteenth century?

A. Leland Stanford
B. Andrew Carnegie
C. J. P. Morgan
D. Henry George
E. John D. Rockefeller

38. Which of the following statements about the antebellum mining frontier is *not* true?

A. Few miners were interested in permanently settling in the West.

B. In spite of the hardships, women flocked to California in large numbers.

C. Miners persecuted the native tribes of the West.

D. Mining towns were often disorderly, lawless communities.

E. Some foreign miners competed with Americans for gold.

39. What best explains the decline in immigration during the years pictured in the following graph?

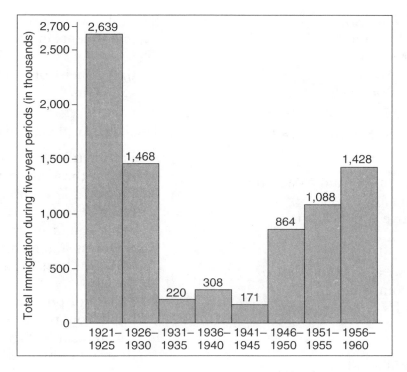

TOTAL IMMIGRATION, 1920–1960

A. Postwar recession ruined the agricultural economy.

B. Slow industrial expansion limited available job opportunities.

C. Nativistic legislation restricted immigration from certain nations.

D. Government land policy favored speculators over individual purchasers.

E. Better employment opportunities existed in Europe rather than in the United States.

40. Which of the following was a foreign affairs issue during the administration of President Jimmy Carter?

A. Iranian hostage crisis
B. Iran-Contra affair
C. North American Free Trade Agreement (NAFTA)
D. Invasion of Panama to arrest Manuel Noriega
E. Fall of Saigon

41. The Annapolis Convention succeeded in

A. resolving a boundary dispute between Maryland and Pennsylvania
B. uniting British colonists against the French
C. convincing Confederation leaders to call a constitutional convention
D. resolving tariff issues
E. settling disputes over the slave trade in North America

42. In the antebellum period, the largest number of women working outside of the home could be found in which of the following professions?

A. Nursing
B. Education
C. Secretarial
D. Textiles
E. Law

43. As part of his "Square Deal," which president signed the Pure Food and Drug Act and the Hepburn Act?

A. Benjamin Harrison
B. Grover Cleveland
C. William McKinley
D. Woodrow Wilson
E. Theodore Roosevelt

44. The Dawes Severalty Act of 1887 attempted to

A. provide economic aid to war-torn European nations
B. force Native Americans to assimilate into white society
C. set lower railroad rates
D. promote western land sales to railroad companies
E. lower tariffs on foreign industrial goods

45. Arthur and William Levitt were responsible for which of the following icons of the 1950s?

A. Standardized suburban communities
B. Polio vaccine
C. *Leave It to Beaver*
D. Hydrogen bomb
E. Electric refrigerators

46. When Congress gained control of Reconstruction policy, Radical Republican leaders

A. hastened the readmission of the seceded states according to President Abraham Lincoln's "10 Percent Plan"
B. redistributed thousands of acres of land formerly owned by slave masters
C. divided the South into military districts to be occupied by the Union army until loyal governments could be created
D. sought only to limit the involvement of the highest Confederate leaders in postwar governments

E. prohibited Northern business investments in the Southern economy as a means of punishing the former Confederacy for secession

47. The "*Sussex* pledge" was

A. President Nixon's promise to release the Watergate tapes
B. President Franklin Roosevelt's promise to provide relief to American farmers
C. a protest statement written by the SDS (Students for a Democratic Society)
D. a plan for postwar Europe stemming from the Yalta Conference
E. a statement by Germany promising to stop unrestricted U-boat warfare

48. Which of the following statements about the Whig party is true?

A. Party members universally opposed the expansion of slavery into the territories.
B. The party succeeded in winning only one election.
C. Party members tended to advocate nationalistic economic policies.
D. The party emerged immediately after the demise of the Federalists.
E. Party members sought to enlist the votes of immigrants.

49. In the late nineteenth century, the growth of cities was caused in part by the

A. settlement house movement
B. rise of public education
C. absence of nativism
D. expansion of industry
E. increasing importance of political machines

50. Racial tensions and fears of espionage led President Franklin D. Roosevelt to

issue Executive Order 9066. As a result, which of the following groups were forced into "relocation" camps?

A. Italian-Americans
B. Japanese-Americans
C. German-Americans
D. Mexican immigrants
E. Socialists

51. The Tet Offensive (1968)

A. demonstrated that the United States was no closer to ending the Vietnam War
B. revealed the success of Nixon's Vietnamization plans
C. temporarily reversed the rising popular opposition to the war
D. improved Johnson's bid for reelection
E. enabled American forces to enter North Vietnam

52. American colonists opposed the passage of the Stamp Act (1765) primarily because it

A. severely limited colonial commerce
B. followed the passage of the unpopular Townshend Acts
C. was too expensive for average colonists
D. did not receive the endorsement of the king
E. imposed a revenue tax

53. Beginning in 1872, mail-order catalogs

A. ruined small businesses
B. promoted the sale of industrial goods in rural areas
C. replaced billboards as the primary means of business advertisement
D. expanded American markets overseas
E. caused the reorganization of the postal system

54. Which of the following statements best asserts the principle of "popular sovereignty?"

A. Congress has the authority to decide where slavery may or may not exist.
B. Political parties provided the best forum for the resolution of the slavery issue.
C. The American people shall decide where slavery will exist by creating a national law in a special legislative convention.
D. The settlers in a given territory have the sole right to decide whether or not slavery will be permitted there.
E. Individual states have the right to reject congressional decisions concerning slavery.

55. All of the following were means of slave resistance during the antebellum period *except*

A. running away
B. breaking tools and slowing down the pace of work
C. field songs
D. adaptations of slave religion
E. frequent bloody slave revolts

56. The Servicemen's Readjustment Act, popularly known as the GI Bill of Rights, granted financial assistance and opened new educational opportunities for veterans. It was passed by

A. Woodrow Wilson.
B. Warren G. Harding
C. Franklin D. Roosevelt.
D. Harry S Truman.
E. Richard Nixon.

57. The Monroe Doctrine (1823) intended to

A. reverse George Washington's neutrality policy

B. eliminate British influence in North America

C. restrict European involvement in the Western Hemisphere

D. facilitate the expansion of American trade in the West Indies

E. open South America to American colonization

58. The federal government promoted the settlement of the Great Plains in the nineteenth century through the passage of the

A. Reclamation Act
B. Homestead Act
C. Gadsden Purchase
D. Webster-Ashburton Treaty
E. Soil Conservation and Domestic Allotment Act

59. One difference between the Middle Colonies and the other British colonies in North America was that

A. residents of the Middle Colonies represented more diverse nationalities
B. the Middles Colonies outstripped their neighbors in the production of tobacco
C. the Middle Colonies developed a primarily industrial economy
D. the residents of the Middle Colonies had little interaction with the native tribes
E. no settlers in the Middle Colonies owned slaves

60. Which of the following was *not* an issue associated with the Kennedy administration?

A. Integration of the University of Mississippi
B. Bay of Pigs Invasion
C. Construction of the Berlin Wall
D. Trade Expansion Act
E. U-2 incident

61. At the turn of the century, the United States favored the Open-Door policy in order to

A. encourage trade among its overseas colonies
B. protect the governments of Latin America
C. ensure that it would have its share in China's trade
D. promote the use of the Panama Canal
E. cripple the Nazi war effort

62. The Northwest Ordinances

A. provided a means to establish new states in the territory ceded in the Treaty of Paris (1783)
B. admitted Oregon and Washington to the Union
C. sanctioned the exploration of the Louisiana Purchase
D. restricted westward expansion
E. were supported mostly by farmers and railroad companies seeking the removal of Indian tribes

63. Breaking with precedent, President Woodrow Wilson went abroad to negotiate a treaty to end World War I. He supported the Treaty of Versailles because it

A. banned submarine warfare
B. blamed Germany for starting the war
C. divided Germany into occupation zones
D. provided for the creation of the League of Nations
E. gave the United States trading privileges in Great Britain

64. The intent of the Alien and Sedition Acts was to

A. weaken the opponents of the John Adams

B. expand the meaning of the First Amendment
C. protect the rights of recent immigrants
D. expel French residents of the Louisiana Purchase
E. require all newspapers to be printed in English

65. Which of the following statements about the First Great Awakening is true?

A. It led to the founding of new colonies in North America.
B. It splintered existing congregations and churches.
C. It found most of its converts in the commercial cities of the East Coast.
D. It strengthened the authority of established religious figures.
E. It cemented the ties between colonial governments and religious denominations.

66. The WPA

A. supported Prohibition during the 1920s
B. was a conservation organization started by John Muir
C. promoted rationing during World War I
D. addressed unfair hiring practices during World War II
E. attempted to revive the economy by creating jobs in the 1930s

67. Harriet Beecher Stowe was notable for

A. organizing an early women's rights convention
B. promoting the reform of prisons and asylums
C. writing the abolitionist novel *Uncle Tom's Cabin*
D. leading slaves to freedom along the Underground Railroad
E. founding a utopian community at New Harmony

68. Which of the following statements is true about the election of 1972?

A. Nixon was the first Republican candidate to carry the "Solid South."
B. Nixon's opponent, Democrat George McGovern, had reunited a party divided since 1968.
C. Nixon benefited from the first economic boom since 1945.
D. Nixon placed Gerald Ford on the ballot to win votes from the Midwest.
E. Nixon struggled to defeat challenger Ronald Reagan in the Republican primary.

69. The term "Dust Bowl" refers to which area of the nation ravaged by drought during the Great Depression?

A. The West Coast
B. South Carolina to Mississippi
C. New England
D. Texas to the Dakotas
E. The Mississippi Delta

70. After the War of 1812, the United States government sought to

A. stimulate trade by lowering tariffs
B. improve commerce with Great Britain in a series of favorable treaties
C. slow the pace of westward expansion
D. redistribute British property seized during the war
E. renew the charter of the Bank of the United States

71. The passage of the first graduated income tax enabled the federal government to rely less upon which of its traditional sources of income?

A. The sale of public lands
B. High tariffs
C. Sale of war bonds
D. Bank loans
E. Corporate taxes

72. In the post-Reconstruction South, white Southerners attempted to circumscribe the citizenship rights of African-Americans by restoring the social customs of the "Old South." Which of the following means of limiting black freedom found its predecessor in the antebellum period?

    A. The Ku Klux Klan
    B. "Grandfather clause"
    C. National legalized segregation
    D. "Black Codes"
    E. Literacy tests for voting

73. The Strategic Defense Initiative ("Star Wars"), which intended to use lasers and satellites to counter Soviet nuclear weapons, was proposed under

    A. Gerald Ford
    B. Jimmy Carter
    C. Ronald Reagan
    D. George Bush
    E. Bill Clinton

74. "It was the best of nationally advertised and quantitatively pro-duced alarm clocks, with all modern attachments, including cathedral chime, intermittent alarm, and phosphorescent dial. Babbitt was proud of being wakened by such a rich device. Socially, it was almost as creditable as buying expensive cord tires."

    In *Babbitt,* which of the following authors criticized the shallow materialism of his or her contemporaries?

    A. Sinclair Lewis
    B. John Steinbeck
    C. Ida Tarbell
    D. Bruce Barton
    E. Jack London

75. The intent of British mercantile legislation before 1750 was to

    A. cripple the colonial economy in North America
    B. promote favorable trade between Great Britain and its colonies
    C. give special trade privileges to its North American colonies
    D. limit the growth of a merchant class in the colonies
    E. prevent the founding of new colonies west of the Appalachian mountains

76. Which of the following diplomatic initiatives during the Cold War best matches the goal of Franklin D. Roosevelt's "Good Neighbor" policy?

    A. Eisenhower Doctrine
    B. Alliance for Progress
    C. Mann Doctrine
    D. SALT II
    E. Warsaw Pact

77. Reform legislation, including stricter building codes and factory inspection acts, followed a horrendous fire in 1911 that claimed 146 lives at the

    A. Triangle Shirtwaist Company (New York)
    B. International Harvester Corporation (Chicago)
    C. Swift meatpacking plant (Chicago)
    D. U.S. Steel Corporation (Pittsburgh)
    E. Bessemer Steel Corporation (New York)

78. Which of the following was *not* a provision of the Compromise of 1850?

    A. Admission of California as a free state
    B. No congressional restriction on slavery in the Mexican Cession

C. Settlement of the Texas and New Mexico boundary issue

D. Prohibition of the slave trade in Washington, DC

E. Appropriation of federal funds for railroad construction in the Southwest

79. Which of the following Supreme Court cases could be viewed as a victory for the opponents of reform?

A. *Swift and Company* v. *United States*, 1905

B. *Lochner* v. *United States*, 1905

C. *National Securities Company* v. *United States*, 1904

D. *Standard Oil of NJ* v. *United States*, 1911

E. *American Tobacco Company* v. *United States*, 1911

80. The following cartoon by Thomas Nast

A. called for reform of American prisons

B. opposed imperialism

C. attacked political corruption

D. demanded improvements in the educational system

E. criticized new child labor laws

The political cartoon, "Tweed-le-dee and Tilden-dum," *Harper's Weekly*, July 1, 1876; courtesy of the Library of Congress.

END OF SECTION I

Section II

Part A

(Suggested writing time—45 minutes)

Directions: The following question requires you to construct a coherent essay that integrates your interpretation of Documents A to H *and* your knowledge of the period referred to in the question. High scores will be earned only by essays that both cite key pieces of evidence from the documents and draw on outside knowledge of the period.

1. At the turn of the century, several nations were competing for international empires. After the Spanish-American War, the United States government sought to extend and solidify its influence in the Western Hemisphere. Analyze the effects of American foreign policy in Latin America in the period 1899 to 1917.

Document A
Source: Platt Amendment, May 22, 1903

> *Article III. The Government of Cuba consents that the United States may exercise the right to intervene for the preservation of Cuban independence, the maintenance of a government adequate for the protection of life property, and individual liberty, and for discharging the obligations with respect to Cuba imposed by the Treaty of Paris on the United States, now to be assumed and undertaken by the Government of Cuba.*

Document B
Source: Hay-Bunau-Varilla Treaty, November 18, 1903

> *The Republic of Panama grants to the United States in perpetuity, the use, occupation and control of a zone of land and land under water for the construction . . . of said canal. . . . The Republic of Panama further grants to the United States in perpetuity, the use, occupation and control of any other lands and waters outside the zone . . . which may be necessary and convenient for the construction . . . and protection of the said Canal.*

Document C
Source: John Wilson Bengough, "Autonomy," *The Public,* January 23, 1904; courtesy of BoondocksNet.com.

Document D
Source: Theodore Roosevelt, Annual Message to Congress, December 6, 1904

> *If a nation shows that it knows how to act with reasonable efficiency and decency in social and political matters, if it keeps order and pays its obligations, it need fear no interference from the United States. Chronic wrongdoing, or an impotence which results in a general loosening of the ties of civilized society, may . . . ultimately require intervention by some civilized nation, and in the Western Hemisphere the adherence of the United States to the Monroe Doctrine may lead the United States, . . . in flagrant cases of such wrongdoing or impotence, to exercise an international police power.*

Document E
Source: W. A. Rogers, "The Full Dinner Pail," *Harper's Weekly,* April 13, 1907; courtesy of Theodore-Roosevelt.com.

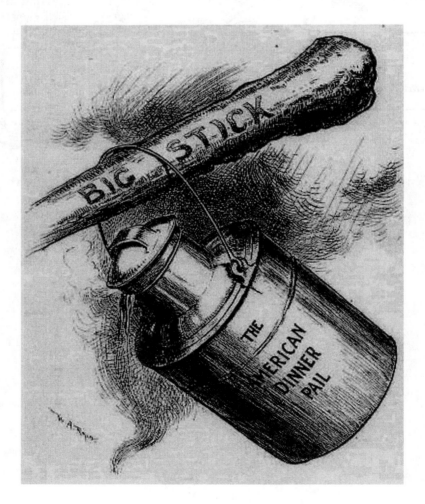

Document F

Source: William Howard Taft, Fourth Annual Message to Congress, December 3, 1912

> *The diplomacy of the present administration has sought to respond to modern ideas of commercial intercourse. This policy has been characterized by substituting dollars for bullets. . . . It is an effort frankly directed to the increase of American trade upon the axiomatic principle that the government of the United States shall extend all proper support to every legitimate and beneficial American enterprise abroad.*

Document G

Source: Erving Winslow, "Aggression in South America," excerpt from Report of the Thirteenth Annual Meeting of the Anti-Imperialist League, 1912

> *It is proposed that in the Honduras and Nicaragua . . . the United States government should be authorized to secure the collection and disbursement of the revenue in the interest of American capitalists who contemplate making loans to those countries. This involves serious risk of complications which may lead to further interferences and ultimate control.*
>
> *The delicacy of these and other foreign relations of the United States is such as should put our citizens upon their guard and confirm their determination to treat with justice all their neighbors and to recognize generally their independent right to govern (or misgovern) their own countries.*

Document H

Source: Nelson Harding, "Uncle Sam: 'I Smell Oil!,' " *Brooklyn Eagle,* reprinted from *American Review of Reviews,* January 1914; courtesy of BoondocksNet.com.

Document I

Source: Woodrow Wilson, Address to Congress, April 20, 1914

A series of incidents have recently occurred which cannot but create the impression that the representatives of General Huerta were willing to go out of their way to show disregard for the dignity and rights of this government, . . . making free to show in many ways their irritation and contempt.

I, therefore, come to ask your approval that I should use the armed forces of the United States in such ways . . . as may be necessary to obtain from General Huerta and his adherents the fullest recognition of the rights and dignity of the United States, even amidst the distressing conditions now unhappily obtaining in Mexico.

Section II

Part B and Part C

(Suggested total planning and writing time: 70 minutes)

Part B

Directions: Choose *one* question from this part. You are advised to spend 5 minutes planning and 30 minutes writing your answer. Cite relevant historical evidence in support of your generalizations, and present your arguments clearly and logically.

2. Evaluate the impact of *two* of the following in diffusing domestic tensions during the nineteenth century:

Compromise of 1820

Compromise of 1833

Compromise of 1877

3. Explain the impact of the Kansas-Nebraska Act upon national politics, 1854 to 1860.

Part C

Directions: Choose *one* question from this part. You are advised to spend 5 minutes planning and 30 minutes writing your answer. Cite relevant historical evidence in support of your generalizations, and present your arguments clearly and logically.

4. Analyze the causes of the Great Depression.

5. Evaluate the success of the containment policies of the Truman administration, 1945 to 1953.

END OF SECTION II

ANSWERS TO PRACTICE EXAM 1

Answers to the Multiple-Choice Questions

1. A	21. A	41. C	61. C
2. C	22. B	42. D	62. A
3. B	23. E	43. E	63. D
4. D	24. D	44. B	64. A
5. E	25. C	45. A	65. B
6. E	26. D	46. C	66. E
7. A	27. B	47. E	67. C
8. D	28. E	48. C	68. A
9. B	29. D	49. D	69. D
10. C	30. B	50. B	70. E
11. C	31. A	51. A	71. B
12. E	32. C	52. E	72. D
13. A	33. E	53. B	73. C
14. E	34. C	54. D	74. A
15. D	35. D	55. E	75. B
16. B	36. A	56. D	76. B
17. D	37. E	57. C	77. A
18. C	38. B	58. B	78. E
19. A	39. C	59. A	79. B
20. B	40. A	60. E	80. C

Explanations of Answers to the Multiple-Choice Questions

1. **A.** The headright system stimulated population growth in colonial Virginia. Planters who helped bring more settlers to the colony received "headrights" of 50 acres. Any planter who imported indentured servants could obtain accumulate sizable tracts of land. The system conferred some political privileges to the holders of large estates.

2. **C.** Similar to the Truman Doctrine, President Eisenhower's policies intended to halt the spread of communism and limit the influence of pan-Arab nationalism. In the wake of the Suez crisis, Eisenhower offered economic and military aid to pro-Western governments. American aid and presence helped Jordan's King Hussein suppress internal strife. In 1958, American marines landed in Lebanon to protect the government of Camile Chamoun.

3. **B.** Garrison, Douglass, Tubman, and Grimke were antebellum abolitionists. Both Garrison and Douglass established newspapers with wide circulations. Douglass established *The North Star;* Garrison founded *The Liberator*.

4. **D.** Before the twentieth century, the labor movement had yet to build significant public support. Government officials at the state and federal level often sent troops to disperse labor strikes. Theodore Roosevelt, William Howard Taft, and Woodrow Wilson resided in the White House during part of the Progressive era. The United Mine Workers, led by John Mitchell, struck against anthracite mine operators in 1902 for higher wages, an eight-hour work day, and, most importantly, recognition of the union. When mine operators refused to compromise, Roosevelt threatened to send in federal troops. The president's position forced operators to agree to arbitration.

5. **E.** Betty Friedan published her attack upon sexism and spurred the modern feminist movement. Gloria Steinem also emerged as one of the principal proponents of women's rights. A conservative journalist, Phyllis Schlafly campaigned against the Equal Rights Amendment. Shirley Chisolm was the first African-American woman to serve in Congress. Geraldine Ferraro ran as the Democratic vice presidential candidate in 1984.

6. **E.** Although many Southerners advocated the annexation of Texas, Jackson was fully aware of the simmering slave controversy. During the last year of his administration, Congress adopted a "gag rule" to prevent discussion of abolitionist petitions. Most Whigs opposed annexation out of fear that it would add another state committed to Jackson. Jackson's land sales policy promoted westward expansion. He saw merit in promoting both the commercial and agricultural economies.

7. **A.** The Nineteenth Amendment established women's suffrage. Prohibition began with the Eighteenth Amendment. The Seventeenth Amendment changed the process for electing senators. The Fourteenth Amendment protected the citizenship rights of African-Americans.

8. **D.** The Great Railway Strike of 1877 began in West Virginia and rapidly spread to other states east of the Mississippi. Still feeling the effects of the Panic of 1873, some Americans embraced the workers' demands for higher wages. However, as union members fought local authorities in a series of highly publicized clashes, public opinion turned against the strikers. Many Americans applauded President Hayes's use of federal troops to quell the violence in West Virginia.

9. **B.** In the early nineteenth century, Great Britain and France resumed hostilities. Sailors deserted British ships to escape the low pay and harsh conditions. The British navy soon began to stop and search American ships for escaped sailors. Impressment often forced native-born Americans into service aboard British ships. James Barron, captain of the *Chesapeake,* refused to allow Admiral Berkley of the HMS *Leopard* to search his ship for deserters. Berkley ordered his men to open fire, killing three and wounding eighteen. Barron relented and the British impressed four of his men. The Chesapeake Incident sparked national outrage.

10. **C.** President Lincoln hoped that a successful strike against Richmond would bring the yearlong war to an end. From the beginning of the campaign, McClelland complained that he lacked sufficient men. At Yorktown, a small detachment of Confederate soldiers (12,000) slowed the advance of McClellan's force of over 110,000 men. McClellan believed that the men marching behind the Confederate earthworks constituted a much larger force. McClellan's trudging pace toward Richmond confirmed Lincoln's assessment that his general "had a bad case of the slows."

11. **C.** After passage of the unpopular Stamp Act, many colonists in New England stopped purchasing British goods. The boycott soon spread to other colonies. British merchants and manufacturers lost considerable profits and urged Parliament to repeal the act. Petitions to the king typically fell on deaf ears. Most colonial governors executed British laws in spite of colonial protest. Although the Sons of Liberty intimidated governors and colonists loyal to the Crown, they had little effect upon parliamentary legislation.

12. **E.** Archibald Cox demanded that President Nixon relinquish the Watergate tapes. Nixon ordered his Attorney General, Elliot Richardson, to fire Cox. Richardson promptly resigned, as did Deputy Attorney General William Ruckelshaus. Nixon's desperate measures raised public indignation and prompted the House of Representatives to pursue impeachment charges.

13. **A.** The slave of an army surgeon, Dred Scott had lived with his master in Illinois and Wisconsin, both which banned slavery. As a result, Scott sued for his freedom after his master's death. Chief Justice Taney wrote one of the majority positions in which he stated that Scott could not sue because he was not a citizen. Taney further ruled that the Missouri Compromise line, imposed by Congress, was "not warranted by the Constitution and is therefore void."

14. **E.** Robert LaFollette served as three terms as governor of Wisconsin. Charles Evans Hughes (NY), Woodrow Wilson (NJ), and Hiram Johnson (CA) also instituted progressive reforms as governor. Eugene Debs ran as the Socialist candidate for president in 1912.

15. **D.** The Constitution granted Congress the sole power to coin money, establish post offices, regulate interstate commerce, and admit new states. While the state government retained the authority to raise a militia, the federal government may nationalize state troops to enforce federal law and maintain order.

16. **B.** The Charles River Bridge Company held a Massachusetts state charter to operate a toll bridge between Boston and Cambridge. The company asserted that the charter ensured a monopoly over bridge traffic. The Warren Bridge Company applied to the state legislature for permission to construct a second bridge. The Charles River Bridge Company argued that John Marshall's Dartmouth

College decision prevented the state from violating contracts. Nevertheless, Chief Justice Roger Taney sided with the Warren Bridge Company and the state of Massachusetts. He argued that the vagueness of the original charter did not specifically confer monopoly rights. Thus, new charters could be granted to expand economic opportunities for the wider community.

17. **D.** Americans of the late nineteenth century embraced new forms of leisure and entertainment. Urban dwellers particularly flocked to vaudeville houses and theaters. Working-class Americans often attended these shows. The movie industry thrived during this era.

18. **C.** The *Brown* v. *Board of Education* decision ordered the desegregation of public schools in 1954. In 1957, nine African-American students attempted to integrate Little Rock Central High School. Governor Orval Faubus ordered the state militia to prevent the students from enrolling. He later withdrew the troops, and an angry mob filled the void. President Eisenhower used federal troops to protect the students and enforce the desegregation of Little Rock Central.

19. **A.** The mass production of the cotton gin increased demand for the Southern staple. Cotton production increased dramatically during the antebellum period. The chilled steel plow and barbed wire helped Great Plains settlers of the late nineteenth century farm and raise cattle.

20. **B.** In *An Economic Interpretation of the Constitution* (1913), Beard asserted that the framers created a government in order to protect private property and promote commerce. Wealthy Americans, who bought bonds during the Revolutionary War, also had a vested interest in the repayment of the public debt.

21. **A.** Lincoln advocated the containment of slavery, not immediate abolition. Although some notable figures such as Wendell Phillips and Ralph Waldo Emerson praised Brown, most Northerners and Republicans condemned his attack on the federal arsenal. In his Cooper Union Speech, Lincoln claimed that "John Brown was no Republican" and assured his listeners that no one could "implicate a single Republican in his Harper's Ferry enterprise."

22. **B.** Roosevelt, Truman, Eisenhower, and Reagan presided over years in which the American economy experienced significant growth. Some had to deal with intermittent problems of inflation. During the early 1970s, Nixon had to battle both inflation and a stagnant economy.

23. **E.** In the late nineteenth century, various state legislatures passed Progressive legislation ranging from child labor regulations to maximum hours. The Fourteenth Amendment forbade states from depriving "any person of life, liberty, or property without due process of law." The Supreme Court construed the meaning of the term "per-

son" to include corporations. If state laws appeared to deprive corporations of property, the Court reasoned, then those acts violated the "due process" clause. For example, the Supreme Court struck down a state law regulating railroad rates. The *E. C. Knight* decision undermined the Sherman Antitrust Act by exempting manufacturing companies from antimonopoly legislation.

24. **D.** Federalists from the New England States met in Hartford in December 1814 to discuss the impact of the War of 1812 on their section. New England opposed war with England because of its impact on commerce. During the war, Federalists did not support the sale of war bonds or federal use of state militias. Moderates at the convention rejected the extremists' proposal for secession and a separate peace. The delegates agreed to a list of grievances and constitutional amendments aimed at protecting the power of the states. However, the signing of the Treaty of Ghent and Jackson's victory at New Orleans turned public opinion against the Federalists.

25. **C.** President Lyndon B. Johnson waged a "War on Poverty" with his "Great Society" legislation. Johnson attempted to extend health care benefits. Medicare provided federally funded medical insurance for the elderly. Medicaid funded medical care for impoverished Americans of all ages.

26. **D.** The Whig party emerged in 1836 to challenge Andrew Jackson's hand-picked successor, Martin Van Buren. Van Buren won the election but soon faced the Panic of 1837. Persistent economic problems affected the next election. The Whigs cast Van Buren as an aristocrat who spent money lavishly while average Americans suffered from the privations of the depression. Furthermore, Whig partisans portrayed their candidate, Indiana Governor William Henry Harrison, as a man of the people. Banners and leaflets pictured Harrison living in a rustic log cabin, consuming hard cider rather than champagne like Van Buren. Harrison defeated Van Buren in the election of 1840.

27. **B.** Many Republicans hoped that the election of Dwight D. Eisenhower would erode the position of Senator McCarthy. However, McCarthy ensured his own fall in 1954. McCarthy's accusations against Secretary of the Army Robert Stevens led to a special congressional inquiry. Television stations broadcasted the Army-McCarthy hearings to a national audience. Viewers witnessed the senator's intimidation tactics. By the end of the year, the Senate censured McCarthy for his conduct.

28. **E.** After his inauguration in 1801, Jefferson refused to renew the Alien and Sedition Acts but did not move to dismantle many economic measures of his Federalist predecessors. Jefferson did not eliminate the national debt but oversaw significant cuts in military and administrative spending. In 1807 Aaron Burr was arrested for an alleged conspiracy to seize lands in the Southwest. Jefferson helped

manage the federal government's case against Burr and urged a conviction for treason. Jefferson refused to pay bribe money to ensure American commerce in the Mediterranean. Without a declaration of war, he ordered the American navy to protect ships in the region. The Louisiana Purchase represents another example of Jefferson interpreting the Constitution loosely.

29. **D.** Colonial assemblies often represented the interests of eastern over western counties. Taxes sometimes fell heavily upon those underrepresented in the legislature. In colonial Virginia, Governor Berkeley sought to restrict white expansion in order to avoid bloody conflicts with Indian tribes. After a number of conflicts with the natives, Bacon raised a rebel army composed mainly of former indentured servants and other unemployed men. The rebels twice marched on Jamestown and evoked a lawlessness Berkeley struggled to contain. Bacon's Rebellion dissipated with the arrival of British troops and Bacon's death from dysentery. The social unrest alarmed propertied Virginians. The Whiskey Rebellion occurred in 1794. Major slave rebellions occurred in 1739, 1800, 1822, and 1832.

30. **B.** The Warren Court made a number of landmark decisions protecting the rights of those accused of crimes. In 1961, Clarence Gideon was arrested for a crime he did not commit. Gideon could not afford a lawyer; the presiding judge refused to provide one. Gideon was subsequently sentenced to five years in prison. He petitioned the Supreme Court, claiming that the judge's refusal to provide a lawyer denied him "due process of law" under the Fourteenth Amendment. The Supreme Court's decision in *Gideon* v. *Wainwright* overturned the conviction and ensured legal representation for the impoverished. The *Escobedo* decision extended access to a lawyer prior to questioning by the authorities. The *Miranda* decision required the police to inform suspects of these rights. Critics argued that the Court protected the rights of the accused at the expense of law-abiding citizens. The Fourth Amendment protects against "unreasonable search and seizures."

31. **A.** Peale and Stuart contributed to emerging cultural nationalism of the early republic. Peale painted several portraits of George Washington and other Revolutionary War heroes. Stuart also produced a wide array of portraits. The "Ashcan school" focused upon the grim realities of urban poverty and city life during the Progressive era.

32. **C.** Americans embraced isolationism in response to world events in the 1930s. Franklin Roosevelt's "quarantine speech" met with extremely mixed emotions. Congress passed a series of laws intended to ensure American neutrality. Japanese airplanes attacked the USS *Panay* and three Standard Oil tankers. Public opinion favored accepting reparations from Japan and removing American ships from foreign waters rather than punitive action. The Neutrality Act of 1935, pro-

hibiting the sale of arms and munitions to belligerent nations, preceded the *Panay* Incident.

33. **E.** During the French and Indian War, American colonists continued to trade with Britain's enemies. Colonial assemblies did not always relinquish control of local militias. However, the colonial governments often failed to cooperate with their neighbors. Parliament began to reexamine its ability to control its North American colonies and passed new regulatory and taxation laws that contributed to the American Revolution. The war weakened France and the Indian tribes. Parliament attempted to check white expansion and limit the colonial trade west of the Appalachians with the Proclamation of 1763. Nevertheless, Indian resistance east of the Mississippi increased as whites migrated across the mountains.

34. **C.** The settlement house movement emerged to address the unhealthy conditions in industrial cities. Jane Addams established Hull House in Chicago, which served as a model for urban reformers. Workers at Hull House strove to help immigrant families adapt to the language and traditions of the United States. Representative Jeannette Rankin voted against the declaration of war in 1917 and 1941. Rachel Carson published *Silent Spring* in 1962. Betty Friedan was the founder and first president of the National Organization of Women. Mary Elizabeth Lease gave several speeches supporting Populist reforms.

35. **D.** President Franklin D. Roosevelt perceived his reelection in 1936 as a popular mandate to extend his New Deal programs. The Supreme Court overturned his Agricultural Adjustment Act and National Industrial Recovery Act in that same year. Roosevelt proposed to raise the number of justices ostensibly to alleviate the workload of older justices. Most people saw the measure as a transparent effort to increase the number of Democrats on the bench. His proposal caused some Democrats to bolt the party and undergirded conservative opposition to the New Deal.

36. **A.** British settlers in North America established permanent settlements in order to take advantage of economic opportunities. The French attempted to exploit trade but did not found as many settled communities. Thus, British settlers outnumbered the French throughout the colonial period. British farmers continually clashed with natives along the frontier. The French tried to form alliances to promote the fur trade and often married native women. Both French and British missionaries attempted to convert the native tribes.

37. **E.** Rockefeller, Carnegie, Stanford, and Morgan each forged lucrative business enterprises in the late nineteenth century. Rockefeller's Standard Oil Trust cornered the refining industry. Carnegie created a vast steel empire. Stanford attempted to monopolize the railroad industry in the West. Morgan dominated the field of banking and investments.

38. **B.** The gold rush drew thousands of immigrants to the West between 1848 and 1852. Prospectors came from abroad, as well from as Eastern states. Many hoped to strike it rich and return home. Most fortune-seekers decided to remain in the West. Miners often clashed with Indian tribes as they staked claims. Some tried to force the native population to work in the mines; others killed local tribes. The population of mining towns remained predominantly male; few women or families traveled to the West. Crime and violence permeated these communities.

39. **C.** Industrial expansion in the late nineteenth century drew millions of immigrants to American cities. While many factory owners sought cheap labor, nativists continually urged Congress to preserve opportunities for American workers. Congress responded with a variety of restrictive laws between 1882 and 1921. The Immigration Restriction Act of 1924 established extremely low quotas for certain nationalities, thus barring numerous immigrants from the United States. Congress extended the act in 1929. The Great Depression paralleled a worldwide economic crisis.

40. **A.** Nationalists and religious fundamentalists forced Shah Reza Pahlevi to flee Iran in January 1979. The deposed Shah sought medical treatment in the United States. An angry mob stormed the American embassy in November, demanding the return of Pahlevi. The militants held 53 American diplomats and service personnel hostage for over a year. A failed rescue attempt exacerbated public frustration with the Carter administration. The United States withdrew from Saigon in 1975. Congress began investigations into the Iran-Contra Affair in 1987. American troops invaded Panama and arrested Manuel Noriega in 1989. Congress ratified the North American Free Trade Agreement in 1993.

41. **C.** In 1786, delegates from five states met in Annapolis to discuss methods to improve interstate commerce. States retained significant power under the Articles of Confederation and often passed high tariffs on each other's goods. Realizing the weaknesses of the existing political structure, the delegates asked Congress to call a general convention in Philadelphia to revise the Articles. The Albany Congress attempted to promote intercolonial unity in 1754.

42. **D.** Enterprises in Lowell and Waltham, Massachusetts, began a trend of employing women in the textile industry in the 1830s. Many women did not enter the fields of education and nursing until after the Civil War. Secretarial work remained a province for men until World War II. Few women made inroads into the law profession until later in the twentieth century.

43. **E.** Roosevelt adopted a more reform-minded domestic program than his Republican predecessors Harrison and McKinley. In 1906, he signed the Hepburn Act to increase the powers of the Interstate

Commerce Commission. The Pure Food and Drug Act passed that same year after public outcry against the food and patent medicine industries.

44. **B.** The Dawes Severalty Act intended to dissolve the tribal system by dividing reservations into 160-acre homesteads. Indian families were encouraged to live on their own farms and abandon native customs. In reality, much of the reservation land was sold to white speculators. The Dawes Plan (1924) provided loans to enable Germany to repay reparations to France after World War I.

45. **A.** The return of World War II soldiers and postwar "baby boom" caused a severe housing shortage. The Levitts introduced mass-produced houses to accommodate the demand. Standardized suburban communities sprang up in New York, New Jersey, and Pennsylvania. Jonas Salk developed a polio vaccine in the 1950s.

46. **C.** Before the Radical Republicans gained control of Reconstruction, the former Confederate states reentered the Union under the moderate conditions imposed by Lincoln and Johnson. New state legislatures enacted "Black Codes" circumscribing the rights of freedmen. Furthermore, most Southern states rejected the Fourteenth Amendment. As a result, Congress passed the Military Reconstruction Act of 1867. The act disbanded the governments created under Lincoln's "Ten Percent Plan" and under Johnson. Military occupation would last until loyal governments ratified the Fourteenth Amendment and registered African-Americans to vote. The act fell short of the hopes of many Radicals by not redistributing land to the freedmen.

47. **E.** During World War I, German submarines sank ships heading to British ports. The German government announced that U-boats would sink all enemy ships. In 1915, a German submarine sank the British luxury liner *Lusitania*, killing nearly 1200 people, including 128 Americans. President Wilson, like many Americans, angrily condemned German actions. He warned Germany not to continue unrestricted U-boat warfare. When an attack on the French ship *Sussex* injured several American passengers, Wilson repeated his warning. In order to keep the United States out of the war, the Germany government gave assurances that it would stop attacking ships without warning.

48. **C.** The Whigs emerged in the 1830s as an anti-Jackson party. The party absorbed elements of the nativistic American ("Know-Nothing") party. They supported the maintenance of the Bank of the United States, road construction, and tariffs to protect American industries. The Whigs found adherents in every region. The Whig presidential candidate won the elections of 1840 and 1848. However, the slavery issue troubled the party. By the 1850s, many Southern Whigs supported the expansion of slavery into the territories, while their Northern counterparts opposed expansion.

49. **D.** After the Civil War, rapid industrial growth created significant demand for labor in American factories. Millions of immigrants, especially from Southern and Eastern Europe, flocked to the cities seeking employment. Nativism increased as Americans feared competition for jobs and the spread of non-Protestant religions.

50. **B.** In response to Pearl Harbor and long-standing racial prejudice, local authorities in the West urged Roosevelt to address the presence of Japanese-Americans (Nisei). Roosevelt issued Executive Order 9066, which allowed military officials to remove the Nisei to relocation centers. No similar policy was followed for first-generation Americans of German or Italian descent.

51. **A.** In late 1967, General William Westmoreland assured President Johnson that American victories portended the surrender of the Vietnamese communists. In reality, North Vietnamese leaders were planning a massive invasion of South Vietnam. The communist offensive began in January 1968 during the Tet holiday. North Vietnamese forces struck 41 cities, including Saigon. The Tet Offensive revealed that the United States was no closer to victory than earlier in the war. As a result, the antiwar movement intensified.

52. **E.** After the French and Indian War, Parliament imposed the Stamp Act to defray the costs of colonial defense. However, the colonists had become accustomed to paying revenue taxes passed by their assemblies. Many believed that Parliament legitimately retained the right to regulate trade but not to raise revenue. Although the tax was not extremely burdensome, it sparked fiery rhetoric and boycotts throughout the colonies. Parliament later rescinded the act but would try to raise revenue with the Townshend Acts in 1767.

53. **B.** Advertising changed in the late nineteenth century to expand the markets of American industries. Chain stores challenged small merchants to market mass-produced goods at a lower price. However, farmers often could not obtain similar products in local country stores. Catalogs such as Montgomery Ward and Sears Roebuck made new items available in rural areas. Farmers soon embraced the newest tools, technologies, and fashions displayed in the catalogs.

54. **D.** The acquisition of new territories in the antebellum period exacerbated the controversy over the expansion of slavery. The Constitutional Convention had banned the further importation of slaves after 1808. Congress established the Missouri Compromise line to limit the expansion of slavery in the Louisiana territory. The Mexican Cession became the target of new debates. Some argued that Congress could extend the Missouri Compromise line to California. Others argued the people residing in a territory should decide the question of slavery. Stephen Douglas and other Democratic politicians promoted "popular sovereignty" as a solution to the slavery question.

55. **E.** Slaves resisted oppressive conditions in many ways. Although laws did not recognize slave marriages, slaves frequently held their own ceremonies. Slaves merged African traditions with Christianity and practiced their own forms of religion. Field songs and religious music challenged the dominance of whites through coded messages. Slaves resisted the pace of work set by masters and drivers by breaking tools or working more slowly. Others ran away from their plantations, especially in the upper South. However, slave revolts did not occur frequently.

56. **C.** Roosevelt signed the GI Bill in 1944. This act provided loans for purchasing homes and grants for education. Millions of veterans took advantage of government funding to pursue higher education and job training. The GI Bill helped fuel postwar prosperity in the 1940s and 1950s.

57. **C.** The United States adopted an official policy of neutrality in the conflicts between Spain and its Latin American colonies. Nevertheless, American businesses supplied the rebels in those colonies. The United States became the first nation to recognize the newly independent governments. Wary of European involvement in the Western Hemisphere, Secretary of State John Quincy Adams urged President James Monroe to adopt a more forceful policy. The Monroe Doctrine opposed future European colonization and efforts to undermine existing governments. Furthermore, it reiterated a traditional policy of noninterference in European affairs.

58. **B.** Congress passed the Homestead Act in 1862. This act offered prospective settlers 160-acre homesteads in the West for a nominal fee if they resided on the land for five years. Thousands of settlers streamed west with hopes of establishing farms on the Great Plains. The Gadsden Purchase provided a potential railroad route in the Southwest. The Webster-Ashburton Treaty settled a boundary dispute along the Maine border. Congress passed the Reclamation Act (1902) to fund irrigation projects in the West. The Soil Conservation and Domestic Allotment Act replaced provisions of the Agricultural Adjustment Act during the New Deal.

59. **A.** English, Scotch-Irish, Dutch, and German settlers resided in the Middle Colonies (New York, New Jersey, and Pennsylvania). The region sustained a thriving agricultural and commercial economy. Although the Quakers of Pennsylvania opposed slavery, some colonists in the region owned slaves. Virginia produced more tobacco than any other colony.

60. **E.** The Soviet Union shot down an American U-2 airplane during the last year of the Eisenhower administration. The Soviets captured the pilot and displayed photographic equipment after the administration denied Soviet charges of espionage. Although the plans for

an invasion of Cuba began under Eisenhower, the Bay of Pigs affair occurred during the first few months of the Kennedy administration. The Berlin Wall was constructed in 1961. In October 1962, Kennedy sent federal troops to protect James Meredith, the first African-American to attend the University of Mississippi. The 1962 Trade Expansion Act lowered tariffs to promote trade between the United States and European nations.

61. **C.** In the late nineteenth century, several European nations established "spheres of influence" in China. These nations protected their provincial commerce with discriminatory port duties, tariffs, and railroad rates. Secretary of State John Hay issued the "Open-Door Notes" in order to convince the European powers to provide equal access to Chinese markets.

62. **A.** The Confederation government passed the Northwest Ordinances to resolve problems with territory ceded by Great Britain at the end of the Revolutionary War. As settlers migrated across the Appalachian Mountains, Congress sought the means to include the region in the new republic. The ordinances established plans for orderly settlement and creation of new state governments.

63. **D.** Wilson traveled to France to ensure passage of his Fourteen Points. Wilson hoped that the conference would not impose a punitive peace treaty upon Germany. However, Allied leaders agreed only to a few his points. The treaty included the creation of the League of Nations, which Wilson believed would prevent future wars. At the end of World War II, the Potsdam Conference finalized plans to divide Germany into occupation zones.

64. **A.** Recent immigrants frequently joined the Jeffersonian Republicans at the close of the eighteenth century. During the "quasi-war" with France, Republican newspapers excoriated the policies of John Adams. Federalists in Congress searched for ways to weaken the opposition. The Alien Act made naturalization of immigrants more difficult. The Sedition Act empowered the federal government to arrest those who printed libelous material. The acts alarmed many who saw them as a direct assault on the Constitution.

65. **B.** The First Great Awakening swept across the colonies in the 1730s and 1740s. Preachers urged people to reestablish a direct relationship with God. Established ministers rejected the message of the evangelicals, splitting denominations between "New Lights" and "Old Lights." The religious revivals were particularly popular along the frontier. The Great Awakening undermined the authority of established churches by diversifying American religion.

66. **E.** One of Franklin Roosevelt's New Deal programs, the Works Progress Administration expanded relief efforts. It financed diverse activities from road and building construction to projects for writ-

ers and artists. The Fair Employment Practices Committee (FEPC) investigated discriminatory hiring practices during World War II.

67. **C.** Stowe wrote *Uncle Tom's Cabin,* the most widely read antebellum novel. Its strident abolitionist message intensified the sectional conflict. However, she did not participate in the organization of the Seneca Falls Convention. Dorothea Dix advocated prison and asylum reform. Harriet Tubman helped other slaves escape to the North. Robert Owen founded New Harmony.

68. **A.** The Republican party stuck with the Nixon-Agnew ticket in 1972. The president had little difficulty winning the primaries. His conservative "Southern strategy," emphasizing his opposition to busing, enabled him to win votes in the solidly Democratic South. Nixon's reelection campaign benefited from lingering divisions within the Democratic party. Nixon won every state except Massachusetts.

69. **D.** Severe drought contributed to widespread erosion on the Great Plains. Windstorms stripped away the rich topsoil, leaving many hard-pressed farmers few options but to move off their land. This ecological distress spawned new cultivation and conservation efforts during the New Deal.

70. **E.** The War of 1812 revealed an array of problems that Republican administrations strove to address. Circulation of state bank notes and fluctuating currency values led Congress to charter the second Bank of the United States. Merchants and manufacturers grew alarmed as Great Britain began to flood American marts with cheap industrial goods. They pleaded with Congress to raise tariffs to protect domestic industries and commerce.

71. **B.** The sale of public lands had diminished by the early twentieth century. Woodrow Wilson used passage of the national income tax as a springboard for tariff reform. Progressives had long demanded reduction of tariffs, which seemed to enrich only the industrialists. Wilson signed the Underwood Tariff, since the federal government gained a new source of income with the Sixteenth Amendment. The government continued to rely upon loans and war bonds.

72. **D.** The "Black Codes" passed in the postwar era resembled the antebellum state laws that restricted the freedoms of African slaves. The Ku Klux Klan menaced African-American who challenged the old order during and after Reconstruction. Southern states enacted literacy tests and "grandfather clauses" in order to limit black suffrage. *Plessy* v. *Ferguson* (1896) legalized segregation.

73. **C.** The Strategic Defense Initiative escalated Cold War tensions during the Reagan administration. The Soviets argued that it undermined arms control agreements. In the United States and Europe, a "nuclear freeze" movement urged the superpowers to halt the construction of nuclear weapons.

74. **A.** Sinclair Lewis mocked the material aspirations of society in the 1920s. Tarbell and London were turn-of-the-century muckrakers. Steinbeck's work addressed the social dislocations of the Great Depression. A prominent advertising executive, Barton published *The Man Nobody Knows* (1925), which portrayed Jesus as a salesman.

75. **B.** Great Britain prospered when goods flowed freely between the colonies and the mother country. The seventeenth-century Navigation Acts attempted to ensure that all colonial trade went to Great Britain. The Woolen Act (1699), Hat Act (1732), and Iron Act (1750) discourage domestic manufacturing so that colonists would purchase British goods.

76. **B.** Roosevelt attempted to improve relations with Latin American nations by rejecting the policy of sending American troops to resolve internal problems. Kennedy's Alliance for Progress also aimed to improve relations by offering economic aid to Latin American nations. The Eisenhower Doctrine offered economic and military aid to Middle Eastern nations. Eisenhower sent troops to restore order in Lebanon. During the 1960s, the Mann Doctrine led to American military intervention to support a right-wing regime in the Dominican Republic.

77. **A.** The disaster at the Triangle Shirtwaist Company heightened public awareness of industrial abuses. Triangle employed mostly women workers. Many perished in the blaze or leapt to their deaths trying to avoid the flames. Investigations revealed that locked exits and the collapse of the main fire escape trapped the women inside.

78. **E.** The rapid increase in California's population escalated sectional tensions. Southerners in Congress agreed to admit California as a free state and ban the slave trade in Washington, DC as long as Congress imposed no direct ban on slavery in the Mexican Cession. Furthermore, they required the passage of a stricter fugitive slave law. The compromise resolved the boundary dispute between Texas and New Mexico but did not provide funding for railroad construction.

79. **B.** The Supreme Court overturned a state maximum-hours law in *Lochner* v. *New York*. However, the Court supported antitrust legislation by ordering the dissolution of monopolies in the other four decisions.

80. **C.** Thomas Nast published cartoons in many of the leading journals of the nineteenth century. He criticized Andrew Johnson and the treatment of African-Americans during Reconstruction. No individual figure incurred Nast's wrath more than Tammany Hall boss William M. Tweed. Nast continually addressed corruption in New York City during the Tweed years.

Summary Response to the Document-Based Question

1. Students might begin the essay with a brief discussion of the Treaty of Paris (1898) and its impact upon Cuba. American military occupation under General Leonard Wood followed ratification of the treaty. Wood oversaw the construction of infrastructure, revamped Cuba's political administration, and pioneered health reforms. However, the United States violated the Teller Amendment by not affording Cuba complete independence. Congress retained the right to intervene in Cuban affairs and curbed Cuban autonomy in the Platt Amendment (Document A). Students may note that the United States sent troops into Cuba in 1906 and 1912 to quell rebellions and maintained a naval base at Guantanamo. Students may also refer to "dollar diplomacy" by discussing how American corporations came to dominate the oil, railroad, and, most importantly, sugar industries. Some might compare American involvement in Cuba to a different policy towards Puerto Rico (Foraker Act of 1900, Jones Act of 1917). Students should identify the policies of Theodore Roosevelt, William H. Taft, and Woodrow Wilson. They should examine how the Venezuela crisis (1902) precipitated the announcement of the "Roosevelt Corollary" to the Monroe Doctrine (Document D). Students will apply their knowledge of this policy to American intervention in the Dominican Republic in 1905. Some might note that U.S. control of Dominican customs undermined the nation's independence. Students might speculate on the results of involvement in the internal affairs of nations. A discussion of American interests in constructing an isthmian canal should include Secretary of State John Hay and overtures to Colombia. Students may discuss Philippe Bunau-Varilla, the USS *Nashville,* and Panamanian Revolution. Students will note how Panama reacted to the Hay-Bunau-Varilla Treaty (Document B). Students may interpret Document C as an allegation that the United States orchestrated the Panamanian Revolution. Others might argue that the Hay-Bunau-Varilla Treaty enabled the United States to direct Panamanian affairs. An examination of "dollar diplomacy" under Taft (Document F) may touch upon his Secretary of State Philander C. Knox. Students will note how the growing influence of American mining companies in Nicaragua resulted in military intervention in 1909. Others might note that American banks financed and owned Nicaragua railroads. American troops returned in 1912 to help maintain the government of Adolfo Diaz. Students might state that Document E reflects the belief that the United States used its military to open or preserve economic opportunities. Some might point to future problems with the Sandinistas or Contras. Students may use Document G to indicate that American imperialism did not enjoy universal support in the United States. Students could observe how the United States continued its involvement in the Dominican Republic and Nicaragua (Bryan-Chamorro Treaty, 1914) under Wilson. They may also touch

upon how intervention in Haiti in 1915 paralleled involvement with its neighbor. Most students will discuss Wilson's relationship with Mexico. Some might begin with the transfer of power from Porfirio Diaz to Francisco Madero to General Victoriano Huerta and Wilson's refusal to recognize the Huerta regime. Students might observe that American businesses wanted to promote stability in Mexico in order to establish favorable trade (Document H). Students should examine the instability related to conflicts between Huerta and Venustiano Carranza. Students should discuss the effects of the Tampico affair (Document I) and seizure of Veracruz. Students should also refer to the tenuous relationship between Wilson and Carranza and the issue of recognition. Some may touch upon Pancho Villa and raids in the American Southwest that caused Wilson to send General John Pershing and an expeditionary force across the border. Students will note that the United States and Mexico approached war and should speculate about the long-term effects of American policy.

Summary Responses to the Standard Free-Response Questions

2. Students might observe that immigration into the Louisiana Territory raised the issue of the expansion of slavery. When Missouri applied for statehood, New York Representative James Tallmadge Jr. proposed an amendment that banned the future importation of slaves into the state and provided for the gradual emancipation of existing bondsmen. The Tallmadge amendment touched off a rancorous sectional debate. Students may comment that this debate revolved around moral issues, political power, or which economic system (slave versus free labor) would predominate. Maine's application for statehood complicated the questions over Missouri. Students may touch upon leading political figures: Henry Clay, John C. Calhoun, and Jesse B. Thomas. The Compromise of 1820 admitted Missouri as a slave state, Maine as a free state, and banned slavery north of the 36 30¢ line. Students might argue that the Missouri Compromise resolved the immediate debate but revealed potential divisions. Domestic tensions over the tariff issue began during Andrew Jackson's first administration. South Carolinians blamed their economic distress on the "tariff of abominations" (tariff of 1828). Some asserted that secession would provide relief from the despised legislation. John C. Calhoun, Democratic vice presidential candidate, hoped to avert secession by asserting the theory of nullification in his anonymously published *South Carolina Exposition and Protest*. He believed a strong statement would induce the federal government to reduce tariff rates. Some students might touch upon the Webster-Hayne debate or Jackson's Jefferson Day dinner speech as evidence of the rift between nationalists and states' rights advocates. The Tariff of 1832 did little to reduce tariff rates or the frustrations of South Carolinians. The South Carolina legislature passed an "ordinance of nullification" and ordered state

officials not to enforce the tariff law. Jackson called nullification trea-son in his *Proclamation to the People of South Carolina* and made military preparations to enforce the law. Congress approved a "force bill" empowering Jackson to use the military to achieve compliance. Passage of the Compromise of 1833, which gradually lowered tariff rates, avoided armed conflict between South Carolina and the federal government. Students might discuss the issue of states' rights versus national supremacy. Electoral irregularities during the election of 1876 raised sectional tensions. Democrat Samuel Tilden held a slight edge in the popular vote over Republican Rutherford B. Hayes. How-ever, electoral votes from Oregon, Louisiana, South Carolina, and Florida remained disputed between both parties. No constitutional provision offered a solution to the problem. Tensions ran high as news-papers and private citizens speculated about the renewal of civil war. Congress appointed a special election commission that awarded the elec-tion to Hayes. In exchange, Republicans promised to remove federal troops from the South and made other concessions. Students may observe that the crisis and compromise spelled an end to Reconstruction.

3. The Kansas-Nebraska Act (1854) divided part of the Louisiana terri-tory into two new territories and repealed the congressional ban on slavery above the Missouri Compromise line. Passage of the act sparked bitter sectional debate. Students might discuss the Sumner-Brooks affair to illustrate the rising passions. The Kansas-Nebraska destroyed the Whig party, which could not breach the divide between its anti-slavery and pro-slavery factions. Some Southern Whigs crossed party lines in support of the act. Others remained opposed to the legislation and ran against Democrats in local elections. The Whig party dis-integrated as a national partisan unit. Students should discuss how Northern Whigs organized the sectional Republican party. The act caused some Northern Democrats to bolt the party. However, the Democratic party preserved a tenuous alliance between its Southern faction and some Northern constituents. Pennsylvania Democrat James Buchanan defeated Republican John C. Fremont in 1856. Sectional strife over "bleeding Kansas," the *Dred Scott* decision, and the Lecompton Constitution stemmed from the act and further unsettled the political atmosphere. Students should discuss how the Democra-tic party failed to contain sectional tensions during the election of 1860. The nomination of Stephen Douglas caused delegates from the Deep South to leave the national convention and nominate John C. Breckinridge. John Bell won the nomination of the Constitutional Union party, which drew significant support from former Southern Whigs. Students will observe how the division among the Democrats led to the election of Abraham Lincoln, who had opposed the Kansas-Nebraska Act.

4. Students should assess the factors leading to the Great Depression and broaden the discussion beyond the stock market crash. World War I

and government policy led to an overproduction that depressed the farm economy early in the 1920s. Many farmers struggled to meet mortgage payments. Over the course of the decade, farmers stopped purchasing industrial goods. The industrial economy would also suffer from overproduction. Students might note how advertising and mass production fostered a consumer mania. Automobiles and construction were the leading industries. Those who could not afford items could purchase them through installment buying. Many people overextended their personal finances. A maldistribution of wealth also contributed to the Depression. Half of all Americans barely made subsistence wages, while 5 percent earned one-third of the nation's income. The Supreme Court overturned minimum-wage legislation in *Adkins* v. *Children's Hospital* in 1923. Students should discuss the importance of money in circulation to maintain the nation's economy. Government policies contributed to the Depression. Students should touch upon the three Republican presidents (Harding, Coolidge, and Hoover) and their administrations. High tariffs (Fordney-McCumber, Hawley-Smoot) led to retaliatory responses from foreign nations. Some students might discuss reparations policy, particularly in relation to Germany. Europe also began producing its own food at the end of the decade. Students should note that domestic production increased, while foreign markets were constricted. Coolidge (Revenue Act of 1926) and Treasury Secretary Andrew Mellon cut taxes on the highest income brackets but not on middle incomes. Banks lowered interest rates, making loans easily available. Consumers and businesses took out loans. Businesses expanded their facilities, but laid off workers if the expansion did not turn a profit. As a result, consumers had less purchasing power by the end of the decade. Many banks kept little reserve as they made loans and speculated on the stock market. When private citizens, farmers, or businesses defaulted on loans, banks closed their doors. The growth of the stock market reflected the false prosperity of the greater economy. Students will observe how overspeculation, reckless investments, and the failure of some investment banks contributed to the stock market crash. Although a large percentage of the population did not invest on the stock market, numerous businesses and banks saw the bulk of their assets disappear. Factories closed; bank failures caused runs on banks. Over a half million people lost their homes. Unemployment rose to over 25 percent of the population.

5. Students might begin a discussion of the early Cold War by examining the Yalta and Potsdam Conferences. Yalta seemed to provide for free elections in nations formerly occupied by the Nazis. Potsdam divided Germany into occupation zones with the intent of reuniting the nation at a later date. Some students might refer to George Kennan's "long telegram" or X Article. Students should focus upon the Marshall Plan and Truman Doctrine as the foundation of containment policy. The Marshall Plan provided over $13 billion to rebuild European industries, combat inflation, and increase European production. Great

Britain, France, Germany, Italy, and the Netherlands received the largest amount of American grants and loans, but several smaller nations also received aid. Most of those nations did not succumb to internal strife or ally with the Soviet Union. The Truman Doctrine had a $400 million budget to provide economic or military assistance to "nations facing armed aggression." Greece received American assistance and suppressed a communist revolt. Turkey solidified its defenses along its border with the Soviet Union. Neither nation fell under Soviet influence during the Truman administration. Stalin perceived a threat to Soviet control of Eastern Europe when the Allies merged their occupation zones in 1948. He imposed a blockade around Berlin in June to force the city to join the Soviet zone. Truman authorized the Berlin Airlift ("Operation Vittles") in order to provide the beleaguered with food and medical supplies. The Soviets lifted the blockade in May 1949. Some students might discuss the formation of NATO. Students might argue that Truman's efforts at containment achieved more success in Europe than in Asia. A discussion of Asian containment policy should address the Chinese Civil War. Some students might refer to George Marshall's mission to China. Chiang Kai-shek was unable to stop the peasants' revolt led by Mao Tse-tung. Chiang fled to Formosa (Taiwan); the Truman administration recognized his government as the legitimate Chinese government. Truman refused to recognize Mao's government. NSC-68 followed Truman's call for a reevaluation of American foreign policy. Truman responded to the North Korean invasion and resolution by the U.N. Security Council by sending American forces under General Douglas MacArthur. Students might discuss the restrictions of "limited warfare" but that American forces kept South Korea from falling under the control of the communist North.

Practice Exam 2

Answer Sheet For Multiple-Choice Questions

1. _____	21. _____	41. _____	61. _____
2. _____	22. _____	42. _____	62. _____
3. _____	23. _____	43. _____	63. _____
4. _____	24. _____	44. _____	64. _____
5. _____	25. _____	45. _____	65. _____
6. _____	26. _____	46. _____	66. _____
7. _____	27. _____	47. _____	67. _____
8. _____	28. _____	48. _____	68. _____
9. _____	29. _____	49. _____	69. _____
10. _____	30. _____	50. _____	70. _____
11. _____	31. _____	51. _____	71. _____
12. _____	32. _____	52. _____	72. _____
13. _____	33. _____	53. _____	73. _____
14. _____	34. _____	54. _____	74. _____
15. _____	35. _____	55. _____	75. _____
16. _____	36. _____	56. _____	76. _____
17. _____	37. _____	57. _____	77. _____
18. _____	38. _____	58. _____	78. _____
19. _____	39. _____	59. _____	79. _____
20. _____	40. _____	60. _____	80. _____

PRACTICE EXAM 2
AP U.S. HISTORY

Section I

Time—55 minutes

80 questions

Directions: Each of the questions or incomplete statements below is followed by five suggested answers or completions. Select the one that is best in each case and write your answer neatly on the answer sheet.

1. The 1968 presidential campaigns of Richard Nixon and George Wallace were similar in that both candidates

   A. actively supported segregation
   B. emphasized law and order
   C. called for the escalation of American involvement in Vietnam
   D. chose running mates from Southern states
   E. emphasized their experience in national politics

2. Many colonial assemblies imposed taxes to support official churches. All of the following colonies had established churches *except*

   A. Massachusetts
   B. Virginia
   C. Georgia
   D. New Hampshire
   E. Rhode Island

3. The Kansas-Nebraska Act (1854) heightened sectional tensions because it

   A. extended suffrage to Irish and German immigrants in the territories
   B. repealed a congressional prohibition on the expansion of slavery
   C. banned slavery in new territories

   D. admitted both territories as slave states which further eroded the political power of the North
   E. overturned the controversial *Dred Scott* decision

4. Hernando Cortes is significant to the history of North America because he

   A. explored the Great Lakes region
   B. established the first Franciscan mission in California
   C. became the first white man to cross the Mississippi River
   D. fought and eventually defeated the powerful Aztecs
   E. established friendly relations with the Iroquois Confederation

5. The Bank War pitted Nicholas Biddle, Henry Clay, and the National Republicans against President Andrew Jackson and Secretary of the Treasury Roger B. Taney. Ultimately, Jackson and Taney destroyed the bank by

   A. revoking the bank charter in 1828
   B. proving that the creation of the B.U.S. was unconstitutional
   C. placing deposits of federal tax money in state banks
   D. failing to enforce Marshall's decision in *Fletcher* v. *Peck*
   E. placing Democrats on the board of directors of the bank

6. The Voting Rights Act, which followed the successful protest march from Selma to Montgomery, was passed during the administration of

   A. Harry S Truman
   B. Dwight D. Eisenhower
   C. John F. Kennedy
   D. Lyndon B. Johnson
   E. Richard M. Nixon

7. In April 1775, "the shot heard round the world" occurred at Lexington when British soldiers clashed with Massachusetts minutemen. The reason that General Gage dispatched troops to Lexington and Concord was to

   A. arrest radical leaders and seize stockpiled weapons
   B. save Governor Thomas Hutchinson after the Boston Tea Party
   C. enlist the support of the colony's committee of correspondence
   D. suppress violent reactions to the Stamp Act
   E. help Benedict Arnold escape capture

8. After World War II, a civil war broke out in China between communists and nationalists (Kuomintang). In order to keep a noncommunist ally in power, the Truman administration supported

   A. Mao Tse-tung
   B. Ngo Dinh Diem
   C. Reza Pahlevi
   D. Kim Il-Sung
   E. Chiang Kai-shek

9. Which of the following benefited most from federal spending during World War II?

   A. Cotton states in the South
   B. Northeastern industrial cities
   C. The West
   D. The "Corn Belt," from Kansas to Ohio
   E. Oil states in the Southwest

10. The primary goal of the American Colonization Society was to

    A. oppose the activities of Irish Catholic immigrants in Northern industrial cities
    B. help freed slaves return to Africa
    C. establish religious colonies in the territories west of the Mississippi River during the Second Great Awakening
    D. get temperance legislation passed in Congress
    E. find new sources of slave labor in the Caribbean colonies of France and Great Britain

11. The "Roosevelt Corollary" empowered the United States to intervene in the governments of nations that were "unable to manage their own affairs." In response to threats by France, Germany, and Italy, Theodore Roosevelt sent marines to seize control of the customs house in

    A. the Dominican Republic
    B. Brazil
    C. Mexico
    D. the Philippines
    E. Cuba

12. Which of the following presidents pursued *détente,* a foreign policy aimed at reducing Cold War friction between the United States and Soviet Union?

    A. Dwight D. Eisenhower
    B. John F. Kennedy
    C. Lyndon Johnson
    D. Richard Nixon
    E. Ronald Reagan

13. John Marshall's decision in the *Marbury* v. *Madison* case was significant because it

    A. guaranteed the sanctity of contracts

B. protected property rights by denying a state the ability to confiscate Tory estates
C. established the principle of "judicial review"
D. set the number of Supreme Court justices at nine
E. reversed his earlier decision in *Gibbons* v. *Ogden*

14. "I, too, sing America.
I am the darker brother.
They send me to eat in the kitchen
When company comes,
They'll see how beautiful I am
And be ashamed-
I, too, am America."

Which of the following was a poet whose work (excerpted above) was a major part of the Harlem Renaissance?

A. Maya Angelou
B. Richard Wright
C. Allen Ginsberg
D. Booker T. Washington
E. Langston Hughes

15. The introduction of the horse to the native tribes of the Great Plains

A. allowed them to make war on the Indians of the Pacific Northwest more easily
B. enabled them to leave their villages and follow the buffalo herds
C. reduced conflict with white settlers
D. forced them to migrate to the Indian Territory along with the Cherokee
E. led to a rapid decline in tribal authority

16. Both Dwight D. Eisenhower and John F. Kennedy employed a Keynesian strategy to manage the nation's economy. Which of the following best expresses the basic principle of Keynesian economics?

A. The government would manipulate money in circulation to promote or slow the pace of economic growth.
B. The government would regulate the economy through direct involvement in private companies.
C. The government would eliminate the "boom-bust" cycle of the American economy by cutting federal subsidies.
D. The government would stabilize the economy by investing in the nation's largest companies.
E. The government would socialize only those industries that failed to turn a profit.

17. Which of the following statements was *not* an argument made by antisuffragists during the Progressive era?

A. Men adequately represented the views of women.
B. Women's suffrage menaced the proper raising of children.
C. Granting women the right to vote would empower immigrants more than natives.
D. Women would advance the causes of temperance and school reform.
E. Women's suffrage would reverse gender roles in America.

18. During the New Deal, President Franklin Roosevelt signed the Social Security Act to provide relief to elderly Americans. President Lyndon Johnson attempted to achieve similar results by initiating which of the following measures?

A. Medicare
B. Revenue Act
C. Economic Recovery Tax Act
D. Gramm-Rudman-Hollings Act
E. Americans with Disabilities Act

19. Reflecting a new focus on individualism, which of the following authors created the character of "Natty Bumppo," a rugged frontiersman who struggled against the disorders of his society?

    A. Frederick Jackson Turner
    B. Henry David Thoreau
    C. James Fenimore Cooper
    D. Henry Wadsworth Longfellow
    E. Theodore Dwight Weld

20. Which of the following statements is true about John Rolfe and his impact upon the economic development of colonial North America?

    A. He defeated the powerful Iroquois Confederation and opened the Great Lakes to white expansion.
    B. He developed a highly successful iron works in New Jersey that served as a model for other colonies.
    C. He established a profitable shipping company that opened commerce with the West Indies.
    D. He introduced a strain of cotton that Southern colonies began to grow.
    E. He experimented with tobacco cultivation, which soon became a profitable export.

21. The Scottsboro case symbolized the

    A. prevalence of xenophobia and fear of radicalism in the 1920s
    B. prevalence of racism and prejudice in the 1930s
    C. persecution of domestic communists in the 1940s
    D. opposition to New Deal in the 1950s
    E. growing liberalism of the Supreme Court in the 1960s

22. Although the Cold War rapidly escalated with the end of World War II, the 1950s were marked by a period of "peaceful coexistence." Tensions between the Soviet Union and United States were alleviated temporarily. Which of the following reinvigorated Cold War hostilities?

    A. Berlin Airlift
    B. Iran Hostage Crisis
    C. Cuban Missile Crisis
    D. U-2 Incident
    E. Suez Crisis

23. Which of the following was a scientific advancement made during the first half of the eighteenth century?

    A. Inoculations against smallpox
    B. Development of commercial fertilizers
    C. Discovery of antibiotics
    D. Pellagra remedy
    E. Steam engine

24. The Freeport Doctrine, which stated that the people of a territory could bar slavery by passing "unfriendly legislation," alienated Southern Democrats and damaged the presidential aspirations of

    A. Abraham Lincoln
    B. John C. Calhoun
    C. Stephen A. Douglas
    D. John C. Breckinridge
    E. James Buchanan

25. The onset of the Panic of 1837 and Great Depression shared which of the following causes?

    A. Overspeculation on the stock market
    B. The lack of standardized currency
    C. Overproduction of war goods
    D. Unregulated banking systems
    E. Overspeculation in western land sales

26. American revolutionaries sought the assistance of France in their war against the British. However, France

initially refused to recognize the sovereignty of the States and withheld military aid until the American victory at

A. Bunker Hill, 1775
B. Trenton, 1776
C. Saratoga, 1777
D. Guilford Courthouse, 1780
E. Yorktown, 1781

27. Which of the following was the main factor that prevented a postwar depression under Truman and Eisenhower?

A. The lack of labor strife
B. Federal spending on relief projects
C. Significant repayment by foreign debtors
D. The revival of the Southern agricultural economy
E. High consumer demand

28. The results of the election of 1800 were unique because

A. a Whig president was elected for the first time
B. the election ended in an electoral tie
C. George Washington was the unanimous choice of the Electoral College
D. the president and vice president came from different parties
E. the president failed to win a majority of the popular vote

29. Which of the following reformers attempted to improve the treatment of the mentally ill?

A. Lyman Beecher
B. Neil Dow
C. Lucretia Mott
D. Elizabeth Cady Stanton
E. Dorothea Dix

30. The Sixteenth Amendment implemented

A. the first national child labor regulations
B. a federal income tax
C. direct election of senators
D. the first anti-lynching law
E. the first national referendum

31. Which of the following was a slave revolt during the first half of the eighteenth century?

A. Stono Rebellion
B. Culpeper's Rebellion
C. Dorr Rebellion
D. Leisler's Rebellion
E. Newburgh conspiracy

32. The Taft-Hartley Act of 1947

A. banned the closed shop (union members only)
B. required communist organizations to register with the federal government
C. desegregated the armed forces
D. established the Federal Employee Loyalty Program
E. raised tariff rates

33. Which of the following individuals was the Seminole chief who resisted the removal of his people along the "Trail of Tears" by fighting a guerrilla war in the swamps of Florida beginning in 1835?

A. Black Hawk
B. Sequoyah
C. Sitting Bull
D. Osceola
E. Pontiac

34. The Zimmermann Telegram

A. insulted President McKinley by calling him "weak and a bidder for the admiration of the crowd"
B. demanded that Great Britain pay reparations for the *Alabama* claims
C. denied American mining companies access to the rich iron mines of Venezuela

D. demonstrated the level of corruption in the Harding administration

E. angered Americans because Germany encouraged Mexico to make war against the United States

35. The Proclamation of 1763

A. outlawed colonial assemblies

B. empowered colonial governors to imprison smugglers

C. attempted to limit colonial expansion

D. restricted colonial manufacturing

E. attempted to halt trade with the West Indies

36. Which of the following sets of authors reflected a growing sense of alienation from modern society during the 1950s?

A. Claude McKay and Countee Cullen

B. Theodore Dreiser and Jack London

C. J. D. Salinger and Ralph Ellison

D. John Dos Passos and John Steinbeck

E. Helen Hunt Jackson and Ida Wells Barnett

37. The emergence of the Populist party demonstrated

A. the grievances of farmers against the railroad companies

B. the opposition of Northerners to the expansion of slavery into the territories

C. popular approval of the acquisition of colonies

D. greater support for the modern civil rights movement

E. the increasing power of labor unions in the twentieth century

38. Early in the Civil War, the *Trent* Affair nearly produced a diplomatic crisis when

A. the USS *Monitor* sank a British ship

B. a British ship broke through the Union blockade around Charleston

C. Union ships seized a delivery of cotton off the coast of Great Britain

D. the HMS *Trent* sank the Confederate vessel *Virginia*

E. Union forces seized Confederate diplomats from a British ship

39. The *Federalist Papers* were

A. a pamphlet written by Patrick Henry to protest passage of the Stamp Act

B. Thomas Jefferson's argument against the Alien and Sedition Acts

C. a criticism of Chief Justice John Marshall's decision in *Dartmouth College* v. *Woodward*

D. essays written to win support for ratification of the Constitution

E. written to expose the weakness of the Federalists after the War of 1812

40. The primary goal of the antebellum Liberty party was to

A. ensure women's suffrage

B. prevent the expansion of slavery into new territories

C. oppose industrial capitalism and ensure the rights of factory workers

D. limit foreign immigration to Northern cities

E. promote free transportation on the new railroads spreading throughout the nation

41. It began at a Carnegie Steel plant. It involved a clash between Pinkerton guards and strikers. It was finally

suppressed by the governor of Pennsylvania, who sent 8000 militiamen to protect strike breakers. Resolution of the strike led to the blacklisting of members of the steelworkers' union. Which strike of the Progressive era is described above?

A. Great Railway Strike of 1877
B. Haymarket Square Strike, 1886
C. Homestead Strike, 1892
D. Pullman Strike, 1896
E. Anthracite Strike, 1902

42. President Dwight D. Eisenhower sent 5000 marines into which of the following nations in order to keep a pro-Western government in power?

A. Iran
B. Lebanon
C. Turkey
D. Vietnam
E. Guatemala

43. The Fifteenth Amendment represented a truly radical part of Radical Reconstruction mainly because it

A. limited the Reconstruction powers of Congress
B. guaranteed property rights for freedmen throughout the Union
C. limited President Johnson's appointment powers
D. guaranteed suffrage for freedmen
E. extended voting rights to women as well as men

44. Which of the following events damaged President William Howard Taft's chances for reelection?

A. The beginning of World War I
B. The passage of the Adamson Act
C. His veto of the Clayton Act and Congress's subsequent override
D. His denunciation of Speaker of the House Joe Cannon
E. Passage of the Payne-Aldrich Tariff

45. In order to "pump prime" the stagnant American economy in the 1930s, President Franklin Roosevelt created the CCC. This agency

A. employed young men to plant trees and develop national park facilities
B. froze prices for consumer goods at the level of the economy in 1925
C. paid writers, artists, and actors to continue to perform
D. drafted young men into the army
E. gave financial aid to local relief programs

46. All of the following statements about the development of railroads in the antebellum period are true except that

A. new towns appeared along the tracks
B. rail lines ran between the North and South as much as between the North and the West
C. the expansion of lines surpassed the construction of canals
D. the federal government gave large land grants to railroad companies
E. the width of track was not standard for all routes

47. Racial violence erupted in New York City in 1863. Angry whites attacked African-Americans and burned an orphanage for black children. What caused this riot?

A. Food shortages
B. The Union defeat at First Manassas
C. President Lincoln's suspension of *habeas corpus*
D. Passage of the Conscription Act
E. The assassination of President Lincoln

48. Which of the following best assesses the results of the election of 1824?

A. It marked the end of the Federalist party.
B. John Quincy Adams won an overwhelming majority of the popular votes.
C. The Whig party won its first presidential campaign.
D. Lingering depression from the Panic of 1819 undermined the candidacy of James Monroe.
E. Jacksonians believed a "corrupt bargain" cost their candidate the election.

49. The circumstances surrounding King Philip's War (1676) suggest that

A. New England settlers clashed with the native tribes over territorial expansion
B. Great Britain had to send troops to protect its colonists against the encroachments of French settlers
C. colonial governors could not protect colonial commerce
D. the colonists refused to share the costs of their own defense
E. British colonists frequently raided Spanish settlements in North America

50. The Ku Klux Klan of the 1920s differed from its nineteenth-century predecessor in that it

A. influenced politics and elections
B. no longer opposed African-American suffrage
C. led an anti-immigrant campaign
D. remained active primarily in the South
E. opposed the temperance movement

51. "Supply-side" economics, which rests on the belief that tax cuts cause economic growth, is associated

with which of the following administrations?

A. Reagan
B. Carter
C. Ford
D. Nixon
E. Johnson

52. All of the following statements about the labor movement after World War II are true *except*

A. the American Federation of Labor (A.F.L.) merged with the Congress of Industrial Organization (CIO)
B. unionized workers in steel and other industries received significant wage increases
C. some unions were charged with corrupt practices
D. the CIO's "Operation Dixie" succeeded in enlisting thousands of members in the South
E. Congress attempted to curb the power of unions

53. In the late nineteenth century, European nations established colonies or "spheres of influence" in Asia and Africa. One reason that the United States did not have a vast empire was that it had a weak, coastal navy. The author who promoted the construction of a powerful steel fleet in his book *The Influence of Sea Power upon History, 1660–1783* was

A. William Randolph Hearst
B. General John J. Pershing
C. Eugene V. Debs
D. George Creel
E. Alfred Thayer Mahan

54. Which of the following was an incident of the Mexican War?

A. *Gaspee* Incident
B. Treaty of New Echota

C. Olive Branch Petition
D. Slidell Mission
E. Ostend Manifesto

55. William Penn

   A. was expelled from the Massachusetts Bay colony for criticizing church leaders
   B. won a pivotal victory when he led colonial troops against the French at Fort Duquesne in 1756
   C. founded a colony that extended a significant degree of religious toleration
   D. led farmers in a rebellion against a whiskey excise tax
   E. wrote the "Fundamental Orders of Connecticut"

56. The 1930s marked which of the following shifts within the electorate?

   A. The Southern states increasingly supported Republican candidates for office.
   B. African-Americans began to support the Democratic party.
   C. The Republican party began to reflect the interests of urban centers.
   D. The Democratic party drew more support from business leaders.
   E. The Republican party began to capture the votes of organized labor.

57. During the Grant administration, the Credit Mobilier scandal centered upon

   A. the distribution of fraudulent state currency, which contributed to the Panic of 1873
   B. the misuse of federal subsidies and bribery of government officials
   C. the failure of a major oil company to pay federal taxes

   D. the misuse of federal funds designed to provide the Freedmen's Bureau with homesteads to distribute among former slaves
   E. inaccurate voting results recorded during the election of 1876

58. Before Pearl Harbor, the nation struggled with unemployment, deflation, and social friction. Although booming wartime production alleviated much of the economic crisis, all divisive tensions were not eliminated. President Roosevelt created the FEPC in order to

   A. ensure that companies did not follow discriminatory hiring practices
   B. conduct war bond drives
   C. convert factories to wartime production
   D. remove Japanese-Americans from the West Coast
   E. redistribute income to prevent class conflict

59. Wounded Knee was significant because

   A. Cherokee Indians helped General Jackson defeat the Creeks
   B. Tecumseh died in the battle thus destroying an inter-tribal confederacy
   C. it marked the end of Indian resistance on the Great Plains
   D. French and Indian forces defeated Colonel George Washington and the Virginia militia
   E. Indians of the Southwest helped Texas troops fight General Santa Anna

60. Which of the following had the greatest impact on the American economy in the early 1970s?

A. Drought and erosion
B. Savings and loan failures
C. The end of price freezes
D. North American Free Trade Agreement
E. Arab oil embargo

61. In the 1820s, Robert Owen's community at New Harmony

    A. rejected the individualism and materialism of industrial capitalism
    B. served as a model for the employment of women in textiles
    C. fostered the revivals of the Second Great Awakening
    D. established the first refuge for Mormons in the United States
    E. was the first settlement of escaped slaves in the Midwest

62. President Lincoln's "10 Percent Plan" was designed to

    A. stop Southern states from seceding
    B. restore 10 percent of the slave population to Southern loyalists
    C. limit westward expansion by requiring an amount of gold for the purchase of land
    D. restore Southern states to the Union quickly
    E. keep Great Britain from recognizing the Confederacy

63. In 1774, Parliament passed the Intolerable (Coercive) Acts, which were intended to

    A. force New York to obey the Quartering Act
    B. punish Massachusetts for the Boston Tea Party
    C. close the port of Philadelphia until John Hancock and Ben Franklin surrendered
    D. empower colonial governors to enforce the Stamp Act

    E. close all Eastern ports after Lexington and Concord

64. Margaret Sanger was significant to the 1920s because she

    A. was a leading advocate of birth control
    B. was the first woman elected to Congress
    C. led a spirited campaign in support of Prohibition
    D. wrote novels critical of contemporary materialism
    E. served as President Coolidge's Secretary of Commerce

65. Which of the following was *not* part of President Lyndon B. Johnson's "Great Society?"

    A. Higher Education Act
    B. Medicaid
    C. Appalachian Regional Development Act
    D. Economic Opportunity Act
    E. Immigration Reform and Control Act

66. Patrick Henry and James Monroe opposed the ratification of the Constitution because it

    A. failed to adequately protect the institution of slavery
    B. resembled the British constitution too closely
    C. did not include a bill of rights
    D. chartered a national bank
    E. allowed the states to retain the power to regulate interstate commerce

67. "Jim Crow" laws were written to

    A. ensure full citizenship rights for freedmen
    B. give investors economic incentive for investing in factories in the South

C. circumscribe the social and legal position of freedmen

D. punish corrupt government officials

E. diversify the Southern economy

68. Which of the following statements best assesses Theodore Roosevelt's impact on the election of 1912?

A. He won his first election after the assassination of President McKinley.

B. He split the Republican vote.

C. He helped his hand-picked successor, William Howard Taft, win the presidency.

D. He frightened all Socialist candidates from the field with his nationalistic speeches.

E. He won fewer votes than when he ran for president in 1900.

69. Secretary of the Treasury Alexander Hamilton supported the passage of the Assumption Act because it

A. enabled the federal government to tax the states in order to repay debts accumulated during the Revolutionary War

B. proposed that all war bonds should be repaid at face value

C. empowered the federal government to create a national bank with branch banks in every state

D. eliminated the high tariffs passed during the Confederation period

E. allowed settlers to purchase land near the Great Lakes

70. The Nye Committee report (1936)

A. called for greater regulation of the nation's financial institutions

B. attacked the complacency of the Coolidge and Hoover administrations

C. countered President Roosevelt's plan to increase the size of the Supreme Court

D. requested the strengthening of the Interstate Commerce Commission

E. claimed that American bankers and munitions makers had drawn the nation into World War I

71. Which of the following treaties granted the American states the land from the Appalachian Mountains to the Mississippi River?

A. Jay's Treaty, 1794

B. Treaty of Paris, 1783

C. Treaty of Tordesillas, 1494

D. Treaty of Guadaloupe Hidalgo, 1848

E. Treaty of New Echota, 1835

72. The most significant problem plaguing the agricultural economy during the 1920s was

A. a severe drought that destroyed crops from California to Pennsylvania

B. foreign competition from Latin America

C. the lack of technology available to farmers of the Midwest

D. overproduction

E. the lack of farm labor in the West

73. The cartoon on page 372 refers to a peace conference in Portsmouth, New Hampshire, in 1905. President Theodore Roosevelt was awarded the Nobel Peace Prize in 1906 for mediating a conflict between which of the following two nations at this meeting?

A. China and Germany

B. Mexico and Spain

C. Nicaragua and Portugal

The political cartoon, "Good Offices," *Harper's Weekly*, August 1898; courtesy of Theodore-Roosevelt.com.

D. Great Britain and Persia
E. Japan and Russia

74. Which of the following presidents oversaw the creation of the Federal Reserve Board, which set interest rates and monitored the behavior of government and some state banks?

A. Grover Cleveland
B. William McKinley
C. Teddy Roosevelt
D. Woodrow Wilson
E. Warren G. Harding

75. In the novel *Progress and Poverty* (1879), which of the following authors prescribed a socialistic "single-tax" strategy on land to address the disparity of wealth between factory owners and workers?

A. Henry George
B. Ida Tarbell
C. Lincoln Steffens
D. Jacob Riis
E. Terence Powderly

76. The Emancipation Proclamation had which of the following effects?

   A. It ended slavery throughout the United States.
   B. It sparked widespread slave rebellions in the Southern states.
   C. It kept Great Britain from recognizing the Confederacy.
   D. It destroyed the Democratic party's chances of winning the election of 1864.
   E. It led to the abolition of slavery in the border states.

77. President Calvin Coolidge vetoed the McNary-Haugen bill primarily because he

   A. did not want to involve the nation in European affairs
   B. supported the continuation of Prohibition
   C. supported the interests of World War I veterans
   D. rejected federal intervention in the economy
   E. believed its provisions restricted stock speculation

78. "In the new code of laws, which I suppose it will be necessary for you to make, I desire you would remember the ladies, and be more generous and favorable to them than your ancestors. Do not put such unlimited power into the hands of husbands. . . . If particular care is not paid to the ladies, we are determined to foment a rebellion, and will not hold ourselves bound by any laws in which we have no voice, or representation."

   As stated in the preceding quotation, which of the following women called for a more equal position after the American Revolution?

   A. Phyllis Wheatley
   B. Abigail Adams
   C. Dolly Madison
   D. Clara Barton
   E. Lucretia Mott

79. During the Cold War, the United States experienced strained relations with Cuba. At one point, the CIA trained Cuban exiles to launch an invasion to topple the Castro regime. Their efforts failed miserably. The Bay of Pigs incident weakened the position of the United States abroad and marred the foreign policy record of which of the following administrations?

   A. Nixon
   B. Truman
   C. Eisenhower
   D. Johnson
   E. Kennedy

80. After the Civil War, the crop-lien system further impoverished farmers, both black and white, by

   A. imposing a state excise on the planting of grains often distilled into alcohol in the mountain regions
   B. regulating the planting of cash crops such as cotton
   C. requiring them to mortgage their crops to local merchants who furnished necessary supplies
   D. denying farmers the right to hold land unless their grandfathers owned property
   E. raising tariff rates on agricultural products

END OF SECTION I

Section II

Part A

(Suggested writing time: 45 minutes)

Directions: The following question requires you to construct a coherent essay that integrates your interpretation of Documents A to H *and* your knowledge of the period referred to in the question. High scores will be earned only by essays that both cite key pieces of evidence from the documents and draw on outside knowledge of the period.

1. To what extent did the Supreme Court advance or inhibit Progressive regulation of corporations in the period 1885 to 1920?

Document A
Source: U.S. v. Debs, et al., 1894 (response to the Pullman Strike)

> *That the original design [of the Sherman Antitrust Act] to suppress trusts and monopolies . . . is clear; but it is equally clear that further and more comprehensive purpose came to be entertained. . . . Combinations are condemned, not only when they take the form of trusts, but in whatever form found, if they be in restraint of trade.*

Document B
Source: U.S. v. E. C. Knight Company, 1895

> *Congress did not attempt . . . to make criminal the acts of persons in the acquisition and control of property which the states of their residence or creation sanctioned or permitted.*
>
> *The contracts and acts of the defendants related exclusively to the acquisition of the Philadelphia refineries and the business of sugar refining in Pennsylvania, and bore no direct relation to commerce between states or with foreign countries. The object was manifestly private gain in the manufacture of the commodity, but not through the control of interstate or foreign commerce.*

Document C
Source: Holden v. Hardy, 1898

We think the [Utah act limiting the hours of miners] may be sustained as a valid exercise of the police power of the state. The act does not profess to limit the hours of all workmen, but merely those who are employed in underground mines. . . . These employments, when too long pursued, the legislature has judged to be detrimental to the health of employees.

[Mine owners] naturally desire to obtain as much labor as possible from their employees, while the latter are often induced by the fear of discharge to conform to regulations which . . . would be detrimental to their health. . . . In other words, the proprietors lay down the rules and the laborers are practically constrained to obey them. In such cases, self-interest is often an unsafe guide and the legislature may properly interpose its authority.

Document D
Source: Smyth v. Ames, 1898

By the 14th Amendment it is provided that no state shall deprive any person of property without the due process of law nor deny to any person within its jurisdiction the equal protection of laws. That corporations are persons within this amendment is now settled.

[The Court] adjudged that the enforcement of the schedules of rates established by the [Nebraska law reducing railroad rates] . . . would deprive the railroad companies of the compensation they were legally entitled to receive.

Document E
Source: *Lochner v. New York*, 1905

> *The act [state law limiting maximum hours of bakers] is not . . . a health law, but is an illegal interference with the rights of individuals, both employers and employees, to make contracts regarding labor upon such terms as they may think best. . . . Statutes of the nature of that under review, limiting the hours in which grown and intelligent men may labor to earn their living, are meddlesome interferences with the rights of the individual, and they are not saved from condemnation by the claim that they are passed upon the subject of the health of the individual whose rights are interfered with.*

Document F
Source: *Muller v. Oregon*, 1908

> *The two sexes differ in structure of body, . . . in the amount of physical strength in the capacity for long-continued labor, . . . the influence of vigorous health upon the future well-being of the race, . . . and in the capacity to maintain the struggle for subsistence. This difference justifies a difference in legislation.*
>
> *For these reasons, and without questioning in any respect the decision in* Lochner v. New York, *we are of the opinion that it cannot be adjudged that the [state law limiting the hours women may work] is in conflict with the Federal Constitution, so far as it respects the work of a female in a laundry.*

Document G
Source: Standard Oil Company of New Jersey v. United States, 1911

The public policy has been to prohibit . . . contracts or acts entered into with the intent to wrong the public and which unreasonably restrict competitive conditions, limit the rights of individuals, restrain the free flow of commerce, or bring about public evils such as the enhancement of prices.

The combination of the defendants in this case is an unreasonable and undue restraint of trade in petroleum and its products moving in interstate commerce, and falls within the prohibitions of the [Sherman Antitrust Act].

Document H
Source: Wilson v. New, 1917

The effect of the [Adamson Act] is not only to establish permanently an eight-hour standard for work and wages as between the [railroad] carrier and employees affected, but also to fix a scale of minimum wages for the eight-hour day and proportionately for overtime.

Viewed as an act establishing an eight-hour day as the standard of service by employees, the statute is clearly within the power of Congress under the commerce clause.

Viewed as an act fixing wages, the statute merely illustrates the character of regulation essential, and hence permissible, for the protection of the public right.

Section II

Part B and Part C

(Suggested total planning and writing time: 70 minutes)

Part B

Directions: Choose *one* question from this part. You are advised to spend 5 minutes planning and 30 minutes writing your answer. Cite relevant historical evidence in support of your generalizations and present your arguments clearly and logically.

2. Before he was elected president, Thomas Jefferson believed that a strict interpretation of the Constitution firmly bound the actions of the federal government. To what extent did Jefferson adhere to this belief during his two terms in office?

3. Explain the impact of manifest destiny upon the 1840s.

Part C

Directions: Choose *one* question from this part. You are advised to spend 5 minutes planning and 30 minutes writing your answer. Cite relevant historical evidence in support of your generalizations and present your arguments clearly and logically.

4. Discuss the effects of New Deal reform legislation by examining *two* of the following acts:

   Social Security Act

   Wagner (National Labor Relations) Act

   Fair Labor Standards Act

5. Compare and contrast the post-World War I Red Scare with the anticommunism crusade after World War II.

END OF SECTION II

ANSWERS TO PRACTICE EXAM 2

Answers to the Multiple-Choice Questions

1. B	21. B	41. C	61. A
2. E	22. D	42. B	62. D
3. B	23. A	43. D	63. B
4. D	24. C	44. E	64. A
5. C	25. D	45. A	65. E
6. D	26. C	46. B	66. C
7. A	27. E	47. D	67. C
8. E	28. B	48. E	68. B
9. C	29. E	49. A	69. A
10. B	30. B	50. C	70. E
11. A	31. A	51. A	71. B
12. D	32. A	52. D	72. D
13. C	33. D	53. E	73. E
14. E	34. E	54. D	74. D
15. B	35. C	55. C	75. A
16. A	36. C	56. B	76. C
17. D	37. A	57. B	77. D
18. A	38. E	58. A	78. B
19. C	39. D	59. C	79. E
20. E	40. B	60. E	80. C

Explanations of Answers to the Multiple-Choice Questions

1. **B.** During the 1968 campaign, both Nixon and Wallace emerged as spokesmen for conservatives. Wallace railed against protestors and civil unrest. Nixon appealed to "Middle America" and the "silent majority" that wanted stability and the enforcement of laws. Only Nixon had political experience at the federal level. Wallace's running mate, General Curtis LeMay of Ohio, stated the way to end the Vietnam War was to "bomb them back to the Stone Age." On the other hand, Nixon called for "peace with honor" and alluded to a plan to end the war. Nixon's vice presidential candidate, Spiro Agnew, previously served as Governor of Maryland.

2. **E.** Only Rhode Island did not establish an official church nor tax residents for its maintenance. Roger Williams, a young Separatist minister, argued that the church and state should be separated completely. As a result, the Massachusetts colonial government exiled him. Williams received a parliamentary charter to establish a new colonial government. He founded Rhode Island as a haven where people of all faiths could practice their religions without interference from the colonial government.

3. **B.** The Kansas-Nebraska Act set off a firestorm of protest in the Midwest and East. The act repealed the prohibition on the expansion of slavery established by the Missouri Compromise. The Wilmot Proviso had attempted to limit the expansion of slavery into territories acquired from Mexico. The *Dred Scott* decision was not rendered until 1857.

4. **D.** Cortes began his conquest of the Aztec empire in 1519. By 1521, he controlled most of the Aztec territory. Cortes and his men set the pattern of relations with natives followed by future conquistadores. Father Junipero Serra established the first Franciscan mission in California. Samuel de Champlain explored the Great Lakes region. The Spanish had no contact with the Iroquois confederation.

5. **C.** The Second Bank of the United States had been chartered in 1816. Although the charter would not elapse until 1836, the National Republicans, led by Henry Clay, attempted to make the bank a major issue in the 1832 campaign. Andrew Jackson, at the height of his popularity, defeated Clay. He saw this victory as a public mandate to destroy the bank. Jackson instructed his Treasury Secretary, Roger B. Taney, to pay federal expenses from the Bank of United States coffers and place all new deposits in selected state banks.

6. **D.** In March 1965, Martin Luther King, Jr. helped organize a protest in Selma to call national attention to a voting system that denied African-Americans equal access. Local police and state troopers attacked the marchers on the Edmund Pettus Bridge. National outrage spurred the passage of Civil Rights Act of 1965, popularly known as the Voting Rights Act, by Lyndon Johnson.

7. **A.** By 1775, Massachusetts was a hotbed of colonial discontent. General Thomas Gage commanded the British troops in Boston. Gage marched west to seize weapons amassed by Massachusetts "minutemen" and, if possible, arrest the outspoken Samuel Adams and John Hancock.

8. **E.** Chiang Kai-shek led the Nationalists against Mao's Communists in China. Kim Il-Sung was a communist leader in North Korea. The United States supported Ngo Dinh Diem in Vietnam until 1963. Shah Reza Pahlevi, a pro-Western dictator, remained in power in Iran until 1978.

9. **C.** Western states received a disproportionate number of federal contracts during World War II. Several roads, power plants, and munitions factories were constructed in the West. The aircraft industry flourished through federal patronage. Furthermore, most of the ships launched to fight Japan disembarked from western ports.

10. **B.** Early opponents of slavery attempted to eliminate slaves from Southern society. The American Colonization Society, organized by a group of wealthy white Virginians, proposed a plan to compensate

masters who volunteered to emancipate their slaves. The ACS would then transport the former slaves to Africa. Congress, private donors, and a few state legislatures donated money to the Society. Slaves liberated by the ACS founded Liberia on the western coast of Africa in the 1830s.

11. **A.** After the Venezuelan crisis (1902), Roosevelt sought to ensure against European involvement in Latin American affairs. The Dominican Republic accumulated over $20 million in debt to several European nations. When those nations threatened action to recover their investments, Roosevelt proclaimed that the United States retained the right to intervene in the internal affairs of Latin American nations. Under pressure from Roosevelt, the Dominican government allowed the United States to assume control of the collection of customs. American supervision of Dominican finances lasted almost 30 years.

12. **D.** Richard Nixon sought to normalize relations with both communist China and the Soviet Union. He visited China in February 1972. American and Soviet diplomats completed talks on the Strategic Arms Limitation Talks (SALT I) during his administration. Nixon traveled to the Soviet Union in May 1972; Leonid Brezhnev visited the United States the following year.

13. **D.** William Marbury sued James Madison to induce the Supreme Court to issue a writ of mandamus. The Judiciary Act of 1789 granted the Court the power to issue these writs, which served as court orders. Marshall declared that part of the Judiciary Act was void, since it exceeded the powers granted to the Court under Article III of the Constitution. Thus, Marshall established the principle of "judicial review." Marshall ruled against the confiscation of Tory estates in *Martin* v. *Hunter's Lessee* (1816) and protected the sanctity of contracts in *Dartmouth College* v. *Woodward* (1819).

14. **E.** African-American artists and authors sparked the cultural movement known as the Harlem Renaissance. Langston Hughes published the poem "I, too" in 1925. Maya Angelou and Richard Wright were African-American authors associated with later time periods. Allen Ginsberg was a Beat poet of the 1950s.

15. **B.** Various theories explain the introduction of the horse to the tribes of the Great Plains. Some historians believe that Europeans provided the first horses. Others assert that different tribes traded horses to the region's Indians. By the mid-eighteenth century, the horse had become a permanent fixture of the Great Plains. Domesticated horses allowed some tribes to pursue buffalo herds. However, the local tribes rarely traveled as far as the Pacific Northwest.

16. **A.** Economist John Maynard Keynes published *The General Theory of Employment, Interest, and Money* in 1936. Eisenhower cut federal expenditures while restricting credit and raising interest rates. These policies caused a business slump. Eisenhower subsequently

adopted a more flexible fiscal policy that allowed for easier credit and deficits. Although initially resistant to an unbalanced budget and deficit spending, Kennedy became a more committed Keynesian than Eisenhower. He occasionally combined tax cuts with federal spending to stimulate growth. Keynesian economics did not propose direct involvement in the affairs of private companies.

17. **D.** Antisuffragists asserted that women's suffrage would invert gender roles. They argued women would abandon the role of caretaker while pursuing involvement in politics. Men would then be forced into a more domestic position. Some opponents linked women's suffrage to contemporary nativism. They asserted that extending the vote to women would swell the ranks of immigrant voters. However, men also supported the temperance and education reform movements and would not want to diminish the number of potential supporters.

18. **A.** Medicare offered relief to elderly Americans in the form of federal aid for medical expenses. President Ronald Reagan signed the Economic Recovery Tax Act (1981) to lower corporate and individual income tax rates and the Gramm-Rudman-Hollings Act (1985) to reduce the federal budget.

19. **C.** Thoreau, Cooper, and Longfellow were antebellum authors who made nature a central theme in their works. Cooper first introduced "Natty Bumppo" in *Pioneers* (1823). Bumppo played a central role in ensuing Cooper novels, representing the archetype of American individualism. Turner formulated his "frontier thesis" at the end of the nineteenth century. Weld wrote abolitionist tracts.

20. **E.** Rolfe began to experiment with a local breed of tobacco in Virginia in 1612. He quickly produced sellable crops and found a ready market in Great Britain. As Virginia planters sought more land to cultivate tobacco, they inevitably clashed with the local tribes. However, the Iroquois resided further north. Peter Hasenclever founded a successful ironworks in New Jersey in the mid-eighteenth century.

21. **B.** Two white women accused nine black youths of rape in 1931. Little evidence indicated that the women had been assaulted. Nevertheless, an all-white jury convicted the nine young men and sentenced eight to death. Although the Supreme Court overturned the convictions in 1932, five would serve jail terms. The Sacco-Vanzetti trial revealed the nativism associated with the 1920s.

22. **D.** Tense relations with the Soviet Union seemed to be improving by the end of the 1950s. Nikita Khrushchev visited the United States in 1959. Eisenhower and the Soviet premier planned a summit conference in Paris for the following year. The president intended to visit Moscow. On May 1, 1960, the Soviets shot down an American U-2 spy plane. The Eisenhower administration attempted to cover up the plane's mission until the Soviets produced the pilot and wreckage of

the plane. Khrushchev rescinded Eisenhower's invitation and withdrew from the summit meeting. The Cuban Missile Crisis occurred two years later. Both the Berlin airlift and Suez Crisis took place before 1957.

23. **A.** British scientists noted that intentional exposure to mild cases of smallpox immunized people against contracting the disease. After an outbreak of smallpox struck Boston in 1720, Puritan theologian Cotton Mather encouraged the city's residents to be inoculated. Many residents resisted the practice initially. Nevertheless, theologians and physicians continued to urge the procedure. Inoculations became a standard medical practice by 1750. The steam engine was developed in the early nineteenth century. Commercial fertilizers came into common use in the late 1800s. Antibiotics emerged in 1928. Scientists and physicians attacked pellagra after World War I.

24. **C.** During his debates with Lincoln in the Illinois senate race, Stephen A. Douglas enunciated the Freeport Doctrine. Douglas hoped to defuse potential national strife by trying to reconcile "popular sovereignty" with the Kansas-Nebraska Act. He asserted that slavery could not survive in a territory where residents passed "unfriendly legislation." Douglas's failure to endorse the Kansas-Nebraska Act unequivocally cost him Southern votes in 1860.

25. **D.** Overspeculation in western land sales only affected the Panic of 1837. A standardized currency had been used for many decades before the onset of the Great Depression. Overspeculation on the stock market contributed to the Great Depression but not the Panic of 1837. However, banking problems contributed to both economic crises. "Runs on banks" resulted in lost savings and the stagnation of industrial and agricultural development.

26. **C.** Although the British army suffered significant casualties at Bunker Hill, the Americans eventually retreated. The victory at Trenton did not convince France that the rebels could sustain a protracted war with Great Britain. Washington's army had been severely defeated in a series of battles in New York during the previous summer and fall. However, Horatio Gates defeated the depleted forces of General Johnny Burgoyne at Saratoga in October 1777. Over 5000 British soldiers surrendered to the Continental Army. American diplomats used the victory as a springboard to hasten a treaty of alliance in 1778.

27. **E.** Many people feared the return of Depression-level unemployment at the end of World War II. The demobilization of hundreds of thousands of soldiers, the immediate end of wartime production, and significant cuts in federal spending portended dire economic consequences. However, pent-up consumer demand, kept in check by wartime rationing and price controls, provided the economic boost to forestall depression. Inflation soon became a greater con-

cern than depression or unemployment. Labor strife escalated after the war, including major strikes in the mining and railroad industries. After Republican victories in the elections of 1946, Congress moved to cut spending for aid to education, Social Security increases, and conservation projects in the West.

28. **B.** In the election of 1800, both Thomas Jefferson and Aaron Burr received 73 electoral votes. Congress broke the deadlock by choosing Jefferson on the 36 ballot. Popular votes were not yet tallied in presidential races. The election of 1796 produced a Federalist president (John Adams) and Republican vice president (Jefferson). In 1840, William Henry Harrison was elected the first Whig president.

29. **E.** In the antebellum period, debtors, the mentally ill, and criminals were often lumped together in prisons. After witnessing these conditions, Dorothea Dix led a nationwide campaign to give the mentally ill better treatment. Mott and Stanton were women's rights advocates who organized the Seneca Falls Convention. Beecher and Dow urged temperance.

30. **B.** Progressives had long been calling for a graduated income tax to equalize the tax burden. The Sixteenth Amendment empowered Congress to levy an income tax. The Seventeenth Amendment changed the process of electing senators. Popular election replaced election by the state legislatures.

31. **A.** The most significant slave uprising of the eighteenth century occurred in South Carolina in 1739. Several slaves met near the Stono River, seized weapons, and attacked local whites before fleeing toward Spanish Florida. Nearly 100 slaves joined the revolt. White planters on horseback caught up with the rebels, and a brief gun battle ensued. Approximately 30 slaves died; most of those captured were executed for their participation. In 1677, Carolinians led by John Culpeper resisted the collection of customs by local proprietors. Jacob Leisler raised a militia to unseat an unpopular New York governor in 1689. In 1783, Continental officers stationed near Newburgh, New York, threatened to mutiny if Congress did not issue back pay and fund pensions. Only George Washington's intercession avoided a crisis. The Dorr Rebellion reflected tensions over the issue of the expansion of voting rights in Rhode Island in 1842.

32. **A.** In response to labor stridency, Congress passed the Taft-Hartley Act. The law prohibited the "closed shop," which kept nonunion workers out of certain factories. It also allowed state legislatures to pass "right-to-work" laws, which further undermined the power of organized labor. The McCarran Internal Security Act (1950) was intended to limit the activities of communist organizations. President Truman's Executive Order 9835 established the Federal Employee Loyalty Program. His Executive Order 9981 began the integration of the armed services.

33. **D.** Jackson's Indian policy forced tribes in the South to move west along the "Trail of Tears." Under duress, some Seminoles agreed to move to the Indian territory. However, Osceola led a band of his tribe against white troops. The Seminole War continued after Osceola's capture in 1837. The federal government halted its pursuit of the Seminoles in 1842. Pontiac fought white expansion into the Great Lakes region in 1763. Black Hawk led an uprising of Sauk and Fox against white settlers in Illinois in 1832. Sequoyah established an alphabet for the Cherokee.

34. **E.** In February 1917, British intelligence agents intercepted a telegram from German foreign minister Arthur Zimmermann. The note instructed a German envoy to offer the Mexicans the opportunity to regain territory lost to the United States if Mexico allied with Germany against the Americans. The Zimmermann telegram outraged an American public already incensed by the resumption of unrestricted U-boat warfare. The de Lome note angered Americans in 1898 by insulting President McKinley and heightened the war fever against Spain.

35. **C.** The French and Indian War vastly expanded the British empire. American colonists sought to expand into the territory acquired from France. Concerned with the financial burdens of protecting new lands, British officials sought to minimize administrative and defensive costs. American expansion required protection against Indian attacks along the frontier. As a result, Parliament issued the Proclamation of 1763, which forbade colonial migration across the Appalachian Mountains. It had limited effects as colonists streamed across the mountains to establish new settlements.

36. **C.** Both J. D. Salinger (*The Catcher in the Rye*) and Ralph Ellison (*Invisible Man*) created characters alienated from the strict conformity of their era. Dreiser, London, Jackson, and Wells-Barnett wrote during the late nineteenth and early twentieth centuries. McKay and Cullen penned works associated with the Harlem Renaissance of the 1920s. Dos Passos and Steinbeck described American society during the Great Depression.

37. **A.** The Populist party emerged from various farmers' organizations of the late nineteenth century. Most farmers bristled at the high rates charged for transportation of crops by the railroad companies. Others urged the monetization of silver to expand the currency and alleviate debts. In the late 1890s, they emerged as a political force to challenge the Republican and Democratic parties. Populists elected some state officials and representatives to Congress. However, they failed to attract significant support from the labor unions.

38. **E.** In late 1861, Charles Wilkes, commander of the USS *San Jacinto*, stopped the British vessel *Trent* off the coast of Cuba. Wilkes seized two Confederate diplomats, John Slidell and James M. Mason, and

sailed to Boston. President Lincoln realized Wilkes had violated international maritime law. The British government irately demanded the release of the prisoners, payment of reparations, and a public apology. Lincoln averted a crisis by releasing Slidell and Mason with a vague apology.

39. **D.** Thirty-nine delegates signed the Constitution on September 17, 1787. Supporters of ratification called themselves "Federalists" and set out to win public approval. Opponents of centralization ("Antifederalists") also attempted to marshal support. Alexander Hamilton, James Madison, and John Jay wrote a series of essays known as *The Federalist Papers*. These documents extolled the virtues of a constitutional government.

40. **B.** The Liberty party fed off the rising tide of antislavery sentiment in the 1830s. Few opponents of slavery advocated immediate abolition. Most favored halting the expansion of the institution into new territories. In April 1840, delegates met in Albany, New York, and nominated Kentuckian James G. Birney for president. Birney believed the party could raise public awareness of the antislavery cause. Although he won only 7000 votes in 1840, Birney polled over 60,000 four years later. Some members of the Liberty party joined the Free-Soil party in 1848.

41. **C.** The Amalgamated Association of Iron and Steel Workers organized workers in Andrew Carnegie's Homestead steel plant near Pittsburgh, Pennsylvania. Henry Frick, manager of the Homestead Plant, announced a series of wage cuts beginning in 1890. In 1892, the Amalgamated Association went on strike. Frick closed the plant and hired 300 Pinkerton guards to break the strike. The arrival of the Pinkertons sparked a violent response from the strikers. Steel workers fought and defeated the guards. Three Pinkertons and 10 strikers died in the melee. Governor Robert E. Pattison sent over 8000 National Guardsmen to quell the strike. Production resumed at Homestead as troops protected replacement workers.

42. **B.** The Eisenhower Doctrine aimed at restricting the communist influence in the Middle East. Some policymakers perceived pan-Arab nationalism as equally threatening. General Gamal Abdel Nasser of Egypt led the pan-Arab movement. In 1958, forces linked to Nasser threatened to topple the government in Lebanon. Eisenhower responded by dispatching 5000 marines to support the Lebanese government.

43. **D.** The Fifteenth Amendment prohibited the federal and state governments from denying freedmen the right to vote. A number of Northern states refused to ratify the amendment. It passed only as a condition of readmission for Southern states. However, the amendment did not apply to women of any race. Reconstruction governments consistently resisted calls for the redistribution of the lands of former slave masters.

44. **E.** Progressives urged a reduction of tariff rates. Taft called a special session of Congress to consider their appeal. However, the president provided little support as conservatives diluted the tariff bill. Passage of the Payne-Aldrich Tariff damaged the president's standing with the reform wing of the Republican party. Taft further alienated reformers by not opposing "Old Guard" Speaker of the House Joe Cannon who had been frustrating progressive legislation. In 1912, many progressive Republicans bolted the party to support the candidacy of Theodore Roosevelt.

45. **A.** The Civilian Conservation Corps hired young men between the ages of 18 and 25 to work in national parks and forests. CCC workers planted trees and constructed irrigation projects. Although the young men wore uniforms and lived in barracks, they were not drafted into the army. The Works Progress Administration (WPA) financed various artistic projects. The Federal Emergency Relief Agency (FERA) supported local relief agencies with cash grants.

46. **B.** Railroad construction expanded rapidly in the antebellum period. The vast majority of lines linked western agricultural states with industrial centers in the East. The federal government promoted track construction by offering land grants to railroad companies. Differing track gauges inhibited the construction of a national railway system.

47. **D.** The Union defeat at First Manassas occurred in 1861. Lincoln suspended habeas corpus in Maryland early in the war. Lincoln's passage of a draft law caused widespread opposition. Immigrants and factory workers objected most strenuously to conscription. Many feared that free blacks would take their jobs. The Conscription Act seemed to confirm their belief that the war was being fought for the benefit of African-Americans. In New York City in July 1863, demonstrations against the draft became violent. Demonstrators attacked free blacks and burned African-American homes and businesses.

48. **E.** Monroe did not run for president in 1824. The election involved four candidates: John Quincy Adams, Andrew Jackson, William Crawford, and Henry Clay. No candidate polled an electoral majority. Jackson received the most votes of any single candidate (99). Adams followed with 84. Popular votes were not yet tallied in every state. The Constitution required the House of Representatives to decide elections that did not yield an electoral majority. Clay had received the fewest electoral votes (37). Nevertheless, as Speaker of the House, he wielded significant influence. Clay cast his lot with Adams, who won the vote in the House. When Adams subsequently named Clay his Secretary of State, a position often leading to the White House, Jackson's supporters became convinced that the two men had conspired to deny their candidate the election. Accusations of a "corrupt bargain" would haunt the Adams administration.

49. **A.** King Philip (Metacomet) led the Wampanoag tribe against white settlers in Massachusetts. Well-organized and armed with guns, King Philip and the Wampanoag raided over 20 towns along the colony's frontier. The British settlers joined forces with the Mohawks, long-time rivals of King Philip's tribe. The war ended when Mohawks ambushed and killed the Wampanoag chieftain.

50. **C.** Unlike its nineteenth-century antecedent, the Ku Klux Klan expanded its activities across the nation in the 1920s. The Klan continued to terrorize African-Americans. The new Klan also responded to changes in the twentieth century. Its members, frequently from rural areas, supported Prohibition because they associated alcohol with the evils of city of life. In the same vein, they advocated immigration restriction in response to the influx of Southern and Eastern Europeans in the preceding decades.

51. **A.** Ronald Reagan's 1980 campaign promised to alleviate the economic problems caused by the stagnation of the 1970s. Reagan believed that high taxes limited the amount of capital that could be used to expand the economy. "Supply-side" economics, commonly called Reaganomics, proposed to cut taxation on corporations and the wealthy who, in turn, would stimulate growth by investing in the economy. Tax cuts also implied a significant reduction in federal spending.

52. **D.** The New Deal strengthened labor unions through favorable legislation such as the Wagner and Fair Labor Standards Acts. After World War II, Congress moved to limit union power in the Taft-Hartley Act. The federal investigations of the Teamsters and United Mine Workers unions revealed corruption and other scandals. Nevertheless, the labor movement achieved some successes. The AFL and CIO merged in 1955. Some unions, particularly the steelworkers, bargained for higher wages. However, the CIO's efforts to organize Southern mass-production workers yielded minimal results.

53. **E.** Mahan asserted that a nation's wealth and influence stemmed from sea power. Industrialization enabled American factories to construct large, steel ships. The development of steam engines required coaling stations if fleets were to reach distant lands. Mahan, Theodore Roosevelt, and Henry Cabot Lodge advocated a "large policy" in which the United States would become more involved in world affairs. Mahan publicized his views in a number of popular journals, which contributed to public support of imperialistic ventures.

54. **D.** President James K. Polk sent ambassador John Slidell to Mexico City to negotiate a new border at the Rio Grande River, as well as to purchase New Mexico and California. However, many Mexican nationalists continued to resent the American response to the Texas revolution. The Mexican government rejected Slidell's offer. Incensed at the Mexican response to Slidell, the Polk administration seized on an incident between Mexican troops and forces under General

Zachary Taylor as a pretext for a declaration of war. The *Gaspee* Incident occurred in 1772 when colonists raided a British merchant ship. The Olive Branch Petition (1775) sought to avert war with Great Britain. The Cherokee ceded millions of acres of land to the federal government in the Treaty of New Echota (1835). The Ostend Manifesto (1854) implied that the United States may use force if Spain refused to sell Cuba.

55. **C.** King Charles II granted Penn a vast proprietary colony in North America. Penn promoted the sale of land in his colony by advertising throughout Europe. Pennsylvania attracted settlers from a variety of nations. A Quaker, Penn did not seek to establish any official religion. Settlers practiced several faiths without interference from the colonial assembly. Church leaders in Massachusetts expelled Roger Williams for insisting on separation of church and state. Williams founded Rhode Island, which also extended a significant degree of religious freedom.

56. **B.** African-Americans that could vote generally cast ballots for Republican candidates, having joined the Republican party during Reconstruction. Beginning with the New Deal, African-Americans increasingly supported Democratic candidates. Richard Nixon made inroads into the Southern electorate in 1968. He would carry the former "Solid South" in 1972.

57. **B.** The Union Pacific Railroad Company hired Credit Mobilier, a construction company, to build its transcontinental route. Some members of Credit Mobilier served on the board of directors of Union Pacific. They subsequently used their positions to shift sizable contracts to the construction company. In the process, they defrauded Union Pacific and the federal government, which had been subsidizing the railroad construction, of millions of dollars. To impede a federal investigation, the directors of Credit Mobilier bribed congressmen and Vice President Schuyler Colfax with stock.

58. **A.** In 1941, A. Philip Randolph, head of the railroad porters' union, began pressuring President Roosevelt to integrate the workforces of companies receiving federal defense contracts. When Randolph planned a massive demonstration for integration in Washington, DC, Roosevelt created the Fair Employment Practices Committee (FEPC). The committee was empowered to examine the treatment of African-Americans in war industries.

59. **C.** A religious revival among the several tribes swept across the Great Plains before 1890. Participants practiced the "Ghost Dance," which they believed foretold the return of the buffalo and exodus of whites. White reservation agents worried that the widespread practice of the "Ghost Dance" indicated an impending rebellion. During an attempt to arrest Sitting Bull, soldiers killed the Sioux chief. In December 1890, a regiment of cavalry attempted to disperse a group

of Sioux at Wounded Knee. When fighting ensued, nearly 200 Indians and 40 soldiers died. Wounded Knee represented the end of resistance by the tribes of the Great Plains.

60. **E.** The Organization of Petroleum Exporting Countries (OPEC) acted as a loose bargaining agent for Third World nations that sold oil. During the Yom Kippur War (1973), Arab members of OPEC announced a boycott of oil to those nations that supported Israel. The United States and some Western European nations had recognized and aided Israel since its founding in 1948. OPEC also raised oil prices by 400 percent. A massive fuel shortage struck the United States and contributed to skyrocketing inflation in the 1970s.

61. **A.** Scottish industrialist Robert Owen founded a utopian community at New Harmony, Indiana, in 1825. Owen argued against harsh factory conditions and sought to create a community based on socialistic principles. Although New Harmony failed as an economic unit, it inspired others to try to form communities free from the abuses of competitive, capitalistic society. The Lowell mills employed a predominantly female workforce early in the antebellum period. Lowell attempted to create a moral atmosphere and required workers to live in supervised dormitories.

62. **D.** By the end of the Civil War, Lincoln sought to readmit former Confederate states to the Union rapidly. His plan offered amnesty to all Southerners, except high Confederate officials, that swore allegiance to the Union and agreed to abolish slavery. When 10 percent of the 1860 electorate affirmed their allegiance, voters could establish a state government within the Union. Louisiana, Tennessee, and Arkansas reestablished state governments before Lincoln's assassination.

63. **B.** The Tea Act of 1773 exempted the British East India Company from taxes imposed on other colonial merchants. This act gave the company a virtual monopoly of the tea trade and threatened a number of colonial businesses. Furthermore, many colonists perceived the act as another example of taxation without representation. As a result, colonists boycotted British goods. In December 1773, Bostonians disguised as Indians boarded British ships and dumped the tea into the harbor. In response, Parliament enacted the Coercive Acts, which included closing the port of Boston until the colonists repaid the company for the costs of the tea.

64. **A.** Sanger pioneered the birth control movement of the 1920s. She published *The Birth Control Review* to disseminate information about contraception. It sold nearly 10,000 copies per issue in 1922. She founded the American Birth Control League and promoted contraception as a cure for urban poverty. Sanger established the first clinic for counseling the public on the advantages of contraception. By the end of the 1920s, she helped found over 800 birth control clinics.

65. **E.** President Ronald Reagan signed the Immigration Reform and Control Act (1986) to control illegal immigration into the United States. Johnson sponsored the other four measures. The Economic Opportunity Act created agencies such as the OEO to combat poverty. Medicaid extended federally sponsored medical insurance for impoverished Americans. The Appalachian Regional Development Act included a $1 billion budget for road construction and other projects in rural areas. The Higher Education Act expanded federal financial aid for college students.

66. **C.** After the signing of the Constitution in 1787, intense ratification battles in the states determined if a new government would be created. Henry and Monroe championed the antiratification forces in Virginia. They believed that the Constitution did not offer the people sufficient protection from the centralized power of the federal government. No provision of the Constitution specifically created a national bank. The debate over creation of a federal bank began after ratification.

67. **C.** The "Jim Crow" system emerged after Reconstruction. White Southerners attempted restrain black freedom after the passage of the Thirteenth, Fourteenth, and Fifteenth Amendments. Various state laws imposed segregation and limited black suffrage. The Supreme Court's decision in *Plessy* v. *Ferguson* (1896) validated the state legislation, which would not be lifted until the 1950s and 1960s.

68. **B.** Roosevelt was elected as William McKinley's vice president in 1900. Roosevelt succeeded to the presidency after McKinley's assassination in 1901. He won the election of 1904 but chose not to campaign in 1908. Roosevelt threw his support behind the candidacy of William Howard Taft. However, Taft departed from a number of Roosevelt's reform policies, inducing the former president to seek the Republican nomination in 1912. The Republican convention, dominated by the conservative wing of the party, gave the nomination to Taft. Progressive Republicans joined Roosevelt in bolting the party. Roosevelt ran on the Progressive ("Bull Moose") ticket in 1912. The split between conservative and liberal Republicans contributed to Democrat Woodrow Wilson's election as president in 1912.

69. **A.** Hamilton designed a fiscal program to establish the new nation on a solid financial foundation. The Assumption Act addressed the outstanding debts accumulated by states fighting in the Revolutionary War. Some states had repaid most of their debts. Others, such as Massachusetts, still owed a significant amount of money. The Assumption Act empowered the federal government to tax all states to repay the remaining state debts. Although some objected to the new tax burdens, the federal government asserted its authority over the states. The new government would also pass a funding bill that would repay, at face value, all bonds held by creditors.

70. **E.** Senator Gerald P. Nye chaired a committee that examined American entry into World War I. The committee alleged that munitions companies made exorbitant profits during the war. Although the committee produced little proof, it convinced many Americans that bankers persuaded President Wilson to involve the United States in the European conflict. The Nye report fostered strong public support for isolationism prior to World War II.

71. **B.** The Treaty of Paris ended the Revolutionary War. Great Britain recognized the independence of the American states and surrendered the territory from the Appalachian Mountains to the Mississippi River. Jay's Treaty (1794) attempted to improve commerce between Great Britain and the states. In the Treaty of New Echota, the Cherokee ceded millions of acres of land to the federal government. The Treaty of Guadalupe Hidalgo ended the Mexican War. The Treaty of Tordesillas settled territorial claims between Spain and Portugal.

72. **D.** The federal government encouraged production of food products during World War I. Farmers enjoyed high prices and steady demand. However, production did not slow after the end of the war. New technology, such as mechanical tractors and fertilizers, enabled farmers to grow more crops. Overproduction depressed agricultural prices during the 1920s. The drought that created the "Dust Bowl" began in 1930.

73. **E.** A heated economic rivalry touched off a war between Japan and Russia in 1904. Japan believed the Russians menaced their interests in China and Korea. The Japanese navy inflicted serious damage upon the Russian fleet. Japan seized Korea and forced the Russian army to retreat into Manchuria. Roosevelt appealed to both powers to end the conflict. Although the peace treaty heavily favored Japan, Roosevelt received the Nobel Peace Prize for ending the war.

74. **D.** Woodrow Wilson signed the Federal Reserve Act in 1913. The act established 12 regional banks, owned and operated by local banks in the district. The regional banks held a percentage of the assets of member banks in reserve. Banks would issue federal reserve notes that served as the nation's currency. A Federal Reserve system would regulate the banking system.

75. **A.** At the beginning of the Progressive era, Henry George published *Progress and Poverty*. His book blamed poverty on the vast amount of property owned by a few wealthy industrialists. Rising land values only enriched the few. As a result, George proposed a "single tax" in place of other forms of taxation. This tax would fall most heavily on industrialists and would redistribute the wealth more equitably. Single-tax associations were established in several cities. In 1886, George nearly won the race for mayor of New York City. Tarbell exposed the monopolistic practices of Standard Oil Company. Riis

published *How the Other Half Lives* based upon his photographs of urban poverty. Steffens attacked urban corruption in *The Shame of the Cities.*

76. **C.** The Emancipation Proclamation only affected those areas of the nation still in rebellion after January 1, 1863. It did not affect the border states. By issuing the proclamation, Lincoln shifted the Union's war goals. The war would now restore the Union without slavery. Great Britain, which had abolished slavery, would not recognize the independence of the Confederacy and would not fight on its behalf. Opposition to the proclamation seemed to favor the Democrats in 1864. No large-scale rebellions followed the issuance of the proclamation.

77. **D.** The McNary-Haugen bill proposed to create parity prices for agricultural products. It required the federal government to purchase surplus crops and sell them abroad in an effort to raise domestic prices. Coolidge vetoed the bill because he believed the federal government did not have the authority to fix prices.

78. **B.** The American Revolution unleashed new forces that called into question the position of women in society. Emphasis on liberty and the rights of men naturally turned to discussions about women. Abigail Adams wrote a letter to her husband John to remind him "to remember the ladies" in the new laws written for the emerging republic. While Abigail Adams did not call for absolute equality, she did seek protection of the rights of women against abusive husbands.

79. **E.** Although the CIA began training Cuban exiles during the Eisenhower administration, Kennedy approved the plan to invade Cuba. The plan was intended to land a small force, with American air support, on Cuba and foment a popular revolt against Castro. However, the United States failed to provide aerial support. All of the exiles were either killed or captured by Castro's army.

80. **C.** Few traditional sources of credit existed in the South after the Civil War. Black and white farmers relied upon local merchants for all of their needs, including seeds, tools, and household items. Short on cash, these farmers would mortgage their crops to the local merchants as collateral for necessary items. These liens established an inescapable cycle of debt for farmers who experienced a poor crop yield.

Summary Response to the Document-Based Question

1. Students should begin with a discussion of the Interstate Commerce Act (1887) and Sherman Antitrust Act (1890). The Interstate Commerce Act attempted to regulate railroad companies. It required railroads to submit their fare schedules with the federal government and publicize

their rates. The act created an Interstate Commerce Commission (ICC) to monitor the industry. The Sherman Act declared illegal all combinations "in restraint of free trade." It empowered the Justice Department to bring suit and break up such monopolies. However, these acts would have to pass the scrutiny of the Supreme Court. Students might comment upon the composition of the Court during the period. They might explain how a conservative Court could thwart the efforts of reformers. Students should discuss the labor movement during the Progressive era. Several strikes occurred in this period, including the Great Railway Strike (1877), Haymarket Affair (1886), or the Homestead Strike (1892). Students must examine the Pullman Strike (1894), in which railroad workers and the American Railway Union, led by Eugene Debs, crippled traffic in several states and territories. Many governors sided with the railroad companies by employing state troops to disperse the strikers. One notable exception was John Peter Altgeld, governor of Illinois. Railroad operators in Chicago appealed to President Cleveland and Attorney-General Richard Olney to intercede on their behalf. The president ordered 2000 federal troops to break up the strike. The Supreme Court further solidified the position of the railroad corporations by applying the Sherman Antitrust Act against unions that threatened free trade (Document A). In *E. C. Knight Company* v. *U.S.*, the Court further inhibited efforts to regulate corporations by putting manufacturing companies outside the purview of the Sherman Act (Document B). Thus, companies continued to form monopolies in various industries that fixed prices without competition. The Court undermined the Interstate Commerce Commission's authority to determine fair railroad rates by applying the "due process" clause of the Fourteenth Amendment to corporations (Document D). Progressives seeking to limit the hours of labor met with mixed results. In *Holden* v. *Hardy* (1898) the Court affirmed the right of state legislatures to regulate maximum hours in the interests of workers' health (Document C). Seven years later, the Court again reinterpreted the Fourteenth Amendment to cast aside a state law. The *Lochner* decision asserted that legislation not directly related to health concerns violated the rights of workers (Document E). However, reformers gained a partial victory in *Muller* v. *Oregon* (1908), which sustained the legislature's authority to pass regulatory legislation to protect women's health (Document F). Students might comment upon the double standard applied to men and women in the early twentieth century. Students might refer to the Elkins (1903) and Hepburn (1906) Acts, which intended to further the federal government's ability to regulate railroads. Others might explain how presidential leadership advanced the cause of reform by briefly discussing Theodore Roosevelt, William Howard Taft, or Woodrow Wilson. Some students might touch upon how the Roosevelt administration implemented the Sherman Act in *Northern Securities Company* v. *United States* (1904) to set the stage for an examination of the decentralization of monopolies. The Court furthered its position by ordering the Standard Oil Company to break up its monopoly of the oil refining industry (Document G). Students may compare the decision with the Court's response to Swift and American Tobacco. To conclude the essay, students might discuss how the Court endorsed the Adamson Act, which established an eight-hour day for interstate railway workers (Document H).

Summary Responses to the Standard Free-Response Questions

2. Students should begin their responses with a discussion of Thomas Jefferson as secretary of state and vice president. During the Washington administration, Jefferson opposed the nationalistic financial program of Alexander Hamilton. He argued that the Constitution did not expressly permit the creation of a federal bank. He opposed excise taxes and the increase in federal debt. Jefferson expanded his conservative approach to federal power when he penned the Kentucky Resolutions in response to the Alien and Sedition Acts (1798). However, the exigencies of his two terms as president contributed to Jefferson's departure from a strict interpretation of the Constitution. Students might begin by noting how Jefferson adhered to his perception of a limited government by cutting spending and abolition of internal taxes. Jefferson reduced the size of the armed forces. However, Jefferson would fight an undeclared war with the Barbary pirates from 1801 to 1805. When Jefferson refused to pay the pirates "tribute" money for use of the Mediterranean Sea, the raiders seized American ships and seized prisoners. Jefferson ordered the naval fleet to the region without a congressional declaration of war. He justified his actions under the principle that he was protecting American lives and ships. Students should also discuss the Louisiana Purchase. Jefferson faced a constitutional dilemma; the Constitution did not directly permit the government to purchase land. Furthermore, the treaty seemed to abridge the naturalization powers of Congress. Nevertheless, Jefferson justified the acquisition of the Louisiana territory through his treaty-making powers. Some students might touch upon Jefferson's involvement in the Burr conspiracy trial, his efforts to remove Federalist judges, or the Embargo Act (1807) as further evidence of his departure from a strict interpretation of the Constitution.

3. Students should begin by defining manifest destiny and discuss its racial, religious, and nationalistic overtones. Some students might mention John L. O'Sullivan, the Democratic newspaper editor who promoted expansionism. The theory rested upon the idea that the United States was destined by God to expand its boundaries for the purpose of extending the blessings of liberty. It implied the superiority of white civilization and government over the native tribes and Mexicans in the West. Nonwhites would be excluded from this rapidly expanding republic. Newspapers attracted public support for westward expansion. Americans moved westward during the early 1840s. Stu-

dents should discuss migration to Oregon and the Pacific Coast. Missionaries and farmers encouraged settlement in the region in spite of conflicting British claims on the location of borders. Students should also discuss how Americans debated the annexation of Texas. Generally, Northerners and Whigs opposed annexation, as it seemed to favor the Democratic party and Southern states. As a result, manifest destiny significantly influenced the election of 1844. Whig candidate Henry Clay did not firmly endorse expansionism. Some students might mention his "Raleigh letter." Democrat James K. Polk, a dark-horse candidate, won popular support by calling for "the re-occupation of Oregon and the re-annexation of Texas." Polk easily carried the election. Not long after his inauguration, Polk faced the possibility of war with both Great Britain and Mexico. The Polk administration began negotiations for the 49th parallel as the border between British and American territory. When the British rejected Polk's first offer, some Americans cried "54 40′ or fight," seeming to support war for all of the Oregon territory. Both nations averted armed conflict when the British government finally relented and agreed on the 49th parallel. However, manifest destiny did lead to war with Mexico. Students might begin by discussing how annexationists perceived Mexicans. Students should touch upon the causes of the war (Slidell mission, the "attack" upon Zachary Taylor's troops south of the Nueces River). Some students may touch upon the "All Mexico" movement in their examination of the Treaty of Guadalupe Hidalgo. Students might conclude by linking manifest destiny to the explosive issue of the expansion of slavery.

4. To introduce the Social Security Act, students might begin by discussing Huey Long and Dr. Francis Townsend. Senator Long promoted the "Share Our Wealth" movement, which would address the needs of the indigent through confiscatory taxation on the wealthy. Under this plan, the federal government would be able to offer families a guaranteed annual wage. Townsend advocated providing federal pensions to the elderly. He believed that the pensions would allow older Americans to retire, thus opening jobs for the unemployed. While Congress endorsed neither plan, these proposals rallied support for the Social Security Act (1935). This act established a pension system for the elderly. Both employers and employees contributed to the pension fund. Although payments would not begin until 1940, recipients could receive up to $85 dollars per month. The act also implemented a program of unemployment insurance funded by contributions from employers. Recipients received temporary federal assistance if they were laid off from their jobs. Supporters perceived the act as a means for correcting the vagaries of a capitalist economy. The act was intended to provide a system of insurance rather than welfare. Workers who fell victim to periodic economic downturns now had a "safety net" to temper the blow of depressions. Nevertheless, the act also granted direct assistance to the needy, including

the disabled and dependent children. In *Schechter Poultry Corporation v. United States* (1935), the Supreme Court overturned the National Industrial Recovery Act. Section 7A of this act allowed workers to form unions and to bargain collectively. The invalidation threatened to undermine gains made by unions. The Wagner Act (1935) guaranteed workers the right to join unions and outlawed interference by employers. It created a National Labor Relations Board, which retained the authority to force employers to recognize and negotiate with unions. The Wagner Act protected the rights of workers to join unions. Union membership increased rapidly as workers sought to address their working conditions. The Fair Labor Standards Act resulted from labor agitation. Students might examine the growing militancy of unions in the 1930s. They could discuss strikes by the UAW or steelworkers that called attention to workers' grievances. Some might also refer to the Walsh-Healy Act (1936), which established minimum wage and maximum hours standards for workers in companies receiving government contracts. The Fair Labor Standards Act (1938) established a national minimum wage (25 cents/hour) and maximum hours (40/week). It also imposed regulations on child labor. The act implemented standards championed by reformers since the nineteenth century.

5. Students might begin this essay with a brief discussion of World War I and the Bolshevik Revolution. Both events heightened a fear of radicalism in the United States. This fear increased as racial violence and strikes among steelworkers, the Boston police, and other laborers erupted across the nation. A series of bombings in 1919 were attributed to a radical conspiracy. Widespread nativism reinforced this emerging antiradicalism. Attorney General A. Mitchell Palmer, whose house was damaged by a bomb, led the charge to purge the nation of radicals. Palmer ordered the investigation of subversives. Over 6000 people were arrested; socialists, IWW members, and feminists became the targets of harassment. Although the "Palmer Raids" intended to discover the source of the bombings, they revealed no nationwide conspiracy. The Red Scare began to subside by the end of 1920 but had lingering effects. Students should discuss the impact of antiradicalism and nativism on the Sacco-Vanzetti case. In spite of circumstantial evidence, Nicola Sacco and Bartolomeo Vanzetti received death sentences. Students might discuss the end of World War II and Soviet influence in Eastern Europe to provide some context for the emergence of anticommunism. Students might compare perceptions of radicals and liberals after World War II with their counterparts during the First Red Scare. Students should examine HUAC (House Un-American Activities Committee) and its investigations of the State Department, motion picture industry, and other liberals. Some students might refer to the rise of Richard Nixon. Unsubstantiated allegations of espionage resulted in the conviction of former State Department official Alger Hiss. The Truman administration implemented a fed-

eral employee loyalty program to root out subversives. Congress passed the McCarran Internal Security Act (1950) to inhibit the activities of communist or other radical organizations. Soviet nuclear testing in 1949 seemed to confirm fears of espionage in the United States. The conviction and execution of Ethel and Julius Rosenberg intensified the pervasive hysteria gripping the nation. Students might link the Rosenberg case with Sacco-Vanzetti. Local communities also became concerned that subversives had infiltrated their neighborhoods. Students might compare Joseph McCarthy to A. Mitchell Palmer. McCarthy boldly asserted that he possessed the names of 205 communists working in the State Department. The public believed his unsubstantiated claims, boosting McCarthy to national prominence. Students should discuss McCarthy's Senate subcommittee that harangued witnesses and ruined careers in public service. McCarthy intimidated members of the federal government who might oppose him. McCarthyism fostered an atmosphere of accusation that influenced elections and employment practices. McCarthy's influence diminished rapidly after his hearings with the Army finally destroyed his credibility. Nevertheless, the impact of McCarthyism lingered for several years. Students might discuss the impact of McCarthyism upon domestic policy and foreign diplomacy.

PART V

"AFTER WORDS"

Glossary

abolitionist movement Movement dedicated to the abolition of slavery that existed primarily in the North in years leading up to the Civil War; had both white and black members.

Albany Congress 1754 meeting of representatives of seven colonies to coordinate their efforts against French and Native American threats in the Western frontier regions.

Advertising Age Term first used to describe America's consumer culture of the 1920s, when advertising began to influence the choices of purchasers.

affirmative action Policies that began in the 1970s to make up for past discrimination and give minorities and women advantages in applying for certain jobs and in applying for admission to certain universities.

affluent society Term used by economist John Kenneth Galbraith to describe the American economy in the 1950s, during which time many Americans became enraptured with appliances and homes in the suburbs.

Agricultural Adjustment Administration (AAA) Established by the Agricultural Act of 1932, a New Deal bureau designed to restore economic position of farmers by paying them *not* to farm goods that were being overproduced.

Agricultural Marketing Act 1929 act championed by Herbert Hoover that authorized the lending of federal money to farmer's cooperatives to buy crops to keep them from the oversaturated market; program hampered by lack of adequate federal financial support.

Alien and Sedition Acts Proposed and supported by John Adams, gave the president the power to expel aliens deemed "dangerous to the country's well-being" and outlawed publication and public pronouncement of "false, scandalous, and malicious" statements about the government

Allied Powers Coalition of nations that opposed Germany, Italy, and Japan in World War II; led by England, the Soviet Union, and the United States

America First Committee Isolationist group in America that insisted that America stay out of World War II; held rallies from 1939 to 1941; argued that affairs in Europe should be settled by Europeans and not Americans and stated that the Soviet Union was a greater eventual threat than Nazi Germany.

American Colonization Society Formed in 1817, stated that the best way to end the slavery problem in the United States was for blacks to emigrate to Africa; by 1822 a few American blacks emigrated to Liberia. Organization's views were later rejected by most abolitionists.

American Expeditionary Force Official title of American army sent to Europe to aid England and France after United States entered World War I; army was commanded by General John J. Pershing.

American Federation of Labor (A.F.L.) National labor union founded by Samuel Gompers in 1886; original goal was to organize skilled workers by craft. Merged with Congress of Industrial Organizations (CIO) in 1955.

American Indian Movement (AIM) Native American organization founded in 1968 to protest government policies and injustices suffered by Native Americans; in 1973 organized armed occupation of Wounded Knee, South Dakota.

American Liberty League Formed in 1934 by anti-New Deal politicians and business leaders to oppose policies of Franklin Roosevelt; stated that New Deal policies brought America closer to fascism.

American System Economic plan promoted by Speaker of the House Henry Clay in years following the War of 1812; promoted vigorous growth of the American economy and the use of protective tariffs to encourage Americans to buy more domestic goods.

Anaconda Copper Company Large mining syndicate typical of many companies involved in mining in the western United States in the 1860s and 1870s; used heavy machinery and professional engineers. Many prospectors who found gold, silver, or copper sold their claims to companies such as this.

Anaconda Plan Critical component of initial Union plans to win the Civil War; called for capture of critical Southern ports and eventual control of the Mississippi River, which would create major economic and strategic difficulties for the Confederacy.

Antifederalists Group that opposed the ratification of the proposed Constitution of the United States in 1787; many feared that strong central government would remove the processes of government "from the people" and replicate the excesses of the British monarchy.

Anti-Imperialist League Organization formed in 1898 to oppose American annexation of the Philippines and American imperialism in general; focused the public on the potential financial, military, and especially moral costs of imperialism.

Anti-Saloon League Organization founded in 1893 that increased public awareness of the social effects of alcohol on society; supported politicians who favored prohibition and promoted statewide referendums in Western and Southern states to ban alcohol.

Appomattox In the courthouse of this Virginia city Robert E. Lee surrendered his Confederate army to Ulysses S. Grant on April 9, 1865.

Army-McCarthy hearings 1954 televised hearings on changes that Senator Joseph McCarthy was unfairly tarnishing the United States Army with changes of communist infiltration into the armed forces; hearings were the beginning of the end for McCarthy, whose bullying tactics were repeatedly demonstrated.

Articles of Confederation Ratified in 1781, this document established the first official government of the United States; allowed much power to remain in the states, with the federal government possessing only limited powers. Articles replaced by the Constitution in 1788.

Astrolabe Instrument that enabled navigators to calculate their latitude using the sun and the stars; allowed more accuracy in plotting routes during the Age of Discovery.

Atlantic, Battle of the Began in spring 1941 with the sinking of an American merchant vessel by a German submarine. Armed conflict between warships of America and Germany took place in September of 1941; American merchant vessels were armed by 1942.

Atlantic Charter Fall 1941 agreement between Franklin Roosevelt and Winston Churchill, stating that America and Great Britain would support a postwar world based on self-determination and would endorse a world body to ensure "general security"; U.S. agreement to convoy merchant ships across part of Atlantic inevitably drew America closer to conflict with Germany.

Aztecs Advanced Indian society located in central Mexico; conquered by Spanish conquistador Cortes. The defeat of the Aztecs was hastened by smallpox brought to Mexico by the Spanish.

Baby Boom Large increase in birthrate in United States that began in 1945 and lasted until 1962; new and larger families fueled the move to suburbia that occurred in the 1950s and produced the "youth culture" that would become crucial in the 1960s.

Ballinger-Pinchot Affair Crisis that occurred when William Howard Taft was president, further distancing him from Progressive supporters of Theodore Roosevelt. Richard Ballinger, Taft's Secretary of the Interior, allowed private businessmen to purchase large amounts of public land in Alaska; Forest Service head Gifford Pinchot (a Roosevelt supporter) protested to Congress and was fired by Taft.

Bank War Political battles surrounding the attempt by President Andrew Jackson to greatly reduce the power of the Second Bank of the United States; Jackson claimed the Bank was designed to serve special interests in America and not the common people.

Bataan Death March Forced march of 76,000 American and Filipino soldiers captured by the Japanese from the Bataan Peninsula in early May 1942; over 10,000 soldiers died during this one-week ordeal.

Bay of Pigs Failed 1961 invasion of Cuba by United States-supported anti-Castro refugees designed to topple Castro from power; prestige of the United States, and of the newly elected president, John Kennedy, was damaged by this failed coup attempt.

Bear Flag Republic Declaring independence from Mexican control, this republic was declared in 1846 by American settlers living in California; this political act was part of a larger American political and military strategy to wrest Texas and California from Mexico.

Beat Generation Literary movement of the 1950s that criticized the conformity of American society and the ever-present threat of atomic warfare; *On the Road* by Jack Kerouac, *Howl* by Allen Ginsberg, and *Naked Lunch* by William Burroughs were key works of the Beat Generation.

Berlin Airlift American and British pilots flew in food and fuel to West Berlin during late 1948 and early 1949 because Soviet Union and East Germany blockaded other access to West Berlin (which was located in East Germany); Stalin ended this blockade in May 1949. Airlift demonstrated American commitment to protecting Western allies in Europe during the early Cold War period.

Berlin Wall Concrete structure build in 1961 by Soviets and East Germany physically dividing East and West Berlin; to many in the West, the Wall was symbolic of communist repression in the Cold War era. The wall finally torn down in 1989.

Bessemer steel First produced in 1856 in converter (furnace) invented by Henry Bessemer; was much more durable and harder than iron. Steel was a critical commodity in the Second Industrial Revolution.

bicameral legislature A legislative structure consisting of two houses, this was adopted by the authors of the U.S. Constitution; membership of the states in one house (the House of Representatives) is determined by population, while in the other house (the Senate) all states have equal representation.

Bill of Rights Added to the Constitution in 1791, the first 10 amendments protected freedom of speech, freedom of the press, the right to bear arms, and other basic rights of American citizens.

Birth of a Nation Epic movie released in 1915 by director D. W. Griffith; portrayed the Reconstruction as a period when Southern blacks threatened basic American values, which the Ku Klux Klan tried to protect; film was lauded by many, including President Woodrow Wilson.

Black Codes Laws adopted by the Southern states in the Reconstruction era that greatly limited the freedom of Southern blacks; in several states blacks could not move, own land, or do anything but farm.

blacklist Prevented persons accused of being communists from getting work in entertainment and other industries during the period of anticommunist fervor of the late 1940s and early 1950s; some entertainers waited until the mid-1960s before working publicly again.

black nationalism Spurred by Malcolm X and other black leaders, a call for black pride and advancement without the help of whites; this appeared to be a repudiation of the calls for peaceful integration urged by Martin Luther King. Race riots in Northern cities in mid-1960s were at least partially fueled by supporters of black nationalism.

Black Panthers Group originally founded in Oakland, California, to protect blacks from police harassment; promoted militant black power; also ran social programs in several California cities. Founded by Bobby Seale and Huey P. Newton.

black power Movement of black Americans in the mid-1960s that emphasized pride in racial heritage and black economic and political self-reliance; term coined by black civil rights leader Stokely Carmichael.

"Bleeding Kansas" As a result of Kansas-Nebraska Act of 1854, residents of Kansas territory could decide if territory would allow slavery or not; as a result, both pro-slavery and antislavery groups flooded settlers into Kansas territory. Much violence followed very disputed elections in 1855.

bonanza farms Large farms that came to dominate agricultural life in much of the West in the late 1800s; instead of plots farmed by yeoman farmers, large amounts of machinery was used, and workers were hired laborers, often performing only specific tasks (similar to work in a factory).

Bonus Army Group of nearly 17,000 veterans who marched on Washington in May 1932 to demand the military bonuses they had been promised; this group was eventually driven from their camp city by the United States Army. This action increased the public perception that the Hoover administration cared little about the poor.

Boston Massacre Conflict between British soldiers and Boston civilians on March 5, 1770; after civilians threw rocks and snowballs at the soldiers, the soldiers opened fire, killing five and wounding six.

Boston Tea Party In response to the Tea Act and additional British taxes on tea, Boston radicals disguised as Native Americans threw nearly 350 chests of tea into Boston harbor on December 16, 1773.

Brown v. *Board of Education* 1954 Supreme Court decision that threw out the 1896 *Plessy* v. *Ferguson* ruling that schools could be "separate but equal"; ruling and began the long and painful process of school desegregation in the South and other parts of America.

Bulge, Battle of the December 1944 German attack that was the last major offensive by the Axis powers in World War II; Germans managed to push forward into Belgium but were then driven back. Attack was costly to the Germans in terms of material and manpower.

Bull Moose Party Name given to the Progressive party in the 1912 presidential campaign; Bull Moose candidate ex-president Theodore

Roosevelt ran against incumbent president William Howard Taft and Democrat Woodrow Wilson, with Wilson emerging victorious.

Bull Run, First Battle of July 21, 1861 Confederate victory over Union forces, which ended in Union forces fleeing in disarray toward Washington; this battle convinced Lincoln and others in the North that victory over the Confederates would not be as easy as they initially thought.

Bull Run, Second Battle of Decisive victory by General Robert E. Lee and Confederate forces over the Union army in August 1862.

Bunker Hill, Battle of June 1775 British attack on colonial forces at Breed's Hill outside Boston; despite frightful losses, the British emerged victorious in this battle.

Calvinism Militant Protestant faith that preached salvation "by faith alone" and predestination; desire by Calvinists in England to create a "pure church" in England was only partially successful, thus causing Calvinist Puritans to come to the New World starting in 1620.

Camp David Accords Treaty between Egypt and Israel brokered by President Jimmy Carter and signed in early 1979; Israel agreed to give back territory in the Sinai Peninsula to Egypt, while Egypt agreed to recognize Israel's right to exist as a nation.

carpetbaggers Term used by Southerners to mock Northerners who came to the South to gain either financially or politically during the Reconstruction era.

Central powers The alliance of Germany, Austria-Hungary, the Ottoman Empire, and Bulgaria that opposed England, France, Russia, and later the United States in World War I.

Chancellor of the Exchequer During the era prior to and during the Revolutionary War, this was the head of the department in the British government that issued and collected taxes; many acts issued by the Chancellor of the Exchequer created great resentment in the American colonies.

Chancellorsville, Battle of Brilliant Confederate attack on Union forces led by Stonewall Jackson and Robert E. Lee on May 2 to 3, 1863; Union defeat led to great pessimism in North and convinced many in the South that victory over North was indeed possible.

Chateau-Thierry, Battle of One of the first 1918 World War I battles where soldiers of the American Expeditionary Force fought and suffered severe casualties.

Checkers Speech Speech made by Richard Nixon on national television on September 23, 1952, where he defended himself against charges that rich supporters had set up a special expense account for his use; by the speech Nixon saved his spot on the 1952 Republican ticket (he was running for vice president, with Eisenhower running for president) and saved his political career.

Cherokee Nation* v. *Georgia 1831 Supreme Court case in which the Cherokee tribe claimed that Georgia had no right to enforce laws in Cherokee territory, since Cherokees were a sovereign nation; ruling by John Marshall stated that Cherokees were a "domestic dependent nation" and had no right to appeal in federal court.

Church of England Also called the Anglican Church, this was the Protestant church established by King Henry VIII; religious radicals desired a "purer" church that was allowed by monarchs of the early seventeenth century, causing some to come leave for the Americas.

Circular Letter In reaction to the 1767 Townshend Acts, the Massachusetts assembly circulated a letter to the other colonies, asking that they work together and jointly issue a petition of protest. Strong-willed response of British authorities to the letter influenced the colonial assemblies to work together on a closer basis.

Civilian Conservation Corps (CCC) New Deal program that began in 1933, putting nearly 3 million young men to work; workers were paid little, but worked on conservation projects and maintaining beaches and parks. CCC program for young women began in 1937.

Civil Rights Act of 1866 Act that struck down Black Codes and defined the rights of all citizens; also stated that federal government could act when civil rights were violated at the state level. Passed by Congress over the veto of President Andrew Johnson.

Civil Rights Act of 1964 Key piece of civil rights legislation that made discrimination on the basis of race, sex, religion or national origin illegal; segregation in public restrooms, bus stations, and other public facilities also was declared illegal.

Civil Service Commission Created by the Pendelton Civil Service Act of 1883, this body was in charge of testing applicants and assigning them to appropriate government jobs; filling jobs on the basis of merit replaced the spoils system, in which government jobs were given as rewards for political service.

Clayton Antitrust Act 1914 act designed to strengthen the Sherman Antitrust Act of 1890; certain activities previously committed by big businesses, such as not allowing unions in factories and not allowing strikes, were declared illegal.

Cold War Period between 1945 and 1991 of near-continuous struggle between the United States and its allies and the Soviet Union and its allies; Cold War tensions were made even more intense by the existence of the atomic bomb.

colonial assemblies Existed in all of the British colonies in America; House of Burgesses in Virginia was the first one. Members of colonial assemblies were almost always members of the upper classes of colonial society.

Committees of Correspondence First existed in Massachusetts, and eventually in all of the colonies; leaders of resistance to British rule listed their grievances against the British and circulated them to all of the towns of the colony.

Committee on Public Information Created by Woodrow Wilson during World War I to mobilize public opinion for the war, this was the most intensive use of propaganda until that time by the United States. The image of "Uncle Sam" was created for this propaganda campaign.

Common Sense Very popular 1776 publication in the colonies written by Englishman Thomas Paine, who had come to America in 1774; repudiated the entire concept of government by monarchy. After publication of this document, public sentiment in the colonies turned decisively toward a desire for independence.

Compromise of 1850 Complex agreement that temporarily lessened tensions between Northern and Southern political leaders, and prevented a possible secession crisis; to appease the South, the Fugitive Slave Act was strengthened; to appease the North, California entered the Union as a free state.

Compromise of 1877 Political arrangement that ended the contested presidential election of 1876. Representatives of Southern states agreed not to oppose the official election of Republican Rutherford B. Hayes as president despite massive election irregularities. In return, the Union army stopped enforcing Reconstruction legislation in the South, thus ending Reconstruction.

Concord, Battle of Occurred on April 19, 1775, between British regulars and Massachusetts militiamen. More than 70 British soldiers died and another 174 were wounded; as a result, a wider conflict between the colonies and the British became much more probable.

Confederate States of America Eventually made up of 11 former states with Jefferson Davis as its first and only president. Was unable to defeat the North because of lack of railroad lines, lack of industry, and an inability to get European nations to support their cause.

Congress of Industrial Organizations (CIO) Group of unions that broke from the A.F.L. in 1938 and organized effective union drives in automobile and rubber industries; supported sit-down strikes in major rubber plants. Reaffiliated with the A.F.L. in 1955.

conscription Getting recruits for military service using a draft; this method was used by the American government in all of the wars of the twentieth century. Conscription was viewed most negatively during the Vietnam War.

consumer society Many Americans in the 1950s became infatuated with all of the new products produced by technology and went out and purchased more than any prior generation; consumer tastes of the decade were largely dictated by advertising and television.

containment policy Formulated by George Kennan, a policy whereby the United States would forcibly stop communist aggression whenever and wherever it occurred; containment was the dominant American policy of the Cold War era, and forced America to become involved in foreign conflicts such as Vietnam.

Continentals Soldiers in the "American" army commanded by George Washington in the Revolutionary War; victory at the Battle of Trenton on December 16, 1776, did much to raise the morale of the soldiers (and convince many of them to reenlist).

Contract with America 1994 pledge by Republican candidates for House of Representatives; led by Newt Gingrich, candidates promised to support term limits, balancing the budget, and lessening the size of the federal government. In 1994 Congressional elections, Republicans won both houses of Congress for first time in 40 years.

convoy system System used to protect American ships carrying materials to Great Britain in 1940 and 1941; merchant ships were protected by American warships. Firing took place between these ships and German submarines, with American losses.

Copperheads Democrats in Congress in the first years of the Civil War who opposed Abraham Lincoln and the North's attack on the South, claiming that the war would result in massive numbers of freed slaves entering the North and a total disruption of the Northern economy.

Coral Sea, Battle of the May 1942 American naval victory over the Japanese; prevented Japanese from attacking Australia. First naval battle where losses on both sides came almost exclusively from bombing from airplanes.

counterculture Youth of the 1960s who espoused a lifestyle encompassing drug use, free love, and a rejection of adult authority; actual "hippies" were never more than a small percentage of young people.

Coxey's Army Supporters of Ohio Populist Jacob Coxey who in 1894 marched on Washington, demanded that the government create jobs for the unemployed; although this group had no effect whatsoever on policy, it did demonstrate the social and economic impact of the Panic of 1893.

creationism Belief in the Biblical account of the origin of the universe and the origin of man; believers in creationism and believers in evolution both had their day in court during the 1925 Scopes Trial.

Crittenden Plan 1860 compromise proposal on the slavery issue designed to defuse tension between North and South; would have allowed slavery to continue in the South and would have denied Congress the power to regulate interstate slave trade. On the advice of newly elected President Lincoln, Republicans in Congress voted against it.

Crusades From these attempts to recapture the Holy Land, Europeans acquired an appreciation of the benefits of overseas expansion and an appreciation of the economic benefits of slavery.

Cuban Missile Crisis 1962 conflict between the United States and the Soviet Union over Soviet missiles discovered in Cuba; Soviets eventually removed missiles under American pressure. Crisis was perhaps the closest the world came to armed conflict the Cold War era.

Currency Act 1764 British act forbidding the American colonies to issue paper money as legal tender; act was repealed in 1773 by the British as an effort to ease tensions between themselves and the colonies.

dark horse candidate A candidate for office with little support before the beginning of the nomination process; James K. Polk was the first dark horse candidate for president in 1844.

Dawes Act 1887 act designed to break up Native American tribes, offered Native American families 160 acres of farmland or 320 acres of land for grazing. Large amounts of tribal lands were not claimed by Native Americans, and thus were purchased by land speculators.

Declaration of Neutrality Issued by President Woodrow Wilson after the outbreak of World War I in Europe in 1914, stating that the United States would maintain normal relations with and continue to trade with both sides in the conflict; factors including submarine warfare made it difficult for America to maintain this policy.

Declaration of Rights and Grievances 1774 measure adopted by the First Continental Congress, stating that Parliament had some rights to regulate colonial trade with Britain, but that Parliament did not have the right to tax the colonies without their consent.

Declaratory Act 1766 British law stating that the Parliament had absolute right to tax the colonies as they saw fit and to make laws that would be enacted in the colonies. Ironically, issued at the same time as the repeal of the Stamp Act.

deficit spending Economic policy where government spends money that it "doesn't have", thus creating a budget deficit. Although "conventional" economic theory disapproves of this, it is commonplace during times of crisis or war (e.g. The New Deal; post-September 11, 2001).

Democratic party Had its birth during the candidacy of Andrew Jackson; originally drew its principles from Thomas Jefferson and advocated limited government. In modern times many Democrats favor domestic programs that a larger, more powerful government allows.

Democratic-Republicans Believed in the ideas of Thomas Jefferson, who wrote of the benefits of a limited government and of a society dominated by the values of the yeoman farmer. Opposed to the Federalists, who wanted a strong national state and a society dominated by commercial interests.

Desert Shield After Iraq invaded Kuwait on August 2, 1990, President Bush sent 230,000 American troops to protect Saudi Arabia.

Desert Storm February 1991 attack on Iraqi forces in Kuwait by United States and other allied forces; although Iraq was driven from Kuwait, Saddam Hussein remained in power in Iraq.

détente The lessening of tensions between nations. A policy of détente between the United States and the Soviet Union and Communist China began during the presidency of Richard Nixon; the architect of policy was National Security Advisor Henry Kissinger.

Dien Bien Phu 1954 victory of Vietnamese forces over the French, causing the French to leave Vietnam and all of Indochina; Geneva Peace Accords that followed established North and South Vietnam.

direct primary Progressive-era reform adopted by some states that allowed candidates for state offices to be nominated by the rank-and-file party members in statewide primaries instead of by the party bosses, who had traditionally dominated the nominating process.

"Dollar Diplomacy" Foreign policy of President William Howard Taft, which favored increased American investment in the world as the major method for instead increasing American influence and stability abroad; in some parts of the world, such as in Latin America, the increased American influence was resented.

domesticity Social trend of post-World War II America; many Americans turned to family and home life as a source of contentment; emphasis on family as a source of fulfillment forced some women to abandon the workforce and achieve "satisfaction" as homemakers.

Dominion of New England Instituted by King James II in 1686, Sir Edmund Andros governed as a single entity the colonies of Massachusetts, Connecticut, Rhode Island, New York, Plymouth, and New Hampshire without an elective assembly; Andros was finally overthrown by militiamen in Boston in April 1689 (after the Glorious Revolution).

domino theory Major tenet of Cold War containment policy of the United States held that if one country in a region turned communist, other surrounding countries would soon follow; this theory convinced many that to save all of Southeast Asia, it was necessary to resist communist aggression in Vietnam.

Double V campaign World War II "policy" supported by several prominent black newspapers, stating that blacks in America should work for victory over the Axis powers but at the same time work for victory over oppression at home; black leaders remained frustrated during the war by continued segregation of the armed forces.

Dred Scott case Supreme Court case involving a man who was born a slave but had then lived in both a nonslave state and a nonslave territory and was now petitioning for his legal freedom; in 1857 the Court ruled that slaves were not people but were property, that they could not be citizens of the United States, and thus had no legal right to petition the Court for anything. Ruling also stated that Missouri Compromise, which banned slavery in the territories, was unconstitutional.

Dust Bowl Great Plains region that suffered severe drought and experienced severe dust storms during the 1930s; because of extreme conditions many who lived in the Dust Bowl left their farms and went to California to work as migrant farmers.

Eisenhower Doctrine Policy established in 1957 that promised military and economic aid to "friendly" nations in the Middle East; policy was established to prevent communism from gaining a foothold in the region. Policy first utilized later that year when United States gave large amounts of aid to King Hussein of Jordan to put down internal rebellion.

Electoral College Procedure outlined in the Constitution for the election of the president; under this system, votes of electors from each state, and not the popular vote, determine who is elected president. As was demonstrated in 2000 presidential election, this system allows a person to be elected president who does not win the nationwide popular vote.

Emancipation Proclamation Edict by Abraham Lincoln that went into effect on January 1, 1863, abolishing slavery in the Confederate states; proclamation did not affect the four slave states that were still part of the Union (so not to alienate them).

Embargo of 1807 Declaration by President Thomas Jefferson that banned all American trade with Europe. As a result of the war between England and Napoleon's France, America's sea rights as a neutral power were threatened; Jefferson hoped the embargo would force England and France to respect American neutrality.

Emergency Quota Act Also called the Johnson Act, this 1921 bill limited immigration from Southern and Eastern Europe by stating that in a year, total immigration from any country could only equal 3 percent of the number of immigrations from that country living in the United States in 1910.

Enlightenment Eighteenth-century European intellectual movement that attempted to discover the natural laws that governed science and society and taught that progress was inevitable in the Western world. Americans were greatly influenced by the Enlightenment, especially by the ideas of John Locke, who stated that government should exist for the benefit of the people living under it.

Enola Gay The name of the American bomber that on August 6, 1945, dropped the first atomic bomb on the city of Hiroshima, thus initiating the nuclear age.

Era of Good Feelings Term used by a newspaper of the period to describe the years between 1816 and 1823, when after the end of the War of 1812 the United States remained generally free of foreign conflicts and when political strife at home was at a bare minimum (because of the collapse of the Federalist party).

Espionage Act World War I-era regulation passed in 1917 that ordered severe penalties for citizens who criticized the war effort or the government; mandatory prison sentences were also proclaimed for those who interfered with the draft process. Nearly 700 Americans were arrested for violating this act.

Essex Junto Group of Massachusetts Federalists who met to voice their displeasure with the policies of Thomas Jefferson during Jefferson's second term, and proposed that the New England states and New York secede from the Union.

Exodusters Large number of Southern blacks who left the South and moved to Kansas for a "better life" after Reconstruction ended in 1877; many failed to find satisfaction in Kansas because of lack of opportunities and open hostility from Kansas residents.

Fair Deal A series of domestic programs proposed to Congress by President Harry Truman that included a Fair Employment Practices Act, a call for government construction of public housing, an extension of Social Security, and a proposal to ensure employment for all American workers.

Farmer's Alliances After the decline of Grange organizations, these became the major organizations of farmers in the 1880s; many experimented with cooperative buying and selling. Many local alliances became involved in direct political activity with the growth of the Populist Party in the 1890s.

Federalists During the period when the Constitution was being ratified, these were the supporters of the larger national government as outlined in the Constitution; the party of Washington and John Adams, it was supported by commercial interests. Federalists were opposed by Jeffersonians, who favored a smaller federal government and a society dominated by agrarian values. Federalist influence in national politics ended with presidential election of 1816.

Federal Deposit Insurance Corporation (FDIC) Passed during the first Hundred Days of the administration of Franklin Roosevelt, this body insured individual bank deposits up to $2500 and helped to restore confidence in America's banks.

Federal Reserve System Established by Federal Reserve Act of 1913, this system established 12 district reserve banks to be controlled by the banks in each district; in addition, a Federal Reserve Board was established to regulate the entire structure. This act improved public confidence in the banking system.

Federal Trade Commission Authorized after the passage of the Clayton Antitrust Act of 1914, it was established as the major government body in charge of regulating big business. The FTC investigated possible violations of antitrust laws.

Feminine Mystique, The Betty Friedan's 1963 book that was the Bible of the feminist movement of the 1960s and 1970s. Friedan maintained that the post-World War II emphasis on family forced women to think of themselves primarily as housewives and robbed them of much of their creative potential.

feminism The belief that women should have the same rights and benefits in American society that men do. Feminism gained many supporters during the Progressive era, and in the 1960s drew large numbers of supporters. The National Organization for Women (NOW) was established in 1966 by Betty Friedan and had nearly 200,000 members in 1969.

Fifteenth Amendment Ratified in 1870, this amendment stated that a persons could not be denied the right to vote because of the color of their skin or whether or not they had been a slave. This extended the rights of blacks to vote to the North (which the Emancipation Proclamation had not done); some in the women's movement opposed the amendment on the grounds that it did nothing for the rights of women.

Final Solution The plan of Adolf Hitler and Nazi Germany to eliminate Jewish civilization from Europe; by the end of the war in 1945, nearly 6 million Jews had been executed. The full extent of Germany's atrocities was not known in Europe and the United States until near the end of World War II.

fireside chats Broadcasts on the radio by Franklin Roosevelt addressed directly to the American people that made many Americans feel that he personally cared about them; FDR did 16 of these in his first two terms. Many Americans in the 1930s had pictures of Roosevelt in their living rooms; in addition, Roosevelt received more letters from ordinary Americans than any other president in American history.

flapper A "new woman" of the 1920s, who wore short skirts and bobbed hair and rejected many of the social regulations that controlled women of previous generations.

Food and Drug Act 1906 bill that created a federal Food and Drug Administration; example of consumer protection legislation of the progressive era, it was at least partially passed as a result of Upton Sinclair's novel *The Jungle*.

Force Act 1832 legislation that gave President Andrew Jackson the power to invade any state if that action was necessary to enforce federal law; bill was in response to nullification of federal tariff regulation by the legislature of South Carolina.

Fordney-McCumber Tariff 1922 act that sharply increased tariffs on imported goods; most Republican leaders of the 1920s firmly believed in "protectionist" policies that would increase profits for American businesses.

Fort Sumter Federal fort located in Charleston, South Carolina, that was fired on by Confederate artillery on April 12, 1861; these were the first shots actually fired in the Civil War. A public outcry immediately followed across the Northern states, and the mobilization of a federal army began.

Fourteen Points Woodrow Wilson's view of a post-World War I that he hoped the other Allied powers would endorse during the negotiations for the Treaty of Versailles; Wilson's vision included elimination of secret treaties, arms reduction, national self-determination, and the creation of a League of Nations. After negotiations, only the League of Nations remained (which the United States never became part of).

Fourteenth Amendment Ratified in 1868, this amendment stated that "all persons born or naturalized in the United States" were citizens. In addition, all former Confederate supporters were prohibited from holding office in the United States.

Franciscans Missionaries that established settlements in the Southwestern United States in the late 1500s; at their missions Christian conversion was encouraged, but at the same time Native Americans were used as virtual slaves. Rebellions against the missions and the soldiers sent to protect them began in 1598.

Fredericksburg, Battle of Battle on December 13, 1862, where the Union army commanded by General Ambrose Burnside suffered a major defeat at the hands of Confederate forces.

freedmen Term used for free blacks in the South after the Civil War. Freedman enjoyed some gains in terms of education, the ability to hold office, and economic well-being during the Reconstruction era, although many of these gains were wiped out after the Compromise of 1877.

Freedom Rides Buses of black and white civil rights workers who in 1961 rode on interstate buses to the Deep South to see if Southern states were abiding by the 1960 Supreme Court ruling banning segregation on interstate buses and waiting rooms and restaurants at bus stations. Buses met mob violence in numerous cities; federal marshals were finally called to protect the freedom riders.

Freeport Doctrine Introduced by Stephen Douglas in the Lincoln-Douglas debates, the idea that despite the Dred Scott Supreme Court decision, a territory could still prevent slavery by electing officials who were opposed to it and by creating laws and regulations that would make slavery impossible to enforce.

Free-Soil party Political party that won 10 percent of the vote in the 1848 presidential election; they were opposed to the spread of slavery into any of the recently acquired American territories. Free-Soil supporters were mainly many former members of the Whig party in the North.

Free Speech Movement Protests at the University of California at Berkeley in 1964 and 1965 that opposed the control that the university, and "the establishment" in general, had over the lives of university students. Protesters demanded changes in university regulations and also broader changes in American society.

free trade The philosophy that trade barriers and protective tariffs inhibit long-term economic growth; this philosophy was the basis for the 1994 ratification by the United States of the North American Free Trade Agreement (NAFTA), which removed trade restrictions between the United States, Mexico, and Canada.

French and Indian War Called the Seven Years War in European textbooks, in this war between the British and the French fought for the right to expand their empire in the Americas. Colonists and Native Americans fought on both sides, and the war eventually spilled to Europe and elsewhere. The English emerged victorious, and in the end received all of French Canada.

Fugitive Slave Act Part of the Compromise of 1850, this legislation set up special commissions in Northern states to determine if an accused runaway slave really was one; according to regulations, after the verdict, commissioners were given more money if the black was found to be a runaway than if he or she was found not to be one. Some Northern legislatures passed laws attempting to circumvent the Fugitive Slave Act.

Gadsden Purchase Strip of territory running through Arizona and New Mexico that the United States purchased from Mexico in 1853; President Pierce authorized this purchase to secure that the southern route of the transcontinental railroad (between Texas and California) would be in American territory.

Geneva Accords After the French were defeated in Vietnam, a series of agreements made in 1954 that temporarily divided Vietnam into a two parts (along the 17th parallel) and promised nationwide elections within two years. To prevent communists from gaining control, the United States installed a friendly government in South Vietnam and saw that the reunification elections never took place.

Gettysburg Address Speech made by Abraham Lincoln at dedication ceremony for a cemetery for Union soldiers who died at the Battle of Gettysburg; in this November 19, 1863 speech, Lincoln stated that freedom should exist in the United States for *all* men, and that "government of the people, by the people, for the people, shall not perish from the earth."

Gettysburg, Battle of The most important battle of the Civil War, this July 1863 victory by Union forces prevented General Robert E. Lee from invading the North. Defeat at Gettysburg, along with defeat at the Battle of Vicksburg during the same month, turned the tide of war firmly in the direction of Union forces.

Ghent, Treaty of 1814 treaty between the United States and Great Britain ending the War of 1812; treaty restored diplomatic relations between the two countries but did nothing to address the issues that had initially caused war.

Ghost Dances Religion practiced by Lakota tribesmen in response to repeated incursions by American settlers. Ghost dancers thought that Native American messiah would come and banish the whites, return the buffalo, and give all former Native American land back to the Native Americans. Worried territorial officials had Sitting Bull arrested (he was later killed under uncertain circumstances) and killed another 240 Lakota at Wounded Knee Creek.

GI Popular term for American servicemen during World War II; refers to the fact that virtually anything they wore or used was "government issued."

GI Bill Officially called the Serviceman's Readjustment Act of 1944, this legislation gave many benefits to returning World War II veterans, including financial assistance for veterans wanting to go to college or enter other job training programs, special loan programs for veterans wanting to buy homes or businesses, and preferential treatment for veterans who wished to apply for government jobs.

globalization Belief that the United States should work closely with other nations of the world to solve common problems; this was the foreign policy approach of President Clinton. Policies that supported this approach included the ratification of NAFTA, the United States working more closely with the United Nations, and "nation building" abroad. Many policies of globalization were initially rejected by Clinton's successor, George W. Bush.

Glorious Revolution English revolution of 1688 to 1689 where King James II was removed from the throne and his Protestant daughter Mary and her Dutch husband William began to rule. Reaction to this in the American colonies was varied: There was a revolt against appointed Catholic officials in New York and Maryland, and in Massachusetts the governor was sent back to England with the colonial demand that the Dominion of New England be disbanded.

gold standard Economic system that bases all currency on gold, meaning that all paper currency could be exchanged at a bank for gold. Business interests of the late nineteenth century supported this; William Jennings Bryan ran for president three times opposing the gold standard, and supported the free coinage of silver instead.

"Gospel of Wealth" The philosophy of steel magnate Andrew Carnegie, who stated that wealthy industrialists had an obligation to create a "trust fund" from their profits to help their local communities. By the time of his death, Carnegie had given over 90 percent of his wealth to various foundations and philanthropic endeavors.

Grange Initially formed in 1867, the Grange was an association of farmers that provided social activities and information about new farming techniques. Some local Grange organizations became involved in cooperative buying and selling.

Great Awakening A religious revival in the American colonies that lasted from the 1720s through the 1740s; speakers like Jonathan Edwards enraptured speakers with sermons such as "Sinners in the Hands of an Angry God." Religious splits in the colonies became deeper because of this movement.

Great Compromise Plan drafted by Roger Sherman of Connecticut that stated one house of the United States Congress would be based on population (the House of Representatives), while in the other house all states would be represented equally (the Senate). This compromise greatly speeded the ratification of the Constitution.

Great Migration Migration of large numbers of American blacks to Midwestern and Eastern industrial cities than began during World War I and continued throughout the 1920s. Additional workers were needed in the North because of the war and during the 1920s because of immigration restrictions; blacks were willing to leave the South because of continued lynchings there and the fact that their economic situation was not improving.

Great Society Aggressive program announced by President Lyndon Johnson in 1965 to attack the major social problems in America; Great Society programs included the War on Poverty, Medicare and Medicaid programs for elderly Americans, greater protection for and more legislation dealing with civil rights, and greater funding for education. Balancing the Great Society and the war in Vietnam would prove difficult for the Johnson administration.

Greenback party Political party of the 1870s and early 1880s that stated the government should put more money in circulation and supported an eight-hour workday and female suffrage. The party received support from farmers but never built a national base. The Greenback party argued into the 1880s that more greenbacks should be put in circulation to help farmers who were in debt and who saw the prices of their products decreasing annually.

"Greenbacks" Paper money issued by the American government during and immediately after the

Civil War that was not backed up by gold or silver.

gridlock Situation when the president is a member of one political party and the U.S. Congress is controlled by the other party, causing a situation where little legislation is actually passed. This is how some describe the situation with President Clinton and the Republican-controlled Congress after the 1994 congressional elections.

Guadalcanal, Battle of Battle over this Pacific island lasted from August 1942 through February 1943; American victory against fierce Japanese resistance was the first major offensive victory for the Americans in the Pacific War.

Guadeloupe-Hidalgo, Treaty of Treaty ending the war with Mexico that was ratified by the Senate in March 1848 and for $15 million gave the United States Texas territory to the Rio Grande River, New Mexico, and California.

Guilded Age, The Some historians describe the late nineteenth century in this manner, describing it as an era with a surface of great prosperity hiding deep problems of social inequity and shallowness of culture. The term comes from the title of an 1873 Mark Twain novel.

Gulf of Tonkin Resolution 1964 Congressional resolution that gave President Johnson the authority to "take all necessary measures to repel" attacks against American military forces stationed in Vietnam. Later, critics would charge this resolution allowed the president to greatly expand the Vietnam War without congressional oversight.

Harlem Renaissance Black literary and artistic movement centered in Harlem that lasted from the 1920s into the early 1930s that both celebrated and lamented black life in America; Langston Hughes and Zora Neale Hurston were two famous writers of this movement.

Hartford Convention Meeting of New England Federalists in the closing months of the War of 1812 where they threatened that New England would secede from the United States unless trade restrictions imposed by President Madison were lifted. American victory in the war made their protests seem pointless.

Hawley-Smoot Tariff In response to the initial effects of the Great Depression, Congress authorized this tariff in 1930; this established tariff rates on imported goods at the highest level of any point in United States history. Some American companies benefited in the short term, although the effect on world trade was disastrous, as many other countries erected tariff barriers on American imports.

Haymarket Square Location in Chicago of labor rally called by anarchist and other radical labor leaders on May 2, 1886. A bomb was hurled toward police officials, and police opened fired on the demonstrators; numerous policemen and demonstrators were killed and wounded. Response in the nation's press was decidedly anti-union.

Head Start One of Lyndon Johnson's War on Poverty programs that gave substantial funding for a nursery school program to prepare children of poor parents for kindergarten.

Heavy industry The production of steel, iron, and other materials that can be used for building purposes; great increase in heavy industry fueled the massive industrial growth that took place in the last half on the nineteenth century.

Hessians German troops who fought in the Revolutionary War on the side of Great Britain; Hessian troops were almost all paid mercenaries.

Holding company A company that existed to gain monopoly control over an industry by buying large numbers of shares of stock in as many companies as possible in that industry. The best example in American history was John D. Rockefeller's Standard Oil corporation.

Holocaust Historical term used for the extermination of 6 million Jewish victims by Nazi Germany during World War II. Much has been written on the reasons for the Holocaust and why it occurred in Germany.

Homestead Act 1862 enactment by Congress that gave 160 acres of publicly owned land to a farmer who lived on the land and farmed it for two years. The provisions of this bill inspired hundreds of thousands of Americans to move westward in the years after the Civil War.

Hoovervilles Groups of crude houses made of cardboard and spare wood that sprung up on the fringes of many American cities during the first years of the Great Depression. These shacks were occupied by unemployed workers; the name of these communities demonstrated the feeling that President Hoover should have been doing more to help the downtrodden in America.

horizontal integration The strategy of gaining as much control over an entire single industry as possible, usually by creating trusts and holding companies. The most successful example of horizontal integration was John D. Rockefeller and Standard Oil, who had at one point controlled over 92 percent of the oil production in the United States.

HUAC (House Un-American Activities Committee) Committee of the House of Representatives that beginning in 1947 investigated possible communist infiltration of the entertainment industry and, more importantly, of the government. Most famous investigations of the committee were the investigation of the "Hollywood Ten" and the investigation of Alger Hiss, a former high-ranking member of the State Department.

Huguenots Protestants in France, who by the 1630s were believers in Calvinism. Few Huguenots ended up settling in the Americas, as French officials feared they would disrupt the unity of colonial settlements.

Hull House Established by Jane Addams and Ellen Gates Starr in Chicago in 1889, this was the first settlement house in America. Services such as reading groups, social clubs, an employment bureau, and a "day care center" for working mothers could be found at Hull House. The Hull House model was later copied in many other urban centers.

"Hun" Term used in allied propaganda during World War I to depict the German soldier; Germans were portrayed as bloodthirsty beasts. World War I was the first war where propaganda was used on a widespread scale.

Hundred Days The period from March through June of 1933; the first 100 days of the New Deal presidency of Franklin Roosevelt. During this period programs were implemented to assist farmers, the banks, unemployed workers, and businessmen; in addition, prohibition was repealed.

hunter-gatherers Early civilizations that existed not by farming but by moving from region to region and taking what was necessary at the time from the land; some early Native American tribes in northern New England lived as hunter-gatherers.

hydrogen bomb Atomic weapons much more powerful than those used at Hiroshima and Nagasaki, these were developed and repeatedly tested by both the United States and the Soviet Union in the 1950s, increasing dramatically the potential danger of nuclear war.

impeachment The process of removing an elected public official from office; during the Progressive Era several states adopted measures making it easier to do this. Presidents Andrew Johnson and William Jefferson Clinton were both impeached by the House of Representatives, but neither was convicted by the U.S. Senate (the procedure outlined in the Constitution of the United States).

impressment British practice of forcing civilians and ex-sailors back into naval service; during the wars against Napoleon the British seized nearly 7500 sailors from American ships, including some that had actually become American citizens. This practice caused increased tensions between the United States and Great Britain and was one of the causes of the War of 1812.

Inca empire Advanced and wealthy civilization centered in the Andes mountain region; aided by smallpox, Francisco Pizarro conquered the Incas in 1533.

indentured servants Legal arrangement when an individual owed compulsory service (in some cases only 3 years, in others up to 10) for free passage to the American colonies. Many of the early settlers in the Virginia colony came as indentured servants.

Industrial Workers of the World (I.W.W.) Established in 1905, this union attempted to unionize the unskilled workers who were usually not recruited by the American Federation of Labor. The I.W.W. included blacks, poor sharecroppers, and newly arrived immigrants from Eastern Europe. Members of the union were called "Wobblies," and leaders of the union were inspired by Marxist principles.

Influence of Sea Power upon History, The Very influential 1890 book by Admiral Alfred Thayer Mahan, which argued that throughout history the most powerful nations have achieved their influence largely because of powerful navies. Mahan called for a large increase in the size of the American navy, the acquisition of American bases in the Pacific, and the building of the Panama Canal.

initiative process Procedure supported by the Populist party in 1890s where any proposed law could go on the public ballot as long as a petition with an appropriate number of names is submitted beforehand supporting the proposed law.

internment camps Controversial decision was made after the bombing of Pearl Harbor to place Japanese-Americans living on the West Coast in these camps. President Roosevelt authorized this by Executive Order #9066; this order was validated by the Supreme Court in 1944. In 1988 the U.S. government paid compensation to surviving detainees.

Interstate Commerce Act Passed in 1887, the bill created America's first regulatory commission, the Interstate Commerce Commission. The task of this commission was to regulate the railroad and railroad rates, and to ensure that rates were "reasonable and just."

Intolerable Acts Term used by anti-British speakers across the colonies for the series of bills passed in Great Britain to punish the Massachusetts colony for the Boston Tea Party of December 1773. These including the closing of Boston harbor, prohibiting local meetings, and mandatory quartering of troops in the homes of Massachusetts residents.

Iran-Contra Affair During the second term of the Reagan administration, government officials sold missiles to Iran (hoping that this would help free American hostages held in Lebanon); money from this sale was used to aid anticommunist Contra forces in Nicaragua. Iran was a country that was supposed to be on the American "no trade" list because of their taking of American hostages, and congressional legislation had been enacted making it illegal to give money to the Contras. A major scandal for the Reagan administration.

Iranian Hostage Crisis On November 4, 1979, Islamic fundamentalists seized the American embassy in Tehran, Iran, and took all Americans working there hostage. This was a major humiliation for the United States, as diplomatic and military efforts to free the hostages failed. The hostages were finally freed on January 20, 1981, immediately after the inauguration of Ronald Reagan.

ironclad ship Civil War-era ships that were totally encased in iron, thus making them very difficult to damage; the ironclad of the Confederate army was the *Virginia* (it had been the *Merrimac* when it was captured from the Union), whereas the Union ship was the *Monitor*. The two ships battled each other in March 1862, with both being badly damaged.

Iron Curtain In a March 5, 1946 speech in Fulton, Missouri, Winston Churchill used this term to describe the division that the Soviet Union had created between itself and its Eastern European allies and Western Europe and the United States. Churchill emphasized the need for the United States to stand up to potential Soviet aggression in the future.

"Irreconcilables" After World War I, a group of U.S. senators who were opposed to a continued U.S. presence in Europe in any form. This group was influential in preventing the passage of the Versailles Treaty in the Senate.

island-hopping A successful American military tactic in the Pacific in 1942 and 1943 of taking strategic islands that could used as staging points for continued military offensives. Increasing American dominance in air power made this tactic possible.

isolationism A policy of disengaging the United States from major world commitments and concentrating on the U.S. domestic issues. This was the dominant foreign policy of the United States for much of the 1920s and the 1930s.

Jay's Treaty 1794 treaty between the United States and Great Britain designed to ease increasing tensions between the two nations; the British did

make some concessions to the Americans, including abandoning the forts they occupied in the interior of the continent. However, Britain refused to make concessions to America over the rights of American ships; tensions over this issue would eventually be a cause of the War of 1812.

Jazz Age Term used to describe the image of the liberated, urbanized 1920s, with a flapper as a dominant symbol of that era. Many rural, fundamentalist Americans deeply resented the changes in American culture that occurred in the "Roaring 20s."

Jazz Singer, The 1927 film starring Al Jolson that was the first movie with sound. Story of the film deals with young Jewish man who has to choose between the "modern" and his Jewish past.

Jesuits Missionary group who established settlements in Florida, New Mexico, Paraguay, and in several areas within French territory in North America. Jesuits were organized with military precision and order.

jingoism American foreign policy based on a strident nationalism, a firm belief in American world superiority, and a belief that military solutions were, in almost every case, the best ones. Jingoism was most evident in America during the months leading up to and during the Spanish-American War.

Judiciary Act 1801 bill passed by the Federalist Congress just before the inauguration of President Thomas Jefferson; Federalists in this bill attempted to maintain control of the judiciary by reducing the number of Supreme Court judges (so Jefferson probably wouldn't be able to name a replacement) and by increasing the number of federal judges (who President Adams appointed before he left office). Bill was repealed by new Congress in 1802.

Judicial Review In the 1803 *Marbury* v. *Madison* decision, Chief Justice John C. Marshall stated that the U.S. Supreme Court ultimately had the power to decide on the constitutionality of any law passed by the U.S. Congress or by the legislature of any state. Many had argued that individual states should have the power to do this; the *Marbury* decision increased the power of the federal government.

Justice Reorganization Bill Franklin Roosevelt's 1937 plan to increase the number of Supreme Court justices. He claimed that this was because many of the judges were older and needed help keeping up with the work; in reality he wanted to "pack the court" because the Court had made several rulings outlawing New Deal legislation. Many Democrats and Republicans opposed this plan, so it was finally dropped by Roosevelt.

kamikaze pilots 1945 tactic of Japanese air force where pilots flew at American ships at full speed and crashed into them, in several cases causing ships to sink. This tactic showed the desperate nature of the Japanese military situation at this time; by July 1945, kamikaze attacks were no longer utilized, as Japan was running out of airplanes and pilots.

Kansas-Nebraska Act 1854 compromise legislation crafted by Stephen Douglas that allowed the settlers in the Kansas and Nebraska territories to decide if those territories would be slave or free. Bill caused controversy and bloodshed throughout these territories; in the months before the vote in Kansas, large numbers of "settlers" moved in to influence the vote, and after the vote (won by pro-slavery forces), violence between the two sides intensified.

Kent State University Site of May 1970 antiwar protest where Ohio National Guardsmen fired on protesters, killing four. To many, this event was symbolic of the extreme political tensions that permeated American society in this era.

Kentucky and Virginia Resolves Passed by the legislatures in these two states, these resolutions maintained that the Alien and Sedition Acts championed through Congress by John Adams went beyond the powers that the Constitution stated belonged to the federal government. These resolves predated that later Southern argument that individual states could "nullify" federal laws deemed unconstitutional by the states.

Kerner Commission Established in 1967 to study the reason for urban riots, the commission spoke at length about the impact of poverty and racism on the lives of urban blacks in America, and emphasized that white institutions created and condoned the ghettoes of America.

King William's War Colonial war against the French that lasted from 1689 to 1697; army from New England colonies attacked Quebec, but were forced to retreat because of the lack of strong colonial leadership and an outbreak of smallpox among colonial forces.

Kitchen Cabinet An informal group of advisors, with no official titles, who the president relies on for advice. The most famous Kitchen Cabinet was that of Andrew Jackson, who met with several old political friends and two journalists for advice on many occasions.

Knights of Labor The major labor union of the 1880s; was not a single large union, but a federation of the unions of many industries. The Knights of Labor accepted unskilled workers; publicity against the organization was intense after the Haymarket Square riot of 1886.

Know-Nothing party Political party that developed in the 1850s that claimed that the other political parties and the entire political process was corrupt, that immigrants were destroying the economic base of American by working for low wages, and that Catholics in America were intent on destroying American democracy. Know-Nothings were similar in many ways to other nativist groups that developed at various points in America's history.

Korean War 1950 to 1953 war where American and other United Nations forces fought to stop communist aggression against South Korea. U.S. entry into Korean War was totally consistent with the U.S. Cold War policy of containment. Negotiated settlement divided Korea along the 38th parallel, a division that remains today.

Ku Klux Klan Organization founded in the South during the Reconstruction era by whites that wanted to maintain white supremacy in the region. KKK used terror tactics, including murder. The Klan was revitalized in the 1920s; members of the 1920s Klan also opposed Catholics and Southern and Eastern European immigrants. The KKK exists to this day, with recent efforts to make the Klan appear to be "respectable."

labor movement The drive that began in the second half of the nineteenth century to have workers join labor unions. Divisions existed in nineteenth-century unions on whether unions should focus their energies on political gains for workers or on "bread and butter" issues important to workers. In the twentieth century, unions have broad political powers, as most endorse and financially support candidates in national and statewide elections.

Laissez-faire economic principles Economic theory derived from eighteenth-century economist Adam Smith, who stated that for the economy to run soundly the government should take a hands-off role in economic matters. Those who have favored policies such as high import tariffs do *not* follow laissez-faire policies; a policy like NAFTA has more support amongst the "free market" supporters of Adam Smith.

land speculation The practice of buying up land with the intent of selling it off in the future for a profit. Land speculation existed in the Kentucky territory in the 1780s, throughout the West after the Homestead Act, and in Florida in the 1920s, when hundreds bought Florida swampland hoping to later sell it for a profit.

League of Nations International body of nations that was proposed by Woodrow Wilson and was adopted at the Versailles Peace Conference ending

World War I. The League was never an effective body in reducing international tensions, at least partially because the United States was never a member of it.

Lend-Lease Act Legislation proposed by Franklin Roosevelt and adopted by Congress in 1941, stating that the United States could either sell or lease arms and other equipment to any country whose security was vital to America's interest. After the passage of this bill, military equipment to help the British war effort began to be shipped from the United States.

Letters from a Farmer in Pennsylvania A 1767 pamphlet by Pennsylvania attorney and land-owner John Dickinson, in which he eloquently stated the "taxation without representation" argument, and also stated that the only way that the House of Commons could represent the colonies in a meaningful way would be for actual colonists to be members of it.

Lever Food and Fuel Control Act August 1917 measure that gave President Wilson the power to regulate the production and consumption of food and fuels during wartime. Some in his administration argued for price controls and rationing; instead, Wilson instituted voluntary controls.

Levittown After World War II, the first "suburban" neighborhood; located in Hempstead, Long Island, houses in this development were small, looked the same, but were perfect for the postwar family that wanted to escape urban life. Levittown would become a symbol of the post-World War II flight to suburbia taken by millions.

Lewis and Clark Expedition 1803 to 1806 mission sent by Thomas Jefferson to explore and map the newly acquired Louisiana territory and to create good relations with various Native American tribes within the territory. Reports brought back indicated that settlement was possible in much of the region, and that the Louisiana territory was well worth what had been paid for it.

Lexington Massachusetts town where the first skirmish between British troops and colonial militiamen took place; during this April 19, 1775 "battle," eight colonists were killed and another nine were wounded.

Liberator, The The radical abolitionist journal of William Lloyd Garrison that was first published in 1831; Garrison and his journal presented the most extreme abolitionist views during the period leading up to the Civil War.

Liberty Bonds Sold to United States civilians during World War I; a holder who paid $10 for a bond could get $13 back if the holder held onto the bond until it matured. Bonds were important in financing the war effort, and celebrities such as Charlie Chaplin made short films encouraging Americans to buy them.

Little Bighorn, Battle of the 1876 Montana battle where Colonel George Custer and 300 of his men were killed by a group of Cheyenne and Lakota warriors. This was the last major victory by Native American forces over a U.S. army unit.

London Company In 1603 King James I gave the London Company a charter to settle the Virginia territory. In April 1607, the first settlers from this company settled at Jamestown.

"Lost Generation" Group of American intellectuals who viewed America in the 1920s as bigoted, intellectually shallow, and consumed by the quest for the dollar; many became extremely disillusioned with American life and went to Paris. Ernest Hemingway wrote of this group in *The Sun Also Rises*.

Louisiana Purchase The 1803 purchase of the huge Louisiana territory (from the Mississippi River out to the Rocky Mountains) from Napoleon for $15 million. This purchase made eventual westward movement possible for vast numbers of Americans.

Lowell System Developed in the textile mills of Lowell, Massachusetts, in the 1820s, in these factories as much machinery as possible was used, so that few skilled workers were needed in the process, and the workers were almost all single young farm women, who worked for a few years and then returned home to be housewives. Managers found these young women were the perfect workers for this type of factory life.

Loyalists Individuals who remained loyal to Great Britain during the years up to and during the Revolutionary War. Many who were Loyalists were from the higher strata of colonial society; when war actually broke out and it became apparent that the British were not going to quickly win, almost all went to Canada, the West Indies, or back to Great Britain.

Loyalty Review Boards These were established in 1947 in an effort to control possible communist influence in the American government. These boards were created to investigate the possibility of "security risks" working for the American government, and to determine if those "security risks" should lose their jobs. Some employees were released because of their affiliation with "unacceptable" political organizations or because of their sexual orientation.

Lusitania British passenger liner with 128 Americans on board that was sunk of the coast of Ireland by a German U-boat on May 7, 1915. This sinker caused outrage in the United States and was one of a series of events that drew the United States closer to war with Germany.

Manhattan Project Program begun in 1941 to develop an atomic weapon for the United States; project was aided by German scientists added to the research team who had been working on a similar bomb in Germany. First test of the bomb took place in New Mexico on July 16, 1945.

manifest destiny Term first used in the 1840s, the concept that America's expansion westward was as journalist John O'Sullivan said, "the fulfillment of our manifest destiny to overspread the continent allotted by Providence for the free development of our yearly multiplying millions."

Man in the Gray Flannel Suit, The Early 1950s book and movie that compares the sterility, sameness, and lack of excitement of postwar work and family life with the vitality felt by many World War II veterans during their wartime experiences.

Marbury v. Madison 1803 decision of this case written by Chief Justice John Marshall established the principle of judicial review, meaning that the Supreme Court ultimately has the power to decide if any federal or state law is unconstitutional.

March on Washington Over 200,000 came to Washington for this August 1963 event demanding civil rights for blacks. A key moment of the proceedings was Martin Luther King's "I have a dream speech"; the power of the civil rights movement was not lost on Lyndon Johnson, who pushed for civil rights legislation when he became president the following year.

Marshall Plan Plan announced in 1947 whereby the United States would help to economically rebuild Europe after the war; 17 Western European nations became part of the plan. The United States introduced the plan so that communism would not spread across war-torn Europe and bring other European countries into the communist camp.

Massacre at Wounded Knee December 28, 1890 "battle" that was the last military resistance of Native Americans of the Great Plains against American encroachment. Minneconjou Indians were at Wounded Knee creek. American soldiers attempted to take their arms from them; after shooting began, 25 American soldiers died, along with 150 men, women, and children of the Indian tribe.

martial law During a state of emergency, when rule of law may be suspended and government is controlled by military or police authorities. During the Civil War, Kentucky was placed under martial law by President Lincoln.

massive retaliation Foreign policy officials in the Eisenhower administration believed the best way to stop communism was to convince the communists that every time they advanced, there would be massive retaliation against them. This policy explains the desire in this era to increase the nuclear arsenal of the United States.

McCarran Internal Security Act Congressional act enacted in 1950 that stated all members of the Communist party had to register with the office of the Attorney General and that it was a crime to conspire to foster communism in the United States.

McCarran-Walter Act 1952 bill that limited immigration from everywhere except Northern and Western Europe and stated that immigration officials could turn any immigrant away that they thought might threaten the national security of the United States.

McCarthyism Named after Senator Joseph McCarthy of Wisconsin, the title given for the movement that took place during the late 1940s and early 1950s in American politics to root out potential communist influence in the government, the military, and the entertainment industry. Harsh tactics were often used by congressional investigations, with few actual communists ever discovered. This period is seen by many today as an era of intolerance and paranoia.

Meat Inspection Act Inspired by Upton Sinclair's *The Jungle,* this 1906 bill established a government commission that would monitor the quality of all meat sold in America and inspect the meat-packing houses for safety and cleanliness.

Medicare Part of Lyndon Johnson's Great Society program, this program acted as a form of health insurance for retired Americans (and disabled ones as well). Through Medicare, the federal government would pay for services received by elderly patients at doctor's offices and hospitals.

mercantilism Economic policy practiced by most European states in the late seventeenth century that stated the power of any state depended largely on its wealth; thus it was the state's duty to do all that it could to build up wealth. A mercantilist country would not want to import raw materials from other countries; instead, it would be best to have colonies from which these raw materials could be imported.

Merrimack Union ironclad ship captured by Confederates during the Civil War and renamed the *Virginia.*

Meuse-Argonne Offensive American forces played a decisive role in this September 1918 Allied offensive, which was the last major offensive of the war and which convinced the German general staff that victory in World War I was impossible.

Middle Passage The voyage across the Atlantic Ocean taken by slaves on their way to the Americas. Sickness, diseases, and death were rampant as slave ships crossed the Atlantic; on some ships over 20 percent of slaves who began the journey were dead by the time the ship landed.

"midnight appointments" Judicial or other appointments made by an outgoing president or governor in the last hours before he or she leaves office. The most famous were the judicial appointments made by John Adams in the hours before Thomas Jefferson was inaugurated as president.

Midway, Battle of June 4, 1942 naval battle that crippled Japanese offensive capabilities in the Pacific; American airplanes destroyed four aircraft carriers and 245 Japanese planes. After Midway, Japanese military operations were mainly defensive.

Missouri Compromise In a continued effort to maintain a balance between free and slave states, Henry Clay proposed this 1820 compromise, which admitted Maine to the Union as a free state, Missouri to the Union as a slave state, and stated that any part of the Louisiana Territory north of 36 degrees, 30 inches would be nonslave territory.

Model T Automobile produced by Ford Motor Company using assembly line techniques. The first Model Ts were produced in 1907; using the assembly line, Ford produced half of the automobiles made in the world between 1907 and 1926.

Molasses Act In the early 1700s colonists traded for molasses with the French West Indies. British traders wanted to reduce trade between the colonies and the French; in 1733 they pressured Parliament to pass this act, which put prohibitively high duties on imported molasses. Colonists continued to smuggle French molasses in the Americas in spite of British efforts to prevent this.

Monitor Union ironclad ship utilized during the Civil War; fought one battle against the *Virginia*, the South's ironclad ship, and never left port again.

Monroe Doctrine President James Monroe's 1823 statement that an attack by a European state on any nation in the Western Hemisphere would be considered an attack on the United States; Monroe stated that the Western Hemisphere was the hemisphere of the United States and not of Europe. Monroe's statement was scoffed at by certain European political leaders, especially those in Great Britain.

Montgomery bus boycott Yearlong refusal by blacks to ride city buses in Montgomery, Alabama, because of their segregation policies. Boycott began in December 1955; Supreme Court finally ruled that segregation on public buses was unconstitutional. Rosa Parks began the protest when she was arrested for refusing to give up her seat for a white man, and Martin Luther King was a young minister involved in organizing the boycott.

Morrill Land Grant Act 1862 federal act designed to fund state "land-grant" colleges. State governments were given large amounts of land in the western territories; this land was sold to individual settlers, land speculators, and others, and the profits of these land sales could be used to establish the colleges.

Ms. Founded in 1972 by Gloria Steinem, this glossy magazine was aimed at feminist readers.

muckrakers Journalists of the Progressive era who attempted to expose the evils of government and big business. Many muckrakers wrote of the corruption of city and state political machines. Factory conditions and the living and working condition of workers were other topics that some muckrakers wrote about.

My Lai Massacre In 1968 a unit under the command of Lieutenant William Called killed over 300 men, women, and children in this small Vietnamese village. The antiwar movement took the attack as a symbol of the "immorality" of United States efforts in Vietnam.

NAFTA (North American Free Trade Agreement) Ratified in 1994 by the U.S. Senate, this agreement established a free trade zone between the United States, Mexico, and Canada. Critics of the agreement claim that many jobs have been lost in the United States because of it.

napalm Jellylike substance dropped from American planes during the Vietnam conflict that horribly burned the skin of anyone that came into contact with it. On several occasions, napalm was accidentally dropped on "friendly" villages.

National American Woman's Suffrage Association The major organization for suffrage for women, it was founded in 1890 by Susan B. Anthony and Elizabeth Cady Stanton. Supported the Wilson administration during World War I and split with the more radical National Woman's Party, who in 1917 began to picket the White House because Wilson had not forcefully stated that women should get the vote.

National Association for the Advancement of Colored People (NAACP) Formed in 1909, this organization fought for and continues to fight for the right of blacks in America. The NAACP originally went to court for the plaintiff in the *Brown v. Board of Education* case, and Thurgood Marshall, the NAACP's chief counsel and later a Supreme Court justice, was the main attorney in the case.

National Bank Planned by Alexander Hamilton to be similar to the Bank of England, this bank was funded by government and private sources. Hamilton felt a National Bank would give economic security and confidence to the new nation; Republicans who had originally opposed the bank felt the same way in 1815 when they supported Henry Clay's American System.

National Consumers League Formed in 1890, this organization was concerned with improving the working and living conditions of women in the workplace.

national culture When a general unity of tastes and a commonality of cultural experience exist in a nation; in a general sense, when a country starts to "think the same." This occurred in America for the first time in the 1920s; as many people saw the same movies, read the same magazines, and heard the same things on the radio, a national culture was born.

National Industrial Recovery Act (NIRA) 1933 New Deal legislation that created the Works Progress Administration (WPA) that created jobs to put people back to work right away and the National Recovery Administration (NRA), who worked in conjunction with industry to bolster the industrial sector and create more long-lasting jobs.

National Labor Relations Board (NLRB) Part of the 1935 Wagner Act, which was a huge victory for organized labor. The NLRB ensured that factory owners did not harass union organizers, ensured that collective bargaining was fairly practiced in labor disputes, and supervised union elections. The NLRB was given the legal "teeth" to force employers to comply with all of the above.

National Origins Act Very restrictive immigration legislation passed in 1924, which lowered immigration to 2 percent of each nationality as found in the 1890 census. This lowered immigration dramatically and, quite intentionally, almost eliminated immigration from Eastern and Southern Europe.

National Security League Organization founded in 1914 that preached patriotism and preparation for war; in 1915 they successfully lobbied government officials to set up camps to prepare men for military life and combat. The patriotism of this group became more strident as the war progressed; in 1917 they lobbied Congress to greatly limit immigration into the country.

National Woman's Party Formed by Alice Paul after women got the vote, this group lobbied unsuccessfully in the 1920s to get an Equal Rights Amendment for women added to the Constitution. Desire for this amendment would return among some feminist groups in the 1970s.

Nation of Islam Supporters were called Black Muslims; this group was founded by Elijah Muhammad and preached Islamic principles along with black pride and black separatism. Malcolm X was a member of the Nation of Islam.

NATO (North Atlantic Treaty Organization) Collective alliance of the United States and most of the Western European nations that was founded in 1949; an attack of one member of NATO was to be considered an attack on all. Many United States troops served in Europe during the Cold War era because of the NATO alliance. To counter NATO, the Soviet Union created the Warsaw Pact in 1955.

Naval Act of 1900 Legislation that authorized a large increase in the building of ships to be used for offensive purposes; this measure helped ensure the creation of a world-class American navy.

Navigation Acts 1660 measures passed by Charles II that were designed to increase the dependence of the colonies on England for trade. Charles mandated that certain goods produced in the colonies, such as tobacco, should be sold only to England, that if the colonies wanted to sell anything to other countries it had to come through England first, and that all trade by the colonies to other countries would have to be done in English ships. These measures could have been devastating to the colonies; however, British officials in the colonies did not enforce them carefully.

nativism Nativism states that immigration should be greatly limited or banned altogether, since immigrants hurt the United States economically and also threaten the social well-being of the country. Nativist groups and parties have developed on several occasions in both the nineteenth and the twentieth century; nativist sentiment was especially strong in the 1920s.

Neutrality Act of 1935 To prevent the United States from being drawn into potential European conflicts, this bill said that America would not trade arms with any country at war, and that any American citizen traveling on a ship of a country at war was doing so at his or her own risk.

Neutrality Act of 1939 Franklin Roosevelt got Congress to amend the Neutrality Act of 1935; new legislation stated that England and France could buy arms from the United States as long as there was cash "up front" for these weapons. This was the first military assistance that the United States gave the Allied countries.

New Deal Series of policies instituted by Franklin Roosevelt and his advisors from 1933–1941 that attempted to offset the effects of the Great Depression on American society. Many New Deal policies were clearly experimental; in the end it was the onset of World War II, and not the policies of the New Deal, that pulled the United States out of the Great Depression.

New Deal Coalition The coalition of labor unions and industrial workers, minorities, much of the middle class, and the Solid South that carried Franklin Roosevelt to victories in 1936 and 1940 and that was the basis of Democratic victories on a national level until this coalition started to break up in the late 1960s and early 1970s. A sizable number of this group voted for Ronald Reagan in the presidential elections of 1980 and 1984.

New Democrat Term used to describe Bill Clinton and his congressional supporters during his two terms in office. A New Democrat was pragmatic, and not tied to the old Democratic belief in big government; New Democrats took both Democratic and Republican ideas as they crafted their policies. Some in the Democratic party maintained that Clinton had actually sold out the principles of the party.

New Federalism A series of policies during the administration of Richard Nixon that began to give some power back to the states that had always been held by the federal government. Some tax dollars were returned to state and local governments in the form of "block grants"; the state and local governments could then spend this money as they thought best.

New Freedom policy An approach favored by Southern and Midwestern Democrats, this policy stated that economic and political preparation for World War I should be done in a decentralized manner; this would prevent too much power falling into the hands of the federal government. President Wilson first favored this approach, but then established federal agencies to organize mobilization.

New Frontier The program of President John Kennedy to revitalize America at home and to reenergize America for continued battles against the Soviet Union. Kennedy asked young Americans to volunteer for programs such as the Peace Corps; as he said in his inaugural speech: "Ask not what your country can do for you—ask what you can do for your country."

"new immigrants" Immigrants that came from Southern and Eastern Europe, who made up the majority of immigrants coming into the United States after 1900. Earlier immigrants from Britain, Ireland, and Scandinavia appeared to be "like" the groups that were already settled in the United States; the "new immigrants" were very different. As a result, resentment and nativist sentiment developed against this group, especially in the 1920s.

New Jersey Plan As the U.S. Constitution was being debated and drafted, large states and small states each offered proposals on how the legislature should be structured. The New Jersey Plan stated that the legislature should have a great deal of power to regulate trade, and that it should consist of one legislative house, with each state having one vote.

New Nationalism The series of progressive reforms supported by Theodore Roosevelt as he ran for president on the Progressive or "Bull Moose" ticket in 1912. Roosevelt said that more had to be done to regulate big business and that neither of his opponents were committed to conservation.

New Right The conservative movement that began in the 1960s and triumphed with the election of Ronald Reagan in 1980. The New Right was able to attract many middle-class and Southern voters to the Republican party by emphasizing the themes of patriotism, a smaller government, and a return to "traditional values."

"New South" Concept promoted by Southerners in the late 1800s that the South had changed dramatically and was now interested in industrial growth and becoming a part of the national economy. A large textile industry did develop in the South beginning in the 1880s.

Nez Perce Plains Native American tribe that attempted to resist reservation life by traveling 1500 miles with American military forces in pursuit. After being tracked and suffering cold and hardship, the Nez Perce finally surrendered and were forced onto a reservation in 1877.

Non-Intercourse Act In response to the failure of France and Britain to respect the rights of American ships at sea, President Madison supported this legislation in 1809, which authorized trade with all countries except Britain and France, and stated that trade exist with those countries as soon as they respected America's rights as a neutral power. The British and the French largely ignored this act.

Northwest Ordinances Bills passed in 1784, 1785, and 1787 that authorized the sale of lands in the Northwest Territory to raise money for the federal government; these bills also carefully laid out the procedures for eventual statehood for parts of these territories.

NOW (National Organization for Women) Formed in 1966, with Betty Friedan as its first president. NOW was at first interested in publicizing inequalities for women in the workplace; focus of the organization later turned to social issues and eventually the unsuccessful effort to pass an Equal Rights Amendment for women.

nuclear proliferation The massive buildup of nuclear weapons by the United States and the Soviet Union in the 1950s and into the 1960s; in the United States this was fostered in the belief that the threat of "massive retaliation" was the best way to keep the Soviet Union under control. The psychological effects of the atomic bomb on the populations of the Soviet Union and the United States were also profound.

nullification The belief that an individual state has the right to "nullify" any federal law that the state felt was unjust. Andrew Jackson was able to resolve a Nullification Crisis in 1832, but the concept of nullification was still accepted by many Southerners, and controversy over this was a cause of the Civil War.

Ocala Platform Platform of the Farmer's Alliance, formulated at an 1890 convention held in Ocala, Florida. This farmer's organization favored a graduated income tax, government control of the railroad, the unlimited coinage of silver, and the direct election of United States senators. Candidates supporting the farmers called themselves Populists and ran for public offices in the 1890s.

Old Age Revolving Pension Plan Conceived by California doctor Francis Townsend in 1934, this plan would give every retired American $200 a month, with the stipulation that it would have to be spent by the end of the month; Townsend claimed this would revitalize the economy by putting more money in circulation. A national tax of 2 percent on all business transactions was supposed to finance this plan. A large number of Townsend clubs were formed to support this plan.

"on the margin" The practice in the late 1920s of buying stock and only paying in cash 10 percent of the value of that stock; the buyer could easily borrow the rest from his or her stockbroker or investment banker. This system worked well as long as investors could sell their stocks at a profit and repay their loans; after the 1929 stock market crash, investors had to pay these loans back in cash.

OPEC Acronym for Organization of Petroleum Exporting Countries, this organization sets the price for crude oil and determines how much of it will be produced. The decision of OPEC to raise oil prices in 1973 had a dramatic economic impact in both the United States and the rest of the world.

Open-Door policy The policy that China should be open to trade with all of the major powers, and that all, including the United States, should have equal right to trade there. This was the official American position toward China as announced by Secretary of State John Hay in 1899.

Oregon Trail Trail that took settlers from the Ohio River Valley through the Great Plains and the Rocky Mountains to Oregon. Settlers began moving westward along this trail in 1842; by 1860 over 325,000 Americans had traveled westward along the trail.

Oregon Treaty Both the United States and Great Britain claimed the Oregon Territory; in 1815 they agreed to jointly control the region. In 1843 the settlers of Oregon declared that their territory would become an independent republic.

Palmer Raids Part of the Red Scare, these were measures to hunt out political radicals and immigrants who were potential threats to American security. Organized by Attorney General A. Mitchell Palmer in 1919 and 1920 (and carried out by J. Edgar Hoover), these raids led to the arrest of nearly 5500 people and the deportation of nearly four hundred.

Panama Canal Crucial for American economic growth, the building of this canal was begun by American builders in 1904 and completed in 1914; the United States had to first engineer a Panamanian revolt against Colombia to guarantee a friendly government in Panama that would support the building of the canal. In 1978 the U.S. Senate voted the return the Panama Canal to Panamanian control.

Panic of 1837 The American economy suffered a deep depression when Great Britain reduced the amount of credit it offered to the United States; American merchants and industrialists had to use their available cash to pay off debts, thus causing businesses to cut production and lay off workers.

Paris, Treaty of The treaty ending the Revolutionary War, and signed in 1783; by the terms of this treaty the United States received the land between the Appalachian Mountains and the Mississippi River. The British did keep their Canadian territories.

Pendleton Civil Service Act 1883 act that established a civil service system; there were a number of government jobs that were filled by civil service examinations and not by the president appointing one of his political cronies. Some states also started to develop professional civil service systems in the 1880s.

Pentagon Papers A government study of American involvement in Vietnam that outlined in detail many of the mistakes that America had made there; in 1971 a former analyst for the Defense Department, Daniel Ellsberg released these to the *New York Times*.

Platt Amendment For Cuba to receive its independence from the United States after the Spanish-American war, it had to agree to the Platt

Amendment, which stated that the United States had the right to intervene in Cuban affairs if the Cuban government could not maintain control or if the independence of Cuba was threatened by external or internal forces.

Plumbers A group of intelligence officials who worked for the committee to reelect Richard Nixon in 1972; the job of this group was to stop leaks of information and perform "dirty tricks" on political opponents of the president. The Plumbers broke into the office of Daniel Ellsberg's psychiatrist, looking for damaging information against him and totally discredited the campaign of Democratic hopeful Edmund Muskie.

pocket veto A method a president can use to "kill" congressional legislation at the end of a congressional term. Instead of vetoing the bill, the president may simply not sign it; once the congressional term is over, the bill will then die.

political machine An organization that controls the politics of a city, a state, or even the country, sometimes by illegal or quasi-legal means; a machine employs a large number of people to do its "dirty work," for which they are either given some government job or are allowed to pocket government bribes or kickbacks. The "best" example of a political machine was the Tammany Hall organization that controlled New York City in the late nineteenth century.

Populist party Party that represented the farmers that scored major electoral victories in the 1890s, including the election of several members of the U.S. House of Representatives and the election of one U.S. senator. Populist candidates spoke against monopolies, wanted government to become "more democratic," and wanted more direct government action to help the working classes.

Port Huron Statement The manifesto of Students for a Democratic Society, a radical student group formed in 1962. The Port Huron Statement called for a greater role for university students in the nation's affairs, rejected the traditional role of the university, and rejected the foreign policy goals that America was embracing at the time.

Potsdam Conference July 1945 conference between new president Harry Truman, Stalin, and Clement Atlee, who had replaced Churchill. Truman took a much tougher stance toward Stalin than Franklin Roosevelt had; little substantive agreement took place at this conference. Truman expressed reservations about the future role of the Soviet Union in Eastern Europe at this conference.

Powhatan Confederacy Alliance of Native American tribes living in the region of the initial Virginia settlement. Powhatan, leader of this alliance, tried to live in peace with the English settlers when they arrived in 1607.

professional bureaucracy Government officials that receive their positions after taking competitive civil service tests; they are not appointed in return for political favors. Many government jobs at the state and national level are filled in this manner beginning in the 1880s.

progressivism A movement that desired political and social reform, and was most influential in America from the 1890s up until World War I. Most popular progressive causes included reforming city government, better conditions for urban workers, the education of newly arrived immigrants, and the regulation of big businesses.

proportional representation The belief that representation in a legislature should be based on population; the states with the largest populations should have the most representatives. When the Constitution was being formulated, the larger states wanted this; the smaller states favored "one vote per state." The eventual compromise, termed the Connecticut plan, created a two-house legislature.

proprietorships Settlements in America that were given to individuals, who could govern and regulate the territory in any manner they desire. Charles I, for example, gave the Maryland territory to Lord Baltimore as a proprietorship.

Puritans Group of religious dissidents who came to the New World so they would have a location to establish a "purer" church than the one that existed in England. The Puritans began to settle the Plymouth Colony in 1620 and settled the Massachusetts Bay Colony beginning in 1630. Puritans were heavily influenced by John Calvin and his concept of predestination.

putting-out system The first textile production system in England, where merchants gave wool to families, who in their homes created yarn and then cloth; the merchants would then buy the cloth from the families and sell the finished product. Textile mills made this procedure more efficient.

Quartering Act 1765 British edict stating that to help defend the empire, colonial governments had to provide accommodations and food for British troops. Many colonists considered this act to be the ultimate insult; they perceived that they were paying for the troops that were there to control the colonies.

Queen Anne's War 1702 to 1713 war, called the War of the Spanish Succession in European texts, pitted England against France and Spain. Spanish Florida was attacked by the English in the early part of this war, and Native Americans fought for both sides in the conflict. The British emerged victorious and in the end received Hudson Bay and Nova Scotia from the French.

Radical Republicans Group of Republicans after the Civil War who favored harsh treatment of the defeated South and a dramatic restructuring of the economic and social systems in the South; favored a decisive elevation of the political, social, and economic position of former slaves.

ratifying conventions In late 1787 and in 1788 these were held in all states for the purpose of ratifying the new Constitution of the United States. In many states, approval of the Constitution was only approved by a small margin; in Rhode Island ratification was defeated. The Founding Fathers made an intelligent decision in calling for ratifying conventions to approve the Constitution instead of having state legislatures do it, since the under the system proposed by the Constitution, some of the powers state legislatures had at the time would be turned over to the federal government.

ration cards Held by Americans during World War II, these recorded the amount of rationed goods such as automobile tires, gasoline, meat, butter, and other materials an individual had purchased. Where regulation in World War I had been voluntary, consumption in World War II was regulated by government agencies.

realpolitik Pragmatic policy of leadership, in which the leader "does what he or she has to do" in order to be successful. Morality has no place in the mind-set of a leader practicing realpolitik. The late nineteenth-century German chancellor Otto von Bismarck is the best modern example of a leader practicing realpolitik.

Rebel Without a Cause 1955 film starring James Dean exploring the difficulties of family life and the alienation that many teenagers felt in the 1950s. Juvenile delinquency, and the reasons for it, was the subtext of this film, as well as the source of countless other 1950s-era movies aimed at the youth market.

recall One of a number of reforms of the governmental system proposed by progressive-era thinkers; by the process of recall, the citizens of a city or state could remove an unpopular elected official from office in midterm. Recall was adopted in only a small number of communities.

reconcentration 1896 Spanish policy designed to control the Cuban people by forcing them to live in fortified camps; American outrage over this leads some politicians to call for war against Spain.

Reconstruction Act Plan of Radical Republicans to control the former area of the Confederacy and approved by Congress in March 1867; former Confederacy was divided into five military districts, with each controlled by a military commander (Tennessee was exempt from this). Conventions were to be called to create new state governments (former Confederate officials could not hold office in these governments).

Reconstruction era The era following the Civil War where Radical Republicans initiated changes in the South that gave newly freed slaves additional economic, social, and political rights. These changes were greatly resented by many Southerners, causing the creation of organizations such as the Ku Klux Klan. Reconstruction ended with the Compromise of 1877.

Reconstruction Finance Corporation Established in 1932 by Herbert Hoover to offset the effects of the Great Depression; the RFC was authorized to give federal credit to banks so that they could operate efficiently. Banks receiving these loans were expected to extend loans to businesses providing jobs or building low-cost housing.

Red Scare Vigorous repression of radicals, "political subversives," and "undesirable" immigrants groups in the years immediately following World War I. Nearly 6500 "radicals" were arrested and sent to jail; some sat in jail without every being changed with a crime, while nearly 500 immigrants were deported.

referendum one of a series of progressive-era reforms designed to improve the political system; with the referendum, certain issues would be decided not by elected representatives as voters are called upon to approve or disapprove specific government programs. Consistent with populist and progressive era desire to return government "to the people."

religious right Primarily Protestant movement that greatly grew beginning in the 1970s and pushed to return "morality" to the forefront in American life. The religious right has been especially active in opposing abortion, and since the 1980s has extended its influence in the political sphere by endorsing and campaigning for specific candidates.

Removal Act of 1830 Part of the effort to remove Native Americans from "Western" lands so that American settlement could continue westward, this legislation gave the president the authorization (and the money) to purchase from Native Americans all of their lands east of the Mississippi, and gave him the money to purchase lands west of the Mississippi for Native Americans to move to.

Report on the Public Credit 1790 report by Secretary of the Treasury Alexander Hamilton, in which he proposed that the federal government assume the entire amount of the nation's debt (including state debt), and that the federal government should have an increased role in the nation's economy. Many of America's early leaders vigorously opposed the expansion of federal economic power in the new republic and the expansion of American industry that Hamilton also promoted.

Republican party Formed in 1854 during the death of the Whig party, this party attracted former members of the Free-Soil party and some in the Democratic party who were uncomfortable with the Democratic position on slavery. Abraham Lincoln was the first Republican president. For much of the twentieth century, the party was saddled with the label of being "the party of big business," although Richard Nixon, Ronald Reagan, and others did much to pull middle class and Southern voters into the party.

"Reservationists" This group in the United States Senate was led by Henry Cabot Lodge and was opposed to sections of the Versailles Treaty when it was brought home from Paris by President Woodrow Wilson in 1919. Reservationists were especially concerned that if the United States joined the League of Nations, American troops would be used to conduct League of Nations military operations without the approval of the Congress.

Resettlement Administration In an attempt to address the problems of Dust Bowlers and other poor farmers, this 1935 New Deal program attempted to provide aid to the poorest farmers, resettle some farmers from the Dust Bowl, and establish farm cooperatives. This program never received the funding it needed to be even partially successfully, and in 1937 the Farm Security Administration was created to replace it.

Revenue Act of 1935 Tax legislation championed by Franklin Roosevelt that was called a "soak the rich" plan by his opponents. Under this bill, corporate, inheritance, and gift taxes went up dramatically; income taxes for the upper brackets also rose. By proposing this, Roosevelt may have been attempting to diffuse the popularity of Huey Long and others with more radical plans to redistribute wealth.

Revenue Act of 1942 Designed to raise money for the war, this bill dramatically increased the number of Americans required to pay income tax. Until this point, roughly 4 million Americans paid income tax; as a result of this legislation, nearly 45 million did.

"revisionist" history A historical interpretation not found in "standard" history books or supported by most historians. A revisionist history of the

origins of the Cold War, for example, would maintain that the aggressive actions of the United States forced the Soviet Union to seize the territories of Eastern Europe for protection. Historical interpretations that may originally be revisionist may, in time, become standard historical interpretation.

revival meetings Religious meetings consisting of soul-searching, preaching, and prayer that took place during the Second Great Awakening at the beginning of the nineteenth century. Some revival meetings lasted over one week.

Rio Pact 1947 treaty signed by the United States and most Latin American countries, stating that the region would work together on economic and defense matters and creating the Organization of American States to facilitate this cooperation.

Roe v. Wade 1973 Supreme Court decision that made abortion legal (except in the last months of pregnancy). Justices voting in the majority in this 5-to-2 decision stated that a woman's right to privacy gave her the legal freedom to choose to have an abortion. Abortion has remained as one of the most hotly debated social issues in America.

Roosevelt Corollary An extension of the Monroe Doctrine, this policy was announced in 1904 by Theodore Roosevelt; it firmly warned European nations against intervening in the affairs of nations in the Western Hemisphere, and stated that the United States had the right to take action against any nation in Latin America if "chronic wrongdoing" was taking place. The Roosevelt Corollary was used to justify several American "interventions" in Central America in the twentieth century.

Rosie the Riveter Image of a woman factory worker drawn by Norman Rockwell for the *Saturday Evening Post* during World War II. Women were needed to take on factory jobs that had been held by departing soldiers; by 1945 women made up nearly 37 percent of the entire domestic workforce.

"Rough Riders" A special unit of soldiers recruited by Theodore Roosevelt to do battle in the Spanish-American War; this unit was composed of men from many backgrounds, with the commanding officer of the unit being Roosevelt (after he resigned as Assistant Secretary of the Navy). The most publicized event of the war was the charge of the Rough Riders up San Juan Hill on July 1, 1898.

Salem Witch Trials 120 men, women, and children were arrested for witchcraft in Salem, Massachusetts, in 1692; 19 of these were executed. A new governor appointed by the Crown stopped additional trails and executions; several historians note the class nature of the witch trials, as many of those accused were associated with the business and/or commercial interests in Salem, while most of the accusers were members of the farming class.

SALT I (Strategic Arms Limitation Talks) 1972 treaty signed by Richard Nixon and Soviet premier Leonid Brezhnev limiting the development of additional nuclear weapon systems and defense systems to stop them. SALT I was only partially effective in preventing continued development of nuclear weaponry.

salutary neglect British policy announced at the beginning of the eighteenth century stating that as long as the American colonies remained politically loyal and continued their trade with Great Britain, the British government would relax enforcement of various measures restricting colonial activity that were enacted in the 1600s. Tensions between the colonies and Britain continued over British policies concerning colonial trade and the power of colonial legislatures.

satellite countries Eastern European countries that remained under the control of the Soviet Union during the Cold War era. Most were drawn together militarily by the Warsaw Pact; satellite nations that attempted political or cultural rebellion, such as Hungary in 1956 or Czechoslovakia in 1968, faced invasion by Soviet forces.

"Saturday Night Massacre" October 20, 1973 event when Richard Nixon ordered the firing of Archibald Cox, the special investigator in charge of the Watergate investigation. Attorney General Elliot Richardson and several others in the Justice Department refused to carry out this order and resigned. This event greatly damaged Nixon's popularity, both in the eyes of the public and in the Congress.

scalawags Term used by Southerners in the Reconstruction era for fellow Southerners who either supported Republican Reconstruction policies or gained economically as a result of these policies.

Scopes Trial 1925 Tennessee trail where teacher John Scopes was charged with teaching evolution, a violation of state status. The American Civil Liberties Union hired Clarence Darrow to defend Scopes, while the chief attorney for the prosecution was three-time presidential candidate William Jennings Bryan. While Scopes was convicted and ordered to pay a small fine, Darrow was able to poke holes in the theory of creationism as expressed by Bryan.

Scottsboro Boys Nine black young men who were accused of raping two white women in a railway boxcar in Scottsboro, Arizona in 1931. Quick trials, suppressed evidence, and inadequate legal council made them symbols of the discrimination that faced blacks on a daily basis during this era.

Scramble for Africa The competition between the major European powers to gain colonial territories in Africa that took place between the 1870s and the outbreak of World War I. Conflicts created by competing visions of colonial expansion increased tensions between the European powers and were a factor in the animosities that led to World War I.

secession A single state or a group of states leaving the United States of America. New England Federalists threatened to do this during first administration of Thomas Jefferson; Southern states did this in the period prior to the Civil War.

Second Continental Congress Meeting of delegates from the American colonies in May 1775; during the sessions some delegates expressed hope that the differences between the colonies and Britain could be reconciled, although the Congress authorized that the Continental Army be created and that George Washington be named commander of that army.

Second Great Awakening Religious revival movement that began at the beginning of the nineteenth century; revivalist ministers asked thousands of worshippers at revival meetings to save their own souls. This reflected the move away from predestination in Protestant thinking of the era.

Second Industrial Revolution The massive economic growth that took place in American from 1865 until the end of the century that was largely based on the expansion of the railroad, the introduction of electric power, and the production of steel for building. By the 1890s America had replaced Germany as the major industrial producer in the world.

Second National Bank Bank established by Congress in 1816; President Madison had called for the Second Bank in 1815 as a way to spur national economic growth after the War of 1812. After an economic downturn in 1818, the bank shrunk the amount of currency available for loans, an act that helped to create the economic collapse of 1819.

Second New Deal Beginning in 1935 the New Deal did more to help the poor and attack the wealthy; one reason Roosevelt took this path was to turn the American people away from those who said the New Deal wasn't going far enough to help the average person. Two key legislative acts of this era were the Social Security Act of May 1935 and the June 1935 National Labor Relations Act (also called the Wagner Act), which gave all Americans the right to join labor unions. The Wealth Tax Act increased the tax rates for the wealthiest Americans.

settlement houses Centers set up by progressive-era reformers in the poorest sections of American cities; at these centers workers and their children might receive lessons in the English language or citizenship, while for women lessons in sewing and cooking were oftentimes held. The first settlement house was Hull House in Chicago, established by Jane Addams in 1889.

Seventeenth Amendment Ratified in 1913, this amendment allowed voters to directly elect United States senators. Senators had previously been elected by state legislatures; this change perfectly reflected the spirit of progressive-era political reformers who wanted to do all they could to put political power in the hands of the citizenry.

Sherman Antitrust Act 1890 congressional legislation designed to break up industrial trusts such as the one created by John D. Rockefeller and Standard Oil. The bill stated that any combination of businesses that was "in the restraint of trade" was illegal. Because of the vagueness of the legislation and the lack of enforcement tools in the hands of the federal government, few trusts were actually prosecuted as a result of this bill.

Shiloh, Battle of Fierce Civil War battle in Tennessee in April 1862; although the Union emerged victorious, both sides suffered a large number of casualties in this battle. Total casualties in this battle were nearly 25,000. General U.S. Grant commanded the Union forces at Shiloh.

Sioux Plains tribe that tried to resist American westward expansion; after two wars the Sioux were resettled in South Dakota. In 1876 Sioux fighters defeated the forces of General Custer at the Battle of Little Bighorn. In 1890 almost 225 Sioux men, women, and children were killed by federal troops at the Massacre at Wounded Knee.

sit-down strikes A labor tactic where workers refuse to leave their factory until management meets their demands. The most famous sit-down strike occurred at the General Motors plant in Flint, Michigan, beginning in November, 1936; despite efforts by company guards to end the strike by force, the workers finally saw their demands met after 44 days.

sit-in Tactic used by the civil rights movement in the early 1960s; a group of civil rights workers would typically occupy a lunch counter in a segregated establishment in the South and refuse to leave, thus disrupting normal business (and profits) for the segregated establishment. During sit-ins civil rights workers often suffered physical and emotional abuse. The first sit-in was at the Woolworth's store in Greensboro, North Carolina, on February 1, 1960.

Sixteenth Amendment 1913 amendment that instituted a federal income tax. In debate over this measure in the Congress, most felt that this would be a fairer tax than a national sales tax, which was proposed by some.

Smith-Connally Act 1943 legislation that limited the nature of labor action possible for the rest of the war. Many in America felt that strikes, especially those organized in the coal mines by the United Mine Workers, were detrimental to the war effort.

Social Darwinism Philosophy that evolved from the writings of Charles Darwin on evolution that stated people inevitably compete with each other, as do societies; in the end the "survival of the fittest" would naturally occur. Social Darwinism was used to justify the vast differences between the rich and the poor in the late nineteenth century, as well as the control that the United States and Europe maintained over other parts of the world.

Social Gospel movement Late nineteenth-century Protestant movement preaching that all true Christians should be concerned with the plight of immigrants and other poor residents of American cities and should financially support efforts to improve the lives of these poor urban dwellers. Progressive-era settlement houses were oftentimes financed by funds raised by ministers of the Social Gospel movement.

Social Security Act Considered by many to be the most important act passed during the entire New Deal, this 1935 bill established a system that would give payments to Americans after they reached retirement age; provisions for unemployment and disability insurance were also found in this bill. Political leaders of recent years have wrestled with the problem of keeping the Social Security system solvent.

Sons of Liberty Men who organized opposition to British policies during the late 1760s and 1770s. The Sons of Liberty were founded in and were most active in Boston, where in response to the Stamp Act they burned the local tax collector in effigy and burned a building that he owned. The Sons of Liberty also organized the Boston Tea Party. Samuel Adams was one of the leaders of this group.

"Southern Strategy" Plan begun by Richard Nixon that has made the Republican party dominant in many areas of the South that had previously voted Democratic. Nixon, Ronald Reagan, and countless Republican congressional candidates have emphasized law and order and traditional values in their campaigns, thus winning over numerous voters. Support from the South had been part of the New Deal Democratic coalition crafted by Franklin Roosevelt.

Spanish-American War War that began in 1898 and stemmed from furor in America over treatment of Cubans by Spanish troops that controlled the island. During the war the American navy led by Admiral Dewey destroyed the Spanish fleet in the Pacific, the American ship the *Maine* was sunk in Havana harbor, and Teddy Roosevelt led the Rough Riders up San Juan Hill. A major result of the war was the acquisition by the United States of the Philippines, which made America a major power in the Pacific.

speakeasies Urban clubs that existed in the 1920s where alcohol was illegally sold to patrons. The sheer number of speakeasies in a city such as New York demonstrated the difficulty of enforcing a law such as prohibition.

special prosecutor An official appointed to investigate specific governmental wrongdoing. Archibald Cox was the special prosecutor assigned to investigate Watergate, while Kenneth Starr was the special prosecutor assigned to investigate the connections between President Clinton and Whitewater. President Nixon's order to fire Cox was the beginning of the famous 1973 "Saturday Night Massacre."

speculation The practice of purchasing either land or stocks with the intent of selling them for a higher price later. After the Homestead Act and other acts opened up the western United States for settlement, many speculators purchased land with no intent of ever settling on it; their goal was to later sell the land for profit.

spoils system Also called the patronage system, in which the president, governor, or mayor is allowed to fill government jobs with political allies and former campaign workers. Political reformers of the 1880s and 1890s introduced legislation calling for large numbers of these jobs to be filled by the merit system, in which candidates for jobs had to take competitive examinations. President Andrew Jackson began the spoils system.

Sputnik First man-made satellite sent into space, this 1957 scientific breakthrough by Soviet Union caused great concern in the United States. The thought that the United States was "behind" the Soviet Union in anything worried many, and science and mathematics requirements in universities across the country increased as a result.

Square Deal The philosophy of President Theodore Roosevelt; included in this was the desire to treat both sides fairly in any dispute. In the coal miner's strike of 1902 he treated the United Mine Workers representatives and company bosses as equals; this approach continued during his efforts to reg-

ulate the railroads and other businesses during his second term.

stagflation A unique economic situation faced political leaders in the early 1970s, where inflation and signs of economic recession occurred at the same time. Previously, in times of inflation, the economy was improving, and vice versa. Nixon utilized wage and price controls and increased government spending to end this problem.

Stamp Act To help pay for the British army in North America, Parliament passed the Stamp Act in 1765, under which all legal documents in the colonies had to be issued on officially stamped paper. A tax was imposed on all of these documents, as well as on all colonial newspapers. The resistance to the Stamp Act was severe in the colonies, and it was eventually repealed.

Stamp Act Congress Representatives of nine colonies went to this meeting held in New York in October 1765; the document produced by this congress maintained the loyalty of the colonies to the Crown but strongly condemned the Stamp Act. Within one year the Stamp Act was repealed.

state's rights The concept that the individual states, and not the federal government, have the power to decide whether federal legislation or regulations are to be enforced within the individual states. The mantle of state's rights would be taken up by New England Federalists during the presidency of Thomas Jefferson, by many Southern states in the years leading up to the Civil War, and by some Southern states again in response to federal legislation during the civil rights era of the 1960s.

Stono Rebellion 1739 slave rebellion in South Carolina where over 75 slaves killed white citizens and marched through the countryside with captured guns. After the rebellion was quashed, discipline imposed by many slave owners was much harsher. This was the largest slave rebellion of the 1700s in the colonies.

Students for a Democratic Society (SDS) Founded in 1962, this group was part of the "New Left" movement of the 1960s. SDS believed in a more participatory society, in a society that was less materialistic, and in university reform that would give students more power. By 1966 SDS concentrated much of its efforts on organizing opposition to the war in Vietnam. The *Port Huron Statement* was the original manifesto of SDS and was written by SDS founder Tom Hayden.

suburbia The area outside of the cities where massive number of families flocked to in the 1950s and 1960s. Suburban parents oftentimes still worked in the cities, but the suburban lifestyle shared little with urban life. Critics of 1950s suburbia point to the sameness and lack of vitality noted by some suburban residents and to the fact that suburban women oftentimes had to forget past dreams to accept the role of "housewife."

Sugar Act Another effort to pay for the British army located in North America, this 1764 measure taxed sugar and other imports. The British had previously attempted to halt the flow of sugar from French colonies to the colonies: By the Sugar Act they attempted to make money off this trade. Another provision of the act harshly punished smugglers of sugar who didn't pay the import duty imposed by the British.

Suffolk Resolves These were sent from Suffolk Country, Massachusetts, to the meeting of the First Continental Congress in September 1774 and called for the citizens of all of the colonies to prepare to take up arms against the British. After much debate, the First Continental Congress adopted the Suffolk Resolves.

supply-side economics Economic theory adopted by Ronald Reagan stating that economic growth would be best encouraged by lowering the taxes on wealthy businessmen and investors; this would give them more cash, which they would use to start more businesses, make more investments, and in general stimulate the economy. This theory of "Reaganomics" went against economic theories going back to the New Deal that claimed to efficiently stimulate the economy, more money needed to held by consumers (who would turn and spend it).

Sussex Pledge A torpedo from a German submarine hit the French passenger liner the *Sussex* in March 1916, killing and injuring many (including six Americans). In a strongly worded statement, President Wilson demanded that the Germans refrain from attacking passenger ships; in the Sussex Pledge the Germans said that they would temporarily stop these attacks, but that they might have to resume them in the future if the British continued their blockade of German ports.

Taft-Hartley Act 1947 congressional legislation that aided the owners in potential labor disputes. In key industries the president could declare an 80-day cooling off period before a strike could actually take place; the bill also allowed owners to sue unions over broken contracts, and forced union leaders to sign anticommunist oaths. The bill was passed over President Truman's veto; Truman only vetoed the bill for political reasons.

Tammany Hall Political machine that ran New York City Democratic and city politics beginning in 1870, and a "model" for the political machines that dominated politics in many American cities well into the twentieth century. William Marcy "Boss" Tweed was the head of Tammany Hall for several years and was the most notorious of all of the political bosses.

Tariff of 1816 An extremely protectionist tariff designed to assist new American industries in the aftermath of the War of 1812; this tariff raised import duties by nearly 25 percent.

Tax Reform Act of 1986 The biggest tax cut in American history, this measure cut taxes by $750 billion over five years and cut personal income taxes by 25 percent. Tax cuts were consistent with President Reagan's belief that more money in the hands of the wealthy would stimulate the economy. Critics of this tax cut would argue that the wealthy were the ones that benefited from it, as little of the money that went to the hands of the rich actually "trickled down" to help the rest of the economy. Critics would also argue that the national deficits of the late 1980s and early 1990s were caused by these tax cuts.

Taylorism Following the management practices of Frederick Winslow Taylor, the belief practiced by many factory owners beginning in 1911 (when Taylor published his first book) that factories should be managed in a scientific manner, with everything done to increase the efficiency of the individual worker and of the factory process as a whole. Taylor describes the movements of workers as if they were machines; workers in many factories resisted being seen in this light.

Tea Act 1773 act by Parliament that would provide the American colonies with cheap tea, but at the same time would force the colonists to admit that Parliament had a right to tax them. The Sons of Liberty acted against this measure in several colonies, with the most dramatic being the Boston Tea Party. Parliament responded with the harsh Coercive Acts.

Teapot Dome Scandal One of many scandals that took place during the presidency of Warren G. Harding. The Secretary of the Interior accepted bribes from oil companies for access to government oil reserves at Teapot Dome, Wyoming; other Cabinet members were later convicted of accepting bribes and using their influence to make millions. The Harding administration was perhaps the most corrupt administration in American political history.

Teller Amendment As Americans were preparing for war with Spain over Cuba in 1898, this Senate measure stated that under no circumstances would the United States annex Cuba. The amendment was passed as many in the muckraking press were suggesting that the Cuban people would be better off "under the protection" of the United States.

temperance movement Movement that developed in America before the Civil War that lamented the effect that alcohol had on American society. After the Civil War members of this movement would become especially concerned about the effect of alcohol on immigrants and other members of the urban poor; out of the temperance movement came the drive for nationwide prohibition.

tenant farmers In the Reconstruction South, a step up from sharecropping; the tenant farmer rented his land from the landowner, freeing him from the harsh supervision that sharecroppers suffered under.

Tennessee Valley Authority Ambitious New Deal program that for the first time provided electricity to residents of the Tennessee Valley; the TVA also promoted agricultural and industrial growth (and prevented flooding) in the region. In all, residents of seven states benefited from the TVA.

Ten Percent Plan Abraham Lincoln's plan for Reconstruction, which would have offered full pardons to persons living in Confederate states who would take an oath of allegiance to the United States (former Confederate military officers and civilian authorities would not be offered this possibility); once 10 percent of the citizens of a state had taken such an oath, the state could take steps to rejoin the Union. Radical Republicans in the U.S. Senate felt that this plan was much too lenient to the South.

Tenure of Office Act 1867 congressional act designed to limit the influence of President Andrew Johnson. The act took away the president's role as commander in chief of American military forces and stated that Congress had to approve the removal of government officials made by the president. In 1868 Johnson attempted to fire Secretary of War Stanton without congressional approval, thus helping set the stage for his impeachment hearings later that year.

Tet Offensive January 1968 attack launched on American and South Vietnamese forces by North Vietnamese and Vietcong soldiers. Although Vietcong troops actually occupied the American embassy in Vietnam for several hours, the end result was a crushing defeat for the anti-American forces. However, the psychological effect of Tet was exactly the reverse: Vietcong forces were convinced they could decisively strike at South Vietnamese and American targets, and many in America ceased to believe that victory was "just around the corner."

Thirteenth Amendment 1865 amendment abolishing slavery in the United States and all of its territories (the Emancipation Proclamation had only ended slavery in the Confederate states). Final approval of this amendment depended on ratification by newly constructed legislatures in eight states that were former members of the Confederacy.

Thirty-Eighth Parallel The dividing line between Soviet-supported North Korea and U.S.-backed South Korea both before and as a result of the Korean War; American forces have been stationed on the southern side of this border continually since the Korean War ended in 1953.

Three-Fifths Compromise As the new Constitution was being debated in 1787, great controversy developed over how slaves should be counted in determining membership in the House of Representatives. To increase their representation, Southern states argued that slaves should be counted as people; Northerners argued that they should not count, since they could not vote or own property. The compromise arrived at was that each slave would could as three-fifths of a free person.

"tight money" Governmental policy utilized to offset the effects of inflation; on numerous occasions the Federal Reserve Board has increased the interest rate on money it loans to member banks; these higher interest rates are passed on to customers of member banks. With higher interest rates, there are fewer loans and other business activity, which "slows the economy down" and lowers inflation.

Timber and Stone Act 1878 bill that allowed private citizens to purchase forest territory in Oregon, Washington, California, and Nevada. Although the intent of the bill was to encourage settlement in these areas, lumber companies purchased large amounts of these land claims from the individuals who had originally purchased them.

Townshend Acts 1767 Parliamentary act that forced colonists to pay duties on most goods coming from England, including tea and paper, and increased the power of custom boards in the colonies to ensure that these duties were paid. These duties were despised and fiercely resisted in many of the colonies; in Boston resistance was so fierce that the British were forced to occupy Boston with troops. The acts were finally repealed in 1770.

Trail of Tears Forced march of 20,000 members of Cherokee tribe to their newly designated "homeland" in Oklahoma. Federal troops forced the Cherokees westward in this 1838 event, with one out every five Native Americans dying from hunger, disease, or exhaustion along the way.

Trenton, Battle of December 26, 1776 surprise attack by forces commanded by George Washington on Hessian forces outside of Trenton, New Jersey. Nearly 950 Hessians were captured and another 30 were killed by Washington's forces; three Americans were wounded in the attack. The battle was a tremendous psychological boost for the American war effort.

Triangle Shirtwaist Fire March 1911 fire in New York factory that trapped young women workers inside locked exit doors; nearly 50 ended up jumping to their death, while 100 died inside the factory. Many factory reforms, including increasing safety precautions for workers, came from the investigation of this incident.

triangular trade system The complex trading relationship that developed in the late seventeenth century between the Americas, Europe, and Africa. Europeans purchased slaves from Africa to be resold in the Americas, raw materials from the Americas were exported to European states, while manufactured products in Europe were sold throughout the Americas.

Truman Doctrine Created in response to 1947 requests by Greece and Turkey for American assistance to defend themselves against potentially pro-Soviet elements in their countries, this policy stated that the United States would be ready to assist any free nation trying to defend itself against "armed minorities or . . . outside pressures." This would become the major American foreign policy goal throughout the Cold War.

trust Late nineteenth-century legal arrangement that allowed owners of one company to own stock in other companies in the same industry. By this arrangement, John D. Rockefeller and Standard Oil were able to buy enough stock to control other oil companies in existence as well. The Sherman Anti-Trust Act and the Clayton Anti-Trust Act were efforts to "break up" the numerous trusts that were created during this period.

Turner Thesis Published by Frederick Jackson Turner in 1893, "The Significance of the West in American History" stated that western expansion had played a fundamental role in defining the American character, and that the American tendencies toward democracy and individualism were created by the frontier experience.

Twelfth Amendment 1804 amendment that established separate balloting in the Electoral College for president and vice president. This amendment was passed as a result of the electoral deadlock of the 1800 presidential election, when Thomas Jefferson and his "running mate" Aaron Burr ended up with the same number of votes in the Electoral College; the House of Representatives finally decided the election in favor of Jefferson.

U-2 American reconnaissance aircraft shot down over the Soviet Union in May 1960. President Eisenhower initially refused to acknowledge that this was a spy flight; the Soviets finally produced pilot Francis Gary Powers, who admitted the purpose of the flight. This incident created an increase in Cold War tensions at the end of the Eisenhower presidency.

Uncle Tom's Cabin 1852 novel by Harriet Beecher Stowe that depicted all of the horrors of Southern slavery in great detail. The book went through several printings in the 1850s and early 1860s and helped to fuel abolitionist sentiment in the North.

unicameral legislature A governmental structure with a one-house legislature. As written in the Articles of Confederation, the United States would have a unicameral legislature, with all states having equal representation.

United Farm Workers Organized by Cesar Chavez in 1961, this union represented Mexican-Americans engaged in the lowest levels of agricultural work. In 1965 Chavez organized a strike against grape growers that hired Mexican-American workers in California, eventually winning the promise of benefits and minimum wage guarantees for the workers.

United States Forest Service Created during the presidency of Theodore Roosevelt, this body increased and protected the number of national forests and encouraged through numerous progress the efficient use of America's natural resources.

Universal Negro Improvement Association Black organization of the early 1920s founded by Marcus Garvey, who argued that however possible blacks should disassociate themselves from the "evils" of white society. This group organized a "back to Africa" movement, encouraging blacks of African descent to move back there; independent black businesses were encouraged (and sometimes funded) by Garvey's organization.

unrestricted submarine warfare The German policy announced in early 1917 of having their U-boats attack all ships attempting to land at British or French ports, despite their origin or purpose; because of this policy, the rights of the United States as a neutral power were being violated, stated Woodrow Wilson in 1917, and America was forced to declare war on Germany.

USS *Maine* American ship sent to Havana harbor in early 1898 to protect American interests in period of increased tension between Spanish troops and native Cubans; on February 15 an explosion took place on the ship, killing nearly 275 sailors. Later investigations pointed to an internal explosion on board, but all of the muckraking journals of the time in the United States blamed the explosion on the Spanish, which helped to develop intense anti-Spanish sentiment in the United States.

Valley Forge Location where General Washington stationed his troops for the winter of 1777 to 1778. Soldiers suffered hunger, cold, and disease: Nearly 1300 deserted over the course of the winter. Morale of the remaining troops was raised by the drilling and discipline instilled by Baron von Steuben, a former Prussian officer who had volunteered to aid the colonial army.

vertical integration Type of industrial organization practiced in the late nineteenth century and pioneered by Andrew Carnegie and U.S. Steel; under this system all of the various business activities needed to produce and sell a finished product (procuring the raw materials, preparing them, producing them, marketing them, and then selling them) would be done by the same company.

Vicksburg, Battle of After a lengthy siege, this Confederate city along the Mississippi River was finally taken by Union forces in July 1863; this victory gave the Union virtual control of the Mississippi River and was a serious psychological blow to the Confederacy.

Viet Cong During the Vietnam war, forces that existed within South Vietnam that were fighting for the victory of the North Vietnamese. Vietcong forces were pivotal in the initial successes of the Tet Offensive, which did much to make many in America question the American war effort in Vietnam and played a crucial role in the eventual defeat of the South Vietnamese government.

Vietnamization The process begun by Richard Nixon of removing American troops from Vietnam and turning more of the fighting of the Vietnam war over to the South Vietnamese. Nixon continued to use intense bombing to aid the South Vietnamese efforts as more American troops were being pulled out of Vietnam; in 1973 a peace treaty was finally signed with North Vietnam, allowing American troops to leave the country and all American POWs to be released. In March 1975, North Vietnamese and Vietcong forces captured Saigon and emerged victorious in the war.

Virginia Plan A concept of government crafted by James Madison and adopted by delegates to the convention that created the United States Constitution, this plan proposed a stronger central government than had existed under the Articles of Confederation; to prevent too much power being placed in the hands of one person or persons, the plan proposed that the powers of the federal government be divided amongst officials of executive, judicial, and legislative branches.

VISTA (Volunteer in Service to America) Program instituted in 1964 that sent volunteers to help poor Americans living in both urban and rural settings; this program was sometimes described as a domestic peace corps. This was one of many initiatives that were part of Lyndon Johnson's War on Poverty program.

voluntarism The concept that Americans should sacrifice either time or money for the well-being of their country; a sense of voluntarism has permeated America during much of its history, especially during the progressive era and during the administration of John Kennedy ("ask not what your country can do for you—ask what you can do for your country"). President George W. Bush called for a renewed sense of voluntarism in the aftermath of the attacks of September 11, 2001.

Wade-Davis Act Congress passed this bill in 1864 in response to the "10 Percent Plan" of Abraham Lincoln; this legislation set out much more difficult conditions than had been proposed by Lincoln for Southern states to reenter the Union. According to Wade-Davis, all former officers of the Confederacy would be denied citizenship; to vote, a person would have to take an oath that he had never helped the Confederacy in any way, and half of all white males in a state would have to swear loyalty to the Union before statehood could be considered. Lincoln prevented this from becoming law by using the pocket veto.

Wagner Act Also called the National Labor Relations Act, this July 1935 act established major gains for organized labor. It guaranteed collective bargaining, prevented harassment by owners of union activities, and established a National Labor Relations Board to guarantee enforcement of its provisions.

war bonds Also called Liberty Bonds, these were sold by the United States government in both World War I and World War II and used by the government to finance the war effort. A person purchasing a war bond can make money if he or she cashes it in after 5 or 10 years; in the meantime, the government can use the money to help pay its bills. In both wars, movie stars and other celebrities encouraged Americans to purchase war bonds.

War Industries Board Authorized in 1917, the job of this board was to mobilize American industries for the war effort. The board was headed by Wall Street investor Bernard Baruch, who used his influence to get American industries to produce materials useful for the war effort. Baruch was able to increase American production by a staggering 22 percent before the end of the war.

Warren Commission The group that carefully investigated the assassination of John F. Kennedy. After hearing much testimony, the commission concluded that Lee Harvey Oswald acted alone in killing the president. Even today many conspiracy theorists question the findings of the Warren Commission, claiming that Oswald was part of a larger group who wanted to assassinate the president.

Warsaw Pact Defensive military alliance created in 1955 by the Soviet Union and all of the Eastern European satellite nations loyal to the Soviet Union; the Warsaw Pact was formed as a reaction against NATO and NATO's 1955 decision to invite West Germany to join the organization.

Washington Conference 1922 conference where the United States, Japan, and the major European powers agreed to build no more warships for 10 years; in addition, the nations agreed not to attack each other's territories in the Pacific. This treaty came from strong post-World War I sentiment that it was important to avoid conflicts between nations that might lead to war.

Watergate Affair The break-in into Democratic campaign headquarters was one of a series of dirty tricks carried out by individuals associated with the effort to reelect Richard Nixon president in 1972. Extensive efforts were also made to cover up these activities. In the end, numerous government and campaign officials spent time in jail for their role in the Watergate Affair, and President Nixon was forced to resign in disgrace.

Webb Alien Land Law 1913 California law that prohibited Japanese who were not American citizens from owning farmland in California. This law demonstrates the nativist sentiment found in much of American society in the first decades of the twentieth century.

Webster-Hayne Debate 1830 Senate debate between Senator Daniel Webster of Massachusetts and Senator Robert Hayne of South Carolina over the issue of state's rights and whether an individual state has the right to nullify federal legislation. Webster skillfully outlined the dangers to the United States that would be caused by the practice of nullification; this debate perfectly captured many of the political divisions between North and South that would increase in the 1830s through the 1860s.

Whig party Political party that came into being in 1834 in opposition to the presidency of Andrew Jackson. Whigs opposed Jackson's use of the spoils system and the extensive power held by President Jackson; for much of their existence, however, the Whigs favored an activist federal government (while their opponents, the Democrats, favored limited government). William Henry Harrison and Zachary Taylor were the two Whigs elected president. The Whig party dissolved in the 1850s.

Whiskey Rebellion Many settlers in Western frontier territory in the early 1790s questioned the power that the federal power had over them. In 1793 settlers in the Ohio territory refused to pay federal excise taxes on whiskey and attacked tax officials who were supposed to collect these taxes; large numbers of "whiskey rebels" threatened to attack Pittsburgh and other cities. In 1794 President Washington was forced to send in federal troops to put down the rebellion.

"White Man's Burden" From the poem of the same name by Rudyard Kipling, this view justified imperialism by the "white man" around the world, but also emphasized the duty of the Europeans and Americans who were occupying new territories to improve the lives of those living in the newly acquired regions.

Whitewater The name of the scandal that got President Bill Clinton impeached but not convicted. Whitewater was the name of real-estate deal in Arkansas that Clinton and his wife Hillary Rodham Clinton were both involved in; opponents claimed the actions of the Clintons concerning Whitewater were illegal, unethical, or both. Independent Counsel Kenneth Starr expanded the investigation to include the suicide of Clinton aide Vincent Foster, missing files in the White House, and the relationship of President Clinton with a White House intern, Monica Lewinsky.

Wilmont Proviso In the aftermath of the war with Mexico, in 1846 Representative David Wilmont proposed in an amendment to a military bill that slavery should be prohibited in all territories gained in the treaty ending that war. This never went into law, but in the debate over it in both houses, Southern representatives spoke passionately in defense of slavery; John C. Calhoun even suggested that the federal government had no legal jurisdiction to stop the existence of slavery in any new territory.

Woodstock Music Festival 1969 event that some perceive as the pinnacle of the 1960s counterculture. 400,000 young people came together for a weekend of music and a relative lack of hassles or conflict. The difficulty of mixing the 1960s counterculture with the radical politics of the era was demonstrated when Peter Townshend of the Who kicked Abbie Hoffman off of the Woodstock stage.

Works Progress Administration (WPA) New Deal program established in 1935 whose goal was to give out jobs as quickly as possible, even though the wages paid by the WPA were relatively low. Roads and public buildings were constructed by WPA work crews; at the same time, WPA authors wrote state guidebooks, artists painted murals in newly constructed public buildings, and musicians performed in large cities and small towns across the country.

writ of habeas corpus Allows a person suspected of a crime not to simply sit in jail indefinitely; such a suspect must be brought to court and charged with something, or he or she must be released from jail. Abraham Lincoln suspended the right of habeas corpus during the Civil War so that opponents of his policies could be contained.

Yalta Conference Meeting between Stalin, Churchill, and Roosevelt held two months before the fall of Nazi Germany in February of 1945. At this meeting Stalin agreed to assist the Americans against the Japanese after the Germans were defeated; it was decided that Germany would be divided into zones (each controlled by one of the victors), and Stalin promised to hold free elections in the Eastern European nations the Soviet army had liberated from the Nazis. Critics of the Yalta agreement maintain that Roosevelt was naïve in his dealings with Stalin at this meeting (he was only months from his own death), and that Churchill and Roosevelt essentially handed over control of Eastern Europe to Stalin.

yellow journalism This method uses accounts and illustrations of lurid and sensational events to sell newspapers. Newspapers using this strategy covered the events in Cuba leading up to the Spanish-American War, and did much to shift American opinion toward desiring war with Spain; some critics maintain that many tactics of yellow journalism were used during the press coverage of the Whitewater investigation of Bill Clinton.

Yorktown, Battle of The defeat of the forces of General Cornwallis in this battle in October of 1781 essentially ended the hopes of the British for winning the Revolutionary War. American and French troops hemmed the British in on the peninsula of Yorktown, while the French navy located in Chesapeake Bay made rescue of the British troops by sea impossible.

Zimmermann Telegram January 1917 telegram sent by the German foreign minister to Mexico suggesting that the Mexican army should join forces with the Germans against the United States; when the Germans and Mexicans were victorious, the Mexicans were promised most of the southwestern part of the United States. The British deciphered the code of this telegram and turned it over to the United States; the release of its content caused many in America to feel that war against the Germans was essential.